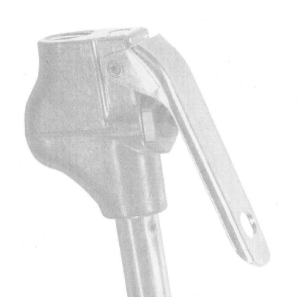

MICROSOFT®

ASP.NET

PROGRAMMING WITH MICROSOFT

VISUAL C#® .NET

STEP BY STEP

Microsoft®
.net™

G. Andrew Duthie

PUBLISHED BY
Microsoft Press
A Division of Microsoft Corporation
One Microsoft Way
Redmond, Washington 98052-6399

Library of Congress Cataloging-in-Publication Data
Duthie, G. Andrew, 1967-
     Microsoft ASP.NET Programming with Visual C# .NET Version 2003 Step by
Step / G. Andrew Duthie.
          p. cm.
     Includes index.
     ISBN 0-7356-1935-2
     1. Active server pages.   2. Web sites--Design.   3. Web servers--Computer programs.   I.
Title.

     TK5105.8885.A26D89   2003
     005.276--dc21   2003042215

Printed and bound in the United States of America.

3 4 5 6 7 8 9   QWE   8 7 6 5 4 3

Distributed in Canada by H.B. Fenn and Company Ltd.

A CIP catalogue record for this book is available from the British Library.

Microsoft Press books are available through booksellers and distributors worldwide. For further information about international editions, contact your local Microsoft Corporation office or contact Microsoft Press International directly at fax (425) 936-7329. Visit our Web site at www.microsoft.com/mspress. Send comments to *mspinput@microsoft.com*.

Acquisitions Editor: Anne Hamilton
Project Editor: Lynn Finnel

Body Part No. X09-45931

Table of Contents

Part 2   ASP.NET Infrastructure

Part 3   ASP.NET Web Forms

Part 4   Beyond the Basics

Part 5   Appendixes

Acknowledgments

I want to express my thanks for the support and assistance provided by my project editor at Microsoft Press, Lynn Finnel, as well as for her persistence and perseverance on the project. Thanks also to the editing team for catching my goofs and helping make my work the best it can be. My thanks especially to Anne Hamilton for her ongoing support for my work.

Last but not least, I thank my wife, Jennifer. Her love, patience, and support make my work possible and worthwhile.

G. Andrew Duthie
March, 2003

Introduction

Finding Your Best Starting Point

Microsoft ASP.NET Programming with Microsoft Visual C# .NET 2003 Step by Step is designed to provide a comprehensive introduction and overview of developing Web applications with ASP.NET. The goal of this book is to help you become competent at the basic skills necessary for creating and using ASP.NET applications. To help you get there as quickly and easily as possible, this book has been divided into four parts, each composed of one or more chapters related to a specific topic. Over the course of these parts and chapters, you'll learn about the new Microsoft .NET development platform and the part that ASP.NET plays in it. You'll also learn the skills necessary to take advantage of ASP.NET Web Forms, Server Controls, and XML-based Web services.

Depending on the skills and experience you bring to this book, you might want to start with a particular part of interest to you or skip over certain parts entirely. The following table can help you decide where to start.

If you are	Follow these steps
New	
To programming	**1** Install the sample files as described in "Installing the Sample Files" on page xvii.
	2 Learn about the background of the Microsoft .NET Framework and ASP.NET by reading Chapters 1–6. Then either work through Part 3 if you want to know more about the technologies underlying ASP.NET or work through Part 4 if you want to get straight into the coding.
	3 Work through the rest of the parts and chapters based on your interest in the various topics.
Switching	
From classic ASP or similar technologies	**1** Install the sample files as described in "Installing the Sample Files" on page xvii.
	2 Read or scan Parts 1 and 2 if you're interested in the background of .NET and ASP.NET.
	3 Work through Part 3 for basic Web Forms skills as well as an introduction to using ASP.NET Server Controls and accessing data with ADO.NET.

If you are		Follow these steps
	4	Work through Part 4 for additional ASP.NET application skills.
Referencing		
This book after working through the chapters	**1**	Use the index to locate information about specific topics, and use the table of contents to locate information about general topics.
	2	Read the Quick Reference at the end of each chapter for a brief review of the major tasks in each chapter.

Corrections, Comments, and Help

Every effort has been made to ensure the accuracy of this book and the contents of the sample files. Microsoft Press provides corrections and additional content for its books through the World Wide Web at the following address:

http://www.microsoft.com/mspress/support

To connect directly to the Microsoft Press Knowledge Base and enter a query about a question you may have, visit:

http://www.microsoft.com/mspress/support/search.asp

If you have problems, comments, or ideas regarding this book or the sample files, please send them to Microsoft Press.

Send e-mail to:

mspinput@microsoft.com

Or send postal mail to:

Microsoft Press
Attn: Developer Step by Step Series Editor
One Microsoft Way
Redmond, WA 98052-6399

Please note that product support is not offered through the above addresses. For help with ASP.NET, you can connect to Microsoft Technical Support on the Web at *support.microsoft.com/directory*, or for additional developer information about ASP.NET, go to *www.microsoft.com/net* and search on ASPNET.

Visit the Microsoft Press World Wide Web Site

You are also invited to visit the Microsoft Press World Wide Web site at the following location:

http://www.microsoft.com/mspress

You'll find descriptions for the complete line of Microsoft Press books (including others by G. Andrew Duthie), information about ordering titles, notice of special features and events, additional content for Microsoft Press books, and much more.

Installing the Sample Files

The sample code used in this book is available on the book's Web site at *http://www.microsoft.com/mspress/books/6724.asp*. To download the sample files, click the "Companion Content" link in the More Information menu on the right side of the Web page. This will load the Companion Content page, which includes the link for downloading the sample files. To install the sample files, run the executable file downloaded from the link and accept the license agreement that is presented.

By default, the files will be copied to the folder C:\Microsoft-Press\ASPNETSBS_CS. The destination folder will also contain a readme.htm file that you'll need to refer to for instructions in setting up and using the sample files.

System Requirements

To use the sample code provided at the Web site, you'll need a computer with the following configuration:

- Microsoft Windows 2000 (SP3 or later recommended), XP Professional, or Windows Server 2003, Web edition.
- Microsoft SQL Server 2000 (Personal, Standard, or Enterprise Edition, SP3 recommended) or the Microsoft SQL Server Desktop Engine (MSDE), which is included with Visual Studio .NET 2003.
- Microsoft Internet Explorer 5.5 or later.
- Internet Information Services (IIS). (To access the ASP.NET features, you must install IIS prior to installing the Microsoft .NET Framework.)

- The .NET Framework SDK, which you can download from the MSDN Web site at *http://msdn.microsoft.com/netframework/downloads/ default.asp*. (Because Microsoft Visual Studio .NET includes the SDK, you don't need to install the .NET Framework SDK separately if you install Visual Studio .NET.) Note that Windows Server 2003 comes with the .NET Framework version 1.1 preinstalled, so you do not need to install this separately.

- Visual Studio .NET 2003 or Visual C# .NET 2003, Professional Edition or higher. You can use the Standard edition, but some chapters (including Chapter 10) use project types only available in the Professional and higher editions.

▶ **Note**   To more easily run some of the command-line tools in the .NET Framework (such as wsdl.exe and the command-line compilers), you might also need to add the paths to these utilities to the PATH environment variable, as described in Appendix C. If you have problems running any of the command-line tools, you can use the Windows Search facility (located on the Start menu) to search for the location of these tools. Then add the path to their location to the PATH environment variable.

Conventions Used in This Book

You can save time when using this book if you take the time to understand how instructions, keys, notes, and so on are used *before* you start the first chapter. Please take a moment to read the following list, which explains the conventions for these and other elements.

- Hands-on exercises for you to follow are given in numbered lists of steps (1, 2, and so on).
- Text that you are to type appears in boldface type.
- As you work through steps, you will occasionally see tables with lists of properties that you will type into Visual C# .NET.
- A plus sign between two key names means that you must press those keys at the same time. For example, Press Alt+Tab means that you hold down the Alt key while pressing the Tab key.
- Notes labeled NOTE provide additional information or tips about a topic.
- Notes labeled IMPORTANT alert you to essential information that you should check before continuing the chapter. This can include information to help you avoid problems such as application crashes or security issues.
- Notes labeled TIP can help save you time and trouble as you use the technologies being described.

Getting Started with ASP.NET

Opening and Running an ASP.NET Web Application

In this chapter, you will learn how to:

- Start Microsoft Visual Studio .NET.
- Open and run an ASP.NET application.
- Work with tool windows.
- Exit Visual Studio .NET.

Microsoft ASP.NET is not just an upgrade—not by a long shot. ASP.NET provides the most advanced Web development platform created to date. What's more, ASP.NET has been rebuilt from the ground up to create an entirely new and more flexible infrastructure for Web development.

What makes ASP.NET so revolutionary is that it's based on Microsoft's new .NET platform, or more accurately the Microsoft .NET Framework. To understand clearly where and when to use ASP.NET, let's take some time to go over the Microsoft .NET platform, the products that it comprises, and where ASP.NET fits within Microsoft .NET.

Understanding Microsoft .NET

Microsoft .NET is an umbrella term that describes a number of recently released technologies from Microsoft. Taken together, these technologies are the most substantial changes to the Microsoft development platform since the transition from 16-bit to 32-bit development.

Microsoft .NET includes the following technology areas:

- The .NET Framework
- .NET languages and language tools

In the next section, you'll learn about these technologies and how you can use them to speed up your development of robust, high-performance Web- or Forms- based applications on the Microsoft Windows platform.

The .NET Framework

The .NET Framework is an essential technology for ASP.NET development. It provides the basic system services that support ASP.NET, as well as Windows Forms development, the new rich client development technology provided by .NET. Much like the Microsoft Windows NT 4.0 Option Pack, which was an add-on to Windows NT 4.0 that added Internet Information Server 4.0 and Active Server Pages technologies to NT 4.0, the .NET Framework is an add-on to Microsoft Windows XP, Windows 2000, Windows NT 4.0, and Windows 98/ME that adds the basic supporting system services for .NET technologies. The framework will also be built into newer releases of the Windows server operating system line, including the Windows Server 2003 line.

▶ **Important**   While Visual Studio .NET is supported on the Windows 98, Windows NT, Windows 2000, and Windows XP platforms, the full .NET framework is not available on all platforms. Most important, while other platforms can be used as ASP.NET clients, ASP.NET applications will run only on Windows 2000 and later.

The .NET Framework consists of two main parts:

- The common language runtime
- The .NET Framework class library

The Common Language Runtime

The common language runtime (CLR) provides a run-time environment for the execution of code written in any .NET language. The CLR manages the execution of .NET code, including memory and object lifetime management. In addition to these management services, the CLR allows developers to perform debugging, exception handling, and inheritance across multiple languages. Performing these tasks requires that the language compilers follow the Common Language Specification (CLS), which describes a subset of the data types supported by the CLR that are common to all of the languages used in .NET.

The individual language compilers compile the code written by developers into an intermediate language called Microsoft Intermediate Language (IL or MSIL). The IL is then Just-In-Time (JIT) compiled at first execution. Optionally, IL assemblies may be compiled to native code by the CLR at install time using a utility called ngen.exe. This can improve startup time, although at some cost to performance, due to optimizations available during JIT compilation. Note that ngen.exe cannot be used for assemblies generated from ASP.NET pages and code-behind classes.

Code that is compiled to IL and managed by the CLR is referred to as *managed code*. It's called this because the CLR takes responsibility for managing the execution of the code, including the instantiation of objects, allocation of memory, and garbage collection of objects and memory.

Components written in managed code and executed by the CLR are referred to as *.NET managed assemblies*, or *assemblies* for short. Assemblies are the basic unit of deployment in the .NET world and are quite similar to COM components. The difference is that whereas a COM component has a type library to describe how clients should interact with it, an assembly contains a *manifest*, which is the set of metadata that describes the contents of the assembly. Among other advantages, the self-describing nature of .NET components means that they don't need to be registered on a computer in order to work!

This metadata also describes the dependencies and version information associated with an assembly. Not only does this make it much easier to ensure that all necessary dependencies of an assembly are fulfilled, but it also means that multiple versions of the same assembly can be run side by side on the same computer without conflict. This is a major step in resolving "DLL Hell," the bane of many developers' existence. Just ask any Web developer who's worked with more than one version of Microsoft ActiveX Data Objects (ADO), and you're sure to get an earful about applications being broken by a new version of ADO. With .NET, this issue should be a thing of the past. As long as the consuming application knows which version of an assembly it's designed to use, it can locate the correct version among multiple versions of the same assembly by querying the assembly's metadata.

There's a great deal more to the CLR, which you'll learn in future chapters. If you need further information on the CLR, do a search on "common language runtime" in either the .NET Framework SDK documentation or the MSDN Library documentation for Visual Studio .NET.

The .NET Framework Class Library

The .NET Framework class library is designed to support the efforts of developers by providing base classes from which developers can inherit. This class library is a hierarchical set of .NET classes that developers can use in their own applications. These classes, which are organized by containers referred to as *namespaces*, provide both basic and advanced functionality that developers can easily reuse. They include classes that support basic common datatypes; classes that provide access to data; and classes that support such system services as drawing (good news for anyone who's had to use a third-party component for dynamically creating graphics in an ASP application), network functionality (including DNS and reverse DNS lookups), and many others.

The library also contains the classes that form the basis of ASP.NET, including the *Page* class (a part of the *System.Web.UI* namespace) from which all ASP.NET pages are derived, as well as many other classes in the *System.Web* namespace and the other namespaces nested under *System.Web*. Later chapters will discuss several of these classes.

▶   **Note**   The ASP.NET QuickStart Tutorial (installed with the .NET Framework SDK samples) contains a useful Class Browser sample application (which can be found at *http://localhost/QuickStart/aspplus/doc/classbrowser.aspx* once you have installed the .NET Framework SDK samples) that you can use to view the various classes of the .NET Framework class library.

Inheritance

Inheritance is a central concept in the .NET Framework. It provides a way for developers to use existing code in classes. A class can expose both properties and methods that clients can use. Classes that are inherited from a particular base class are said to be *derived* from that class. By inheriting from a class, a developer can reuse the functionality that it exposes without having to rewrite the code.

In addition (and more important), a developer creating a derived class can override one or more of the methods exposed by the parent class in order to provide a specialized implementation of that functionality. This capability will come in handy when you learn about custom server controls in Chapter 10.

.NET Languages and Language Tools

One of the best things about the .NET platform is that whereas classic ASP restricted developers to using scripting languages (with their inherent limitations), ASP.NET lets you work with *any* .NET-compliant language. This means that the code you write in ASP.NET is compiled for better performance, and you can take full advantage of advanced language features.

For the .NET platform, languages (and the development tools with which you'll use them) are probably one of the most important topics to discuss. Let's take a high-level look at some of the languages and tools that will be available for developing .NET applications.

Notepad and Other Text Editors

Believe it or not, many developers, particularly ASP developers, still do much of their development in Microsoft Notepad (which I used to lovingly refer to as "Visual" Notepad) or other free or inexpensive text editors. While Notepad has the substantial advantage of being ubiquitous, it's not exactly what you'd call a robust development environment. That said, if you're working with the .NET Framework SDK (rather than Visual Studio .NET), there's no reason you can't use Notepad (or another favorite text editor) to do all of your .NET development. The .NET Framework SDK includes command-line compilers for Microsoft Visual Basic .NET, Microsoft Visual C# (pronounced "C sharp"), and Microsoft JScript .NET. So, you can create your classes, ASP.NET pages, and so on in Notepad, and then you can either compile them explicitly using the command-line compilers or, in the case of ASP.NET, allow the ASP.NET runtime to dynamically compile the page when it's requested for the first time.

Visual Studio .NET

For simpler and faster development, most developers will probably want to work in Visual Studio .NET, which provides a single integrated development environment (IDE) for all of Microsoft's .NET languages (with the exception of Microsoft Visual FoxPro 7.0, which does not use the CLR or the .NET Framework). This means that developers of Visual Basic, Microsoft Visual C++, and C# all share the same IDE, including the capability to perform debugging and exception handling across languages, in the same environment.

Visual Studio .NET provides a substantial number of new features, including

- A single, unified programming model for all .NET languages and for both Windows and Web applications
- Drag-and-drop development for the server using the Server Explorer
- Dynamic Help
- A robust customization and extensibility model for the IDE
- Strong support for XML
- Web services with dramatically easier cross-platform application integration

You'll learn more about the Visual Studio .NET environment later in this chapter.

C#

A new member of the Visual Studio family, C# is a descendent of the C language. It's much like C++, but designed with greater simplicity and ease of use in mind. Although C# isn't necessarily as easy to learn as Visual Basic, it's far easier than

C++ and provides nearly all of the power available to C++ developers. It also doesn't require you to manage the allocation and deallocation of memory, as C++ does. Because C#, like Visual Basic .NET, is a managed language, all of the memory management is taken care of by the CLR. This is an important advantage because memory management is one of the most troublesome areas of C++ development and is responsible for many application crashes.

Developers familiar with C, C++, and Java will quickly become productive using C#. This book will include some code examples in C# to give you a taste of this exciting new language.

Additional .NET Languages

Visual Studio .NET also ships with JScript . NET, Visual C++, and the managed extensions for Visual C++, which allow C++ developers to target their applications to the CLR.

Visual Studio .NET also provides an extremely flexible plug-in architecture that allows other languages written for or ported to the .NET platform to easily use the power of the Visual Studio IDE. The current list of third-party languages planned for Visual Studio .NET includes

- APL
- COBOL
- Eiffel
- FORTRAN
- Haskell
- Mercury
- Mondrian
- Oberon
- Pascal
- Perl
- Python
- RPG
- Scheme

It's important to point out that while some of the languages shown in the preceding list will be commercial implementations, some others are research projects being conducted by universities and might never reach commercial status. Still, between the languages that ship with Visual Studio .NET and the third-party languages that are or will be available, there should be a language to please just about any developer.

Getting Started with Visual Studio .NET

Although this book will focus on building ASP.NET applications with Visual C# .NET, the development environment you'll be working in is Visual Studio .NET. Because Visual Studio .NET now supports all of the .NET languages in a single IDE, many of the tasks you'll learn in this book are applicable to Visual Basic .NET, Visual C++, and JScript .NET, as well as to Visual C# .NET.

Visual Studio .NET Basics

You'll begin your tour by starting the Visual Studio .NET IDE. Next, you'll learn about some of the features of the IDE designed to help you get started. You'll finish this section by learning how to open an ASP.NET Web application project.

▶   **Important**   The exercises in this chapter require that you have installed at minimum the Visual C# .NET Standard Edition, as well as the practice files for the book, which you can download from the book's Web site at *http://www.microsoft.com/mspress/books/6724.asp*. If you have not installed both, please do so now and then return to this chapter.

Start Visual Studio .NET

1   Click the Start button, point to All Programs (or Programs in Windows 2000), and then point to Microsoft Visual Studio .NET 2003.

 start

The icons for Visual Studio .NET will be displayed.

2   Click the icon for Microsoft Visual Studio .NET 2003.

The Visual Studio .NET IDE will start. The Start Page is displayed by default whenever you start Visual Studio .NET, and provides links and tools to help you configure the IDE, open recent projects, create new projects, and many other tasks. By default, the IDE will display the Projects tab of the Visual Studio .NET Start Page. This tab allows you to quickly open a recent project or to create a new project. The Online Resources tab allows you to find sample code, access online community resources, find .NET downloads, and more. You'll see more of this tab in a bit. The My Profile tab of the Start Page, shown in the following illustration, allows you to configure the layout of the tool windows in Visual Studio .NET, as well as the keyboard shortcuts used to accomplish common tasks.

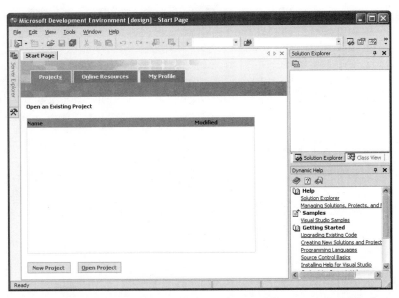

3   Select the My Profile tab, and then change the main *Profile* drop-down list from Visual Studio Developer to Visual C# Developer.

This will configure the IDE windows and keyboard configuration to match those shown in the following illustration.

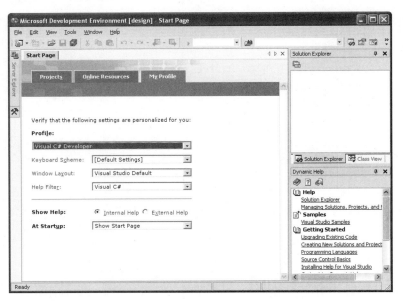

4   Change the *Profile* drop-down list back to Visual Studio Developer
to restore the original settings.

Search for sample code

1   Click the Online Resources tab.

By default, the Get Started section will be selected (if it's not, click
Get Started). Here you can search for samples based on the developer
profile (Visual Studio, Visual Basic, Visual C++, or Visual C#) and
filtered by keyword or type, as shown in the following illustration.

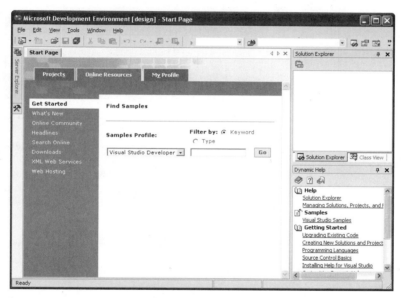

2   Type **ASP.NET** in the text box, and then click Go.

A list of matching samples will be displayed, as shown in the following illustration.

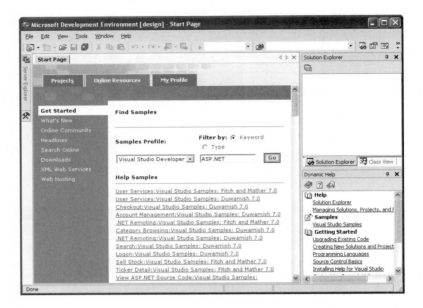

▶ **Important**   Sample applications and code can be useful tools for learning how to develop applications, including ASP.NET applications. But keep in mind that samples are often designed to illustrate a limited set of specific concepts, and might not always use best practices for security and design. Before using sample code in your applications, be sure that you understand the security and architectural implications of doing so.

Open a Web application project

1   Switch back to the Projects tab and then click Open Project.

The Open Project dialog box will be displayed, as shown in the following illustration.

2   Browse to the location where you installed the practice files (the default is C:\MS Press Books\ASPNETSBS_CS), open the Chapter_01 folder, select the Chapter_01.csproj file, and then click Open. (Alternatively, you can open all the projects installed with the practice files by selecting the aspnetsbs.sln file located in the aspnetsbs_cs folder.)

The Chapter_01 project will be loaded. Note that if you open a project originally created with Visual Studio .NET 2002 in Visual Studio .NET 2003, you will be prompted to convert the project file to the newer format. Once this conversion is done, you will not be able to open the project in older versions of Visual Studio .NET.

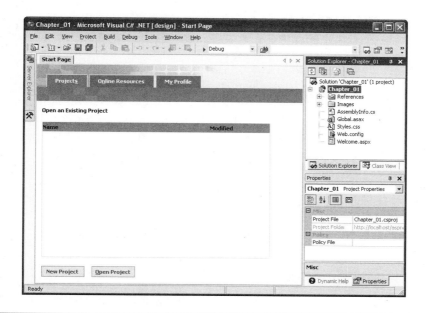

▶ **Note**   By default, Windows 2000 and Windows XP hide file extensions for known file types. If this setting is turned on, you will not see the .csproj and/or .sln extensions to the files mentioned earlier. You can modify this setting in the Windows Explorer Folder Options dialog box. From the Windows Explorer Tools menu, select Folder Options and then click on the View tab. Uncheck the Hide Extensions For Known File Types check box, and then click OK or Apply. The file extensions will now appear in the Open Project dialog box.

Solutions and Projects

Applications in Visual Studio .NET are organized into containers called *projects* and *solutions*. Projects are containers for the files associated with a single application type, such as a Web application or control library, while solutions are containers for one or more projects. The projects that make up the sample files for this book are contained in a single solution named aspnetsbs.sln. Solutions are a useful tool for organizing all of the projects associated with a larger application, such as Web applications, and the control projects or component projects associated with them.

Running Web applications is a little different than running Windows applications or console applications. With Windows applications and console applications, running the application in the IDE is as simple as clicking the Start button, shown in the following illustration, on the Visual Studio .NET toolbar. Although you can also run a Web application using this technique, it's more common to simply browse to the page in the application that you want to test. If you want to run a Web application using the Start button (or by selecting Start from the Debug menu), you need to select a page in your application that will be the start page, or the first page loaded when the application is run. You'll learn about these techniques in Chapter 14, which covers debugging ASP.NET applications. For now, let's just test a page by browsing it.

Test a Web Forms page

1   Load the Chapter_01 project. (If you've been following along in the book, you might have already loaded the Chapter_01 project; if so, skip to the next step. If not, return to the previous section, follow the steps to load the project, and then return to this section.)

2   In the Solution Explorer window, right-click the Welcome.aspx file, and then select View In Browser.

The Welcome.aspx page, shown in the following illustration, will be loaded into a browser window that is integrated into the IDE. You can browse pages in a Microsoft Internet Explorer external browser window or with browsers other than Internet Explorer by right-clicking a page, selecting Browse With, and then choosing your desired browser and other options.

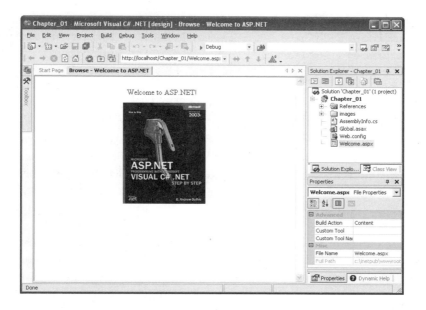

The Visual Studio .NET IDE

The Visual Studio .NET environment includes a wide array of tool windows, toolbars, and menus to provide developers with a great deal of flexibility in performing development tasks. You can perform any given task, such as adding an item to a project, by using a tool window, a toolbar button, or a menu selection. While this flexibility is a good thing, it can be a little overwhelming at first. To make it easier for you to find your way around, let's take a tour through the new enhancements, tool windows, toolbars, and menus of the Visual Studio .NET IDE.

IDE Enhancements

The new enhancements you'll find in the Visual Studio .NET IDE include the following:

- **Start Page**   The Start Page, which we saw earlier in the chapter, is the default page that's displayed each time you start Visual Studio .NET. It allows you to set your preferences for the IDE, access recent and existing projects, and create new projects.

■ **Multilanguage IDE**   Unlike Visual Studio 6, which used different IDEs for each programming language (although Microsoft Visual InterDev and Microsoft Visual J++ shared an IDE), all languages in Visual Studio .NET share the same IDE. This means that standard features such as Find and Replace, debugging, and so on work consistently across different languages. This alone will be a big productivity enhancer from Visual Studio 6.

■ **Command window**   A cross between Visual Basic's Immediate window and a command line, the Command window lets you execute Visual Studio commands or code statements, depending on the mode of the window. The illustration below shows a Command window that's been switched to immediate mode using the *immed* command. The Command window has two modes:

  ■ Command mode allows you to execute Visual Studio commands without using the menu system, or to execute commands that don't appear in any menu.

  ■ Immediate mode, used in debugging, allows you to evaluate expressions, check the value of variables, execute program statements and functions, and so on.

■ **Tabbed Documents**   Designed to simplify the management of multiple files being edited simultaneously, the Tabbed Documents interface allows you to see all of the files you're editing at once. This makes it much simpler to switch back and forth between open editing windows. You can still set up Visual Studio .NET to use the old method used by Visual Studio 6, however. Just click the Tools menu, select Options, then select the General option in the Environment folder, switch from Tabbed Documents to MDI environment, and then click OK. You'll need to restart Visual Studio .NET for this change to take effect.

- **Auto Hide** My personal favorite, Auto Hide works much like the feature of the same name in the Windows toolbar. To enable auto-hide for a window, click the pushpin icon, shown in the following illustration, in the window's title bar. Now the window will hide itself at the side of the IDE, where it's docked when the mouse moves away from the window, leaving only a tab with the window title visible. Moving the mouse pointer over the tab will cause the window to reappear. This is a great feature for preserving the maximum amount of screen real estate for the code window, and it can make life much easier in terms of managing multiple windows in the IDE.

- **Improved HTML editor** Like Visual InterDev before it, the Visual Studio .NET HTML editor provides both a design view and an HTML (source) view. Visual Studio .NET has done away with the Quick View window provided by Visual InterDev. Instead, you preview pages in an embedded browser window, which provides a truer view of how a page will really look. The improved editor also supports specifying the HTML schema you're writing for via the *targetSchema* property. Setting *targetSchema* determines which elements will be made available via the editor's statement completion features and allows the IDE to provide you with feedback on syntax that's incorrect in the context of your chosen target schema.

Use tabbed documents

1 With the Chapter_01 project opened in the IDE, double-click the Welcome.aspx file in the Solution Explorer window.

A new tab will be added to the editor, as shown in the following illustration.

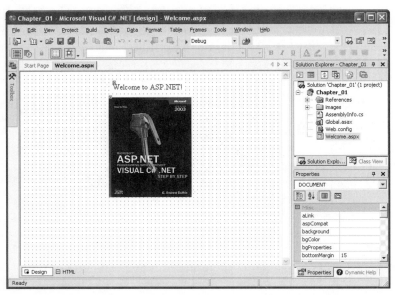

2   Switch between open documents (including the Start Page) by clicking on the tab for the document you want to switch to.

If there are more tabs than will fit onscreen, you can scroll to view the hidden tabs using the Scroll buttons, as shown below, at the top of the editor window. You can close the currently selected document by clicking the Close button, as shown below, at the top of the editor window.

◁ ▷

☒

New Features

In addition to the IDE enhancements, a number of entirely new features have been added to the Visual Studio .NET IDE.

- **XML editor**   This allows you to edit XML data (.xml) and schema (.xsd) files in source, data, or schema views, depending on the type of XML file you're editing.

- **Dynamic Help**   Dynamic Help provides context-sensitive help while you work in the IDE by suggesting topics of interest as you add files, controls, and code to your project, as shown in the following illustration.

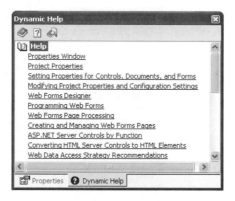

▶ **Note** While the Dynamic Help window can be very useful, it also imposes a performance penalty—each time you perform some action in the IDE, the Dynamic Help window searches for topics of interest related to that action. If you're familiar with most of the tasks you need to perform, or if you're running Visual Studio .NET on an older machine, closing the Dynamic Help window (by clicking the Close button in the upper right-hand corner of the window) can make the IDE more responsive.

■ **Support for Windows Installer** Visual Studio now supports this much-improved set-up technology for Windows applications, including support for installation rollback in case of installation issues. You can even create deployment packages for Web applications that will allow you to install and run ASP.NET applications on a machine that does not currently have the .NET Framework installed. The deployment package will install all necessary run-time files for you.

IDE Windows

While you work with Visual Studio .NET, you'll encounter a wide variety of windows in the IDE, used for a wide variety of purposes. Some are new, like the Dynamic Help window described in the previous section, while some will be familiar to users of previous versions of Visual Studio. In this section, we'll take a look at the most commonly used windows.

■ **Designer/Source Editor** This is where you'll spend most of your time in the Visual Studio environment. This window integrates almost all of the designers and source-code editors that you'll use in Visual Studio, including the Web Forms, XML schema, and HTML designers, as well as a unified source-code editor that provides support for XML, HTML, SQL, cascading style sheets (CSS), and all of the .NET languages. The editor provides enhanced features specific to each language. Two new features of the HTML and CSS editors that are particularly exciting are IntelliSense statement completion for both HTML and CSS, and better control over how (or if) the editor modifies the format of your HTML and CSS documents. To change the formatting settings, from the Tools menu, select Options. In the Options dialog box, select the Text Editor folder, then select the HTML (or CSS) folder, and then select the Format option. Buttons at the bottom of the designer/editor window allow you to change between Design and HTML views of ASP.NET pages, as well as between different modes for other document types.

■ **Solution Explorer**   The Solution Explorer window should be familiar to anyone who's used Visual InterDev 6. It's one of the primary tools you'll use to manage project files and resources, including adding, removing, opening, renaming, and moving files, as well as setting a start-up page or project, switching between code and design view for a file, and viewing status information (for example, Source Code Control status) on your files. The following illustration shows the Solution Explorer.

■ **Class View**   The Class View window (shown in the following illustration), which by default shares a window with the Solution Explorer, contains a listing of all classes (contained in .vb or .cs modules) in your projects and the methods, properties, and interfaces implemented in those classes.

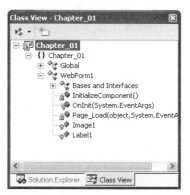

- **Server Explorer** The Server Explorer, as shown in the following illustration, is a new feature of Visual Studio .NET that allows you to view resources on both your local machine and remote servers, including configured data connections, event logs, message queues, and performance counters. The Server Explorer also lets you drag and drop resources onto Web Forms pages or .NET components, allowing some of the most productive server-side development available to date. In the Standard edition of Visual C# .NET, the Server Explorer is limited to connecting to and viewing database objects.

- **Properties** The Properties window should be immediately familiar to anyone who's used any of the Visual Studio suites of development tools. It provides access to the properties of the object currently selected in the IDE. The Properties window allows you to collapse or expand categories of properties to better view the categories you're interested in. You can also view the properties in alphabetical order by clicking the Alphabetic (AZ) button, as shown in the following illustration, just below the object selection drop-down menu.

1

Running ASP.NET Applications

■ **The Visual Studio .NET Toolbox**   The Visual Studio .NET Toolbox is another element modeled closely on the Visual InterDev environment. It provides access to a wide variety of controls, components, and HTML elements. You can add Toolbox items (essentially, the HTML tags or text elements used to implement controls or components) to Web Forms or components by either double-clicking the item name in the Toolbox (in which case the item is inserted at the current cursor location) or by using drag-and-drop (allowing you to place the item where desired). Note that some items do not have a visual representation when used in a Web Form. These items will usually be displayed in a separate window area at the bottom of the Designer window. The following illustration shows the Toolbox displaying the Web Forms controls.

▶ **Tip**   You can add your own items or categories (called tabs) in the Toolbox. To add a tab, simply right-click in the Toolbox, select Add Tab, and give the tab a name. To add your own items, make sure the proper category tab is selected, select the desired item in the Designer (or text in the code editor), and then drag it to the Toolbox. You can give the new item a descriptive name by right-clicking it and selecting Rename Item.

■ **Task List**   An underrated and often underutilized tool from Visual InterDev, the Task List window allows developers to create, sort, and track tasks to be completed for the current solution. The

Task List also can contain tasks automatically generated by Visual Studio to help developers locate and correct build errors. Tasks can be categorized and prioritized according to the developer's needs. Categories include Comment tasks (indicated by comment tokens such as *TODO, UPGRADE_TODO,* and so on), User tasks, Build Errors, Shortcuts (created by right-clicking a line of code in the editor and selecting Add Task List Shortcut), and IntelliSense tasks, which are displayed when IntelliSense detects an error in your code. The following illustration shows a Task List with a Shortcut task, a User task, and a Comment task.

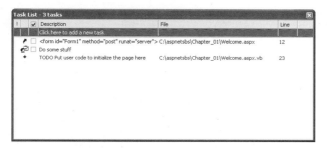

- **Output**   The Output window will be familiar to developers who've used Microsoft's Visual C++ or Visual J++ tools. One of the primary purposes of the Output window is to display messages related to project builds. (A *build* is the process of compiling all of the code files that make up a project.) Since you need to build your ASP.NET Web application before code modifications will appear, you'll be seeing a lot of this window. The following illustration shows the output of a build of a sample project. In this case the build was successful, with no errors or warnings. Had there been build errors or warnings, they would have been displayed in this window.

Now that you've seen some of the main windows in the IDE, put your knowledge to work by following these procedures.

Switch views in the Editor

1   Open the Welcome.aspx page, if it's not already open, by double-clicking the file in the Solution Explorer window. (You can tell if the file is open by reading the tab labels along the top of the editor.)

2   Click the HTML button, as shown in the following illustration, to switch to HTML view for the page (you can switch back by clicking the Design button, as shown below).

When you click the HTML button, the HTML code for the page will be displayed, as shown in the following illustration.

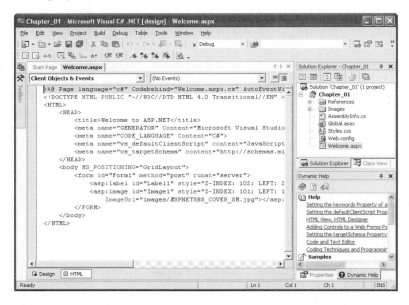

Use the Properties window to modify properties

1   Open the Welcome.aspx file, if it isn't already open, by double-clicking the file in the Solution Explorer window. Make sure you're in Design view—if not, click the Design button to switch to Design view.

2   Click the text "Welcome to ASP.NET!" to select the control it represents. This is an ASP.NET *Label server* control. (You'll learn more about ASP.NET server controls in later chapters.) When you select the

control, its properties are displayed in the Properties window, as shown in the following illustration.

3   Click the + symbol next to the *Font* property to expose its sub-properties.

4   Select the *Bold* property, and then click its drop-down list to change the property value to True.

5   Select the *Size* property, and then click its drop-down list to change the property value to Large.

Note how the text displayed is modified in the following illustration.

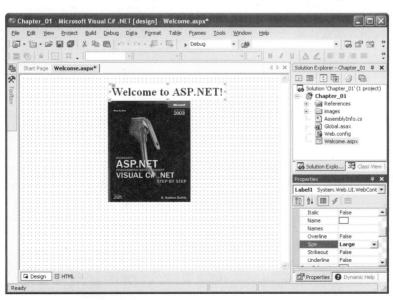

6   Center the *Label* control over the image by clicking and dragging the control in the designer window, and then save the file by clicking the Save button, as shown in the following illustration, on the toolbar.

7 Browse the page by right-clicking Welcome.aspx in Solution Explorer and selecting View In Browser.

The result should look similar to the following illustration.

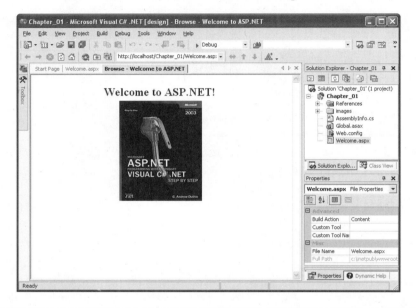

Toolbars

To accomplish tasks in Visual Studio .NET, you'll most likely use a combination of the IDE's toolbars and menus. This section will take a look at the most commonly used toolbars, and the next section will look at the most commonly used menus. You can view the full list of available toolbars by right-clicking any toolbar (or empty toolbar area). In keeping with the customizable nature of the Visual Studio .NET IDE, all toolbars can be customized by adding, removing, or rearranging buttons, moving toolbars, and showing or hiding toolbars.

▶ **Note**   Given the flexibility of the Visual Studio .NET toolbars, it's easy to end up with your toolbars looking nothing like they did when you installed Visual Studio. For some developers this might be a good thing, but if you want to restore your toolbars to their original configuration, click the Toolbar Options button (which looks like the arrow of a drop-down list control) found at the right end of each toolbar, then click Add Or Remove Buttons, then click the menu item for the toolbar name, and then click Reset Toolbar.

- **Standard**   The Standard toolbar, shown in the following illustration, contains buttons for common file and project commands, including opening files and projects, creating new files and projects, and accessing various windows in the IDE.

- **Formatting**   The Formatting toolbar, shown in the following illustration, contains buttons related to the formatting of text, including font and font size, text alignment options, and background and foreground colors. This toolbar is enabled only when you're entering or editing text in Design view.

- **Text Editor**   The Text Editor toolbar, shown in the following illustration, contains buttons related to the operation of the Text Editor, including access to IntelliSense features, indenting and commenting of code, and bookmarks. (You can use these to navigate quickly to specific sections of your code.)

- **Debug**   The Debug toolbar, shown in the following illustration, contains buttons related to Debugging commands, from Start, Stop, and Break commands to buttons for accessing the various Debug windows. Debugging is covered in Chapter 14.

Menus

A great many menus are available in Visual Studio .NET, depending on the task you're working on at any given time. While we won't go over all of them, the menus you'll encounter most frequently in your Visual Studio travels are listed here.

- **File menu**   The File menu is used to create, open, and save files and projects, as well as to print files and to exit the program.
- **Edit menu**   The Edit menu is used for working with text and objects such as Cut, Copy, and Paste, as well as text-specific commands such as Find and Replace, and formatting commands such as Make Uppercase or Make Lowercase.

- **View menu**   The View menu is used to access windows or views that are currently hidden. Use this menu to switch from source code to design view or to open up windows such as the Task List, as well as to choose which toolbars are displayed.

- **Project menu**   The Project menu is used to add items to a project, add references to assemblies or Web services, and set the start page and start-up project used for debugging.

- **Build menu**   The Build menu is used for building and rebuilding a project or projects, as well as commands for deploying projects.

- **Debug menu**   The Debug menu is used to start, stop, and pause (break) debugging, and to set breakpoints and access debugging windows.

- **Table menu**   The Table menu is used for working with HTML tables. Use this menu to insert or delete tables, rows, columns, and cells, as well as to merge or split cells.

- **Tools menu**   The Tools menu contains commands related to customizing the IDE and external tools. You can use this menu to access the Customize dialog box discussed earlier, as well as the Options dialog box, discussed in the next section.

- **Query menu**   The Query menu is used for creating and running database queries using Visual Studio's database tools.

- **Window menu**   The Window menu is used to navigate and manage the open document windows being used by the application.

- **Help menu**   The Help menu is used to access the Visual Studio .NET documentation, as well as to access product support. This menu also contains a link to the Visual Studio .NET start page that appears by default when you open Visual Studio. So if you accidentally close it, you can use this menu item to get it back.

▶ **Tip**   In addition to these menus, you can create your own custom menus. To create a custom menu, right-click anywhere in the menu bar and select Customize. In the Customize dialog box, click the Commands tab. Under Categories, select New Menu. Under Commands, click and drag the New Menu item to the desired location in the menu bar. Next, right-click the new menu heading and use the Name entry to give your new menu a name. Now you can drag items from the other menu categories to your new menu. To create a submenu, drag another copy of the New Menu item into the desired location on your menu.

Options

One of the most dramatic areas of improvement in Visual Studio .NET is in customization. Much of the customization available in Visual Studio .NET is controlled from the Options dialog box, shown in the following illustration. As mentioned earlier, you can access this dialog box by selecting Tools, and then Options. Not only has the number of options increased significantly, but the degree of control over particular options has increased as well.

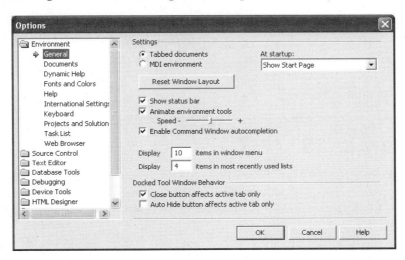

One good example of this increased control is in the area of code formatting. Visual InterDev developers will no doubt remember the frustration of having the Visual InterDev editor reformat their ASP code when switching from Design view to Source view. Visual Studio .NET still performs code formatting, but the developer has language-by-language control over how this formatting is done. (Note that not all languages use auto-formatting, so they won't all have these options.) Go to the Text Editor option folder, choose the language (for example, HTML or CSS), and set the options to your preferred setting. In this way, you can determine how formatting is applied to your code or, for some languages, you can turn off reformatting entirely.

▶ **Note**   One new option that will appeal to longtime BASIC users is having the IDE display line numbers in the text editor. Unlike BASIC, however, the line numbers are only for reference; they're not actually a part of the code. You can turn this option on or off for individual languages, or you can turn it on globally for all languages.

Exiting Visual Studio .NET

When you're finished working with a given project, naturally you'll want to exit from Visual Studio .NET.

Exit Visual Studio .NET

1   Save any open files, using the Save All button, as shown in the following illustration, on the toolbar or by selecting Save All from the File menu.

2   From the File menu, select Exit.
Visual Studio .NET shuts down.

What's New in ASP.NET

While there are plenty of familiar features in ASP.NET, some significant changes have been made to the ASP.NET architecture, including many improvements and new features. The following section will take a high-level look at what's new in ASP.NET.

Familiar Features

It's important to note that many things in ASP.NET will be familiar to Web developers who've used classic ASP. The much-used *Request* and *Response* objects are still there, as are the *Application*, *Session*, and *Server* objects, albeit with some new properties and methods. You can still use either <script runat="server"> blocks or the <% %> ASP script delimiters to denote server-side script. In fact, for the most part you can write an ASP.NET page exactly the same way you would write a classic ASP page. Once you get used to the new programming model of ASP.NET, though, you'll never go back to coding your ASP applications the way you do today.

Also, you don't need to migrate all of your existing ASP applications at once. ASP.NET is designed to run side by side with classic ASP. So while you're working on your first new ASP.NET application, your current ASP applications can still be running right alongside.

What's New

There's a lot of new stuff in ASP.NET, and it will take time to learn all of it. But once you've learned it, your productivity will be far greater than it was with classic ASP. Let's look at a list of some of the new features of ASP.NET.

■   **Web Forms**   This is the new programming model of ASP.NET. Web Forms combines the best of ASP with the ease of development and productivity of Visual Basic. You can drag controls onto a page and then write code to provide interactivity, call business objects, and more. You'll learn about Web Forms in Chapter 7.

- **Server controls**   A major component of the Web Forms programming model, the ASP.NET server controls map approximately to HTML elements (plus some additional controls you'll learn about later) and provide powerful server-side programmability. Server controls are run on the server and can output HTML that's tailored for uplevel browsers, such as Internet Explorer 5.x or later, or for any HTML 3.2–compliant browser. Chapter 8 and Chapter 10 will cover server controls in depth.

- **Web Services**   This is a key part of ASP.NET that allows developers to make programmatic services available to other developers over the Internet (or a local intranet). Web Services are based on the emerging SOAP standard, so they will allow relatively painless interoperation across diverse platforms. You'll learn more about Web Services in Chapter 11.

- **Caching**   ASP.NET includes a powerful new caching engine that will allow developers to improve the performance of their applications by reducing the Web server and database server processing loads. You'll learn more about caching in Chapter 12.

- **Configuration improvements**   ASP.NET uses a new method of storing configuration information for Web applications. Instead of having IIS store this information in a hard-to-access database, it's stored in XML-based human- and machine-readable configuration files, which also make deployment easier. You'll look at how these configuration files work in Chapter 5.

- **State management improvements**   If you've had to build an ASP application to run on a Web farm, you know all too well that there were major limitations to state management in classic ASP. ASP.NET overcomes these limitations, providing support for distributing session state across Web servers, persisting state information in a Microsoft SQL Server database, and providing state management without the use of cookies. You'll learn how to take advantage of these features in Chapter 4.

- **Security**   This is an extremely important function in today's Web applications. The security model in ASP.NET has been substantially improved, including new and improved authentication methods, code access security, and role-based authorization. You'll look at the ASP.NET security model and how to implement security in your ASP.NET applications in Chapter 6. New in version 1.1 of ASP.NET is a feature called Request Validation. This feature, which checks form input for scripts or HTML and throws an exception if such data is found, is designed to help developer prevent cross-site scripting attacks .

■ **Mobile Web Application Support**   Version 1.1 of ASP.NET adds built-in support for the ASP.NET Mobile controls (formerly the Microsoft Mobile Internet Toolkit), which offer support for building Web applications for mobile devices such as Personal Digital Assistants (PDAs) and cell phones. Enhancing this support is a new designer in the Visual Studio .NET IDE for mobile ASP.NET applications.

We've only scratched the surface in describing some of the new offerings of the .NET platform and the substantial advantages offered by ASP.NET. In subsequent chapters, you'll get detailed information on using ASP.NET to create faster, more robust, and more functional Web applications. In the next chapter, you'll learn about the various development tools that you can use to create your Web applications, from simple text editors to powerful IDEs such as Visual Studio .NET.

Chapter 1 Quick Reference

To	Do this	Button
Start Visual Studio .NET	Click the Windows Start button, point to All Programs, point to Microsoft Visual Studio .NET, and then click the Microsoft Visual Studio .NET icon.	start
Change how the IDE tool windows are configured	Click the My Profile link on the Visual Studio .NET Start Page, and modify the settings as desired.	
Switch to and from Design and HTML views of an ASP.NET page	Click the Design or HTML buttons below the designer/editor window.	Design HTML
Save a file	Click the Save button, or select Save *<filename>* from the File menu.	

Creating an ASP.NET Web Application

In this chapter, you will learn how to:

■ Create a new Web application with Microsoft Visual Studio .NET.

■ Add a Web Forms page to a Web application project.

■ Add Server Controls to a Web Forms page and modify their properties.

■ Write code in event handlers.

■ Build and test a Web application.

Now that you've learned about some of the features of Visual Studio .NET, the next step is to take advantage of them in your own applications. Conveniently enough, that's precisely what you're going to learn how to do in this chapter.

You'll begin with an overview of the two major project types used for ASP.NET applications. Then you'll look at the file types used in ASP.NET and the purpose of each. Next, you'll learn how to create a new Web application, add a new Web Forms page, and add controls to the page and manipulate their properties. Finally, you'll learn how to add event-handler code to the page, build the project, and test the page.

ASP.NET Project Types

There are three basic types of ASP.NET applications, each with a distinct purpose. *ASP.NET Web Applications* are for a Web application that will provide its own HTML-based user interface. *ASP.NET Web Services* are for Web-based functionality that will be accessed programmatically. *ASP.NET Mobile Web*

Applications, new in Visual Studio .NET 2003, are designed for creating Web applications targeted at Personal Digital Assistants (PDAs), cell phones, and other mobile devices. You can develop all of these application types with or without Visual Studio .NET, although the Visual Studio environment makes developing them significantly easier and faster. The following illustration shows the Visual Studio .NET New Project dialog box displaying the ASP.NET Web Application, ASP.NET Web Service, and ASP.NET Mobile Web Application project templates for Visual C# .NET (some of the project templates shown might not appear in all editions of Visual Studio .NET).

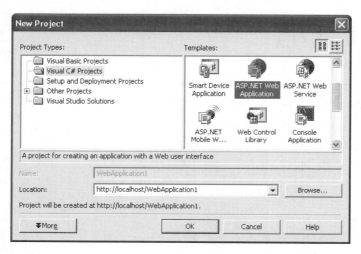

ASP.NET Web Applications

ASP.NET applications, at their simplest, are much like classic ASP applications. The elements of a simple ASP.NET application are

- A virtual directory in IIS, configured as an application root, to hold the files that make up the application and to control access to the files.
- One or more .aspx files.
- A Global.asax file (analogous to the Global.asa file in classic ASP) to deal with Session and Application startup and clean-up logic. This file is optional.
- A Web.config file used to store configuration settings. This file is optional, and is new for ASP.NET.

For Visual Studio .NET users, the good news is that all of the preceding files are created for you when you create a new Web application project.

ASP.NET Web Forms

Web Forms are an important part of any ASP.NET Web application. Put simply, they are ASP.NET pages that use ASP.NET Server Controls. The Web Forms programming model makes it possible (and relatively easy) to develop Web-based applications in much the same way that today's Microsoft Visual Basic programmers develop Microsoft Windows–based applications that have a GUI.

Web Forms in Visual Studio .NET allow you to create rich, interactive applications simply by dragging and dropping controls onto a page and then writing minimal code to handle user interaction, events, and so on. In addition, the Visual Studio .NET environment lets you work on your pages either visually—using the Web Forms Designer—or textually, using the powerful Visual Studio .NET source-code editor.

You can write code in your Web Forms in one of two ways: inline in the .aspx file (as is typical of a classic ASP page), or using a code-behind module. Although it's possible to write your application with code in the actual .aspx file and still take advantage of compiled code and the other improvements of .NET, I recommend that you get in the habit of using code-behind modules. Visual Studio .NET defaults to using code-behind for UI-specific programming logic.

Code-Behind

Code-behind is a new feature in ASP.NET that allows developers to truly separate the HTML and tag-based UI elements from the code that provides user interaction, validation, and so on. Code-behind modules offer developers a number of advantages:

- **Clean separation of HTML and code**   Code-behind allows HTML designers and developers to do what they do best independently, thereby minimizing the possibility of messing up one another's work (something that happens all too frequently when developing classic ASP applications).

- **Easier reuse**   Code that isn't interspersed with HTML in an .aspx page can be more easily reused in other projects.

- **Simpler maintenance**   Because the code is separated from the HTML, your pages will be easier to read and maintain.

- **Deployment without source code**   Visual Studio .NET projects using code-behind modules can be deployed as compiled code (in addition to the .aspx pages), allowing you to protect your source code. This can be very useful if you're creating applications for clients but want to retain control of your intellectual property.

All in all, it's worthwhile to get into the habit of using code-behind. You'll see examples of code-behind throughout the book.

ASP.NET Web Services

Although no one would deny that Web applications created with ASP.NET (or even with classic ASP) can be very useful, one feature that has long been missing is an easy way to provide programmatic functionality over the Internet or an intranet without tying the client to a specific UI. This is where ASP.NET Web services come in.

A Web service, at its simplest, is a chunk of programming code that is accessible over the Web. Web services are based on the World Wide Web Consortium's (W3C) SOAP specification. This allows computers on varying platforms, from Windows servers to UNIX workstations, to offer and consume programmatic services over the HTTP protocol.

▶ **Note** SOAP can use other protocols, such as FTP or SMTP, but HTTP is the most common protocol used with SOAP and Web services because most firewalls allow communication via the HTTP protocol.

ASP.NET makes it remarkably easy to implement Web services. In fact, all it takes is adding an appropriate declaration to any method you want to make available as a Web service. Visual Studio .NET makes it even easier by taking care of all the work necessary to make your Web service available to potential clients. Part IV will discuss Web services in greater detail.

ASP.NET Mobile Web Applications

Like standard ASP.NET Web applications, ASP.NET Mobile Web applications contain a number of standard elements:

- A virtual directory in IIS, configured as an application root, to hold the files that make up the application and to control access to the files.

- One or more .aspx files. Visual Studio .NET creates a single Web form by default with the name MobileWebForm1.aspx. The default Web Form contains a special *<mobile:form>* element, which acts as a container for mobile Web server controls (formerly part of the Microsoft Mobile Internet Toolkit). These controls allow you to design a UI for your application that automatically adapts to a wide variety of mobile devices.

- A Global.asax file to deal with Session and Application startup and clean-up logic. This file is optional.

- A Web.config file used to store configuration settings. In a Mobile Web Application project created with Visual Studio .NET, this file also contains a set of filters that help tailor page output to various mobile devices. This file is optional.

As with the ASP.NET Web Application template, Visual Studio .NET creates all of the preceding files when you create a new ASP.NET Mobile Web application project. You'll learn more about developing ASP.NET applications for mobile devices in Chapter 8.

ASP.NET File Types

You'll see a number of new file types in your ASP.NET applications. To avoid any confusion, let's take a minute to go over the ones you'll see most often and discuss how they're used.

- **.aspx**   The extension you'll see most often. Analogous to the .asp extension in classic ASP, .aspx is used for Web Forms pages.

- **.ascx**   The extension used for Web Forms user controls. User controls provide one of the many ways available in ASP.NET to reuse code. Similar to include files in classic ASP, .ascx files can be as simple as a few HTML tags or can include complex logic that the author might want to reuse in many pages. User controls are added to a Web Forms page using the @ *Register* directive, which is discussed in Part III.

- **.asmx**   The extension used for files that implement Web services. Web services can be accessed directly through .asmx files, or the .asmx file can direct the request to a compiled assembly that implements the Web service.

- **.cs**   The extension for Visual C# .NET code modules. All Web Forms pages (.aspx) added to a Visual Studio .NET Web application that are written in Visual C# .NET will have a corresponding .cs code-behind module with the same name as the Web Form page to which it's related (*pagename*.aspx.cs).

- **.resx**   Denotes a resource file. These files are used primarily in Windows Forms applications, but are also available to Web application developers for storing resources such as alternative text strings for internationalization of applications.

- **Global.asax**   Used to define Application- and Session-level variables and startup procedures. Global.asax is used the same way as Global.asa is used in classic ASP. Note that while Global.asax can be structured like Global.asa, with startup procedures such as *Session_OnStart* (*Session_Start* in ASP.NET) coded directly in the Global.asax file in a *<script runat="server">* block, Visual Studio implements these procedures in a .cs (or .vb, for Visual Basic projects) code-behind module (global.asax.cs) rather than in the Global.asax file itself.

In addition to the functionality available in a classic ASP Global.asa file, which was used for handling Application and/or Session start and end events and declaring Application- and/or Session-level variables, ASP.NET also allows you to import namespaces, link to assemblies, and perform other useful tasks. You'll learn more about Global.asax in Chapter 7.

- **Web.config**   A new file type in ASP.NET, used to solve one of the major hassles with classic ASP applications: configuration. The Web.config file is a human- and machine-readable XML-based file that stores all of the configuration settings for a given application (or segment of an application). Web.config files are interpreted hierarchically—a Web.config file in a subdirectory of your application will override the settings of the Web.config file (or files) in its parent directories. The advantage is that configuration settings can be inherited where that is desirable, but you also have very granular control over configuration.

Visual Studio .NET

It's certainly possible to create ASP.NET Web applications in Notepad or another text editor, but if you're doing serious ASP.NET or component development, you'll probably want to work within the Visual Studio .NET environment. The advantages of Visual Studio .NET over simple text editors include

- Robust management of project files and multiple projects
- Integration with the Microsoft Visual SourceSafe source-code control environment
- Visual Tools for working with Web services, Web Forms server controls, and database tools
- Packaging and deployment services for Web applications
- Support for multiple languages within a single IDE, including cross-language inheritance and debugging

That's just a brief list. There's much more to the tool than can be covered in a single chapter. So without further ado, let's look at how to create projects and pages in the Visual Studio .NET environment.

Creating Applications

One of the first things you're going to want to do in order to work with ASP.NET in Visual Studio .NET is create a new project, or in Visual Studio .NET parlance, a Web application.

Create an ASP.NET Web application

1   Launch Visual Studio .NET using the techniques you learned in Chapter 1.

2   Open the New Project dialog box using one of the following methods:

   ■   Click the Create A New Project link on the Visual Studio .NET Start Page (displayed by default when you first open Visual Studio .NET).

   ■   Click the New Project button (shown in the following illustration), located on the standard toolbar.

   ■   From the File menu, select New, and then Project.

3   In the New Project dialog box (see the following illustration), under Project Types, select the Visual C# Projects folder, then select the appropriate template (ASP.NET Web Application). Type the location as **http://localhost/Chapter_02**, and then click OK.

Visual Studio .NET will create a new Web application along with physical and virtual directories for the project.

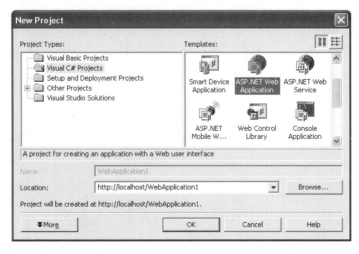

That's it! You've created your first ASP.NET Web application. Note that this application is separate from the Chapter_02 project included with the practice file installation, which is contained in the aspnetsbs solution. Next we'll look at how to add new pages.

In your new Web application, you'll notice that Visual Studio .NET has already added a page named WebForm1.aspx to the project for you and opened it in the editor. Your Visual Studio .NET screen should look similar to the following illustration. However, since one page is rarely enough for most sites, let's look at how to add a new page to your Web application.

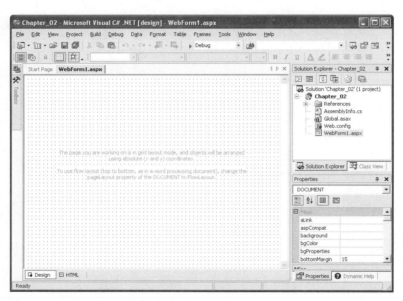

Create a new ASP.NET page (Web Form)

1   Add a new Web Form to your application.

As with creating a new project, there are several ways to add a new ASP.NET page (Web Form) to your application. The method you choose depends largely on how you like to work. Here are three ways to accomplish this task, although there are others:

■   In the Solution Explorer window, right-click the application name, then select Add, and then select Add Web Form, as shown in the illustration on the following page.

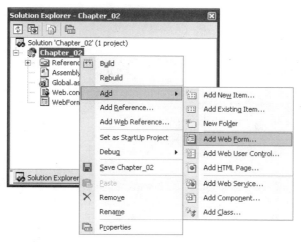

- On the Visual Studio .NET toolbar, click the Add New Item button (shown in the following illustration) and then select Web Form from the Templates list.

- From the Project menu, select Add Web Form.

Any of these methods will open the Add New Item dialog box, shown in the following illustration.

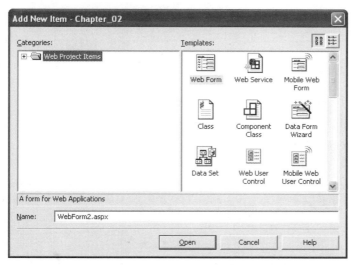

2   In the Add New Item dialog box, verify that the Web Form template is selected and name the new page Hello.aspx. Click Open.

Visual Studio .NET creates the page, adds it to the project, and opens it in the Web Forms Designer, as shown in the following illustration.

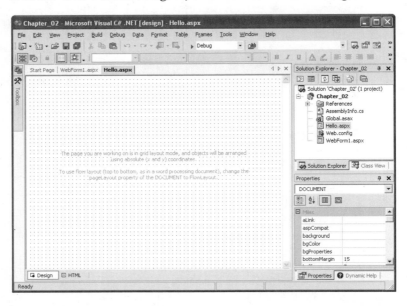

▶ **Tip**   While in the Add New Item dialog box, a brief description of each template is displayed along the bottom of the list window. If you decide to browse the different templates, don't forget to select the proper one (Web Form) before clicking Open.

Adding Server Controls

Now that you've created a page for your new application, what can you do with it? Well, let's begin by making it display a "Hello World!" greeting to the client. By default, Web Forms are opened in *GridLayout* mode. Since *GridLayout* relies on cascading style sheets (CSS), which are not supported in all browsers, you might want to change the page layout to *FlowLayout* mode.

Modify Web Form properties

1   With the Web Form open in the Visual Studio .NET designer, click the Web Form page to ensure it is selected.

When the page is selected, the word *DOCUMENT* should appear in the drop-down box at the top of the Properties window.

2   Select the *pageLayout* property from the Properties window, and
then use the drop-down list to change its value to *FlowLayout*, as
shown in the following illustration.

3   Save the page by selecting File, and then Save (or by clicking the Save
button on the toolbar).

Until you add controls (or HTML elements), the page will display the
following message in Design view.

Add controls to a Web Form

1   With the Web Form open in Design mode, place your mouse over the Toolbox tab. (By default, it's found to the left of the code editor/designer window.)

2   When the Toolbox appears, ensure that the Web Forms palette is active. (The title bar of the active palette is shown immediately above the controls displayed in the Toolbox.) If it isn't active, click on its title bar to activate it. Note that the Web Forms palette is available only when a page is in Design mode.

3   With the Web Forms palette active, double-click the *Label* control entry to add an *ASP.NET Label* control to the page. (You might have to let the toolbox hide itself by moving the mouse pointer away from it to see the label on the form.) Once you've added the label, it should be selected by default.

4   To make the *Label* control display the text you want, you need to change its *Text* property. Select the *Text* property in the Properties window, and then change the text (by default, Label) to **Enter a name:**, as shown in the following illustration.

5   Click the background of the page to place the cursor after the *Label* control you added to the page.

6   Using the Toolbox as in step 3, add a *TextBox* control to the page, and then add a *Button* control to the page.

7   Using the same technique as in step 4, change the *Text* property of the *Button* control to **Submit**.

8   Save the page by clicking the Save button (shown in the following illustration) on the toolbar. You can also save by selecting Save *<file-name>* from the File menu.

Add event handler code

1   To make the page do anything useful, you need to add some code, so double-click the *Button* control.

This will open up the code-behind module for the Web Form and create an event handler procedure called *Button1_Click*.

2   Add the following code to the *Button1_Click* procedure:

```
Label1.Text = "Hello, " + TextBox1.Text + "!";
TextBox1.Visible = false;
Button1.Visible = false;
```

3   Save the code-behind module, which should now look like the following illustration.

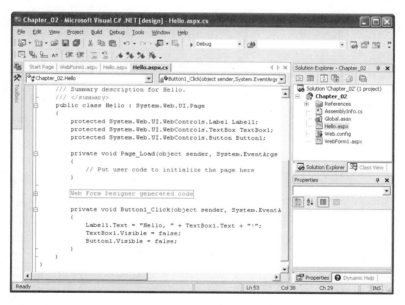

Building and Testing Your Page

Because you modified the code-behind module for the Web Form, you need to build your project before you can browse the page. (You'll learn more about code-behind in later chapters.) *Building* is the process of compiling all of the code modules in the project so they'll be available to the pages and modules that call them. To build the project, from the Build menu, select Build Chapter_02 (or Build Solution, which will build all projects in the solution).

Once you've saved the Web Form page and its code-behind module and built the application, you can test the page.

Test your page

1   Right-click the page in Solution Explorer and select View In Browser. The result should look like the following illustration. (You can close the Output window if you want to see more of a page.)

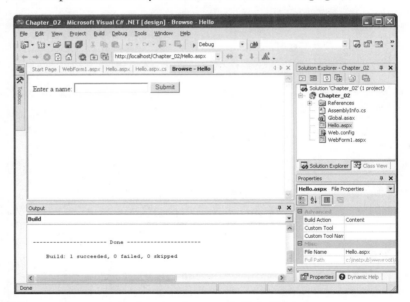

2   Enter your name in the text box and click Submit.

The result should be similar to the following illustration. (Note that the Web toolbar shows the address of the page being browsed. You can enter this address in a browser window on your machine to view the page in a non-embedded browser window.)

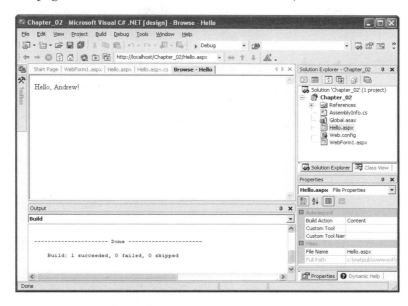

Chapter 2 Quick Reference

To	Do this	Button
Create a new project in Visual Studio .NET	Click the New Project button, select the project language and template, and then provide the name and location for the new project.	
Create a new Web Forms page	Click the Add New Item button (or click the arrow to the right and select Add Web Form). Provide a name for the new Web Form and click OK.	
Save a file	Click the Save button, or select Save *<filename>* from the File menu.	

Understanding Programming Basics

In this chapter, you will learn how to:

- Use expressions, variables, and constants.
- Use methods.
- Use flow control statements.
- Handle errors.
- Use object-oriented programming techniques.

This chapter is intended for readers who have little or no direct programming experience. It's designed to give a brief overview of some basic programming concepts that will help you better understand the examples presented throughout the book. Readers with programming experience might wish to skip this chapter and move on to Chapter 4.

Although this chapter provides an overview of basic programming concepts, I encourage readers with little hands-on programming experience to use other resources to supplement this information. These resources include books on programming basics, Web sites such as the Microsoft Developer Network site (*http://msdn.microsoft.com*), and newsgroups and mailing lists that can be helpful to the inexperienced. (Microsoft maintains a large number of newsgroups on development topics related to Microsoft tools at *http://msdn.microsoft.com/newsgroups/*. You can read from and post to these newsgroups using a newsreader such as Outlook Express.) And the ASP.NET development team at Microsoft has just launched a set of discussion forums on ASP.NET that promise to be a great resource as well.

These forums can be found at *http://www.asp.net/forums/*. Of course, one of the best (and most overlooked) resources for programming concepts in C# is the MSDN documentation that ships with Microsoft Visual C# .NET (a subset of which is also available as part of the quarterly MSDN library, which can be ordered from *http://msdn.microsoft.com/subscription*). The MSDN documentation contains samples, tutorials, language references, and specifications for C#, Microsoft Visual Basic .NET, managed extensions for C++, and JScript .NET.

This chapter will discuss how these basic programming concepts apply to ASP.NET, and how you can use them to create effective ASP.NET applications. Although most of these concepts aren't language-specific, there are some subtle differences in how they're implemented in C# vs. Visual Basic .NET or other .NET languages.

▶   **Note**   In ASP.NET, all code is contained in either Web Forms pages, code-behind modules, or modules that make up class libraries that are external to your ASP.NET applications. The term *module* in this sense refers to the .cs file that contains the code.

A *class*, as you'll see in "Using Classes as Containers for Code" later in this chapter, is a special type of code container that provides a number of useful features. Classes are contained within modules (that is, files with the extension .cs).

A *namespace* contains one or more classes and can be defined in one or more modules. Namespaces can be used to prevent name collisions when two classes have the same name.

Expressions, Variables, and Constants

Expressions, variables, and constants are some of the most basic building blocks of computer programs, and you'll use them all extensively in your ASP.NET applications.

Expressions

Expressions are central to virtually all computer programs. Expressions enable you to:

- Compare values to one another
- Perform calculations
- Manipulate text values

An expression can be as simple as the following:

```
1 + 1
```

An expression like this isn't very useful by itself, however. Unlike people, who can easily recognize "one plus one" and fill in the blank ("equals two"), computers aren't capable of that kind of leap of logic. For the expression to be useful, it needs to tell a computer not just to add one and one, but to store the result somewhere so that we can make use of it later (either by displaying it to the user or using it in another expression later). This is where variables come in.

Variables

As with the preceding example, at some point during the execution of most programs, you'll need to store values of some sort. Examples include the results of mathematical operations (as in the preceding example), text input from users, and the results of comparisons. Simply put, *variables* are storage areas for data. This data can be numeric, text, or any one of a number of special data types.

Data Types

The *data type* variable defines the type of data that can be stored in it, as well as the format in which that data is stored (and the amount of memory that the system needs to allocate for the variable). The following table lists the data types supported by C# and Visual Basic .NET, as well as the Microsoft .NET Framework SDK types to which they map. The data types marked with an asterisk don't have a native representation, but you can still access these data types by using the appropriate *System* type when declaring the variable. Why cover Visual Basic .NET types? If you are creating a class to be used by other developers, knowing how the types match between C# and Visual Basic .NET is critical, both to ensure that the correct type is used, and to document the class in a Visual Basic .NET programmer-friendly way. The good news is that, unlike in the 32 bit Win32 world of Visual Basic 6 and Visual C++ 6, an integer in both environments is the same size and has the same numeric range.

The data type of a variable is determined at the time the variable is declared. This will be discussed further in the section titled "Declaring Variables" later in this chapter. Some data types (such as the *Date* type) do not have language specific implementations. In Table 3-1, there is an asterisk (*) in the cells of types without the corresponding language-specific data types. Some data types are not Common Language Specification (CLS) compliant, and are noted with a cross (†) in the .NET data type column.

Table 3-1. Data Types

C# data type	VB.NET data type	.NET data type	Size
bool	*Boolean*	*System.Boolean*	1 byte
byte	*Byte*	*System.Byte*	1 byte
sbyte	*	*System.SByte †*	1 byte

Table 3-1.   Data Types

C# data type	VB.NET data type	.NET data type	Size
char	Char	System.Char	2 bytes
*	Date	System.DateTime	8 bytes
decimal	Decimal	System.Decimal	12 bytes
double	Double	System.Double	8 bytes
int	Integer	System.Int32	4 bytes
uint	*	System.UInt32 †	4 bytes
long	Long	System.Int64	8 bytes
ulong	*	System.UInt64 †	8 bytes
object	Object	System.Object	4 bytes
short	Short	System.Int16	2 bytes
ushort	*	System.UInt16 †	2 bytes
float	Single	System.Single	4 bytes
string	String	System.String	10 bytes, plus (2 x string length)
struct	User-Defined Type	System.ValueType (inherited)	Sum of member sizes

▶ **Important**   ASP.NET contains both framework-specific data types and language-specific data types for specific .NET languages, such as C# and Visual Basic .NET. To take advantage of some of the multilanguage features of the .NET environment, you need to limit your use of data types to those supported by the CLS, a subset of the data types supported by the common language runtime. In the preceding table, data types marked with a † are not CLS-compliant. Avoid using them in classes that you want to make available for use with other .NET languages.

Note that C# does not have a native type that maps to the *DateTime* data type, but using the .NET data type is just as easy.

Value Types vs. Reference Types

In .NET development, there are two categories of data types: value types and reference types. Although understanding the distinction between these types isn't absolutely necessary if you want to develop ASP.NET applications, it can help you better understand how these data types operate and how to deal with error messages resulting from coding errors. (Not that those ever happen, right?)

Value types are data types that store their data directly as values in memory. They include all the numeric types (*int32*, *short*, *single*, and so on), structures (custom data types based on *System.ValueType*), and enumerations (custom types that represent a defined set of values), as well as *boolean*, *char*, and *date* types. Value types are accessed directly, as in the following example:

```
int myInt; // C# declaration for an int32
// Expression to assign the value 123 directly to the variable
myInt = 123;
```

> ▶ **Note**   C++ programmers will recognize all the syntax used to declare and assign variables, as well as comment delimiters. If instead you are using C# and have a Visual Basic background, several elements of C# syntax might require explanation.
>
> Virtually all C# statements end with semicolons (;). Multiple C# statements can appear on a single line as long as all statements are terminated with semicolons. Unlike Visual Basic .NET, you can spread a single statement over as many lines as needed without using any sort of line extender (such as the underscore character (_) used by Visual Basic .NET). C# ignores whitespace characters, such as spaces, tabs, and new lines.
>
> Comments in C# can be single line comments that begin with two slash characters (//) or multiline comments that begin with slash-star (/*) and end with star-slash (*/).

Reference types are data types that store a reference to another memory location that contains the data, which is usually based on a class, such as the *String* class in the .NET Framework. Reference types include *Object* (which acts as a replacement for Visual Basic's *Variant* type, no longer supported in .NET), *String*, and all *Arrays*, as well as instances of custom classes. Reference types are accessed through members of the class to which the type holds a reference, as in the following example:

```
// Define a class
class myClass {
  public int myInt;
}
// declare an instance of the class
myClass myClassInstance;
// Allocate space for the class
myClass = new myClass();
// Expression to assign the value 123 to myClass member myInt
myClass.myInt = 123;
```

Unlike value types, in which all you need to do is declare the variable and set a value, reference types must be declared and then have space allocated for them, using the new keyword in the example.

▶ **Note**   Conversion between value types and reference types is accomplished through a process called boxing and unboxing. *Boxing* is the process of creating an instance of the reference type object and assigning the value of a value type to the object (as well as storing information on the value's data type). *Unboxing* is the process of assigning the value of the boxed object type to a variable of the appropriate type (or a compatible type, such as assigning a boxed *int16* to a variable of type *int32*). Boxing and unboxing variables enables you to use the most lightweight variable possible, while still being able to box that variable into an object. An example follows:

```
int myInt = 42; // declare and set value of variable
object myObj = myInt; // myInt now boxed as an object containing
// both the value 42 and the type int
int myOtherInt = (int)myObj; // value 42 unboxed into
// value type myOtherInt
```

Declaring Variables

Before you can use variables in your programs, you need to declare them. *Variable declaration* is the process of specifying the characteristics of the variable (data type, lifetime, scope, and visibility) so that the runtime system knows how much storage space to allocate for the variable, which actions to allow on the variable, and who can take those actions. A variable declaration takes the following form in C#:

```
int x; // Declares a variable of type int
```

▶ **Note**   The previous example uses *x* as the name of the variable. Although this is perfectly acceptable as far as the language compilers are concerned, you should consider giving your variables more meaningful names, such as *FirstName* (for a string variable holding a first name), *LoopCount* (for a numeric variable used in a looping structure), or *Person* (for a reference to a class representing data on a person). This naming convention makes it much easier to remember the purpose of a variable, and it will make your code much easier to maintain. You can find naming guidelines for use in .NET class libraries at *http://msdn.microsoft.com/library/en-us/cpgenref/html/cpconnetframeworkdesignguidelines.asp*.

The preceding declaration specifies a variable of type *int* (which maps to the System.Int32 type). In addition to simple declarations like these, you can use the placement of the declarations, as well as C# keywords, to modify the lifetime, scope, and accessibility of your variables.

Lifetime

Lifetime refers to the span of time from when the variable is declared to when it is destroyed. The lifetime of a variable depends on where it is declared.

▶ **Note**   The following examples in this chapter write text into the *Text* property of a label control named *Message*. Labels and other server controls will be explained more completely in Chapter 8.

For example, the lifetime of a variable declared inside a procedure is limited to the execution of the procedure. After the procedure has finished executing, the variable is destroyed and the memory it occupied is reclaimed. An example is shown here:

```
// C# method
private void HelloWorld()
{
  String HelloString;
  string hellostring;
  HelloString = "Hello World!";
  hellostring = HelloString;
  Message.Text += HelloString;
  Message.Text += "<br/>";
  Message.Text += hellostring;
  // Both HelloString and hellostring will disappear
  //   after the next line...
}
```

▶ **Important**   There are two strings in this example, one declared as a *String* and the other declared as a *string* to remind you that C#, like C++, is case sensitive. In this example, the first string, *HelloString*, is declared as a *System.String* because in searching for the type *String* (note the uppercase S), C# will find *System.String*. The second variable, *hellostring*, is declared as a string (note the lowercase s). This means that *hellostring* is declared using the C# alias for *System.String*. C# considers *HelloString* and *hellostring* to be entirely different objects. This is an important point to remember if you are a beginning C# programmer.

When this procedure completes, the variables HelloString and hellostring no longer exist. Their lifetime has ended. If HelloString had been declared outside the procedure, as in this next fragment of code, its lifetime would be until the instance of the class containing it was destroyed.

```
// Declare string outside of method
String HelloString;
// C# method
void HelloWorld()
{
```

```
HelloString = "Hello World!";
Message.Text += HelloString;
// HelloString will still exist
//  after the next line...
}
```

C# variables can also be declared as *static*. Static variables exist for the life of the class, and even if there are many instances of the class, there is only a single instance of the static variable. Static variables must be declared as members of the class rather than inside a single method.

▶ **Note** The C# documentation recommends using whole words when naming your variables. You should use mixed case, with the first letter of each word capitalized, as in *HelloString*. This is called *Pascal case*. This is one of many possible naming conventions you can use for variables and other elements in your programs. *Naming conventions* are simply agreed-upon standards for how elements will be named in a program. For instance, making the first character of the first word in a phrase lower case and capitalizing the first character of each subsequent word is called *Camel case*. The particular naming convention you choose isn't important, but you must choose one and use it consistently. Doing so will make it easier for you to maintain your code and will help others understand what it's doing.

Scope

Scope, also known as *visibility*, refers to the region of code in which a variable can be accessed. The scope of a variable depends on where the variable is declared, and in Visual C# .NET it can include the following levels.

- **Block-level**   Variables declared within curly braces, {}, for instance in an *if* or *while* statement, are referred to as block-level variables. Although the scope of block-level variables is limited to the block in which they're declared, their lifetime is that of the procedure in which the block appears.

- **Procedure-level**   Also known as local variables, these are visible only within the procedure in which they're declared.

- **Module-level**   In modules, classes, or structures, any variable declared outside of a procedure is referred to as a module-level variable. The accessibility of module-level variables is determined by any accessibility keywords used in their declaration (see the section titled "Accessibility" later in this chapter).

- **Namespace-level**   Variables declared at module level but given public accessibility (*public* or *internal*), are referred to as namespace-level variables. They're available to any procedure in the same namespace that contains the module in which the variable is declared.

Namespaces

A namespace is a container used for scoping. Namespaces can contain classes, structures, enumerations, interfaces, and delegates. By using namespaces, you can have more than one class in a given program with the same name, so long as the classes reside in different namespaces. Using namespaces can help ensure that code created by multiple teams of developers can be combined to create larger systems without name collisions.

Namespaces declared in C# use the *namespace { }* syntax, where the classes and other types to be contained within the namespace are bracketed by the curly braces.

Namespaces can also be nested within other namespaces, forming a hierarchical tree structure. This structure enables you to combine classes in logical groupings, making it easier for those using your namespaces to find the classes they're looking for.

Following these guidelines will make your application more memory-efficient and will make maintaining your code easier.

There is one significant difference in how scope works in C# vs. C++. The following code would work in C++, but fail in C#:

```
private void ScopeTest()
{
    int foo;
    foo = 2;
    if ( foo != 2 )
    {
        // This would work in C++, fail in C#
        int foo;
        foo = 7;
    }
    // In C++, foo would now be equal to the number 2, and the
    //foo declared inside the if statement is not visible
    //or available.
    /* In C#, if the only instance of foo was declared inside
    the if statement, foo would not be visible or
    available, but you would still be unable to
    declare a variable named foo.
    */
}
```

In this contrived example, even though the second copy of foo is declared within the braces of the *if* statement, the compiler will generate an error and fail to compile the code because that second instance of foo would hide the first instance. In C++, the second declaration of foo would declare a variable visible only inside the *if* statement, hiding the previous value of foo. You can, however, declare a variable at the class level and then declare a variable of the same name, even with a different type, within a method of that class.

There are a couple of guidelines to follow regarding lifetime and scope:

- Limit your variables to the narrowest possible scope that will allow you to accomplish your objectives.

- Avoid using the same name for variables of different scope within the same module even where it is allowed. Using the same name in such situations can lead to confusion and errors.

- Because module-level and *static* variables all continue to consume memory as long as the class or module is running, you should use them only when necessary.

Accessibility

The last important concept in variable declaration is accessibility. The accessibility of a variable determines whether it can be accessed from outside the module (or application) in which it's declared. In C#, accessibility is determined through the use of one the following modifiers.

- *public*   Variables declared with the *public* keyword are accessible from anywhere in the same module (or class) in which they're declared, the namespace containing that module, and any other applications that refer to the application in which they're declared. They can only be used at the module or class level.

- *internal*   Variables declared with the *internal* keyword are accessible from anywhere in the same module (or class) in which they're declared, as well as the namespace containing that module.

- *protected*   Variables declared with the *protected* keyword are accessible only within the class in which they're declared or a class that inherits from that class. (See the section titled "Using Inheritance" later in this chapter.) The *protected* keyword can be combined with the *internal* keyword and can be used only to declare class members.

- *private*   Variables declared with the *private* keyword are accessible only from the module, class, or structure in which they're declared. In classes or modules, declaring a variable with no modifier or as *private* has the same effect on the variable's accessibility, but *private* makes your intentions more explicit. The *private* keyword cannot be used within a procedure.

▶ **Note**   In C#, all variables must be declared before they can be used. Failure to declare a variable will result in a compiler error. In Visual Basic .NET and some other languages, it's possible (but not advisable) to use variables without first declaring them.

Operators

In addition to the normal operators you are familiar with ('+' for addition, '-' for subtraction, '/' for division, '*' for multiplication, and '=' for assignment), there are several operators borrowed from C and C++ that require some explanation.

- ++ Increment operator, incrementing the value by 1 (i++ is the same as i=i+1)
- — Decrement operator, decrementing the value by 1 (i— is the same as i=i-1)
- += Increment assignment operator (i+=5 is the same as i=i+5)
- -= Decrement assignment operator (i-=5 is the same as i=i-5)
- == and != Equality and Inequality operator
- % Modulus (remainder) operator. (17%5 equals 2)

There are other, less essential operators that are fully described in the MSDN documentation, and even the common operators can have other meanings. For instance, the plus sign (+) is also used as a string concatenation operator. In addition, operators can be overloaded, enabling you to define new meanings for them when used in combination with your class.

Constants

Constants are similar to variables, except for one important detail: After a constant has been declared and initialized, its value cannot be modified. Constants are very useful when you have a literal value that you want to refer to by name. For example, if you're a fan of Douglas Adams, you might want to create a constant to refer to the literal value *42*.

```
const int TheAnswer = 42;
```

Anywhere within your program (subject to the same scope, lifetime, and accessibility rules as variables) you can use the constant name *TheAnswer* instead of the literal value *42*.

Constants are particularly handy in place of literal values used as the arguments to methods of components you might use. For example, in classic Microsoft ActiveX Data Objects (ADO), the data types of stored procedure parameters were represented by numeric values. Trying to remember all those values would be unrealistic, so the developers of ADO also made it possible to use constants (*adInteger*, *adVarChar*, and so on) in place of the literal values.

In other words, constants let you substitute easy-to-remember names for difficult-to-remember literal values. This can make your code easier to write and maintain.

Enumerations

Many constants used with ASP.NET are actually created using enumerations. Using enumerations, you can locate all related constants together, and the enumerations can be used in a type-safe way. For example, enumerations would be handy if you have a method that accepts numeric values representing a color numbered between 1 and 3. For instance, you might want to set a color:

```
private void SetColor(int color);
```

This method will, in fact, happily accept any integer value. You could declare an enumeration as follows:

```
enum ColorType {
Red = 1,
Green,
Blue
}
```

By default the first element of an enumeration is equal to 0. In this example, because I need an enumeration that contains 1 through 3, I set the first value in the enumeration to 1, and then the subsequent values are each incremented by one. So Green is 2 and Blue is 3. Now, rather than the previous method declaration, you could use the following:

```
private void SetColor(ColorType color);
```

This method will require an instance of the ColorType enumeration passed as the parameter, ensuring that the value is a valid member of the enumeration, and thus that the value represents a valid color. The following is an example of calling SetColor with a ColorType enumeration member:

```
SetColor(ColorType.Blue);
```

Methods

Methods (functions inside of a class—all functions must be inside a class in C#) are an important tool in ASP.NET development because they enable you to determine at the time you write the code the order in which sections of code will run at runtime. Methods also enable you to better organize your code into discrete units based on the functionality provided by each one. For example, if you write code that multiplies two numbers and returns the result, that code is much more useful if it's wrapped in a procedure. Using a method allows the code to be called from more than one place in your application as necessary, which enables you to reuse the code rather than rewrite it each time you need to multiply two numbers. Unlike Visual Basic, which has a *Sub* and a *Function* as distinct concepts, C# has only a single type of method, a function. Of course, you can create a method in C# without returning a value by declaring the function return type *void*. A special "type" in C#, *void* is used to specify that a method does not return a value as in this example:

```
// C# procedure that writes output to the browser
private void WriteHello1(string FirstName)
{
   Message.Text += "Hello, " + FirstName + "!<br/>";
}
```

Receiving Input Parameters

Note that in a C# function, the name of the procedure is followed by a set of empty parentheses. These parentheses have a purpose other than simply taking up space. You can place code between these parentheses to define one or more parameters that users must pass when they call the procedure. Parameters can be passed either by value (a copy of the value is passed to the procedure) or by reference (a reference to the location of the value is passed to the procedure, which allows the procedure to modify the original value). You use the keyword *ref* to specify that the parameter is to be passed by reference. If no keyword is used, the parameters will be passed by value. The following code shows some examples:

```
private void ModifyInt(int MyInt)
{
   MyInt += 42;
   // Modified value will not be available
   // once this method returns.
}
private void ModifyInt(ref int MyInt)
{
   MyInt += 42;
   // Modified value will be available to
   // calling method.
}
```

You can pass more than one parameter to a procedure simply by separating each parameter with a comma, as in the following example:

```
private void WriteHello(string Name1, string Name2)
{
   Response.Write("Hello to both " + Name1 + " and " + Name2)
}
```

Note that you explicitly type the parameters by declaring the data type of each parameter as *string*. If any data type other than *string* is passed to the procedure, the method will not compile. Because the C# *string* type is just an alias for the *System.String* type, you could pass in a *System.String* instance as a parameter and there would be no type violation.

Early vs. Late Binding

One difference between C# and Visual Basic .NET is that C# forces early binding whereas Visual Basic .NET allows late binding by default. Late vs. early binding is a concept that is difficult to grasp without an example. Imagine the following method in Visual Basic .NET (don't worry—this is a very simple function that requires no Visual Basic .NET experience):

```
Private Sub foo(ByRef bar As Integer)
   bar = 2
End Sub
```

This method is very straightforward; accept a single parameter as an integer and set it equal to the number 2. Because the variable is passed by reference (note the ByRef keyword), the changed value will be available to the calling method.

Imagine now that you call the method as follows:

```
foo("1");
```

Will this work? That depends. With the default settings, Visual Basic .NET will compile this and work at runtime. This is late binding. One consequence of this (beside the overhead of converting the string "1" to a number at runtime) is that it is possible that a failure can occur that will not be detected at compile time. For instance, if you call foo as follows:

```
foo("One");
```

What we intend here is clearly less obvious. The string literal "One" cannot be converted to a number, and so if Visual Basic .NET is set up to use late binding, an exception will be thrown at runtime.

The moral of the story is that using C# (with its forced early binding) is a good thing!

Function Overloading

C# does not allow optional parameters, however, much of the same effect can be realized by using function overloading. Function overloading means that there is more than one method with the same name, but different parameters.

For instance, imagine that you have a method that accepts a person's first name, like so:

```
private void WriteHello( string FirstName)
{
  Message.Text += "Hello, " + FirstName + "!<br/>";
}
```

Now let's say that you embed this all over an application and then discover that you really need to make the last name available in some cases. One solution would be to create an additional method, as follows:

```
private void WriteHello(string FirstName, string LastName)
{
  Message.Text += "Hello, " + FirstName + " " + LastName + "!<br/>";
}
```

Now you can call WriteHello and pass in either a single string or two strings. In a more complex example, rather than having each overloaded method actually do some work, you would likely make all methods except one (the one that passes the largest number of parameters) into shell methods that simply call the version with the most parameters, adding default values when called. So you might re-create the WriteHello method that accepts a single string as follows:

```
private void WriteHello(string FirstName)
{
  // Call the two-parameter method and default

  // to an empty string for last name
  WriteHello(FirstName, "");
}
```

This is not quite as convenient as optional parameters as implemented in Visual Basic .NET, but does allow the same functionality.

Returning Values from Functions

All the previous examples used the void return type, meaning that no value was returned from the method. There are two ways of getting values back from a method call. The first is by declaring a non-void return type. For instance, to safely divide two numbers we could do the following:

```
private int Divide(int Numerator, int Divisor)
{
  if ( Divisor != 0 )
  {
    // the return keyword returns the value that follows it

    //   to the caller
    return(Numerator/Divisor);
```

```
    }
    else
    {
        return(0);
    }
}
```

This method prevents me from dividing by 0, and returns 0 if division by 0 is requested. One thing to remember about returning values from a C# method is that there is no default return value. Every logical path in the method must return a value of the correct type. Thus, if I rewrite the method as follows, it will fail to compile:

```
private int Divide(int Numerator, int Divisor)
{
    if ( Divisor!=0 )
    {
        return(Numerator/Divisor);
    }
    else
    {
        Response.Write("Error! Division by 0 requested!");
    }
}
```

The compile time error that C# will return for this method is "Not all code paths return a value." If you say a method will return an int, it really must return one! This example returns an integer, but you can return any type, including complex types like classes and structures. The second way to return a value from a method is to use a *ref* parameter. When you say a parameter is passed by ref, rather than the actual value being passed to the method, a reference (very much like a pointer) is passed, so that changes to the parameter's value will be visible back in the calling method. For instance:

```
private void RefTest(ref int Number)
    {
        Number += 5;
    }


private void CallRefTest()
{
    int foo = 5;
    RefTest(ref foo);
    // Now foo is 10!
}
```

Note that when you pass a ref parameter you must precede the variable name with the keyword *ref*. When calling by reference, you must pass a variable, not a constant. Thus, the following will be invalid:

```
RefTest(ref 5);
```

The compiler message related to this error is "An out or ref argument must be an lvalue." An *lvalue* is an expression that can be placed on the left side of an equal sign used for assignment. Saying 5 = x (where we are using the single equal sign for assignment rather than the double equal sign used for testing equality) makes no sense, so 5 is not an lvalue.

In addition to ref, you can pass a parameter as an *out* parameter. This is similar to a ref, but unlike a ref, the parameter need not be initialized before being passed to the method. For example:

```
private void OutTest(out int Number)
{
    Number = 5;
}
private void CallOutTest()
{
    int foo;
    // Now foo is not initialized!
    // If I tried to use foo here, a compile time error
    //will occur.
    OutTest(out foo);
    // Now foo is 5!
}
```

In this example, foo is declared but not initialized in CallOutTest. In OutTest, foo is assigned a value, and OutTest makes no assumptions about the value of Number being passed as a parameter. If rather than assigning a value to Number, I tried to use the value first, or even tried to increment the value using += rather than just assigning a value, a compile time error occurs.

Finally, you can change the accessibility of a method using the public, private, internal, and protected keywords. Methods are private by default, which means they can be called only from the module, class or struct they reside in. This is the exact opposite of the default in Visual Basic .NET, where methods are public by default.

Flow Control

Another important part of any program is flow control, which enables you to determine at runtime which sections of your code will run, and in what order.

Flow control statements are the foundation of business logic and consist of conditional logic (including *if* and *case* statements), looping structures (*for...* and *do...* loops), and error-handling statements.

if Statements

if statements are the form of conditional logic, also known as decision structures, that you will probably use most in your programs. They enable you to look for a defined logical condition in your program and execute a specific block of code if that condition is *true*. The following code checks a *Session* variable for the logged-in user name (set in the login page) to prevent a user who has not logged into your ASP.NET application from viewing pages that require a login:

```
if ( Session["LoggedInUserName"] == "" )

{

  Response.Redirect("Login.aspx");

}
```

In C#, *if* statements consist of the keyword *if* (case sensitive!), a *predicate* or condition expression, followed by the expression or block to be executed if the predicate evaluates to true. The *if* keyword is self-explanatory.

> ▶ **Note**   To index into the ASP.NET objects such as Session and Application, C#
> uses square brackets ([and]) rather than parentheses. If you use parentheses
> instead, you will get the compile time error message " 'Session' denotes a
> property where a 'method' was expected.", which may seem a little confusing.
> What this is telling you is that Session is a property that needs to be indexed
> using square brackets rather than a method, called with parentheses.

A predicate is an expression that can be simple (as in the previous example) or quite complex, spanning multiple lines as needed. (Recall that C# ignores white space such as spaces, tabs, and newlines.) A predicate can contain multiple expressions that evaluate to *true* or *false* chained by && (logical AND) or || (logical OR) operators. For instance, the following predicate checks for the same *Session* variable as the previous example AND that a variable called *Tries* is not equal to 7:

```
if ( Session["LoggedInUserName"] == "" && Tries != 7 )
{
  Response.Redirect("Login.aspx");
}
```

In this example, if Session ["LoggedInUserName"] is not equal to an empty string, the test for Tries != 7 will not be evaluated. This is called *Short-Circuit Evaluation*. After C# determines that no matter whether an expression evaluates to *true* or *false*, the predicate will still evaluate to *true* or *false*, the additional expressions are not evaluated. In this example it would not matter, but in other examples one of the expressions might have a side effect of being evaluated (changing some variable or calling a method that does). Short-Circuit Evaluation also enables you to test expressions that might run quickly first, and then test those expressions that might take some time to run only if testing the expression could make a difference.

If the predicate evaluates to *true*, the single line or the block immediately below the *if* statement is executed. The following example would work exactly the same as the previous example:

```
if ( Session["LoggedInUserName"] == "" && Tries!=7 )
    Response.Redirect("Login.aspx");
```

This *if* statement is different from virtually all other examples in this book in that it does not use curly braces. Why do I always use curly braces and have a single line *if* statement enclosed within a block? Imagine that I added one more line of code and ended up with the following:

```
// Bad example of what can happen when your indentation says one
// thing, but the code something else.
if ( Session["LoggedInUserName"] == "" && Tries!=7 )
    Tries++;
    Response.Redirect("Login.aspx");
```

Although my indentation means "If there is no logged in user and *Tries* is not equal to 7, increment *Tries* and redirect to Login.aspx," what will really happen is that *Tries* will be incremented only if the predicate evaluates to *true*, and the user will *always* be redirected to Login.aspx. You should always use curly braces, no matter how simple the expression, as this will make your intent explicit, and make your code easier to read.

You can also provide code that will execute if the defined condition is *false* by adding the *else* statement. You can nest *if* and *else* statements as needed. These techniques are shown in the following example:

```
if ( Session["LoggedInUserName"] == "" )
{
    Response.Redirect("Login.aspx");
}
else
{
```

```
if ( Session["LoggedInUserName"] == "SuperUser" )
{
    Response.Write("You are a superuser!");
}
else
{
    Response.Write("Hello, " + Session["LoggedInUserName"] + "!");
}
}
```

▶ **Note**   C# enables you to place en entire *if* statement on a single line, such as the following:

```
if ( 1 < 2 ) Response.Write("1 is less than 2");
```

This syntax should only be used for very simple *if* statements because it is inherently harder to read and debug single-line *if* statements. On occasion I might use such a construct when I need to have lots of *if* statements in a row and want to conserve space. Generally, rethinking the logic to find another way to conserve space is a better solution than placing all of the code for an *if* statement on a single line.

switch case Statements

Another form of conditional logic you'll use frequently is the *switch case* statement. This statement is useful in situations where you can reasonably expect the defined condition you're testing to evaluate to one of a limited number of values (or ranges of values). Unlike *switch case* statements in C++, C# *switch case* statements can switch not only on integer values, but on strings as well. For example, the following code checks to see which item of a listbox was chosen by a user and then it takes appropriate action:

```
switch(ColorString)
{
case "Red":
  Message.Text += "< font color='" + ColorString + "'>";
  Message.Text += "You chose Red";
  Message.Text += "</font>";
  break;
case "Green":
  Message.Text += "<font color='" + ColorString + "'>";
  Message.Text += "You chose Green";
  Message.Text += "</font>";
  break;
case "Blue":
  Message.Text += "<font color='" + ColorString + "'>";
```

```
    Message.Text += "You chose Blue";
    Message.Text += "</font>";
    break;
}
```

You can also add a *default* statement to execute specific code when the tested expression doesn't match any of your listed values, as the following code demonstrates:

```
switch(ColorString)
{
  case "Red":
  // ...
  case "Green":
  // ...
  case "Blue":
  // ...
  default:
    Message.Text += "<font color='black'>";
    Message.Text += "You did not chose a color";
    Message.Text += "</font>";
    break;
}
```

It's good programming practice to always have a *default* statement just in case there are unexpected values for the expression you're testing (such as *ColorString* in this example). Note also that *default* is a C# keyword, so naming a class *default* (with a lowercase *d*) can be a problem. You might inadvertently end up trying to use *default* as a class name if you create a page default.aspx. Use Default.aspx (note the upper-case *D*) to avoid this, or better yet, use a different page name!

▶ **Note**   C++ programmers are used to sometimes not using a *break* statement at the end of every *case* to allow processing to "drop through" to the next *case*. Although there are some cases in which C# does allow this (documented in the C# Language Reference in the MSDN documentation), it is always safer to just include the *break*.

Let's actually use the *switch case* statement in a real Web Form. I will use several components that will be explained later in Chapter 9.

Use the *switch case* Statement

1   Open Visual Studio .NET.

2   On the File menu, choose New, and then click Project.

3   In the New Project dialog box, click the ASP.NET Web Application icon from the C# Project Type.

4   Name the project Chapter_03 as shown in the following illustration, and click OK.

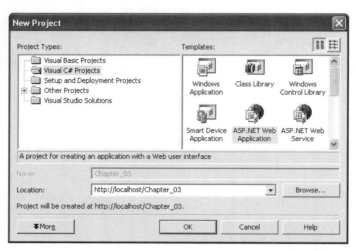

5   You should see the Visual Studio .NET screen, as shown in the following illustration.

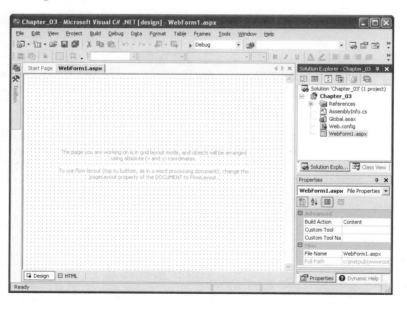

6 Move the mouse pointer over the Toolbox along the left side of the screen. It will expand. Drag a *Label* control onto the form, and then drag a *DropDownList* control onto the form and place it next to the label. Add another label to the form below the drop-down list and the other label. The form should look like the following illustration.

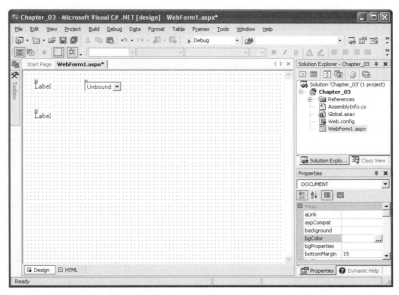

7 Click the drop-down list, and then in the Properties pane, change the *ID* from *DropDownList1* to **Color**. Change *AutoPostBack* from False to True. In the drop-down list, scroll down to the *Items* property, click the ellipsis (...), and enter items for the drop-down list by clicking the Add button four times. Then click the Text box in the Properties pane for the first item and change it to **Select a Color**. Change the text box of the second item to **Red**, the third item to **Green**, and the fourth item to **Blue**. When the screen looks like the illustration on the following page, click OK.

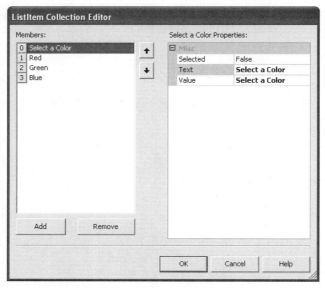

8 Change the text of the label next to the drop-down list to **Color**. Change the *ID* of the label below the drop-down list to **Message**.

9 Double-click the drop-down list and a screen will appear, as shown in the following illustration.

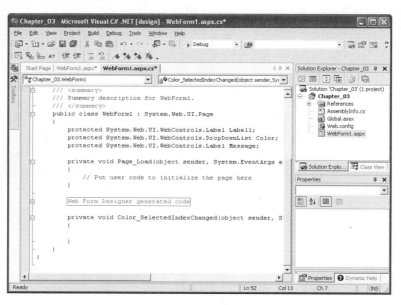

This is the event handler that is called when the selected item in the drop-down list is changed by the user. This is covered more fully in Chapter 9.

10 Add the following code to the *Color_SelectedIndexChanged* event handler:

```
// Initialize label.
Message.Text = "";
switch(Color.SelectedItem.Text)
{
  case "Red":
  Message.Text += "<font color='" + Color.SelectedItem.Text + "'>";
  Message.Text += "You chose Red";
  Message.Text += "</font>";
  break;
  case "Green":
  Message.Text += "<font color='" + Color.SelectedItem.Text + "'>";
  Message.Text += "You chose Green";
  Message.Text += "</font>";
  break;
  case "Blue":
  Message.Text += "<font color='" + Color.SelectedItem.Text + "'>";
  Message.Text += "You chose Blue";
  Message.Text += "</font>";
  break;
  default:
  Message.Text += "<font color=\"black\">";
  Message.Text += "You did not chose a color";
  Message.Text += "</font>";
  break;
}
```

11 On the File menu, click Save All to save the page, and then on the Build menu, click Build Chapter_03 to compile the application.

12 Browse the page by right-clicking it in Solution Explorer, and then selecting View In Browser (or Browse With).

13 To select a color other than the default, click the down arrow to the right of the drop-down list, and click a color. A screen similar to the one shown in the following illustration will appear.

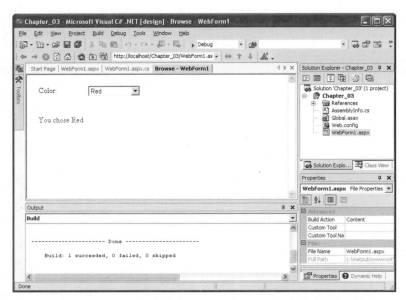

This simple example shows several features of ASP.NET and C# within Visual Studio .NET, including:

- **RAD development**   Drop controls on the form, and then handle events.
- **Codeless development**   The ability to set many properties on controls without any coding.
- **Automatic postbacks by controls other than buttons**   Every time you select an item from the list, the form actually posts back to the server. This allows for a much richer user interface than classic ASP.

Looping Statements

Looping statements are useful features that enable you to perform actions repeatedly, by either specifying explicitly at design time the number of times the code should loop, deciding at runtime how many times to loop, or looping through a collection of objects and taking a specific action on each item. There are several different types of looping statements, each of which has its own particular syntax and is useful for a different situation. Loop types include

- *for...* loops
- *foreach...* loops, a special case of *for...* loops
- *do...while* loops
- *while...* loops

Using *for*... Loops

for... loops are useful for repeating a given set of statements a number of times. The number of times the statements are executed can be determined either explicitly or by evaluating an expression that returns a numeric value. The following example (from the *ASP.NET QuickStart Tutorial*) uses a *for*... loop that counts from 1 to 7, and for each pass of the loop, outputs a message with a font size equal to the counter variable:

```
int i;
for ( i = 0 ; i<7 ; i++ )
{
    Message.Text += "<font size=\"" + i + "\">Welcome to ASP.NET</font><br/>";
}
```

▶ **Note** In this example, I use a backslash (\) inside the string to escape the quotation mark ("). Quotation marks around the font size are required for properly formed HTML because they are used as the string delimiter.

In this example, in addition to using the variable *i*, *i* could also be declared within the *for*... loop, as in this example:

```
for ( int i = 0 ; i < 7 ; i++ )
{
    Message.Text += "<font size=\"" + i + "\">Welcome to ASP.NET</font><br/>";
}
```

Every *for*... loop in C# consists of three parts, any of which can be empty:

- **Initialization**   In the previous example, *int i = 0*
- **Expression**   The test expression, evaluated like the predicate in the *if* statement
- **Iterators**   A statement to be run during each iteration of the loop

You can also use a *for*... loop to loop through the elements of an array by specifying the length of the array as the loop count expression, as follows:

```
string[] s = new string[5];
s[0] = "A";
s[1] = "B";
s[2] = "C";
s[3] = "D";
s[4] = "E";
for (int i = 0 ; i < s.Length ; i++ )
{
  Message.Text += "<font size=\"" + i + "\">";
  Message.Text += s[i];
  Message.Text += "</font><br/>";
}
```

▶ **Note**   Unlike Visual Basic .NET, declaring an array as I do in the example just shown creates an array of 5 elements, *not* an array with 0 as the lower bound and 5 as the upper bound (in fact 6 elements).

Using *foreach...* Loops

foreach... loops are a specialization of *for...* loops that enable you to loop through a collection or group of elements and take action on each item. The following example demonstrates looping through the items in an array of dates:

```
DateTime[] Dates;
Dates = new DateTime[3];
Dates[0]=DateTime.Now;
Dates[1]=Dates[0].AddDays(7);
Dates[2]=Dates[0].AddYears(1);
foreach (DateTime dt in Dates)
{
   Message.Text += dt.ToShortDateString() + "<br/>\n";
}
```

This code outputs each date to the browser using *Response.Write*. Because the *DateTime* type contains a date and a time, I use *ToShortDateString* to format the date in away that shows only the date. Using *foreach...* loops completely eliminates any problem with indexing outside the bounds of the array.

Using *do...while* Loops

do...while loops enable you to execute a set of statements repeatedly for as long as a test condition remains true. The condition contained in the *while* part of the statement is evaluated at the end of each cycle, and so code inside the loop is executed at least once. For example:

```
// doÉwhile syntax:
int i = 1;
do
{
   Message.Text += "<font size=\"" + i + "\">Welcome to ASP.NET</font><br/>";
   i++;
} while ( i <= 5 );
```

Using *while...* Loops

while... loops do essentially the same thing as *do while...* loops; they enable you to execute a given set of statements while a given condition is true. A *while...* loop that does the same thing as the preceding *do...while* loop would look like the following:

```
// while syntax:
i = 1; // Declared previously
```

```
while ( i <= 5 )
{
  Message.Text += "<font size=\"" + i + "\">Welcome to ASP.NET</font><br/>";
  i++;
}
```

Most programs will use a variety of loop types. No matter which loop type you choose, the important thing is that you use it correctly and consistently for a given task. This will make your code easier to read and maintain.

Error Handling

In any application, one challenge faced by developers is dealing with the inevitable errors. Application errors come in three varieties:

- **Syntax errors**   These include misspelled or missing keywords or symbols (such as a missing *closing bracket*), or other mistakes relating to the syntax of the language you're using. Syntax errors are typically flagged by the IDE and can be easily fixed at design time.
- **Runtime errors**   These are errors that appear after your code is compiled and running. Runtime errors are caused by code that appears correct to the compiler, but that cannot run with certain values. For example, code that divides one integer variable by another will appear to be correct to a compiler, but it will cause a runtime error if the second variable is zero.
- **Logic errors**   These are errors in which a program that works correctly under some (or most) circumstances gives unexpected or unwanted results based on certain input values. This type of error can be extremely difficult to track down and fix because it doesn't stop the execution of the program.

One thing all three types of errors have in common is that they must all be handled in some fashion, lest they provoke grave dissatisfaction on the part of your users. An important first step is prevention.

Selecting C# as your language to develop ASP.NET pages is the first step in eliminating some classes of errors that have plagued classic ASP applications. A properly compiled ASP.NET application will not contain undeclared variables or method calls that will compile correctly but could fail with type violations at runtime.

Ways to Handle Exceptional Situations

No matter how careful you are when developing an application, eventually there will be a situation that your application is not prepared to handle. For instance, your application might request access to a database when the database is unavailable. There are two general ways to react to this situation in C#:

- Check return codes from methods that could fail
- Use Structured Exception Handling

Checking return codes to all methods is the way that COM implemented error handling. Checking for HRESULT was a significant part of any COM program written in C or C++. C# allows Structured Exception Handling, where the flow of control is more straightforward. Exception handling brackets the section of code, allowing explicit handling of specific types of exceptions, as well as code that will always run, regardless of whether an exception occurs.

Checking Return Values

Checking return values seems initially to be the easiest way to handle errors. You can, in a very straightforward way, know exactly what failed and react to it in code very close to where the error occurs. The problems that occur are:

- The error handling code interrupts the clean flow of what is happening in the normal case where the process proceeds without error.
- It is too easy to forget about checking for error return codes.
- Given a large number of operations that require checking, the level of nesting can become ungainly.

For example, the code to check three levels of return values shows how confusing this kind of error handling can get:

```
if ( OpenDB() == NO_ERROR )
{
   if ( OpenTable() == NO_ERROR )
   {
      if ( FetchRow() == NO_ERROR )
      {
         // Actually do something
      }
   }
}
```

This type of error handling is best suited for the sort of errors that would occur often. For instance, if you are prompting a user for the name of a file, the method that does that might best be handled by checking a return code.

Using Structured Exception Handling: *try...catch...finally*

The *try...catch...finally* form of exception handling, also known as structured exception handling, should be familiar to C++ and Java developers. In C#, the *try...catch...finally* syntax enables you to enclose code that can cause an exception in such a way as to catch and deal with specific exceptions and/or provide generic exception handling. The following code shows a simple *try...catch* block:

```
int a, b; // declare two ints, a and b
double c;
try // Start monitoring for exceptions
{
  //Code that may cause an exception
  a = 1;
  b = 0;
  c = a / b;
}
catch ( DivideByZeroException )
{
  // Code to handle divide by 0 exception
}
finally
{
  // Code that executes after any code in the Catch block(s)
}
```

You can define *catch* blocks for as many specific errors as you want to handle. The *finally* block can be used for any code you want to run after the exception-handling code, including cleanup code, such as code to close a file. The *finally* block of code is always run, whether or not an exception has occurred.

In addition to catching exceptions, your code can actually throw an exception. To do so, you use the *throw* keyword. For example, if you wanted to catch only the divide by 0 exception and then rethrow any other exception, you could use the following code:

```
int a, b;
double c;
try // Start monitoring for exceptions
{
  //Code that may cause an exception
  a = 1;
  b = 0;
  c = a / b;
}
catch ( DivideByZeroException )
{
  // Code to handle divide by 0 exception
}
catch ( Exception e )
{
throw(e);// Rethrow exception e
}
```

```
finally
{
  // Code that executes after any code in the Catch block(s)
}
```

One thing worth noting is that in the second *catch* block, rather than just declaring the exception type, I specify an instance of the exception that I can then manipulate. In this example, I get a named instance of the exception so that I can rethrow it. This can also be useful when you have exceptions that contain details that you need to look at to properly handle the exception. It is also worth noting that the most specific *catch* blocks should be first, followed by any more general *catch* blocks. If the *catch* for the most general exception type (*Exception* in this example) was first, all exceptions would be caught in that block, including the more specific exception, the *DivideByZeroException*.

What happens if an exception is thrown and your code does not catch it? Probably not what you would like. This next example will step you though the process of creating a page that generates an unhandled exception, and then adding exception handling to properly handle the exception.

Add Exception Handling

1   Open Visual Studio .NET if it's not already open.

2   If Chapter_03 is not already open, on the File menu, choose Open, and then click Project. Click the project Chapter_03 created earlier in this chapter. This project can also be selected by pointing to Recent Projects on the File menu and clicking the project.

3   Right click the Chapter_03 project in the Solution Explorer on the right side of the screen. On the shortcut menu, choose Add, and click Add Web Form. When prompted, type the name of the form as **Exceptions.aspx**, and click the Open button.

4   Position the mouse pointer over the Toolbox until it expands. Drag a *Button* control from the Toolbox onto the form. Drag a label onto the form just below the button.

5   In the Properties pane on the right side of the screen, change the text of the button from Button to **Divide By Zero**, and click Enter. The button conveniently expands to show all the entered text.

6   Change the *ID* of the label from Label1 to **Message**. The screen should look like the following illustration.

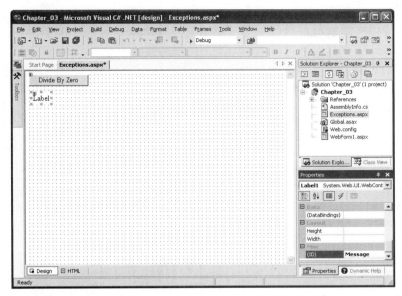

7   Double-click the button in the designer, and you will see the code view showing the *Button1_Click* event handler.

8   Add the following code to the handler:

```
int divisor = 0;
Message.Text = (4/divisor).ToString();
```

9   On the File menu, click Save All to save the page, and then on the Build menu, click Build Chapter_03 to compile the application.

10 Browse the page by right-clicking it in Solution Explorer, and then selecting View In Browser (or Browse With). When you see the screen with the Divide By Zero button, click the button. You will see a screen similar to the following illustration, in which the Output window is closed to allow you to see more of the error page.

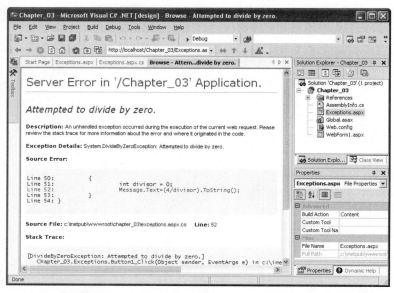

11 Close the application. Find the *Button1_Click* event handler and change the code to the following:

```
int divisor = 0;
try
{
  Message.Text = (4/divisor).ToString();
}
catch(DivideByZeroException)
{
Message.Text = "Cannot divide by 0!";
}
```

12 On the File menu, click Save All to save the page, and then on the Build menu, click Build Chapter_03 to compile the application.

13 To run the application, on the Debug menu, click Start, click the Divide By Zero button and the Message label will display a message telling you that you cannot divide by 0.

You'll see more examples of exception handling throughout the book.

Understanding Object-Oriented Programming Basics

Object-oriented programming will probably be new to some C# programmers, as well as to those new to programming entirely. C++ allows object oriented programming, but C#, with the .NET Framework as a model really encourages object orientation. C++ allows code to exist outside of any class, whereas C# mandates that all code must exist inside classes. The .NET Framework is not a perfect model for studying how to structure classes to achieve best object orientation, but it is a place to start.

This section provides an overview of object-oriented programming, particularly as it relates to the .NET development platform. Object-oriented programming is a substantial topic, so it's highly recommended that you do some additional reading to supplement the material provided here. There are also many books on both object-oriented programming and *design patterns*, related subjects.

In the simplest terms, an *object* is an instance of a class in object-oriented languages such as C++, C#, and Visual Basic .NET. Objects typically mirror their real world counterparts: employees, invoices, and purchase orders are all examples of real world entities that can be modeled as objects in your programs. Objects typically provide both *properties*, which describe some attribute of the object (for example, an employee might have an *EmployeeID* property), and *methods*, which allow actions to be taken by the object (for example, an *Invoice* object might expose a *Process* method). Properties and methods make it easier for programmers to know how to use a given object.

In addition to properties and methods, object-oriented programming offers three helpful features: inheritance, polymorphism, and encapsulation.

- *Inheritance* is the ability to create new classes that are derived from existing classes. A derived class "inherits" all the properties and methods of the class from which it is derived (referred to as the *parent class*). Programmers can then add additional properties and methods to the derived class, or in some cases override the implementation of an existing method inherited from the parent class.

- *Polymorphism* lets programmers have identically named methods in different classes, and it allows the correct method to be executed based on the context of the call. For example, a programmer could define an *Invoice* class with a *Process* method. The programmer could then define separate *TimeInvoice* and *MaterialsInvoice* classes that derived from the *Invoice* class, but which might or might not use the same implementation of the *Process* method exposed by the parent class. A method calling the *Process* method on a class that is descended from Invoice does not need to know exactly which implementation of *Process* will be called.

■ *Encapsulation* allows objects to be treated as "black boxes" in that only the properties and methods defined by the programmer as publicly available are visible outside of the object. Internal object state and the implementation of the publicly available methods are hidden by encapsulation. This limited visibility lets developers freely modify the internal state and implementation of their objects, as long as they don't change the publicly defined interface used to access the object. For instance, an *EmployeeList* class might expose methods *FirstEmployee*, *NextEmployee* and so on. Internally, such a list could be managed using a simple array, a linked list (in which each item points to the next item in a list), or a database table. To the consumer of the class, it should not matter exactly how the list is maintained internally, so long as the public methods such as *FirstEmployee* return the correct information.

Using Classes as Containers for Code

Classes are the basic unit of an object-oriented application. A class in C# typically contains property and method definitions, as well as event handlers (a special class of methods). Classes are often grouped into useful collections through the use of namespaces. *Namespaces* can contain classes and other namespaces. For example, the *System.Web* namespace defined by the .NET Framework SDK contains not only classes such as the *HttpRequest*, *HttpResponse*, and *HttpServerUtility* classes (which provide the equivalent functionality of the ASP Request, Response, and Server intrinsic objects), but also a number of namespaces, including the *System.Web.UI*, *System.Web.Caching*, and *System.Web.SessionState* namespaces, each of which also contains classes and/or namespaces.

By using classes as containers for code and namespaces, the .NET architecture makes it very easy to create a rich, yet intuitive application hierarchy that can make your code easier to use, debug, and maintain.

▶ **Note**   When you develop applications in the Visual Studio .NET environment, a root namespace will be created with the same name as your project. If you specify additional namespaces within your code modules, these will become child namespaces of the root namespace. You can change the root namespace by right-clicking your project in Solution Explorer and clicking Properties. The *Root Namespace* property appears under Common Properties, General.

Using Inheritance

Now that you know a bit about object-oriented programming, let's take a look at a simple example of how to put it to use. First let's define a class based on a real world entity, an animal.

```
public class Animal
{
    public virtual void Eat()
    {
        Console.WriteLine("Yum!");
    }
    public virtual void Sleep()
    {
        Console.WriteLine("Zzzzz");
    }
}
```

You use the *virtual* modifier to let C# know that the behavior can be overridden by a derived class.

▶   **Note**   Unlike C++, C# allows only single inheritance. Although some C++ programmers will find this to be a problem, the reality is that in virtually all cases, there are better alternatives to using multiple inheritance. C# does enable you to implement multiple interfaces, something that is often useful.

Next create a more specific animal class, *Cat*, that derives from the Animal class. Note the use of the listing of the Animal class after the name of the new class and a colon on the first line of the declaration. This is how you let C# know that the class inherits from another class. Inheriting from another class is really that simple. This class will override the behavior of the Eat method, but not the Sleep method, as follows:

```
public class Cat : Animal
{
    public override void Eat()
    {
        Console.WriteLine("Yum, Yum...Meow, Meow!");
    }
}
```

The *override* modifier is used to let C# know you intend to override the method in the base class.

You'll also create a *Dog* class that derives from *Animal* and that overrides the *Sleep* method, but not the *Eat* method, as follows:

```
public class Dog : Animal
{
    public override void Sleep()
    {
        Console.WriteLine("Zzzzzz...woofwoofwoofwoof...zzzzzz!");
    }
}
```

Finally, use the *Cat* and *Dog* classes in the following code. Note that you use the imports statement to access the members of the *Animals* namespace without fully qualified names (such as *Cat* instead of *Animal.Cat*).

```
class UseAnimals
{
    static void Main(string[] args)
    {
    Cat cat;
        Dog dog;

        cat = new Cat();
        cat.Eat();
        cat.Sleep();

        dog = new Dog();
        dog.Eat();
        dog.Sleep();
    }

}
```

This code, when compiled and run from a command line, provides the following output:

```
Yum, Yum...Meow, Meow!
Zzzzz...
Yum!
Zzzzzz...woofwoofwoofwoof...zzzzzz!
```

Even though you called the same two methods on both the *Cat* and *Dog* classes, when you overrode a method of the parent *Animal* class, you got the behavior that you specified for the particular animal. When you didn't override, the output shows that you got the behavior inherited from the parent *Animal* class. You can find the full source code for this example, including a batch file for compiling the classes, in the source folder for this chapter (Chapter_03) in the source archive for this book.

Inheriting from the .NET Base Classes

The preceding example might not seem terribly useful, and admittedly, creating your own *Cats* and *Dogs* by inheriting from *Animal* won't help you much in your development efforts. Fortunately, the same principles demonstrated in that example apply to the classes that make up the .NET Framework. Many of these classes can be used to derive your own specialized classes. You'll see specific examples of this in Chapter 10.

Inheriting Across Languages

Another nifty feature of the .NET Framework and the common language runtime is that they enable you to inherit from classes written in other languages. Why is this important? Because it means that development teams can make better use of the existing skill sets of their developers, as well as the company's existing code base. For example, a company with experienced Visual Basic developers (and existing code in Visual Basic) can have those developers continue to write in Visual Basic .NET. If the company also has a group of skilled Java developers, they can easily make the transition to C# and use the existing class resources created by the VB developers through inheritance.

Chapter 3 Quick Reference

To	Do this	Code
Declare a variable	Use the data type, followed by the variable name.	`int MyInt;`

Modify the accessibility of a variable or procedure	Use the *public*, *private*, *internal*, or *protected* keywords	```public void myProc()```
		```{```
		```}```

To use structured exception handling	Create a *try...catch...finally* block.	```try```
		```{```
		```// Code to try```
		```}```
		```catch (System.Exception)```
		```{```
		```// Handle error```
		```}```
		```finally```
		```{```
		```// Code that will ALWAYS run```
		```}```

To	Do this	Code
Inherit from a base class	Append the base class name to the name of the derived class, separated by a colon	```class Dog : Animal
{
}```
Declare a method that will be overridden in classes that descend from the current class	Use the *virtual* modifier	```public virtual void myProc()
{
}```
Override a method declared in a base class	Use the *override* modifier	```public override void
myProc()
{
}```

ASP.NET Infrastructure

Managing State

In this chapter, you will learn how to:

- Store and retrieve application state.
- Store and retrieve session state.
- Configure session state storage.
- Use client-side cookies for state storage.

Most applications of any significance will use pieces of data, or variables, that need to be maintained across a series of requests or shared between multiple users of an application. This data is referred to as *state*. In a rich client application, it's relatively simple to maintain individual user state simply by allocating space in memory on the client machine. In Web applications, managing user and application state is more challenging. The primary reason for this is that the Hypertext Transfer Protocol (HTTP)—the protocol used to send and receive requests through a Web browser—is inherently stateless. That is, HTTP doesn't inherently provide a way for the Web server to identify a series of requests as coming from the same user, making it difficult for the Web server to maintain state and associate it with an individual user.

In classic ASP, this limitation was overcome through an in-memory collection of key-value pairs associated with the intrinsic *Session* object. This collection, however, had a number of important limitations of its own, which are discussed later in this chapter.

In addition to individual user state, many applications need to store and retrieve *application-level* state information that is global to all users of the Web application. To maintain application state in classic ASP, the intrinsic *Application* object exposed a collection similar to that of the *Session* object's collection.

Using Application State

Application state refers to any data that you want to share among multiple users of your application. This can include connection string information for databases (although this information is often better to limit to the business tier of an application), shared variables, and cached datasets (although these might be better stored using the ASP.NET cache engine, which is discussed in more detail in Chapter 12). In fact, one of the difficulties of managing application state is choosing from the many available options for storing such state.

Like classic ASP, ASP.NET provides a collection of key-value pairs that developers can use to store values and object instances. This collection can be accessed as shown in the following code example:

```
Application["MyApplicationVar"] = "MyValue";
MyLocalVar = Application["MyApplicationVar"];
```

Application state storage in ASP.NET is supplied by the .NET *HttpApplicationState* class (which resides in the *System.Web* namespace), an instance of which is exposed as the *Application* property of the *Page* class. Because every ASP.NET page inherits from the *Page* class, you can access the *Application* property as if it were an inherent property of the page, as shown in the preceding code.

For backward-compatibility with classic ASP, the ASP.NET *Application* object exposes a *Contents* property that can be used to access individual values, using the appropriate key.

```
Application.Contents["MyApplicationVar"] = "MyValue";
MyLocalVar = Application.Contents["MyApplicationVar"];
```

New in ASP.NET is the ability to add items to the *HttpApplicationState* collection using the *Add* method exposed by the *Application* object. You can use the *Remove* method to remove items from the *Application* collection. (In classic ASP, the *Add* and *Remove* methods are exposed by the *Application.Contents* collection.)

```
Application.Add("MyApplicationVar", "MyValue");
Application.Add("MyOtherApplicationVar", "MyOtherValue");
Application.Remove("MyOtherApplicationVar");
```

You can also clear the contents of the *Application* collection by using the *Clear* method exposed by the *Application* object (or the *RemoveAll* method, which is provided for backward-compatibility with classic ASP).

```
//Either line below will clear the application state
Application.Clear();
Application.RemoveAll();
```

The *Application* object exposes several other ways to access and modify the values stored in the *Application* collection, as shown in Table 4-1.

Table 4-1. *Application* Object Methods and Properties

Method or Property	Use
AllKeys property	Returns a collection of all of the keys by which *Application* collection values can be accessed.
Count property	Returns the number of objects stored in the *Application* collection.
Get method	Returns an item from the *Application* collection by key or by index.
Set method	Updates an item in the *Application* collection by key or by index.
GetKey method	Returns the key for an item based on a supplied index.
ToString method	Returns a string that represents an item in the *Application* collection. Useful when a string value is required, rather than an object reference.

In addition to storing values in the *Application* collection, you can instantiate and store references to .NET components, such as DataSets, in application state using the *<object runat="server">* tag syntax in the Global.asax file (or its associated code-behind file). These objects then become part of the *Application* object's *StaticObjects* collection and can be referenced in your ASP.NET Web Form pages by referring to the *id* attribute associated with the object.

```
// Global.asax
<object runat="server" id="MyClassInstance" class="MyClassName"
   scope="Application">
</object>

// Web Forms page
Response.Write("Value = " + MyClassInstance.MyValue);
```

▶ **Note**   Global.asax (or its associated code-behind file) is the only mechanism for creating object instances with *Application* scope.

▶ **Tip**   When you're using either the *Application* or *Session* collections, it's a good idea to initialize the variables you're using to a default value (such as "" for a string or 0 for a numeric) in the *Application_Start* or *Session_Start* event handlers in Global.asax. You can then test for the default value as a way of determining whether it has been altered.

Synchronizing Access to Application State

One challenge in managing state information that's shared between multiple users is ensuring that no two users can attempt to update the state information simultaneously, which could lead to corruption of the data being stored. Like classic ASP, the ASP.NET *Application* object provides *Lock* and *UnLock* methods that developers can use to ensure that only a single user can update application state information at any given time. Developers should call *Application.Lock()* prior to modifying any data stored in the *Application* collection, and call *Application.UnLock()* once the modification is complete. Keep in mind that while the application is locked, no other users can modify data stored in the *Application* collection, which can cause scalability problems. For this reason, you should make sure to keep the application locked for the shortest time possible, and perform as little work as possible while the application is locked.

Reading and writing application state is easy. The output for this example will be written into an ASP.NET Label server control.

Read and write application state

1   Open Visual Studio .NET and create a new Web Application project called Chapter_04.

2   Place your mouse pointer over the Toolbox on the left side of the screen. When the Toolbox appears, select a label and drag it onto the screen.

3   With the label control selected, change the *ID* of the label from Label1 to **Message**. The screen should look something like the following illustration.

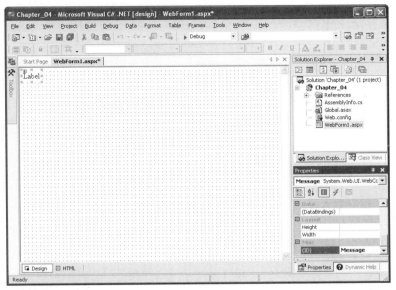

4 From the View menu, select Code, or press F7 to open the code editor.

5 Locate the *Page_Load* method, and add the following code:

```
//Initialize looping variable
int loopCount = 0;

//Lock the application object before we manipulate it
Application.Lock();
Application["TestString"] = "Hello";
Application.Add("TestNumber", 43);

//Now unlock the Application, since we will now
//just read from the Application object.
Application.UnLock();

Message.Text = "There are " + Application.Count.ToString() +
               " items in the Application collection.<br/>";
while (loopCount < Application.Count)
{
    Message.Text += "Application(" + loopCount.ToString() +
                    ") = " + Application[loopCount] + "<br/>";
    loopCount += 1;
}
```

6   Save the page and its code-behind module by selecting File, then Save
    All (or by pressing CTRL+SHIFT+S).

7   Select Build Chapter_04 from the Build menu to build the application.

8   Test the page by right-clicking WebForm1.aspx in Solution Explorer,
    and then selecting View In Browser. The resulting screen should look
    similar to the following illustration.

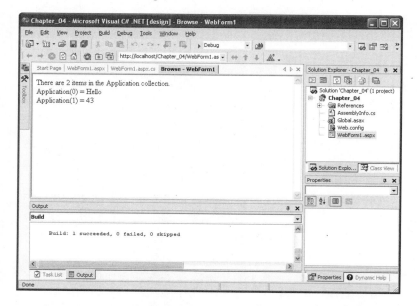

Recommendations for Application State

Information stored in application state can be easily shared among all users of
an application. This can make it very tempting to use application state to store
all manner of data, from application settings such as database connection
strings to cached datasets containing frequently used data. In many cases, there
are more efficient means of storing this data than application state. Table 4-2
shows some examples of when you might or might not want to store information in application state, as well as alternatives for storing such information.

Table 4-2. **Application State Recommendations**

State Information	Issues	Alternative
Database connection strings or other application configuration settings	Typically, these settings are accessed infrequently. Storing this information in application state is not very efficient.	Use the Web.config configuration file to store this information, and retrieve with the *AppSettings* property of the *ConfigurationSettings* Class, as discussed in Appendix B.
Datasets containing frequently read data	Caching frequently used data at the application level can be efficient, but there's little automatic control over when the data is refreshed.	Use the ASP.NET cache engine to cache expensive or frequently read data. The ASP.NET cache engine provides fine-grained control over how and when data is refreshed or purged from the cache. (See Chapter 12 for more information.)
Shared application flags or counter variables	Shared values that can be updated by multiple users of an application can present major scalability issues, as discussed in "State and Scalability" later in this chapter.	Consider storing shared application flags in a database, which will provide finer-grained control over the reading and updating of individual values.
References to object instances	Storing references to objects with the wrong threading model (such as legacy COM components created with Visual Basic) can have a severe impact on the scalability of an application.	If it's absolutely necessary to store a reference to an object instance, ensure that the class from which the object is created is thread safe.

Limitations of Application State

Application state has several limitations that you should consider when deciding how to manage your state information.

- **Durability** Application state lasts only as long as the Web application is running. If the Web application or Web server is shut down or crashes, any state information stored at the application level will be destroyed. Any information that needs to persist between application restarts should be stored in a database or other persistent storage.

- **Web farms**   Application state is not shared across multiple servers in a Web farm (nor across multiple processors in a Web garden). If you need to store values that must be available to all users in these scenarios, application state is not an appropriate choice.

- **Memory**   Any given server has only a limited amount of physical memory available. Overuse of application state can result in information being swapped to virtual memory (a location on a hard drive used to provide supplemental "memory" storage). This can reduce performance significantly.

▶ **Note**   Web farms are groups of identically configured servers that share the load of serving user requests for a given Web application. Each server contains the same content and can fulfill any request. Requests are routed to individual servers by a hardware- or software-based load-balancing algorithm that either determines which server is least loaded or assigns requests to a given server randomly.

Web gardens are a new concept in ASP.NET in which an application can be set to run on specific processors on a multiprocessor server.

Using Session State

As challenging as it can be to manage application-state information, the statelessness of HTTP makes maintaining state for individual users even more challenging. First, the Web server needs to be able to identify a series of requests as coming from a single user. Then the Web server must associate these requests with the state information for that specific user.

In classic ASP, these challenges were met with the intrinsic *Session* object. Each user had his or her own session instance, identified by a session ID, which could be used to store per-user state information. The session ID, a unique generated value for that run of the application, was then stored in a cookie on the client machine. It would then be passed back to the server with each subsequent request, allowing the server to identify the session associated with that user.

Unfortunately, session state in classic ASP had several inherent limitations that made it less than ideal, particularly for applications requiring high scalability. These included the following:

- **Web farms**   In classic ASP, session state could not be scaled across multiple servers in a Web farm, limiting its usefulness in high-scalability situations.

- **Durability**   In classic ASP, session state would be destroyed by a server restart or crash. This made it a poor choice for such uses as shopping carts, whose contents should survive such events.

- **Cookie reliance** Classic ASP offered no inherent solution for supporting session state with browsers that could not or would not accept cookies. Although aftermarket solutions were available, they often involved unacceptable performance trade-offs.

ASP.NET solves each of these limitations, providing per-user state storage that's scalable, reliable, and available on browsers that don't support cookies (or for users who choose not to accept cookies). For more information on the available options for ASP.NET session state and how they solve these limitations, see "Configuring Session State Storage" later in this chapter.

As with the ASP.NET *Application* object, the ASP.NET *Session* object is exposed as a property of the *Page* class, from which all ASP.NET pages inherit. This allows direct access to the *Session* object.

```
Session["MySessionVar"] = "MyValue";
MyLocalVar = Session["MySessionVar"];
```

The *Session* object functionality is provided by the *HttpSessionState* class, an instance of which is created for each user session that session state has been enabled for.

Like the *Application* object, the *Session* object exposes a *Contents* collection for backward-compatibility with classic ASP. Any values stored in the *HttpSessionState* collection can also be accessed through the *Contents* collection alias.

```
Session.Contents["MySessionVar"] = "MyValue";
MyLocalVar = Session.Contents["MySessionVar"];
```

The *Session* collection can also be used to store references to object instances, using similar syntax to that used to store object references at the application level. These objects then become part of the *Session* object's *StaticObjects* collection and can be referenced in your ASP.NET Web Form pages by referring to the *id* attribute associated with the object.

```
// Global.asax
<object runat="server" id="MyClassInstance" class="MyClassName"
   scope="Session">
</object>

// Web Forms page
Response.Write("Value = " + MyClassInstance.MyValue);
```

Table 4-3 lists some of the additional properties and methods provided by the *Session* object to retrieve and manipulate *Session* collection values.

Table 4-3. *Session* Object Properties and Methods

Method or Property	Use
Keys property	Returns a collection of all of the keys by which *Session* collection values can be accessed.
Count property	Returns the number of objects stored in the *Session* collection.
SessionID property	Returns a string containing the session ID for the current session.
Timeout property	Returns an *Integer* value representing the current *Session Timeout* setting.
Abandon method	Destroys the current user session.
Clear method	Removes all items from the *Session* collection.
RemoveAt method	Removes a specific item from the *Session* collection, based on its index within the collection.
ToString method	Returns a string that represents an item in the *Session* collection. Useful when a string value is required rather than an object reference.

Enabling Session State

Unlike application state, which is always available to Web applications, session state must be enabled before you can use it. The good news is that the default configuration file at the server level (machine.config) automatically enables session state, so you don't need to take any additional steps to enable it. Nonetheless, you should be aware that the settings in the machine.config configuration file, as well as in the Web.config configuration file for your application, determine whether session state is enabled or disabled. The pertinent settings are detailed in Appendix B.

If you want to delay the creation of a session until it's necessary, you can add the *EnableSessionState* attribute to the @ *Page* directive of all pages not requiring session state:

```
<%@ Page EnableSessionState="False" %>
```

Any attempt to access the *Session* object from a page on which *enableSessionState* has been set to *False* will result in an error. Note that once a session has been created for a given user, setting the *enableSessionState* attribute to *False* doesn't result in the destruction of the existing session. It only prevents access to the *Session* object from that page.

You can set the session state to read-only for a given page by setting the *enableSessionState* attribute to *ReadOnly*. Any attempts to update values stored in the *Session* collection from that page will be ignored.

Enabling Session State in Visual Studio.NET

Microsoft Visual Studio .NET makes it even easier to enable (or delay enabling) session state in your applications by exposing the *enableSessionState* attribute as a property of the *Document* object. This allows you to view and modify its value using the Visual Studio .NET Properties window, shown in the following illustration.

To change its setting, select the *enableSessionState* entry in the Properties window, click the drop-down list containing the values, and select the desired value. This will update the @ *Page* directive that appears in the .aspx page currently being edited.

Just as with application state, using Visual Studio .NET to read and write session state is easy. The output for the following example will be written into an ASP.NET Label server control.

Read and write session state

1 Open Visual Studio .NET. Reopen the Chapter_04 project created earlier.

2 Add a new page to the project by right-clicking the project root in Solution Explorer, and then selecting Add, then Add WebForm from the context menu. When prompted, change the name of the file from WebForm2.aspx to **SessionState.aspx** and click Open.

3 Add a label control to the page.

4 With the label control selected, change the *ID* of the label from Label1 to **Message**.

5 From the View menu, select Code or press F7 to open the code editor.

6   Locate the *Page_Load* method, and add the following code:

```
//Initialize looping variable
int loopCount = 0;

Session["TestString"] = "Hello";
Session.Add("TestNumber", 43);

Message.Text="There are " + Session.Count.ToString() +
            " items in the Session collection.<br/>";

while (loopCount < Session.Count)
{
   Message.Text += "Session(" + loopCount.ToString() +
                ") = " + Session[loopCount] + "<br/>";
   loopCount += 1;
}
```

7   Save the application by using the File, Save All menu option (or by pressing CTRL+SHIFT+S).

8   From the Build menu, select Build Chapter_04 to build the application.

9   Test the page by right-clicking SessionState.aspx and selecting View In Browser. The resulting screen should look similar to the following illustration.

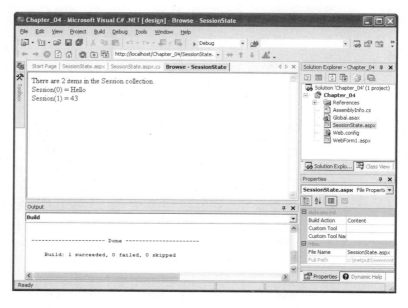

Recommendations for Session State

Session state's ease of use makes it easy to overuse or abuse. Table 4-4 lists examples of when you might or might not want to store information in session state, as well as alternatives for storing such information.

Table 4-4. Session State Recommendations

State Information	Issues	Alternative
User-specific settings	Depending on how frequently these values are accessed, session state might not be the most efficient way to store these settings.	For infrequently accessed values, consider storing user-specific settings in a database.
Datasets containing frequently read data	Caching frequently used data at the session level can be efficient, but there's little automatic control over when the data is refreshed. It's very important to consider the cost of storing a dataset for each user session over the cost of retrieving the dataset from the database.	Use the ASP.NET cache engine to cache expensive or frequently read data. The ASP.NET cache engine provides fine-grained control over how and when data is refreshed or purged from the cache. See Chapter 12 for more information on caching.
References to object instances	Storing references to objects with the wrong threading model (such as legacy COM components created with Visual Basic) can severely affect the scalability of an application. It's important to consider the cost of storing a reference to an object for each user session.	If it's absolutely necessary to store a reference to an object instance, ensure that the class from which the object is created is thread safe.

Limitations of Session State

Thanks to a number of new features in ASP.NET, the primary limitation of session state in ASP.NET is that of memory. As with application state, session state is limited by the memory available on the Web server. Once the available physical memory on the Web server has been exhausted, information will be stored in much slower virtual memory.

State and Scalability

How and where you choose to store state information for your application can have a major impact on how scalable your application is. *Scalability* refers to the ability of an application to service requests from increasing numbers of users without any significant decrease in performance or response time.

The following conditions are among the factors affecting application scalability that result from poor decisions in state management:

- **Failure to disable session state when not used**   If you're not using session state within your application, disable it by changing the *mode* attribute of the *sessionState* configuration section of Web.config to *off*. For applications that make limited use of session state, ensure that any pages that don't use session state include the *EnableSessionState=false* attribute as a part of the page's *@ Page* directive.

- **Misuse of *Application.Lock( )***   The *Application.Lock( )* method prevents access to all application values for any user other than the user whose request resulted in the call to *Application.Lock( )*. This continues until the *Application.Unlock( )* method is called. You should minimize the time that these values are locked by calling *Application.Lock( )* immediately prior to updating a value and calling *Application.UnLock( )* immediately afterward. If there is a value to be added to application state that might require some time to calculate, calculate the value and save the value into a variable, and then lock the application, add the value from the variable, and unlock the application.

- **Storing references to single (or apartment) threaded objects**   Storing references to non-free-threaded objects at application or session level can interfere with IIS thread management capabilities and can result in severe scalability problems. Avoid storing non-free-threaded objects at application or session level.

- **In-process session state**   To scale a Web application beyond a certain point, it's often necessary to use a Web farm to allow multiple servers to handle requests. In-process session state, the default, is not available to all servers on a Web farm. To use session state with a Web farm, you should set your application's *Session* mode to either *State-Server* or *SQLServer* as described in the next section.

- **Overuse of session or application storage**   Storing numerous object references or large datasets at the application level, and particularly at the session level, can rapidly exhaust the physical memory on a

Web server, causing it to substitute virtual memory for storing additional information. This can have a dramatic effect on the performance of an application. You should always ensure that any use of application state (and more important, session state) will not exceed the physical memory resources available on the Web server. Also remember that other applications will be using some of these resources.

Configuring Session State Storage

ASP.NET provides several new possibilities for storing session state. Each is designed to overcome one or more of the limitations of session state in classic ASP. The available settings include the following:

- **In-process (*InProc*)**   This is the default setting. Its behavior is essentially the same as in classic ASP.
- **Out-of-process (*StateServer*)**   This setting specifies that session state will be stored by a server running the ASP.NET state service. The state server to connect to is specified by an attribute, as described in the section "Storing Session State Out-of-Process" later in this chapter.
- **SQL Server (*SQLServer*)**   This setting specifies that session state will be stored in a Microsoft SQL Server database. The SQL Server to connect to is specified by an attribute, as described in the section "Storing Session State in SQL Server" later in this chapter.
- **Cookieless Sessions**   This setting allows you to maintain session state even for users whose browsers cannot handle cookies.

The following sections describe how to configure each of these settings.

Storing Session State In-Process

By default, Web applications, whether created in Visual Studio .NET or created manually, will store session state in-process. As noted, this setting has several inherent limitations, including lack of scalability and durability. For applications requiring neither scalability beyond a single server nor durability of session state across server restarts or crashes, however, this setting might work just fine. And it's the simplest to deal with because it doesn't require any changes to the application configuration file.

Storing Session State Out-of-Process

The first solution to the problems of scalability and durability for session state is to store session state out-of-process in a separate dedicated ASP.NET state process running as a service on a specified server. One advantage of this method is that the ASP.NET State Service can service requests from multiple servers, making it possible to scale session state across a Web farm. Another advantage is that the ASP.NET State Service runs in a separate process (or even on a separate machine), so state information can survive restarts or crashes of a specific Web application process. Note that session state information stored by the ASP.NET State Service does *not* survive a restart or crash of the machine on which the state service is running.

Store session state out-of-process

1   Open the Web.config configuration file for your application by double-clicking it in the Solution Explorer window, and then locate the *sessionState* configuration section.

2   Change the *mode* attribute from InProc to **StateServer**.

3   Modify the *stateConnectionString* attribute so that it reflects the server name (or IP address) of the state server and the port that the ASP.NET State Service is monitoring. (By default, this is 42424. The value is stored in the registry key *HKEY_LOCAL_MACHINE\SYSTEM\CurrentControlSet\ Services\ aspnet_state\Parameters* under *Port*.) Save Web.config.

4   The complete *sessionState* configuration section that uses the ASP.NET State Service on the local machine would look like the following code. (Note that the *sqlConnectionString* attribute, which is not used in this example, and the *cookieless* and *timeout* attributes have been omitted. The full list of attributes is available in Appendix B.)

```
<sessionState
    mode="stateserver"
    stateConnectionString="tcpip=127.0.0.1:42424"/>
```

5   Start the Services Microsoft Management Console (MMC) snap-in by clicking Start, then selecting All Programs, then selecting Administrative Tools, and then selecting Services. Note that you must be logged in as an administrator to see the Administrative Tools folder (if you are not logged in as an administrator, you can still access this folder from the Control Panel, but you will need to use the Run As feature to run the Services MMC snap-in using an administrative account).

6   Start the ASP.NET State Service on the desired server from the Services MMC snap-in. The Windows XP Professional Services snap-in is shown in the following illustration.

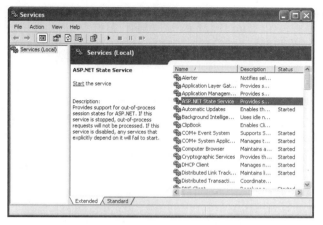

ASP.NET will automatically connect to the specified state server to store session state for your application. If the state service on the specified server is not running or the server is not accessible, you will receive an error message.

Keep in mind that although storing session state in a dedicated server process can improve the overall scalability of your application, moving session state out-of-process has inherent performance implications. Retrieving state information from a different process (and especially from a different machine) is significantly more costly than retrieving it from within the same process. You should test the impact on the type and amount of session data you plan to store before implementing this type of session state storage in a production application.

Storing Session State in SQL Server

The second solution to the problems of scalability and durability for session state is to store it out-of-process in a SQL Server database. One advantage of this method is that the specified SQL Server can service requests from multiple servers, making it possible to scale session state across a Web farm. Also, the session state information is stored in a SQL Server database, so state information can survive restarts or crashes of any Web application process, any Web server, or even the SQL Server itself.

Store session state in SQL Server

1   Set up the SQL Server session state database by running the InstallSqlState.sql SQL script file (located in the Microsoft .NET Framework install directory, by default *%windir%*\Microsoft.NET\Framework*%version%*) against

the SQL Server you plan to use. (For more information on running SQL script files, check with your database administrator or the SQL Server Books Online.)

2   Open the Web.config configuration file for your application and locate the *sessionState* configuration section.

3   Change the *mode* attribute from InProc to **SQLServer.**

4   Modify the *sqlConnectionString* attribute so that it reflects the IP address of the desired SQL Server and the user ID and password used to access the SQL Server, and then save Web.config.

5   The complete *sessionState* configuration section that uses a SQL Server on the local machine would look like the following. (Note that the *stateConnectionString* attribute and the *cookieless* and *timeout* attributes have been omitted.)

```
<sessionState
  mode="SQLServer"
  sqlConnectionString="data source=127.0.0.1;
  user id=sa;password=""/>
```

▶   **Important**   There are security implications to placing the SQL Server user ID and password in the connection string in Web.config. A better practice, where possible, is to use a trusted connection to SQL Server. Chapter 9 describes the steps necessary to use a trusted connection with SQL Server, as well as other connection techniques. Chapter 6 further explores the topic of security in ASP.NET, including good practices for storing connection string information.

Using Cookieless Sessions

One ongoing challenge for Web developers using classic ASP is how to handle session state for users whose browsers can't or won't accept cookies. Classic ASP provided no intrinsic solution for this situation. In ASP.NET, it's relatively simple.

Configure cookieless sessions

1   Open the Web.config configuration file for your application and locate the *sessionState* configuration section.

2   Change the cookieless attribute from false to **true.**

3   The complete *sessionState* configuration section would look like the
    following. (Note that the *stateConnectionString*, *sqlConnection-*
    String, and *timeout* attributes have been omitted.)

```
<sessionState
    cookieless="true"/>
```

When the *cookieless* attribute is set to *true*, ASP.NET will automatically embed the *SessionID* value in the URL for all requests. For best
results, always use relative URLs for internal links within your application. Relative URLs contain only the path and file information for
the requested resource, not the protocol and domain, which are
assumed to be the same as the current page.

Formatting URLs for Cookieless Sessions

ASP.NET provides automatic embedding of session IDs in the relative URLs
within your application, but not for absolute URLs, nor for URLs from applications outside yours. If a request for a page within an application set up for
cookieless sessions is received that doesn't contain an embedded session ID,
ASP.NET will create a new session ID and embed it in the URL for that request.

To prevent this problem, you can manually format URLs by calling the
ApplyAppPathModifier method of the intrinsic *Response* object, and passing it
a virtual path. The method will return an absolute URL containing the embedded SessionID for use with cookieless sessions. An absolute URL includes the
protocol, domain, path, and file name necessary to request a given resource.
The syntax for this method is as follows:

```
string myAbsoluteURL;
myAbsoluteURL = Response.ApplyAppPathModifier("foo.aspx");
```

Using Client-Side Cookies for State Storage

A discussion of state management would be incomplete without at least a brief
mention of another option for storing application state: client-side cookies. This
method doesn't work with users whose browsers cannot handle cookies (or who
have turned off cookies), but it's the most lightweight method for storing certain
types of state data because it requires no resources on the Web server. In cases
where users have cookies turned off, the code that sets the cookie will simply be
ignored. If your code expects the cookie to be present, however, you might get an
error when attempting to access the cookie. For this reason, you should always
wrap code that accesses values in a cookie within a *Try...Catch* block to ensure
that your application can gracefully recover from a missing cookie.

Store user state in a nonpersistent cookie

1   Create a new instance of the *HttpCookie* class.

```
HttpCookie MyCookie = New HttpCookie("MyCookieName");
```

2   Set the *Value* property of the cookie to the desired value.

```
MyCookie.Value = "MyValue";
```

3   Add the cookie to the *Cookies* collection of the *Response* object (exposed by the *Page* class).

```
Response.Cookies.Add(MyCookie);
```

This sets a cookie called "*My Cookie*" that lasts until the user closes the browser.

Using Persistent Cookies

To store user state that will persist across multiple browser sessions, you need to use persistent cookies. In order for a cookie to be persistent, its expiration must occur in the future. To make the cookie created in the previous example persist for two days, add the following line of code, just prior to adding the cookie to the *Response.Cookies* collection:

```
MyCookie.Expires = DateTime.Now.AddDays(2);
```

Here are some things to consider about using persistent cookies.

- Cookies have a bad reputation because of their misuse by some Web companies to track the surfing habits of Web users. It's a good idea to explain to your users exactly how and why you're using persistent cookies, and describe the benefits of accepting those cookies.

- Keep the expiration of persistent cookies within a reasonable amount of time. For most sites, cookie expiration should be measured in hours or days or, at most, months. Setting your cookie expiration to years in the future is likely to result in more users refusing your cookie.

- *Never* store user data in a cookie (for example, credit card numbers or other data that could be at risk if intercepted or otherwise compromised).

▶ **Important**   Although it might seem obvious to avoid storing information such as credit card numbers in cookies, it's equally important to consider the security implications of storing such information on the server side, whether in session state in memory or in a database server. Although there's no single right answer to how to store sensitive data, here are some guidelines you should follow:

- Store sensitive data only if you must, and then only for the minimum length of time necessary.
- Encrypt sensitive data to better protect it from being compromised.
- When possible, archive sensitive data on systems that are not connected to the Internet (and are thus less vulnerable to being compromised).
- Make sure that you follow good security practices on all of your servers, particularly those exposed to the Internet. (We'll cover security in greater detail in Chapter 6.)

▶ **Note**   Although following these guidelines won't guarantee that your Web applications will never be compromised by crackers, they'll help you limit the damage.

ASP.NET Server Control State

Finally, another kind of state that is managed by ASP.NET is server control state. Developers who used classic ASP to create data-driven applications had to figure out how to maintain the state of the various HTML form elements on their ASP pages from one page to the next, or even between submissions of a page that submits to itself. HTML provides no built-in mechanism for maintaining the state of individual form elements, so developers were left to come up with their own methods of maintaining and restoring this information.

ASP.NET provides a solution to this challenge with the server control architecture. All ASP.NET server controls are capable of maintaining their own state through a mechanism known as ViewState. ViewState is maintained on a page-by-page basis as a hidden form field that contains all of the state information for all of the form elements on that page.

ViewState and server controls are discussed in detail in Chapter 8 and Chapter 10.

Chapter 4 Quick Reference

To	Do this	Example

Store information in the *Application* collection	Use either the *Application* object or the *Application.Contents* collection to add the item to the collection, or use the *Application.Add* method.	```Application[key] = value;```
		```Application.Contents[key] = value;```
		```Application.Add(key, value)```

Modify information in the *Application StaticObjects* collection	Add an *<Object>* tag in Global.asax with the *runat="server"* attribute and the scope= *"application"* attribute.	```<object runat="server" id="myObject" scope="Application" class="myClassName"> </object>```
Store session state in a dedicated server process	Modify the *sessionState* configuration section of your application's Web.config file, changing the *mode* attribute to *StateServer* and the *stateConnectionString* attribute to the appropriate IP address and TCP port for the state server being used.	```<sessionState mode="State Server"stateConnectionString="tcpip=127.0.0.1:42424"/>```
Store session state in a SQL Server database	Modify the *sessionState* configuration section of your application's Web.config file, changing the mode attribute to *SQLServer* and the *sqlConnectionString* attribute to the appropriate data source name, user ID, and password for the SQL Server being used.	```<sessionState mode="SQLServer"sqlConnection String= "data source=127.0.0.1;user id=sa;pass word="/>```
Provide support for session state without cookies	Modify the *sessionState* configuration section of your application's Web.config file, changing the *cookieless* attribute to *true*.	```<sessionState cookieless="true"/>```

Configuring an ASP.NET Application

> **In this chapter, you will learn how to:**
>
> ■ Edit ASP.NET configuration files.
>
> ■ Configure an ASP.NET application.
>
> ■ Override parent configuration settings.
>
> ■ Lock down configuration settings.

One of the most important new features of ASP.NET, given the advantages it provides developers, is its new configuration system. This configuration system uses human- and machine-readable XML-based files to store configuration information. This chapter will look at how these configuration files work and how you can use them in your applications.

Understanding ASP.NET Configuration

Configuration in ASP.NET is based on a series of XML-based files that are hierarchical in nature. Each server contains a master (or root) configuration file called machine.config that is stored at the path *%windir%*\Microsoft.NET\ Framework*%version%*\CONFIG\machine.config. (See the following illustration, which shows how the path would look for the Visual Studio .NET Final Beta on Windows Server 2003. The version number for the final release will be different.) This master configuration file contains the default settings for all ASP.NET applications on that server. This file also contains settings for machine-wide configuration (such as assembly binding and remoting channels), as well as other settings. Use caution when you edit this file to avoid inadvertently making changes that affect other applications.

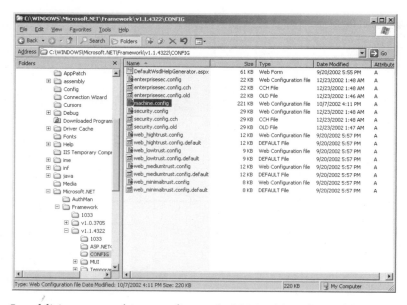

In addition to machine.config, each ASP.NET Web application can have one or more files called Web.config (one per folder) in its folder hierarchy. Each Web.config file overrides any settings of the configuration files in parent folders. Settings in Web.config apply only to content within the folder in which the file resides, and any content in child folders. This allows you to set up a hierarchy of configuration files that lets you set application-wide configuration options at the highest levels, while still allowing you to override those settings at a lower level. For example, if you have a group of files whose access must be restricted, you can place those files in a separate folder within your application and then add a Web.config file that implements tighter security restrictions. You'll see how to do this later in this chapter.

▶ **Note**   If you decide to use multiple levels of configuration files within your application, you should consider using comments to make it clear where you're overriding settings from parent Web.config files or from machine.config. This way, those who need to maintain the application can understand your intent. Comments in ASP.NET configuration files use the same syntax as HTML comments: <!– –>.

Keep in mind also that many of the settings configured in Web.config and machine.config can also be overridden at the page level using attributes of the @ *Page* directive. Take care to ensure that all developers on a project (as well as those who will maintain the application) understand this, to avoid confusion.

Changes to configuration file settings are detected automatically by the ASP.NET runtime and integrated into the cached configuration settings for the application. When a change is made, all new requests for resources within the scope of a given configuration file use the new configuration settings automatically.

Introducing Web.config

Like the machine.config file, Web.config is XML based. This means that each Web.config file is made up of tags and attributes, similar to HTML. (XML is a markup language based on Structured Generalized Markup Language, or SGML, the same language HTML is based on.) Unlike machine.config, however, most Web.config files will not contain elements for every available configuration setting. In fact, an ASP.NET application doesn't actually require a Web.config file in order to function. If Web.config is omitted from an application, it simply inherits its configuration settings from the master configuration file, machine.config.

A Web.config file has the following basic structure:

```
<?xml version="1.0" encoding="utf-8" ?>
<configuration>
    <system.web>
        <elementName1>
            <childElementName1
                attributeName1=value
                attributeName2=value
                attributeNameN=value />
        </elementName1>
        <elementName2
                attributeName1=value
                attributeName2=value
                attributeNameN=value>
        </elementName2>
        <elementNameN
                attributeName1=value
                attributeName2=value
                attributeNameN=value />
    </system.web>
</configuration>
```

Each Web.config file should begin with the standard XML declaration, though it will work without it. The file also contains opening and closing *<configuration>* tags. Nested within those tags are the opening and closing *<system.web>* tags, indicating that the content within is ASP.NET-specific configuration information. This configuration information is supplied in tags referred to as *elements*. Each element consists of an opening and closing tag. Any attributes are defined within the opening tag and any child elements are defined between the opening and closing tags. If an element doesn't have child elements, you can omit the closing tag by adding the forward slash (/) character at the end of the opening tag. (This is standard XML syntax.) You'll see this format in action later in this chapter, as well as in Appendix B.

> ▶   **Note**   Many developers found it frustrating when Microsoft Visual InterDev 6 reformatted code according to its preferred style. That feature was difficult, if not impossible, to turn off. In Microsoft Visual Studio .NET, not only can you control how code is validated and formatted, but in most cases you can also turn off autoformatting entirely.
>
> To view or change the formatting settings for a given language, from the Tools menu select Options, and then click the Text Editor folder. Click the folder for the language of your choice. Note that for some languages, the formatting settings appear on more than one option page. For example, HTML/XML formatting options are set on the Format page, the HTML Specific page, and the XML Specific page, all under the HTML/XML folder.

Editing Configuration Files

At the time of this writing, the Visual Studio .NET environment's tools for editing configuration files are limited to syntax coloring, XML validation, and code formatting. Because the ASP.NET configuration files are XML based, you can also use your favorite XML editor (or text editor) to edit them.

Open Web.config

1   Either open the Chapter_05 project from the practice files, or create a new project named Chapter_05, using the steps you learned in Chapter 2.

2   Locate the Web.config file in the Solution Explorer window and double-click it.

   The Web.config file will be opened for editing using the Visual Studio .NET XML editor, as shown in the illustration on the following page. We'll look at examples of editing this file later in the chapter, so you might want to leave it open.

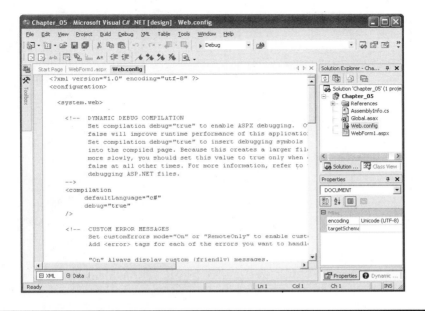

In addition to syntax coloring and validation, Visual Studio .NET provides a default Web.config file for each new Web application project that you create. This default file contains the most commonly used elements, as well as comments that explain the available options for each element, as shown in the previous illustration. The default Web.config file is useful as a template for any additional Web.config files you want to place in subfolders of your Web application. Keep in mind that when you're using configuration files in subfolders of your application, it's a good idea to include only the elements for the configuration settings from the parent file that you want to override. This helps prevent the accidental overriding of a configuration setting, and it might help reduce parsing overhead for the configuration of your application.

Editing the Master Configuration File

Not only does the master configuration file, machine.config, contain the default settings for all ASP.NET applications on the machine, but it also has machine-wide configuration settings. Be cautious when editing this file. It is prudent to create a backup copy of the file before you edit it. Also keep in mind that unless you're the only one who uses the machine on which you're developing, any changes that you make to machine.config will also affect other ASP.NET developers using the machine. Unless you enjoy dealing with unhappy colleagues, you should discuss any proposed changes with them first.

Configuring an ASP.NET Application

At the time of this writing, no GUI tools are available for editing the Web.config files and modifying configuration settings. Fortunately, the default Web.config file created by Visual Studio .NET Web Applications contains comments specific to the most commonly used settings. These comments provide guidance for using the available parameters for a given configuration element (although not all configuration elements appear in the default Web.config file). Complete documentation is provided in the Visual Basic .NET help files installed by default with Visual Studio .NET.

In addition to the comments found in the Web.config file generated by Visual Studio .NET, the machine.config file contains comments with specific settings for certain elements. These comments can guide you when you make configuration changes. Appendix B describes the available ASP.NET configuration elements and their settings.

To illustrate how to configure ASP.NET applications, let's look at two examples. The first example shows how to use the *<customErrors>* element to define a custom page to handle 404-Not Found errors when a user requests a page that doesn't exist in your application. The second example shows how to use the *<httpModules>* element to remove the *SessionStateModule* for applications that do not use session state.

Configure a custom 404 handler

1   Create a new project named Chapter_05 if you didn't do so in the previous exercise.

2   Add a new Web Form to the project. Name the file **fnf.aspx**.

The new Web Form will be displayed in Design view, as shown in the illustration on the following page.

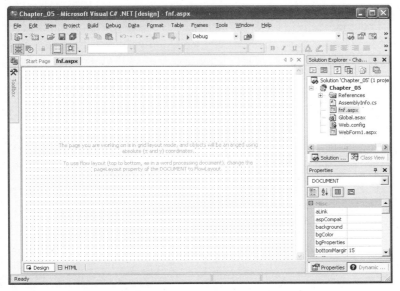

3   Add a *Label* control to the page, as shown in the following illustration.

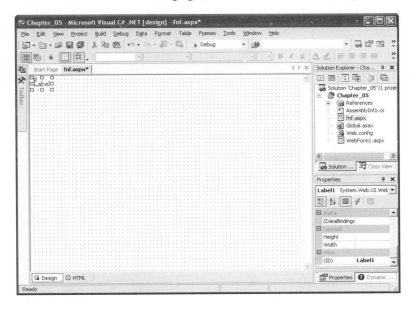

4 Double-click the Web Form in the Design view window.

The code-behind module for fnf.aspx will be displayed in the code editor window, with the cursor automatically moved to the *Page_Load* event handler. Note that a local declaration (highlighted in the following illustration) has been added to the code-behind for the *Label* control to allow programmatic access to the control by its name, *Label1*:

```
protected System.Web.UI.WebControls.Label Label1;
```

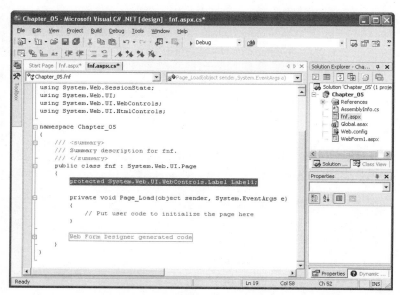

5 Replace the placeholder comment in the *Page_Load* event handler with the code in the illustration on the following page. (The ASP.NET runtime adds the *aspxerrorpath* query string variable automatically and populates it with the path requested by the user when redirecting from an HTTP error.)

```
Label1.Text = "We're sorry. The page you requested: " +
    Request.QueryString["aspxerrorpath"] + " does not exist. ";
```

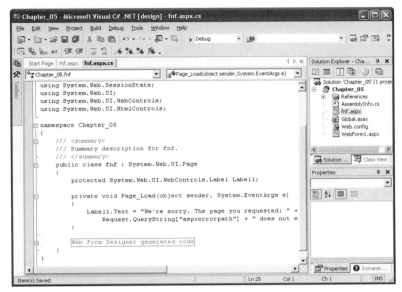

6   Save fnf.aspx and fnf.aspx.vb.

7   If it is not already open, open Web.config by double-clicking it in
    Solution Explorer.

8   Modify the *<customErrors>* element to look like the code in the illus-
    tration on the following page, and then save the file. (The *<error>*
    child element maps the HTTP 404 error code to redirect to the Web
    Form created in a previous step.)

```
<customErrors mode="On">
    <error statusCode="404" redirect="fnf.aspx"/>
</customErrors>
```

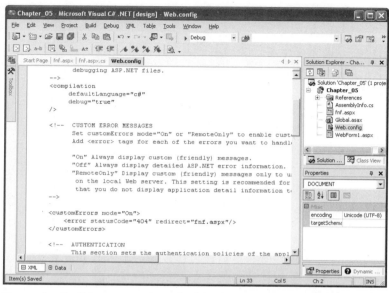

9   From the Build menu, select Build Chapter_05 to build the project.

10   Right-click WebForm1.aspx (the default Web Form added to the
     project when it was created), select Browse With, then select
     Microsoft Internet Explorer from the Browser List window, and then
     click Browse, as shown in the following illustration. (This will open
     the page in a separate browser window, rather than one embedded in
     the IDE.)

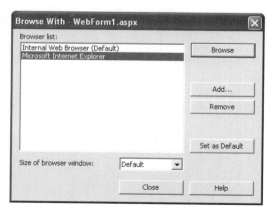

11 Using the Internet Explorer address bar, change the file portion of the URL from WebForm1.aspx to WebForm.aspx (a file that does not exist), and then click the Go button.

The page will redirect to fnf.aspx, and display a message similar to the following. (The path can vary depending on how you set up your project.)

You can use this technique to provide useful error messages to your users, as in this example, or you can expand on it by using the redirect page to send a notification to an administrator of the error, using the Microsoft .NET Framework's *SmtpMail* class. (You'll learn how to use the *SmtpMail* class in Chapter 8.)

HttpModules are classes that participate in the processing of every request made to an application. The built-in *HttpModules* in ASP.NET include *SessionStateModule* and *OutputCacheModule*, as well as modules for each of the built-in authentication methods in ASP.NET. These modules are added by default in machine.config using the *<httpModules>* element. You can use the *<httpModules>* element in your Web.config file to remove any of these modules that you're not using, or to add additional *httpModules* (including your own custom *httpModules*).

Remove an HttpModule

1 Open Web.config (if it isn't already open) by double-clicking it in Solution Explorer.

2 Just under the *<system.web>* tag, add an *<httpModules>* element to the file, as shown in the illustration on the following page:

```
<httpModules>
    <remove name="Session"/>
</httpModules>
```

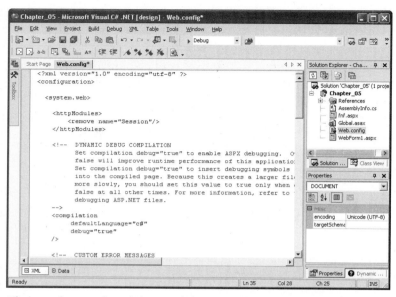

3 Change the *mode* attribute of the *<customErrors>* element to *Off*. (You'll see why in a few steps.)

4 Double-click the file WebForm1.aspx in Solution Explorer, and then double-click the page in the editor.

   The code-behind module for WebForm1.aspx will be displayed for editing, as shown in the following illustration.

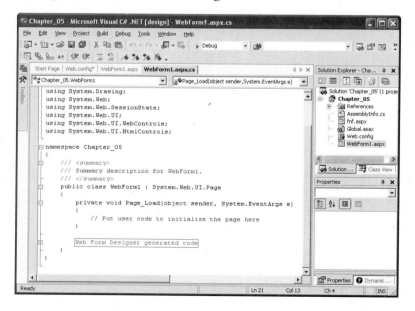

5   Replace the comment in *Page_Load* with the following code, shown
in the following illustration:

```
Session["foo"] = "Bar";
```

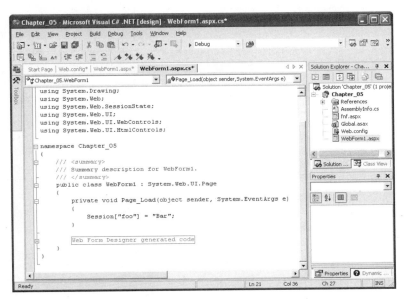

6   Save all open files and build the project.

7   In Solution Explorer, right-click WebForm1.aspx, and then select
Browse With to browse the page in a separate browser window.
(Select Internet Explorer as you did in the previous exercise.)

The request will result in an exception, because you've removed the
SessionStateModule from the application. Had you not modified the
<customErrors> element in Step 3, you would see a generic error
message instead of the detailed message shown on the next page.

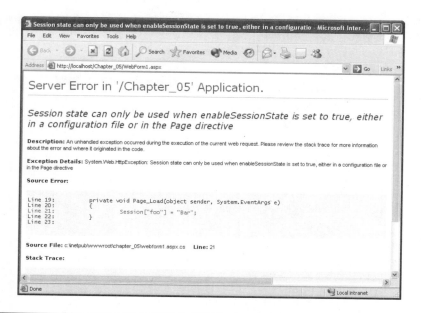

Overriding Configuration Settings for Subdirectories

Once you've created the application-level Web.config file (or Visual Studio .NET has created it for you when you created a project) and modified its settings to suit your needs, you might want to modify the configuration settings for a subset of your application. For example, you might want to apply more stringent security requirements to a particular set of files. In ASP.NET, it's simple to override the application-level configuration settings—it takes only three steps.

Override parent configuration settings

1   Create a subfolder in your application and place in it the content that the new configuration settings will apply to.
2   Create a new Web.config file in the new folder.
3   Add the configuration settings you want to override to the new Web.config file.

Include only the configuration elements that you want to override in the new Web.config file. All other settings are inherited from the Web.config file of the parent folder or, if that file doesn't exist (or doesn't contain settings for all available configuration elements), from the machine.config file for your Web server.

Locking Down Configuration Settings

Clearly, there will be times when Web developers or administrators want to configure settings for an entire server or site and prevent those settings from being overridden. This might be desirable in the case of authentication and authorization settings, or to prevent the overriding of security policy settings. Fortunately, ASP.NET provides the *<location>* tag for just this purpose.

The *<location>* tag has two attributes: *path* and *allowOverride*. The *path* attribute allows you to specify a path to which the settings within the *<location>* tag pair apply. This attribute allows you to use a single configuration file, such as machine.config, to apply configuration settings for multiple applications, virtual directories, or files on the same machine. Some settings can be set only at the machine or application level. If you attempt to apply these settings at the directory or file level using the *path* attribute, an exception will be thrown.

> ▶ **Note**   When you're using the *path* attribute to apply configuration settings to multiple locations, use comments to clarify the intended purpose of each set of *<location>* tags. In shared server environments, use comments to indicate the person responsible for a given set of configuration settings.

The *allowOverride* attribute determines whether the settings within the *<location>* tag pair can be overridden by settings applied in a child configuration file. If this attribute is set to *False*, any attempt to change the specified setting in a child configuration file will result in an exception.

Use the *<location>* tag to lock down configuration settings

1   Open the configuration file (Web.config or machine.config) from which you want to lock down a particular setting.

2   Add the following code within the *<configuration>* and *</configuration>* tags:

```
<location path="path to lock down" allowOverride="false">
   <system.web>
      <!-- Configuration elements to be locked down -->
   </system.web>
</location>
```

The *path* attribute should be the name of a subdirectory. The elements that appear inside the *system.web* tags will be treated as if they were in the Web.config file in that subdirectory.

3   Add the desired configuration elements between the *<system.web>* and *</system.web>* tags.

Running Against a Specific Framework Version

Starting with ASP.NET 1.1, ASP.NET applications can be configured to run using a specific version of the .NET Framework, as long as that version is installed on the target machine. This is referred to as *side-by-side execution*. Why is this important? Because as new versions of the .NET Framework are released, there might be times when security or other concerns require that a later version be incompatible with previous versions. Side-by-side execution allows you to install multiple versions of the .NET Framework on a single machine, and then to configure each application to use the desired version, for compatibility or other reasons.

For executable programs written for the .NET Framework, configuring an application to run against a specific version of the framework is accomplished using the *<assemblyBinding>* configuration element (see the MSDN documentation for Visual Studio .NET for more information on side-by-side execution and the *<assemblyBinding>* element). For ASP.NET applications, you must modify the application mapping in IIS for the desired application. By default, applications created after installing version 1.1 of the .NET Framework will be mapped to ASP.NET 1.1. The following steps show how to configure an application to run against version 1.0 of ASP.NET.

Configure an application to run against ASP.NET 1.0

1   While logged in as an administrator (or using the Run As feature to run using an administrative account), open a command line window, and navigate to the directory containing the version of the framework you want to run against, in this case, C:\WINDOWS\Microsoft.NET\ Framework\v1.0.3705 (change the drive letter and/or the name of the Windows directory to match your setup).

2   Run the ASP.NET Registration tool (aspnet_regiis.exe) using the following command line, substituting the desired application path for **W3SVC/1/ROOT/TestWeb** (*W3SVC/1/ROOT/* represents the root of the first Web site configured in IIS, while *TestWeb* represents the application with that name in that Web site):

```
aspnet_regiis.exe -s W3SVC/1/ROOT/TestWeb
```

▶   **Note**   The path to aspnet_regiis.exe may not be registered in the Path environment variable on your machine, in which case you will need to either include the full path to the executable (you can locate it using the Windows search tool) or follow the instructions in Appendix C for adding the path to aspnet_regiis.exe to the Path environment variable.

3   To verify that the configuration was successful, open the IIS Manager, navigate to the application in question, right-click the application and select Properties, and then click the Configuration button. In the Mappings tab, scroll down to the .aspx extension, and hover the mouse over the Executable Path column for that extension. The version number in the tooltip that displays the path to the executable should look like the one in the following illustration (from the Windows Server 2003 version of the IIS Manager).

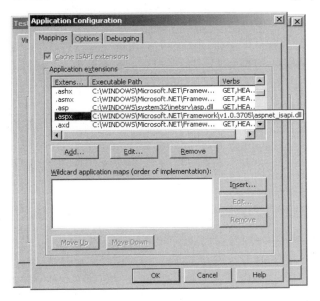

▶ **Important**   In Windows Server 2003 with Internet Information Services 6.0, a new process model is used in which a number of applications are run in one or more processes using an application pool designation. Applications using different application pool designations never share the same process. The reason this is important is that if you try to configure an application to run against a different version of ASP.NET than other applications in the same application pool, you might get an error message similar to the following in the Event Log:

It is not possible to run different versions of ASP.NET in the same IIS process. Please use the IIS Administration Tool to reconfigure your server to run the application in a separate process.

To resolve this issue, you must create a new application pool and assign it to the application that is to be configured differently from the others in the existing pool.

Chapter 5 Quick Reference

To	Do this
Edit Web.config in Visual Studio .NET	Double-click the Web.config file in Solution Explorer, edit as desired, and save.
Override parent configuration settings	Add a new folder to which the new settings will apply, add a new Web.config file to that folder, edit the Web.config to reflect the desired configuration elements, and save. Add the associated content to the same folder.
Lock down configuration settings	Wrap the settings to be locked down with a *<location>* *</location>* tag pair with the *allowOverride* attribute set to *False*.

Security in ASP.NET

In this chapter, you will learn how to:

- Remove unused services to reduce security exposure.
- Create and apply security policies to simplify the configuration of OS security settings.
- Secure the system administrator account for an MSDE database instance.
- Validate and restrict user input.
- Enable logging of Web requests.
- Enable SSL encryption of Web requests.
- Enable Windows or Forms authentication for ASP.NET.
- Use ACL or URL authorization to control access to resources.
- Use trusted connections with SQL Server or MSDE databases.

In days gone by, there were primarily two types of applications: single-user applications in which presentation, business logic, and any necessary data handling all occurred on the client machine of the user; and client/server applications, which removed much or all of the data handling to a separate database server. Back then, security was largely a matter of making sure that in a client/server situation, users made modifications only to data that they were authorized to change. The typical application developer seldom had to face issues such as denial-of-service attacks, port sniffing, and so on.

The Internet has changed all that forever. Applications that are exposed to the Internet are inherently vulnerable to a host of issues, ranging from attempts at stealing data to the defacing of Web sites to denial-of-service attacks. No matter what operating system or other software you run, that vulnerability will never go away entirely. Software is an imperfect science, and unfortunately, an operating system invulnerable to attack has yet to be created.

The good news is that most software, including Microsoft Windows 2000, Microsoft Windows XP, IIS, and Microsoft Windows Server 2003 can be made quite secure if you follow best practices (a recognized set of recommended procedures and policies) for security, such as keeping track of and installing security patches as soon as they are released. One of the remarkable things about security practices in our industry is just how many servers (both Microsoft-based and otherwise) are sitting out there exposed to the Internet, without patches installed that have been available for months, or even years!

The Importance of Security

Security should be one of the first concerns a Web developer thinks about when designing and implementing an application. In many ways, designing an application without *considering* security is the same as designing an application *without* security. It is much harder to add security to an application after the fact than it is to do so up front.

Of course, there are different levels and types of security. The type and level you need for your application will vary depending on what your application does, the type and value of data (if any) that you store, the amount of risk you are comfortable with, and the amount of time, effort, and money you are willing to expend to have a secure application. The security needs of a personal home page, for example, are very different from those of a corporate intranet site or a retail e-commerce site. Table 6.1 describes the kinds of threats that are out there and the consequences of being underprepared for them.

Table 6-1. Security Threats

Type of Threat	Primary Target	Consequence
Web server compromise Defacement Substituting incorrect or misleading information for valid information Unauthorized access to internal networks Installation of Trojan or Distributed Denial of Service (DDoS) code	All Web sites	This threat might be embarrassing for an individual, but can be costly to a corporation, not only in terms of repairing damages, but also in the cost to the company's reputation of having its site defaced or, worse yet, having inaccurate or misleading information posted. Compromised systems can also be used to mount DDoS attacks on other systems—a potential source of liability.

Table 6-1. Security Threats

Type of Threat	Primary Target	Consequence
Denial of service	Higher-profile sites	A denial-of-service attack can prevent users from accessing your site by flooding it with illegitimate requests, among other techniques. These attacks can be difficult to prevent.
Data loss or compromise Data compromised through packet sniffing Server data compromised through user impersonation or data forgery	All sites transmitting and receiving sensitive data	Consequences of not addressing this threat include compromise of credit card or other sensitive data and illicit modification of server data.

▶ **Note**   A more complete discussion of this topic is available in Chapter 14 of William Stallings', *Cryptography and Network Security: Principles and Practice,* 2d ed. (Prentice Hall, 1998).

Security Basics

With so many potential threats against Internet applications, it's often difficult to know just where to start in designing a secure application. This section will discuss some of the strategies you can use to get started.

Server Setup and Application Design

One of the first areas to concentrate on is how you set up your server. Designing an application that implements authentication and authorization properly is futile if someone can simply bypass all that security through some vulnerability that you haven't applied the patch for. This section will discuss a number of good practices for server setup and application design, but it's no substitute for a solid understanding of Windows and IIS security. You should consult other sources for server security, such as the Microsoft TechNet site (*http://www.microsoft.com/technet/*) and the security guides for Windows 2000 and Windows XP offered by the United States' National Security Agency at *http://nsa2.www.conxion.com/*. The books of Michael Howard are an especially good source of information on IIS (and Web application) security. Howard has been a security program manager for Microsoft IIS 4.0 and 5.0, was on the Windows XP team, and is currently a Senior Program Manager for Microsoft's Secure Windows Initiative. His books include *Designing Secure Web-Based Applications for Microsoft Windows 2000* (Microsoft Press, 2000) and *Writing Secure Code*, 2d ed. (Microsoft Press, 2002), *http://www.microsoft.com/MSPress/books/5957.asp*. *Writing Secure Code*, in particular, contains information on threat modeling and other important techniques for designing and developing secure applications that are beyond the scope of this chapter.

Choosing an Operating System

When you're choosing an operating system (OS), the first thing to ask yourself is just how much security you need. As with many issues related to the design of a Web application, there are trade-offs to be made between security and cost. Although client operating systems such as the Windows $9x$ series might be able to act as Web servers on a limited basis through Personal Web Services (PWS), they are not acceptable when security is an important factor.

Workstation or server operating systems, such as Windows Server 2003, Windows 2000, and Windows XP Professional, offer more robust scalability and better security features, including better access control (see "Access Control" on page 158), logging, and encryption.

▶   **Note**   One reason to choose Windows 2000, Windows XP, or Windows Server 2003 to develop and/or host a Web application is that these operating systems can use the NTFS file system; the Windows 9x series cannot. NTFS allows you to provide robust access control at both the file and folder level, and it also provides built-in support for file encryption. The FAT and FAT32 file systems (available in the 9x series) are poor choices for Web applications requiring robust security.

Server operating systems offer the most robust security features, as well as better scalability, greater ease of configuration, and better features for developers.

Your evaluation should include an analysis of features (in this case, security features), cost, and the existing environment, with the goal of determining which OS meets your security needs (features), while allowing you to work within the constraints of cost and existing environment (if any).

▶   **Important**   Windows 2000 and Windows XP provide a number of major security improvements, including built-in support for file system encryption, security policies and templates (discussed later in this section), and a Security Configuration and Analysis tool. This tool can be very useful in determining whether your system will meet your security needs as configured, and can help you easily configure it if it doesn't. For these reasons, Windows 2000 (or later) should be the default choice for secure Web applications on the Microsoft platform. Additionally, the Web Server edition of Windows Server 2003 contains many security improvements that should make it the first choice for building new ASP.NET Web applications, whenever possible.

Choosing a Purpose

Another important point to consider when choosing your operating system is the purpose of the server. For smaller applications with low scalability requirements, it can be acceptable to run your Web server, database server, and components all on the same machine. Because IIS and most databases make significant demands on both RAM and processor power, this model does not scale particularly well for larger applications. More important, however, placing a database on a Web server that is exposed to the Internet greatly increases the security risks to the data stored in that database. This can also be true for other server and application software, from mail-server software to productivity applications such as Microsoft Office. The important point is that as you add more functionality to a server, you are also adding more security exposure. Keep all of this in mind as you configure your servers and decide the purpose for each one.

Too Much Service

The next important set of decisions comes when you install your operating system of choice (Windows 2000, for example), or when you add on services to be used by your application. You should be very conscious of exactly which services are installed by default with your chosen operating system, and understand the vulnerabilities that can result.

Unused services running on your server can be a significant security risk. For example, if you install the FTP or SMTP services and have not protected the ports those services use, an attacker can detect the services and attempt to use them to compromise your server through various known vulnerabilities. (You can reduce the risk of compromise through diligent application of patches. See "Patching" on page 155 for more information.)

If you are not using a service, you should avoid installing it, or use the Add Or Remove Programs Control Panel applet to remove it. The following steps, which are specific to Windows Server 2003, show how to do so. (The procedure for Windows 2000 and Windows XP is similar.)

> ▶ **Tip**   The Microsoft Baseline Security Analyzer (MBSA) tool, which is discussed later in this chapter (see "Patching" on page 155), can assist you in identifying some of the more common unnecessary services that you might consider removing.

Remove unused services

1 Log in using an administrative account.

2 Click Start, click Control Panel, and then click Add Or Remove Programs. (In Windows 2000 and Windows XP, click Control Panel, and then click the Add Or Remove Programs icon.)

3 In the left side of the window, click the Add/Remove Windows Components button.

4 Review the list of installed components (shown in the following illustration).

   Of particular interest is the Application Server node. Select that node and click the Details button. Next, select the Internet Information Services (IIS) node, and click the Details button. (Note that in Windows 2000 and Windows XP, the IIS node is in the first dialog box, so you won't see an Application Server node.)

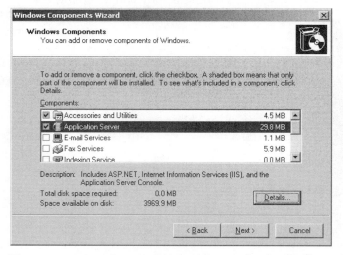

5 To remove a service or component, uncheck (deselect) the check box next to it, as done for the SMTP service shown in the illustration on the following page. Click OK to close the Details dialog box, and again to close the Application Server dialog box (this is not necessary in Windows 2000 and Windows XP).

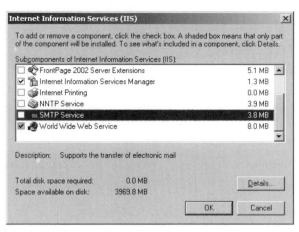

6 Click Next to apply your changes.

7 Click Finish to complete the process, as shown in the following illustration.

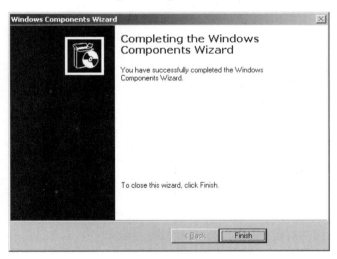

If you need to install services that are not used all the time, you should set them to be started manually rather than automatically. This way, you have control over when these services are running. Be aware, however, that in some cases, even services configured for manual startup can be started because other services are dependent on them. If you have a service you really do not want to ever start, you can set the startup type to disabled, and the service will not start, and cannot be started as a dependent service.

▶ **Important**   Removing unused services is one way of reducing the so-called surface area that a potential attacker has to work with. This technique applies not just to services, but to any software running on a given machine. You should *never* install unnecessary software, whether file sharing software, productivity software, or third-party utilities on a server unless you absolutely must and you understand the security impact that installing them entails.

Be a Policy Maker

One unheralded feature of Windows 2000 and later is a robust set of tools for setting up a machine's security settings quickly and relatively painlessly. A full discussion of these tools is beyond the scope of this book (and could take up a book of its own), but let's look at a couple of them.

The Security Templates tool and the Security Configuration and Analysis tool, when used together, let you create, edit, and apply templates for defining security policies, from minimum password length to file system auditing policy. Both tools, shown in the following illustration, are implemented as Microsoft Management Console (MMC) snap-ins.

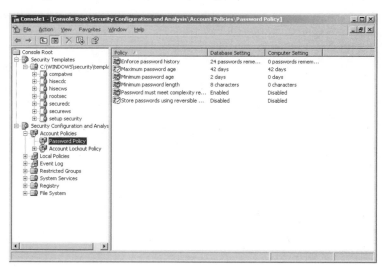

▶ **Note**   You can also define security policies manually by using the Local Security Policy editor, which you can find by opening the Control Panel (and switching to Classic View, if required) and then double-clicking Administrative Tools and then the Local Security Policy icon. This tool allows you to adjust individual local security policy settings as well as apply security templates to the local machine.

Access the Security Templates tool

1 Either open an existing MMC console or create a new one by clicking Start, and then selecting Run. Type **mmc** and click OK.

2 From the File menu (Console menu in Windows 2000), select Add/Remove Snap-In (Ctrl+M), and then click the Add button.

3 From the list of available snap-ins, select the Security Templates snap-in, and then click the Add button.

4 Click the Close button to close the Add Standalone Snap-in dialog box, and then click OK to close the Add/Remove Snap-In dialog box.

5 If desired, from the File (or Console) menu click Save (Ctrl+S) or Save As to save your new or modified MMC console.

▶ **Note**   An infrequently used but helpful feature of the MMC is creating and saving custom consoles that contain the MMC snap-ins you use most frequently. You can use the procedure outlined in the preceding list to add the Security Configuration and Analysis snap-in (or any other snap-in) to a console.

The advantage of using the Security Templates tool to create and edit your security templates is that it allows you to create security policy templates separately from applying the template to the local machine.

Create a new security template

1 Expand the Security Templates node by clicking the + symbol to its left, as shown in the illustration on the next page.

This will display the template path folder(s) available on the machine.

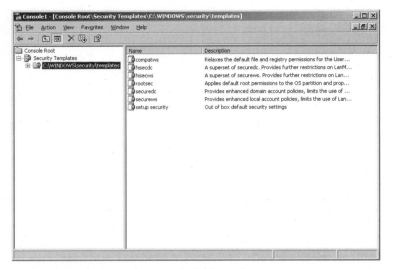

2   Right-click the template path folder where you want to store your new template, and then select New Template.

The following dialog box will be displayed.

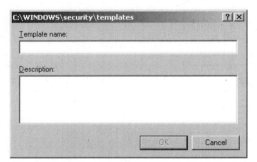

3   Type the name **TestTemplate** and the description **This is a test template** for the new template and click OK. The new template will be displayed under the path folder you selected in Step 1, as shown in the illustration on the following page. (You might need to expand the node for the template folder to view the new template.)

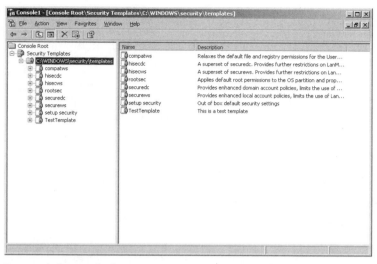

4   Expand the node for your new template by double-clicking it, or click the + sign next to it to display the options available for configuration with the template.

5   Expand the policy area you want to customize, such as the Password Policy (which can be found under the Account Policies node). Select the policy to view its available Policy attributes in the right pane of the console window.

6   Double-click Minimum Password Length policy.

7   Check Define This Policy Setting In The Template, as shown in the following illustration. Edit the value to your desired setting.

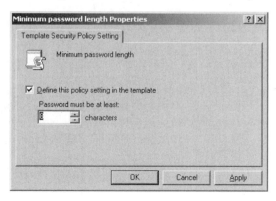

6

8   Click OK to close the Template Security Policy Setting dialog box and apply your change to the template.

9   After making any additional changes to the template, save it by right-clicking the TestTemplate node and selecting Save.

Of course, once you've created your custom template, you might want to use it to configure security for one or more machines. You can do this by using the Security Configuration and Analysis tool, which you can also use to determine which settings on the local machine are not in compliance with the template you've defined (or one of the predefined templates).

▶   **Important**   As with many security-related tasks, you must be logged in as an administrator to successfully analyze the current security settings and apply security templates. Non-administrators can start up the Security Templates and Security Configuration and Analysis tools, but will receive errors if they attempt to perform actions for which they do not have the necessary permissions.

You can also use templates to define security settings for development, staging, and production security requirements. A development or staging server's security requirements are usually less restrictive than those for a production server environment, where the completed application ultimately will be deployed. Unfortunately, when an application is moved to the more restrictive environment of the production server, security restrictions can prevent the application from working. You can define security templates for development, staging, and production environments and then apply those templates to your development and/or staging servers to test whether the application will work with the greater restrictions of those environments. Once testing is complete, you can restore the previous template to continue development work.

▶   **Important**   Because the Security Templates tool can affect a large number of security settings on a machine, it is very important that you configure and test your templates on development or staging systems before applying them to production systems. Certain security restrictions can prevent Web applications from functioning properly (for example, by restricting access on accounts used by the application), so you should always make sure your application works properly under the security policy defined by the template before applying the template to a production system.

Apply a security template

1   Open a console containing the Security Configuration and Analysis MMC snap-in. If prompted, create a test database for this exercise. (For the purposes of this exercise, it doesn't matter which template you create the test database from.)

2   Before selecting a new template, you might want to save your current settings as a template so you can restore them after applying a different template. To save a template containing the current settings, right-click the Security Configuration and Analysis node, select Export Template, provide a name for the exported template, and then click Save.

▶   **Note**   If the Export Template menu option is unavailable on the context menu of the Security and Configuration Analysis node in MMC, you need to create or open a Security Database, Import a template, and then run Analysis. Once you do this, you will be able to run the Export. Follow these steps to enable the Export Template menu option:

   1   Right click on Security and Configuration Analysis in MMC, and select Open Database.

   2   Type the name of a new database, and click Open.

   3   In the Import Template dialog that will appear, select one of the templates and click Open.

   4   Right click on Security and Configuration Analysis in MMC and select Analyze Computer Now from the context menu.

   Once the analysis is complete, Export Template and most other options should be available on the context menu of the Security and Configuration Analysis node in MMC.

3   Right-click the Security Configuration and Analysis node and select Import Template.

4   Select the desired template from the dialog box and click OK. For this example, select the built-in hisecws.inf template.

▶   **Note**   Microsoft has made available a template called hisecweb.inf for configuring a high-security Web server. You can use this template as a starting point for creating your own security templates. You can download it from *http:// download.microsoft.com/download/win2000srv/SCM/1.0/NT5/EN-US/hisecweb.exe.*

5   You can compare the settings in the template to those currently con-
    figured on the local machine by right-clicking the Security Configura-
    tion and Analysis node, selecting Analyze Computer Now, and then
    clicking OK in the Perform Analysis dialog box.

6   Expand the Account Policies node to display the Password Policy
    node. Select the Password Policy node to view its settings, as shown
    in the following illustration. A green check mark indicates where
    local settings match the template; a red X indicates where the settings
    do not match.

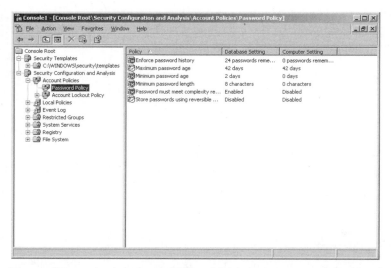

7   To configure the local machine with the settings specified in the tem-
    plate, right-click the Security Configuration and Analysis node, select
    Configure Computer Now, and then click OK in the Configure Sys-
    tem dialog box.

    If you want to view the settings modified by the template, you will
    need to reanalyze the computer as described in Step 5.

Keep in mind that only settings for which a value has been defined in the template will be applied. All other settings will remain as they were previously configured. Also note that when a server that you're configuring is part of a
Windows 2000 or Windows Server 2003 domain, any settings configured in the
domain-wide security policy will override settings in the local security policy.

Passwords, Please

One of the most commonly (and dangerously) overlooked areas in Web server security is password protection. Problems in this area include weak or nonexistent passwords for sensitive information or services, and passwords placed in plain-text files such as ASP and ASP.NET pages, Global.asa or Global.asax files, or configuration files in the Web space.

Weak or Blank Passwords

A simple rule of thumb for sensitive information on your Web server is that it should be protected by a password—a strong one. Too often, developers wrongly assume that it's sufficient to put Web pages that are to be accessed only by certain authorized users (or other sensitive content) in a separate directory that is accessible only by entering the URL directly. And worse, Web developers who are not sufficiently familiar with Microsoft SQL Server might install these databases on a Web server or another server on the network without understanding the security ramifications. The same security ramifications apply to MSDE, which can be installed with the Microsoft .NET Framework Quickstart samples or Microsoft Visual Studio .NET.

SQL Server and MSDE both contain an extended stored procedure called *xp_cmdshell* that allows command-line commands to be run on the server. Why is this important? Because in many cases, people still install SQL Server or MSDE with a blank password for the *sa* (system administrator) account. For a server connected to the Internet, this is like begging to be hacked. In fact, one Web-hosting company that hosts a site devoted to ASP and ASP.NET articles fell prey to precisely this problem because of the default configuration of MSDE in the Beta 2 .NET Framework QuickStart samples, which included a blank sa password, a situation which has been corrected in the release version. This highlights the inherent risk of both beta software and of samples, which are rarely designed for high security. The result was that some malcontents used *xp_cmdshell* to delete much of the content on the affected server. The Web-hosting company was fortunate enough to have backups of the content and was able to restore the server, but the damage could have been much worse.

> ▶ **Important**   I cannot emphasize this strongly enough: You must have a strong password on the *sa* account of any SQL Server or MSDE databases on your network. A malicious user with access through the *sa* account can do anything to your server that could be accomplished from a command line, including adding or deleting user accounts, installing and executing malicious code, and deleting content or system files.

Change the MSDE *sa* password

1   On the machine where MSDE is installed, open a command prompt. (See Appendix C for instructions on installing MSDE.)

2   Type the following command, which uses the osql command-line utility to connect to the \VSdotNET named instance of MSDE that can be installed by the QuickStart samples, and then press the ENTER key:

```
osql -S(local)\VSdotNET -E
```

3   If the connection is successful, you'll see the following prompt. (If the login fails, you'll get a failure message.)

```
1>
```

4   If the login is successful, enter the following commands to modify the password for the *sa* account. Make sure that you memorize the new password so you won't forget it. (Avoid writing it down if possible. But if you must, make sure you put it somewhere secure so prying eyes won't find it.) Replace *<new password>* with the new password you've chosen, and follow the *go* command by pressing the ENTER key:

```
1> sp_password NULL, '<new password>', 'sa'
2> go
```

5   If the result is successful, you should see the message shown in the following illustration. Also note that, in this example, a password containing letters, numbers, and symbols has been chosen.

▶   **Important**   Although it might seem obvious, you should not use the password shown in this example as the sa password for your SQL Server or MSDE instance. Instead, choose a unique value that will be difficult to guess.

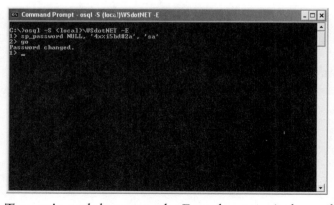

6   Type **exit**, and then press the Enter key to exit the osql utility.

You can also use the SQL Server Enterprise Manager utility, if it is available, to modify the login accounts and passwords for an MSDE database.

Almost as bad as blank passwords are passwords that are weak (easily guess-able), such as

- Names or places
- Dates, such as birthdays or anniversaries
- Words found in a dictionary
- Short passwords (8 characters or fewer)
- Passwords that are all letters, all lowercase, all uppercase, or all numeric

Weak passwords make it much easier for someone trying to hack a server to guess the password for an account. So-called *dictionary attacks* use a dictionary of common terms or words to rapidly attempt to log in to an account. *Brute force attacks* attempt every possible value until they find the correct one. While a strong password won't necessarily eliminate brute force attacks, it can increase the time needed for such an attack to succeed. In combination with appropriate auditing and logging, this can give you time to deal with the attack.

Strong passwords meet minimum requirements for length and complexity. You can require secure passwords using a security template, such as the hisecweb.inf template, or by using the Security Configuration and Analysis tool as described earlier in this chapter. The hisecweb.inf template sets minimum and maximum password age, enforces password history (preventing users from reusing old passwords), sets minimum password length to eight characters, and requires passwords to meet minimum complexity requirements, including requiring passwords to include three of the following four categories of characters:

- Uppercase characters
- Lowercase characters
- Numeric characters
- Nonalphanumeric symbols (such as punctuation and special charac-ters such as *, #, and $)

Note that these settings control passwords only for NT security accounts. If you use your own authentication credentials in your application, you will need to implement your own solution for enforcing strong passwords, such as using the RegularExpressionValidator Server Control to perform pattern matching. (See Chapter 8 for more information on validation controls.)

▶ **Important**   One of the best things an application developer can do to encourage users to use strong passwords is to help reduce the *number* of passwords that users must remember. Too many times, we design applications without any consideration for the host of passwords users must remember for other applications or Web sites. The more passwords users have to remember, the more likely they are to choose simple (and easily guessed) passwords or to write passwords down on sticky notes attached to their monitors.

So what should you, as an application developer do? Find ways to reduce the number of passwords you require your users to remember. A couple of ideas for this include:

- Consolidate authentication for multiple applications under your control, whenever possible. Allowing a single sign-on to multiple applications can reduce the overhead of managing logins (authentication), while application rights can still be assigned on a per-user basis (authorization).

- Use Windows Authentication whenever possible. Using Windows authentication means that users do not need to remember a separate username and login for your application. Of course, if you're going to use Windows authentication, you should encourage the use of strong password policies in your organization so your application will be less vulnerable to easily guessed passwords.

Other practices, such as limiting the length of passwords or making certain characters invalid in a password, can discourage users from reusing passwords that they have memorized for other applications. Here, there's a balancing act between the desirable practice of having unique passwords and the reality that more passwords to remember often means shortcuts like writing down passwords. In cases like these, ask yourself which is worse: users reusing existing passwords (assuming these meet your requirements for strong passwords) or users writing down new passwords because they aren't going to be able to remember them. Just remember that while security is a very important goal, if you make security too hard for your users to deal with, you might end up encouraging practices that make your application *less* secure in the end.

Unsafe Storing of Passwords

Another common problem in Web applications is the storing of passwords or other sensitive data in unsafe locations: plain-text files such as ASP and ASP.NET pages, Global.asa or Global.asax files, and configuration files in the Web space (files that are accessible by HTTP requests to the Web server). The problem usually occurs when developers place database login information, including the password, in a plain-text file on the Web server. These developers assume that since users are prevented from viewing the source of .asp, .aspx, .asa, and .asax files by default, this information will be safe. Unfortunately, this is true only if the Web server is not compromised by a security vulnerability. If a server is compromised, a malicious user might be able to read any file in the Web space for an application and gain the password(s) stored there.

You can protect sensitive information such as database passwords by using one of the following options.

- If you're using SQL Server or MSDE, use a trusted connection to connect to your database. This method uses the *Trusted_Connection* attribute of a connection string to tell SQL Server to use the current user's NT login information to log in. This is most useful in intranet scenarios where users log in to your application via NTLM with an NT username and password. This method gives you the advantage of not needing to store a password at all.

- Store the connection string information in the machine.config file, which is not directly in the Web space of the application, using the appSettings configuration section (described in Appendix B). Although this method is still not ideal because password information is still being stored in plain text, the fact that the machine.config file is stored outside of the Web space makes it that much harder for a malicious user to get to this file. For better security with this method, the directory containing machine.config and the directory containing your Web application should reside on different drives.

- For passwords used with Forms Authentication, you can use the aptly (if awkwardly) named *HashPasswordForStoringInConfigFile* helper method of the *FormsAuthentication* class to hash a password for storing in a configuration file or in a database or XML file. You can then use the same method to hash the password entered by the user at run time and compare the two hashes to determine whether to allow the login to succeed. You'll learn how to store hashed passwords later in this chapter.

In addition, you can use such techniques as encryption (using the classes in the System.Security.Cryptography namespace) to make a would-be hacker's job more difficult. The bottom line is that there is really no 100-percent-secure place that you can store passwords, but some methods are more secure than others. Balance your need for security against other factors when choosing how and where to store sensitive information.

▶ **Note**   Using a trusted connection with SQL Server requires either using Windows authentication and impersonation, as described in "Using Impersonation" on page 181, or setting up the default ASPNET account (the account used to run the ASPNET worker processes) as a login account in the SQL Server database being accessed. This process is described in Chapter 9.

Limit Those Accounts

Account limitations are an important security strategy from the standpoint of Windows accounts, database accounts, and any custom accounts you might create for your application. You should configure each account to have only the capabilities necessary for the type of user it represents. For example, it is usually a good idea to set up a database account with read-only access for pages (or components) in your application that only need to read and display data.

This concept is sometimes referred to as the *principle of least privilege*. Central to this concept is the notion of performing a given task with only the security privileges *required* for that task, and no more. Using an account with more privileges than necessary can result in unfortunate consequences if you have a security bug in your code.

A good example of this practice is Microsoft's decision to change the default account for running ASP.NET worker processes. In the early betas of ASP.NET, the default account was the SYSTEM account, which has numerous privileges and can perform almost any action on a machine. Had this setting remained the default, then any vulnerability found in ASP.NET or in your code could provide an attacker with SYSTEM-level access to the vulnerable machine.

In ASP.NET 1.0 under IIS 5.0, the default is the ASPNET account (specified by the *MACHINE* value for the *username* attribute of the *<processModel>* configuration element in machine.config), which has very few privileges on the system. This change makes certain techniques more difficult to use, but it also reduces the likelihood that a single compromised application can compromise an entire system or an entire network.

> ▶ **Note**   When running IIS 6.0 on Windows Server 2003 in native mode (the default), the IIS 6.0 process model settings (accessed through the Properties dialog box of the application pool containing your application) are used and the settings contained in the *<processModel>* element in machine.config are ignored.
>
> Since the default identity of an application pool process in IIS 6 is the new Network Service built-in account, rather than the ASPNET account, any applications that use Impersonation and grant rights to the ASPNET account would need to be modified to grant those same rights to the Network Service account to run on IIS 6 in native mode.

Another example of a major violation of the principle of least privilege is running database code using the SQL Server *sa* account. *Never* do this, *ever*! If you run your database code (whether raw SQL or stored procs) using the *sa* account, it takes only one coding error on your part for your entire database server to be compromised. And once an attacker has control over one machine in your network, it is far easier for the same outlaw to break into others. Don't let this happen to you. Always use accounts with the minimum necessary privileges to access and update database data.

No Samples, Thank You

Another area of danger for the unwary IIS administrator or Web developer is sample applications. By default, some versions of IIS are installed with a set of sample applications designed to help developers learn to develop applications on an IIS server. The .NET Framework SDK also has samples that can be installed to help developers learn to develop .NET applications. These and other sample applications have their place, but *not* on a production Web server.

Sample applications are not designed to run on production servers, so typically they do not use best practices to prevent servers or applications from being compromised. For example, samples installed with one version of IIS included a utility that allowed users to view the source of ASP pages. Unfortunately, if this utility was installed on a server containing production applications, it could be used to view the source code and make those applications vulnerable to attack.

As mentioned earlier, the .NET QuickStart samples install an instance of the MSDE database software. In the Beta 2 release, this instance was installed with a blank password for the *sa* account. Installing these samples on a server that is exposed to the Internet would result in a major vulnerability.

Additionally, some sample applications demonstrate extremely poor practices when it comes to security. Early versions of the ASP.NET QuickStart samples used the *sa* account with a blank password for database connections. This is an extremely bad practice. Not only does it reinforce the bad habit of leaving the *sa* account with no password, but it also uses an account for data access that has much wider permissions than are necessary for data access alone. The good news is that the current versions of the QuickStart samples follow the best practice of using an MSDE account created especially for the sample applications. This account has permission only to access the databases used by the samples, and only the permissions on those databases necessary for the samples.

Although the changes in the .NET Framework QuickStart samples indicate that Microsoft is committed to demonstrating better security practices in sample applications, you should never install them on a production server (or any other server that is exposed to the Internet, for that matter) without a very clear understanding of the risks entailed, and without undertaking efforts necessary to mitigate those risks.

▶ **Tip**   The MBSA tool (mentioned earlier in "Too Much Service" and discussed later in "Patching") can assist you in identifying samples commonly installed by default in some versions of IIS. It does not, however, identify the .NET Framework QuickStart samples as a security risk. Nonetheless, to reduce the available attack surface you present to potential attackers, you generally should avoid installing the QuickStart samples on a production server exposed to the Internet.

You Need Validation

Validation is another area that is often overlooked in Web application security. For example, developers might include validation code to ensure that users enter an e-mail address or phone number in the correct format. But they might not consider that other text fields, particularly large text fields or those that might be used for display elsewhere in the application, can expose the application to unacceptable risks.

The problem with not validating all text input by the user is that a malicious user can enter text, such as script commands, ASP.NET <% %> render blocks, or other text that, in the wrong context, could be allowed to execute rather than being treated as plain text to be displayed. Additionally, input fields used to construct SQL statements for data access can be vulnerable to unexpected commands. Validation can help you prevent this problem, as well as prevent nuisance problems such as users attempting to post profanity in guest book or discussion list applications built with ASP.NET. In fact, ASP.NET makes it very easy to implement robust validation using a set of server controls designed specifically for this purpose.

The most important thing to take from this discussion is that you should always treat any input from a user as suspect until it has been proven otherwise. Validate that the input from the user is what you're expecting *before* you use, store, or display it. You can do this in a variety of ways, but the most effective is by using regular expressions to test for valid input. In ASP.NET, you can use the *RegularExpressionValidator* control to validate input using a regular expression of your choice. The following code snippet shows the declaration for a multi-line TextBox control, and an associated RegularExpressionValidator control that limits input to a small subset of HTML tags and punctuation characters. The regular expression used in the code example is taken from Chapter 13 of Michael Howard and David LeBlanc's *Writing Secure Code*, 2d ed. (Microsoft Press, 2002).

▶ **Important**   You should always check for valid input, rather than checking for invalid input. The inherent problem with checking for invalid input or data is that it is far too easy to miss a particular type of invalid input. Checking for valid input according to rules you define and rejecting any other input is more likely to ensure that you don't accept malicious input by accident.

```
<form id="Form1" method="post" runat="server">
   <!-- &lt; and &gt; represent < and > -->
   <asp:Label id="Label1" runat="server">Enter text to display (&lt;b&gt;,
&lt;i&gt;, &lt;hr&gt; acceptable):</asp:Label>
      <asp:Button id="Button1" runat="server"
         Text="Display"/>
      <asp:TextBox id="TextBox1" runat="server"
         TextMode="MultiLine" Height="112px" Width="432px"></asp:TextBox>
      <asp:RegularExpressionValidator id="RegularExpressionValidator1"
         runat="server"
         ErrorMessage="Invalid Input Found!"
<!-- This validation expression will allow only <i>, <b>, and <hr> tags,
   spaces, any text A-Za-z0-9, and the following punctuation: ?!,.'".
   All other input will cause the validation to fail.
   Note that this expression does not validate for well-formed HTML -->
ValidationExpression="^([\s\w\?\!\,\.\'\&quot;]*|(</?(i|I|b|B|hr|HR)>))*$"
         ControlToValidate="TextBox1"></asp:RegularExpressionValidator>
      <asp:Label id="Label2" runat="server"></asp:Label>
</form>
```

You'll learn more about using the ASP.NET validation controls in Chapter 8. You can learn more about using regular expressions for validating user input in Chapter 11 and Chapter 13 of *Writing Secure Code*, 2d ed., by Michael Howard and David LeBlanc (Microsoft Press, 2002). A good source for regular expressions for a variety of purposes is *http://www.regexlib.com/*, a site run by Steven A. Smith, a noted leader in the ASP.NET community.

ASP.NET Request Validation

Cross-site scripting (XSS) attacks are a type of attack in which a variety of techniques are used to attempt to execute malicious script code by injecting it into form input, querystrings, or cookies. If an attacker can successfully inject script into one of these areas, and your code processes it without validating or filtering the data, the script code can be executed, exposing your application data and more. (A detailed overview of XSS can be found at *http://www.microsoft.com/ technet/security/topics/csoverv.asp*.) To protect against XSS attacks, the ASP.NET team added a new feature to ASP.NET 1.1 called *Request Validation*. Request Validation checks the query string, form input, and other input data for indications of HTML elements, script blocks, or other potentially dangerous data. If such data is found, an exception of type *HttpRequestValidationException* is thrown.

Request Validation is enabled by default, and can be disabled either at the application level using the *validateRequest* attribute of the *<pages>* configuration element:

```
<pages
   validateRequest="false"/>
```

or at the page level using the *validateRequest* attribute of the @ *Page* directive:

```
<% @ Page ValidateRequest="false" %>
```

> ▶ **Important**   It is highly recommended that you do not disable Request Valida-
> tion unless you have first ensured that all input to the page or application is
> being appropriately validated and/or filtered for potentially dangerous data. Fail-
> ure to heed this recommendation can result in data loss or other serious secu-
> rity problems.

Mind Those Ports!

Internet applications communicate via the TCP/IP protocol, which is the basis
for all communication between computers on the Internet. TCP/IP uses two
pieces of information to find the endpoints for a given communication: the
IP address, which is a unique number assigned to a given machine, and a TCP
(or UDP) port number, which for most applications is a well-known number
used consistently by all applications of that type. For example, all Web servers
use TCP port 80 as the default port for HTTP (Web) communications. The
well-known nature of these port numbers and the services found on them makes
it much easier for Web servers and clients to find one another.

Other well-known ports include File Transfer Protocol (FTP, port 21), Simple
Mail Transport Protocol (SMTP, port 25), and POP3 (port 110). The full list of
well-known ports and the services assigned to them can be found at *http://
www.iana.org/assignments/port-numbers*.

Why is this important to the discussion of security and Web server setup?
Because the very ease of discovery that well-known port numbers make possible
also presents a security risk for the unwary. For example, on Windows 2000,
the ports for services such as FTP, SMTP, and POP3 (among others) are left
open by default. This gives hackers an engraved invitation to probe these ports
and see if the software behind them is vulnerable to attack. Given the many vulnerabilities discovered in FTP, SMTP, and other Internet-based services, it is
essential to close all ports that are not in use by your application.

Closing ports can be accomplished in a number of ways, the most common
being through the use of firewall software or a hardware router with firewall
functionality, or using the IP Security Policy Management MMC snap-in in
Windows 2000 or Windows XP. For many applications, the preferred solution
is to set up a hardware firewall between the Web server and the Internet that
allows traffic only on port 80 (HTTP), and optionally port 443 (HTTPS) if
secure sockets Web traffic is required. (See "Using SSL to Protect Communications" on page 161 for more information on Secure Sockets Layer communication.) Then a second firewall is added between the Web server and the

internal network that allows traffic only on ports necessary for the Web server to reach other servers (such as the database server), and also blocks ports 80 and 443 (and any other ports open in the other firewall). This method places the Web server in what is referred to as a DMZ (demilitarized zone), which is designed to prevent direct communication between the Internet and an internal network. This protects servers on the internal network from attack.

> ▶ **Important**   Whichever method you use to close unused ports on your Web server, it is imperative that you block traffic to any ports that your applications do not use. Remember, however, that the ports that remain open are still a security risk. Effective logging of server activity, frequent monitoring of logs, and prompt patching of vulnerabilities in software operating on the open ports are all important means of defending your server(s) from attacks.

A full discussion of packet filtering, routing, and IPSec management is beyond the scope of this chapter. Consult the manual for your firewall or router, or the Windows 2000/XP Help files, for more information on implementing these solutions.

Patching

Once your server is set up correctly and securely, and you've considered how the design of your application affects security, you might think you're home free. Not so! Even the most securely configured server and securely designed application can be compromised by a lax attitude toward ongoing maintenance. One of the most important aspects of ongoing maintenance of servers and applications is staying on top of patches released by vendors of any software you're using.

In an ideal world, the software we use would be perfect from the start. However, the reality is that there are few, if any, programs that do not contain vulnerabilities. When these vulnerabilities are discovered, typically the vendor of the program will issue a patch designed to correct the problem. Unfortunately, many server administrators do not apply these patches consistently, leaving their servers vulnerable to attack.

This is inexcusable. Most patches can be applied easily, and there are many ways that you can be notified automatically about new ones for Microsoft software, including the following sources of information about patches:

■   The Windows Update site (*http://windowsupdate.microsoft.com/*) lets you analyze the updates available for a given system and determine which of them are currently installed. Microsoft Windows 98 and later and Windows 2000 and later install a link to Windows Update in the Start menu by default.

- The Microsoft Product Security Notification service lets you sign up for e-mail notification of vulnerabilities and available patches. This method is useful for administrators who need to keep track of patches without visiting multiple machines. You can sign up for this service at *http://www.microsoft.com/technet/treeview/ default.asp?url=/technet/security/bulletin/notify.asp*.

- The Microsoft Baseline Security Analyzer (MBSA) is a utility that will scan the local machine, or machines on the local network, for uninstalled patches for Microsoft Windows NT 4.0, Windows 2000, IIS 4.0 and IIS 5.0, Microsoft SQL Server 7.0 and Microsoft SQL 2000 (and MSDE), and Microsoft Internet Explorer 5.01 and later, as well as checking for numerous other potential security problems, such as weak passwords, installed samples for IIS, and security issues related to Internet Explorer and Microsoft Office products. MBSA 1.1 is downloadable from *http://www.microsoft.com/technet/ security/tools/tools/mbsahome.asp*.

Scanning for Missing Patches with MBSA 1.1

Once installed, MBSA is quite easy to use. Simply follow these steps to start MBSA 1.1 and scan your local machine.

1   Click the Start button, choose All Programs (Programs in Windows 2000), and then select Microsoft Baseline Security Analyzer. The MBSA welcome screen will be displayed, as shown in the following illustration.

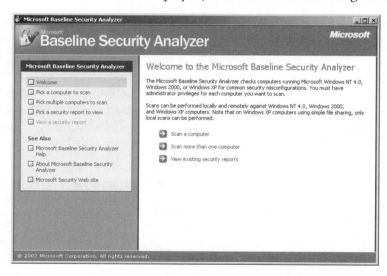

2   Click Scan A Computer. The resulting interface, shown in the following illustration, allows you to select a computer to scan, as well as to specify the types of vulnerabilities to scan for.

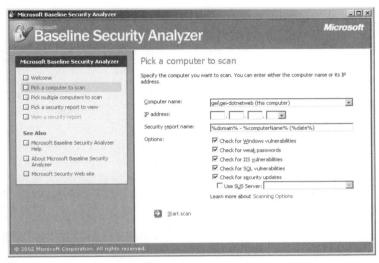

3   Leave the settings as they are, and click Start Scan. When the scan is complete, MBSA will display a report of the vulnerabilities it has found, as shown in the illustration on the next page.

A green check mark next to an entry indicates that no problems were found for that issue. A yellow X indicates a non-critical security warning. These are issues that warrant further investigation, but do not necessarily indicate a vulnerability. A red X indicates a critical security issue requiring action to correct an identified vulnerability. The other two icons you might see are a blue asterisk, indicating recommended best practices, and an i icon, indicating that additional information is available for a given issue. Also, each issue includes links indicating what was scanned, any additional details on the results, and most important, instructions for how to correct a vulnerability found by the tool.

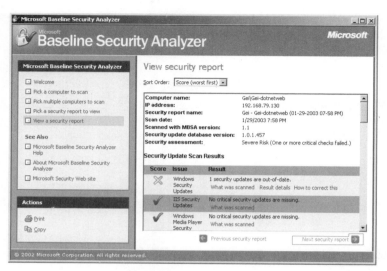

4   Locate an entry with a yellow or red X icon.

5   Click How To Correct This Link and follow the instructions provided to correct the issue, including links to required patches, and so on.

6   Repeat Step 5 for all warnings or critical issues.

7   Once you have finished correcting issues (rebooting when necessary), start MBSA again, and rescan the machine to confirm that the issues have been corrected.

▶ **Note**   Starting with MBSA 1.1, there is an issue with nonsecurity-related patches installed by the Windows Update functionality built into Windows XP, or from the Windows Update Web site. Because the XML file used by MBSA to identify the file versions to scan for does not include nonsecurity-related patches, you might run into a situation in which MBSA highlights a file whose version is higher than expected as a security warning because that file has been updated by Windows Update.

For this reason, keep track of the patches that are installed from Windows Update so that you know when the warning given by MBSA is indicative of a potential problem rather than of a nonsecurity-related patch.

Access Control

Access control is the process of determining who can access resources on your server. This includes both authentication (determining the identity of a user making a request) and authorization (determining whether that user has permission to take the action requested). For an ASP.NET application, there are several different authentication and authorization methods. You'll learn how to implement authentication and authorization in ASP.NET later in this chapter.

It is important not to forget that access control also includes physical access to the machine being secured. The best authentication, authorization, and password practices won't help you a bit if someone can gain physical access to a machine and circumvent your security barriers, or simply damage the machine beyond repair. Any machine that has value to you should be secured physically, as well as via software, from unauthorized use.

Auditing and Logging

As mentioned earlier in this chapter, even the best security practices and strongest passwords cannot provide 100-percent protection against attacks. For this reason, it is imperative to enable auditing and logging on exposed servers.

Auditing is the process of monitoring certain activities, such as login attempts, for success or failure, and then logging the results of this monitoring to the Windows event log. Auditing (and proper monitoring of the logs) allows you to determine when someone is attempting to attack your machine, such as by trying numerous incorrect passwords. In this case, by auditing login failures, you would be able to see the failed login attempts in the Security event log and take appropriate action to foil the would-be intruder (such as disabling the account being attacked). As with many of the other settings discussed in this chapter, the auditing policy for a Windows 2000, Windows XP, or Windows Server 2003 machine can be set using a security template via the Security Configuration and Analysis MMC snap-in.

Logging is the process of writing information about the activities being performed on a machine to a known location for later review. For our purposes, the most important logging (after the logging of audit information) is done by IIS for the Web, FTP, and SMTP services. Logging is performed at the site level. The following steps are for enabling logging for a Web site, but the steps for FTP, SMTP, and other IIS services are similar.

Enable logging in IIS

1   Open Internet Information Services MMC snap-in (known as the Internet Services Manager MMC snap-in in Windows 2000) by clicking Start, and then clicking Control Panel (in Windows 2000, the Control Panel is under the Settings menu selection). In Windows XP, switch to classic view, if that is not already selected. In the Control Panel folder, double-click the Administrative Tools icon. In the Administrative Tools folder, double-click the Internet Information Services icon (the Internet Services Manager icon in Windows 2000). In Windows Server 2003, click Start, choose Administrative Tools,

and then select Internet Information Services (IIS) Manager. If you are not logged in as an administrator you will need to right-click the icon and select Run As, and then specify an administrative account.

2   Select the server you want to manage, and expand the tree to find the site you want to manage. Right-click the desired site and select Properties. The following dialog box will be displayed (the illustration is from IIS 6.0 on Windows Server 2003).

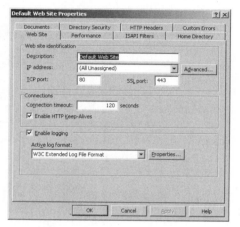

3   In the Web Site tab of the *<sitename>* Properties dialog box, ensure that the Enable Logging check box is checked.

4   Modify the format of the logs by using the Active log format drop-down list You can click the Properties button to modify where logs are kept, how frequently a new log file is created, and the specific information that is logged.

▶   **Note**   It is considered a good practice to modify the location of the Web server logs from their default of %WinDir%\System32\LogFiles because that makes it more difficult for hackers who gain access to your system to cover their tracks. If the log files are in their default location, hackers can more easily alter them or delete them to hide their activity. Make sure to set appropriate ACLs on the log file location, since it might still be possible for an attacker to locate these files.

Using SSL to Protect Communications

By default, information sent via HTTP requests and responses is sent as clear text. This means that someone could capture the packets that make up these requests and responses and then recreate them, including any data passed from form fields on a submitted page. If such a form contained sensitive data, such as passwords or credit card numbers, this data could be stolen.

Encryption is an important tool for keeping this kind of information secure. The most commonly used form of encryption in Web applications is the Secure Sockets Layer (SSL) protocol. Sites requiring secure communications between the Web server and the browser use SSL to create and exchange a key used to encrypt communications between the client and server, thereby helping to protect this information from prying eyes. This is typically done by e-commerce sites to protect credit card information, for example. SSL can also be useful for protecting other information, including SessionID cookies and login information when using basic authentication, or ASP.NET Forms-based authentication. (See "Enabling Authentication" on page 165 for more information on basic authentication.)

By default, SSL communications occur on port 443 (as opposed to non-SSL Web communications, which are on port 80 by default), using the *https://* prefix for URLs that use SSL. Enabling SSL for your Web server requires obtaining a server certificate and binding that certificate to the Web sites on which you want to use SSL. Certificates are issued by several companies, including VeriSign (*http://www.verisign.com/products/site/index.html*), that are presumed to be trustworthy.

Request an SSL certificate

1   Open Internet Information Services (Internet Services Manager in Windows 2000). (If you are not logged in as an administrator, you will need to use the Run As feature of Windows 2000 or Windows XP to run the Internet Services Manager using an administrative account.)

2   Right-click the site you want to protect via SSL and then select Properties.

3   In the Directory Security tab, shown in the illustration on the next page, click the Server Certificate button. This will start the Web Server Certificate Wizard.

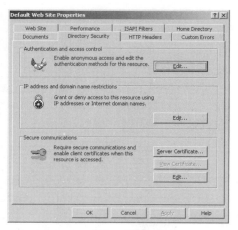

4   Use the Web Server Certificate Wizard to create a new certificate request. This method is useful if you want to create a certificate request to send to a third-party certificate authority, such as VeriSign or Thawte, who will verify the information in the request and send you a server certificate. Alternatively, if you have Certificate Services installed on a machine on your network, you can use that service to create a certificate. (Note that your clients must have your Certificate Services CA listed in their browser as a trusted certificate authority in order to use this method.) See the Certificate Services documentation for more information on creating and installing your own certificates.

▶   **Note**   No matter which method you use to generate a certificate request, the common name of the certificate (identified by the Certificate Services Web request pages as Name) must match the fully qualified domain name of the site the certificate will be installed on. Otherwise, users will get a warning that the server's certificate is valid but the name on the certificate doesn't match the requested URL.

Once you've received the response from the certificate authority containing your certificate, follow these steps to install the certificate for use in IIS.

Install an SSL certificate

1   Locate the certificate file you received from the certificate authority. Right-click the file and select Install Certificate.

2 Open Internet Information Services (or Internet Services Manager on Windows 2000). (If you are not logged in as an administrator, you will need to use the Run As feature of Windows 2000 or Windows XP to run the Internet Services Manager using an administrative account.)

3 Right-click the site you want to protect via SSL and select Properties.

4 On the Directory Security tab, click the Server Certificate button. This will again start the Web Server Certificate Wizard.

5 Click Next to advance to the second page of the wizard.

6 On the Server Certificate page of the wizard, shown in the following illustration (IIS 6.0 version shown), select Assign An Existing Certificate and then click Next.

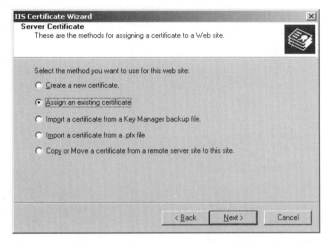

7 The Available Certificates page should list all of the certificates on the current machine, including the certificate you just installed. Select the desired certificate and then click Next.

8 Review the Certificate Summary information to ensure you are assigning the correct certificate. Then click Next.

9 Click Finish to complete the wizard.

Once you've installed the certificate for a given site, you can use SSL to encrypt communications on any of the virtual directories under that site by having users request pages with *https://* rather than *http://*. To ensure that pages cannot be viewed without SSL, however, you must require SSL for the page or directory you want to protect.

Require SSL

1   Open Internet Information Services (or Internet Services Manager if you are using Windows 2000). (If you are not logged in as an administrator, you will need to use the Run As feature of Windows 2000 or Windows XP to run the Internet Services Manager using an administrative account.)

2   Right-click the site, virtual directory, or file you want to protect and then select Properties.

3   On the Directory Security or File Security tab, in the Secure Communications section, click the Edit button, which should now be available. This will open the Secure Communications dialog box, shown in the following illustration.

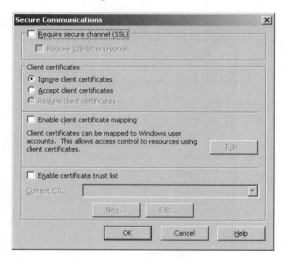

4   In the Secure Communications dialog box, check the Require Secure Channel (SSL) check box. You could check the Require 128-bit Encryption check box for greater security, but this requires that the client browser support 128-bit encryption.

5   Click OK to close the Secure Communications dialog box, and then click OK again to close the Properties dialog box for the site, directory, or file you are protecting. The resource should now be accessible only by using *https://*.

▶ **Important**   Using SSL encryption is an important tool for protecting information sent from the browser to the server, but it is only one of many tools you
need to use to secure your application. SSL alone is not enough. If the only
security tool you use is SSL, your site is almost guaranteed to be vulnerable in
some other area.

Enabling Authentication

As discussed earlier in this chapter, authentication is the process of validating
the identity of the user making the current request. ASP.NET applications work
with IIS to carry out authentication based on one of several authentication
types, which are discussed in the following section.

Authentication and authorization in ASP.NET work hand-in-hand and operate
on two distinct levels: the operating system/IIS level and the ASP.NET level.
Here's an overview of how IIS and ASP.NET interact:

1   A request comes in to IIS for a resource associated with ASP.NET
(such as a Web Form).

2   If one of the IIS authentication methods is enabled, IIS performs authentication, and adds the authentication information to the request.

3   IIS passes the request to the ASP.NET run time. From this point on,
IIS plays no further role in the request.

4a If Windows authentication is enabled, authorization is performed on
the request using the authenticated identity passed by IIS, and if
the authorization (typically ACL authorization) succeeds, the request
is processed.

4b If Forms authentication is enabled, ASP.NET checks for the forms
authentication cookie. If no cookie exists, the user is redirected to the
configured login page. Once the user successfully logs in, an authentication cookie is set, and if the authorization (typically URL authorization) succeeds, the user is redirected to the requested resource.

4c If Passport authentication is enabled, ASP.NET checks for a Passport
cookie, and if it does not exist, redirects the user to the Passport login
page for the site. Once the user successfully logs in, the Passport
cookie is set, and the user is redirected to the requested resource.

Selecting an Authentication Type

Three basic types of authentication are available for ASP.NET applications: Windows-based, Forms-based, and Passport. The authentication method you choose depends on the types of clients you're dealing with, the level of control you have over the client browser choice, and a number of other factors. The next several sections will discuss the available authentication methods, how they're implemented, and why you might choose one particular method over another.

> ► **Note**   The interaction between IIS and ASP.NET in terms of authentication and authorization may be somewhat confusing if you're inexperienced with these features. Until you understand how the various options work, you should practice the techniques and procedures discussed in this section on a machine that is not exposed to the Internet or other potential sources of compromise.

Requests for resources in an ASP.NET application go through two distinct levels of authentication: the IIS level and the ASP.NET application level. The type of authentication you choose determines which of these levels is used to determine whether the request is properly authenticated. As mentioned earlier, authorization also occurs on two levels, so it is important to choose the appropriate authorization method for the authentication type you're using.

The authentication type is determined by the *<authentication>* element in the Web.config file for an application. You'll see examples of this element later in this section. The full syntax of the *<authentication>* element is explained in Appendix B.

Using Windows-Based Authentication

In Windows-based authentication, ASP.NET relies on IIS to authenticate the incoming request by using one of its available authentication methods:

- **Basic authentication**   This method is compatible with most browsers, but the password is sent in clear text. Use this only if you can protect the communication with SSL encryption.

- **Digest authentication**   This authentication method was introduced as a feature of HTTP 1.1, so it may not be supported by all browsers. It sends a hashed value instead of a clear-text password, making it more secure than basic authentication. This method requires a Windows 2000 Domain Controller. You have to store a clear-text version of the password on the Domain Controller used to validate the password, so the Domain Controller must be secured from physical and network intrusions. If no Windows 2000 Domain Controller is available, this option will be unavailable, as seen in the Authentication Methods dialog box shown later in this chapter.

■ **Integrated Windows (NTLM) authentication**   This method is available only with Internet Explorer. It's the most secure method because it never sends the username or password over the network. Use this method if you require your clients to use Internet Explorer to access your application. Note also that Integrated Windows authentication will not work over an HTTP proxy connection, which can make it impossible for clients on a corporate network using a proxy to log in to an application over the Internet. It also requires each person that logs in to your site to have an NT account either on the Web server or on a domain controller trusted by the Web server.

If more than one authentication type check box is checked, Digest and Integrated Windows authentication will always take precedence over basic authentication.

Once IIS has authenticated the user, it passes the authenticated identity to ASP.NET, which can then use that information to allow or deny access to resources within the application. See "Authorizing Users and Roles" on page 179 for more information on this type of authorization.

Change the authentication method used by IIS

1   Open Internet Services Manager.

2   Right-click the site, virtual directory, or file for which you want to modify the authentication method. Select Properties.

3   On the Directory Security (or File Security) tab, in the Anonymous Access And Authentication Control section, click the Edit button. This will open the Authentication Methods dialog box.

4   In the Authentication Methods dialog box, uncheck the Anonymous Access check box. Then check the check box for the desired authentication method, as shown in the illustration on the next page (IIS 6.0 shown). Note that .NET Passport authentication is not available as an option in IIS versions earlier than IIS 6.0.

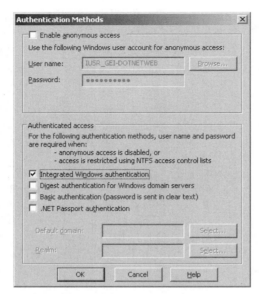

5   Click OK to close the Authentication Methods dialog box, and then click OK to close the Properties dialog box for the resource you selected in Step 2.

Configure Windows authentication for ASP.NET

1   Open the Web.config file for the application in Visual Studio .NET.

2   Modify the *<authentication>* element as follows. (Note that you can set the authentication method only at the application or server level. Attempting to add the *<authentication>* element to a Web.config in a subdirectory that is not configured as an IIS application will result in an error.)

```
<authentication mode="Windows" />
```

3   If desired, you can have ASP.NET impersonate the logged-in user (so that resource requests are made in the security context of the logged-in user) by adding the *<identity>* element as follows. (See "Using Impersonation" on page 181 for more on impersonation.)

```
<identity impersonate="true">
```

4   Save the Web.config file.

Once you have set the authentication mode to Windows, you need to set the authorization method to protect the desired resources.

Using .NET Passport Authentication

Passport authentication uses the centralized Passport authentication service provided by Microsoft. Passport authentication gives users a single login to use with any Passport-enabled site. To use Passport authentication with ASP.NET, you must download and install the Passport SDK, which is available at *http://www.passport.com/business*. ASP.NET provides a wrapper around the Passport authentication service, so you can use it simply by setting the appropriate value for the Web.config *<authentication>* element.

Configure ASP.NET to use .NET Passport authentication

1   Open the Web.config file for the application in Visual Studio .NET.

2   Modify the *<authentication>* element as follows:

```
<authentication mode="Passport" />
```

3   If desired, you can set up an internal redirect URL for Passport authentication by adding a *<passport>* child element as follows. This will redirect users who have not authenticated to the specified internal URL rather than the default Passport login site.

```
<authentication mode="Passport">
   <passport redirectUrl="<URL>">
</authentication>
```

4   Save the Web.config file.

▶ **Note**   To download and install the Passport SDK and use Passport authentication on your site, you will need to register on *http://www.passport.com/business* and pay a license fee.

▶ **Tip**   In IIS 6.0, you can configure an application to use .NET Passport authentication using the IIS Manager applet, as described earlier in this chapter in the steps showing how to change the authentication method used by IIS. See the ".NET Passport Authentication" topic in the IIS 6 documentation for more information on configuring .NET Passport authentication for IIS 6.0.

Using Forms-Based Authentication

Forms-based authentication allows developers to easily implement "roll-your-own" security in their applications. In classic ASP you would need to add an include file or component to every page to look for an authentication cookie, and then redirect to a login page if the cookie didn't exist. ASP.NET Forms-based authentication takes care of all this for you.

All you need to do is create the login page, tell ASP.NET where to find it (via settings in Web.config), and set the desired authorization restrictions. In your login page, you can verify the username and password credentials entered by the user against a database, Windows 2000 Active Directory, or another credential store of your choice, such as an XML file. Once you've verified the user's credentials, you can use the methods exposed by the *FormsAuthentication* class to set or remove an authentication cookie, redirect the user to the original page they requested, or renew the authentication cookie.

▶ **Important**   In Forms-based authentication, the username and password are sent as clear text. To ensure the security of this information, you should always use an SSL-enabled connection for your login page.

Let's take a look at an example. We'll create two pages—a login page and a page to display the username of the currently logged-in user—and we'll add the necessary elements and attributes to Web.config, including authentication credentials against which we'll authenticate requests.

Create a login page

1   Open Visual Studio .NET, and create a new ASP.NET Web Application project named Chapter_06.

2   Add a new Web Form. Type the name of the form as **Login.aspx**.

3   Use the Web Form toolbox palette to add four label controls, two textbox controls, a checkbox control, and a button control to the page. The result should look similar to the illustration on the following page. Note the glyphs in the upper left corner of each control. These indicate that the controls are server controls (as opposed to standard HTML elements that are simply rendered by the client).

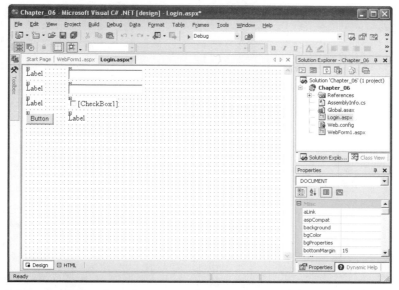

4   Make the following changes to the properties of the specified controls:

Control	Property	Value
Label1	Text	**Username:**
Label2	Text	**Password:**
Label3	Text	**Persist Cookie?**
TextBox2	TextMode	**Password**
Button1	Text	**Login**
Label4	Text	**<blank>**

The result should look similar to the illustration on the next page.

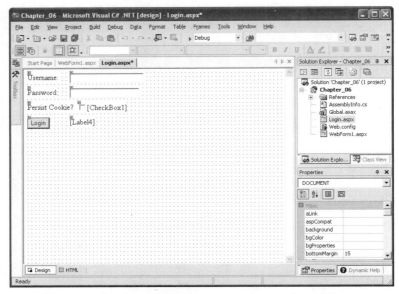

5   Double-click the Button control in the designer. This will open up the code-behind module for the page and add the *Button_Click* event handler.

6   Add a using clause for System.Web.Security to the top of the code-behind module, before the namespace declaration for the Chapter_06 namespace, as shown here (other using clauses not shown).

```
using System.Web.Security;

namespace Chapter_06
{
    // class code
```

This will allow you to use the methods of the *FormsAuthentication* class without explicitly naming the *System.Web.Security* namespace each time.

7   Add the following code to the *Button_Click* event handler. (The completed code-behind module should look similar to the illustration that follows the code.)

```
if (FormsAuthentication.Authenticate(TextBox1.Text, TextBox2.Text))
{
    FormsAuthentication.RedirectFromLoginPage(TextBox1.Text,
CheckBox1.Checked);
}
else
{
    Label4.Text = "Incorrect username or password!";
}
```

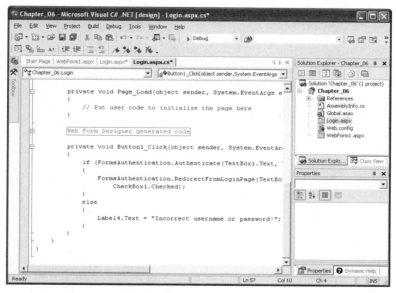

8 Save the page and code-behind module.

Configure Forms authentication

1 Open the Web.config file for the Chapter_06 project.

2 Modify the *<authentication>* and *<authorization>* elements of Web.config as follows, replacing *<username>* with the desired user-name and *<password>* with a hashed password of your choice. (A helper page for hashing passwords named HashPwd.aspx is included with the practice files for this chapter.)

```
<authentication mode="Forms">
    <forms name="formsauth" loginUrl="login.aspx"
        protection="All" timeout="60">
        <credentials>
            <user name="<username >" password="<password>"/>
        </credentials>
    </forms>
</authentication>

<authorization>
    <deny users="?" />
</authorization>
```

▶ **Note**   In addition to the attributes shown in the preceding example, the *<forms>* configuration element exposes several other attributes, including two new attributes introduced in ASP.NET version 1.1, *requireSSL* and *slidingExpiration*. The *requireSSL* attribute specifies whether a secure connection is required to protect data stored in the authentication cookie. If set to *true*, compliant browsers will return the cookie only if the request is made over an SSL connection. The *slidingExpiration* attribute specifies whether the timeout value for the authentication cookie is reset with each request in a given browser session. The default is *false*, which specifies that the cookie will expire after the interval specified by the *timeout* attribute. You can find out more about the attributes available in the *<forms>* element in Appendix B.

By default, you will need to know the password in order to use any page on the site because of the way it is secured. To avoid this and allow you to use the hashpwd.aspx page, add the following section to the Web.Config file just below the closing *<system.web>* tag:

```
<location path="hashpwd.aspx">
   <system.web>
      <authorization>
         <allow users="?" />
      </authorization>
   </system.web>
</location>
```

This section allows the hashpwd.aspx file to be accessed by even unauthenticated users. The *<location>* tag is described more fully in the section titled "Authorizing Users and Roles" on page 179.

3   Save Web.config. The application is now configured to use Forms authentication and to refuse all requests from anonymous users.

Create a page to display the username

1   Add a new Web Form to the Chapter_06 project. Type the name of the form as **ShowUsername.aspx**.

2   Add a Label control and a Button control to the page. The result should look similar to the illustration on the following page.

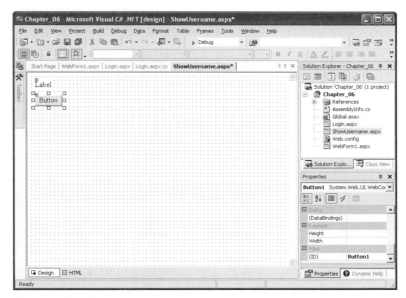

3 Change the Text property of the Button control to **Logout**.

4 Double-click the Button control in the designer. This will open up the code-behind module for the page and add the *Button_Click* event handler.

5 Add the using clause to the top of the code-behind module, as you did for login.aspx. This will allow you to use the methods of the *FormsAuthentication* class without explicitly naming the *System.Web.Security* namespace each time.

```
using System.Web.Security;

namespace Chapter_06
{
    // class code
```

6 Add the following code to the *Button_Click* event handler. The call to the *Signout* method of the *FormsAuthentication* helper class removes the forms authentication cookie, while the *Response.Redirect* call ensures that the user is redirected to the login page.

```
FormsAuthentication.SignOut();
Response.Redirect("ShowUsername.aspx");
```

7 Replace the comment in the *Page_Load* event handler with the following code:

```
Label1.Text = "Username is: " + User.Identity.Name;
```

8 Save the page and code-behind module. The completed code-behind module should look similar to the illustration on the next page.

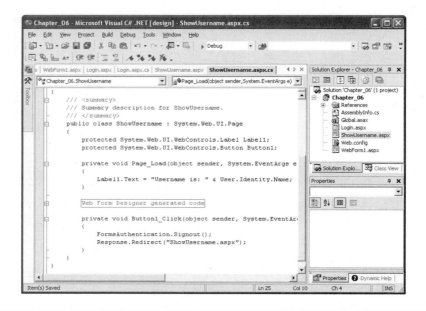

Build and test the project

1   Build the project using the Build Chapter_06 command from the Build menu.

2   Right-click ShowUsername.aspx, then select Browse With, then select Microsoft Internet Explorer, and then click Browse. You should be automatically redirected to the login page, as shown in the following illustration. Note the *ReturnUrl* query string argument in the address box at the top of the browser, which contains the path to the page you originally requested.

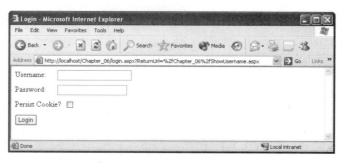

3   Enter the username and password (unhashed) that you configured in Web.config and then click Login. If you choose to check the Persist Cookie? check box, the forms authentication cookie will be a persistent, rather than session, cookie. Persistent cookies are cookies that will remain on the machine and will be there even after the browser session closes out. By persisting the authentication cookie, the user won't need to login the next time they access the page (subject to the timeout limitations set in Web.config). Assuming the credentials you enter match those in Web.config, you will be redirected to ShowUsername.aspx, as shown in the following illustration. Otherwise, an error message will be displayed.

4   Click the Logout button. You will be redirected to the login page.

▶   **Tip**   For the sake of simplicity, we left the ID properties of the controls in the preceding example at their defaults (Label1, Button1, and so on). In a real application, it's best to give controls more meaningful names, such as PasswordBox, LoginButton and so on.

The MSDN documentation provides helpful guidelines for structuring your code and naming objects and variables. You can find these guidelines by entering the words **coding conventions** in the Index pane of the MSDN documentation window.

▶   **Note**   In this example Web.config file, the URL for the login page is specified with the *loginUrl* attribute of the *<forms>* element. (For more information on all of the attributes of the *<forms>* element, see Appendix B.) However, if you leave this attribute out, ASP.NET supplies the name *login.aspx* (which happens to be the same as in the example) as the default.

ASP.NET also supplies a default value of default.aspx for the redirect page when FormsAuthentication.RedirectFromLoginPage is called with no RedirectUrl query string argument. So in the preceding example, if you call the login page directly and authenticate successfully, ASP.NET will attempt to redirect you to default.aspx. If there's no such page, you'll get a "file not found" error.

Using Authorization

After you've authenticated the user making the request, the next step is to authorize the request. *Authorization* means deciding whether to permit the user to access the requested resource.

Authorization in ASP.NET takes two major forms: authorization against NTFS Access Control Lists (ACLs) and URL-based authorization.

Using NTFS ACLs for Authorization

ACL-based authorization is useful when you're using Windows-based authentication in ASP.NET. With ACL-based authorization, you use tools such as the Properties dialog for a file or folder in Windows Explorer to set the list of users or groups that are allowed to access a given resource, and what rights each one has (read, write, execute, and so on). The primary advantage of using ACL-based authorization with Windows-based authentication is that it does not require writing any security-specific code in your ASP.NET application. All security settings can be taken care of administratively.

When a request for a resource (such as an ASP.NET page) comes in, IIS authenticates the request, using whichever method (basic, digest, integrated Windows) has been configured for the application. IIS passes the identity of the logged-in user (or the configured anonymous user account, if anonymous access is enabled) to ASP.NET, which then uses the identity of the user to check the ACL for the requested resource to see if the user has the required permission. If so, ASP.NET fulfills the request.

Configure ACL-based authorization

1   Configure your ASP.NET application to use Windows authentication and to impersonate the logged-in user by adding the following sections to the application's Web.config file.

```
<authentication mode="Windows" />
<identity impersonate="true" />
```

2   Using Windows Explorer, right-click a file or folder in your application's physical directory that you want to restrict access to, and then select Properties. (You must be logged in as either an administrator or an account with ownership rights on the resource to be configured.)

3   Click the Security tab and add or remove users or groups as desired. Note that you should remove the Everyone group if it is present. If you want ASP.NET to be able to access a resource when not impersonating, the ASPNET account should be given access to the resource. When you're finished applying permissions, click OK to close the dialog box.

4   Browse to the protected resource. You should be prompted to log in using your Windows username and password. If you enter credentials for one of the accounts you configured in Step 3, you should be able to access the resource.

Using URL-Based Authorization

URL-based authorization, which is new in ASP.NET, lets you use the *<authorization>* element to grant or deny access to resources in your application based on their URL (hence the name). Unlike the *<authentication>* element, which cannot be used in or applied to a subdirectory of an application, the *<authorization>* element can be applied to subdirectories and even individual files, either by creating Web.config files in the subdirectories or by using the *path* attribute of the *<location>* element to specify the URL for the resource to be protected. URL-based authentication also allows you to specify the HTTP method for which a particular rule applies.

Authorizing Users and Roles

The most basic form of ASP.NET URL-based authorization looks like this:

```
<configuration>
   <system.web>
      <authorization>
         <allow users="Andrew" />
         <deny users="*" />
      </authorization>
   </system.web>
</configuration>
```

When the *<authorization>* element shown here is added to the Web.config for an application, it allows Andrew to access resources in the application's root directory and in any subdirectories that do not have conflicting *<authorization>* permissions set, as well as denying access to all other users. The *users* attribute of the *<allow>* and *<deny>* elements allows you to specify comma-separated lists of users to be allowed or denied access to the URL being protected. (Note that if no path is specified, ASP.NET will apply the settings to the directory in which the Web.config containing the settings resides, as well as its children.) ASP.NET provides the following two wildcards for allowing and denying access:

- ■   * This wildcard lets you allow or deny all users.
- ■   ? This wildcard lets you allow or deny anonymous users.

You can also specify a comma-separated list of roles (equivalent to NT groups) to allow or deny by adding the roles attribute to an *<allow>* or *<deny>* element:

```
<allow roles="Administrators, Users">
```

Note that authorization settings for child directories override those of the parent, unless the parent settings are locked down using the optional *allowOverride* attribute of the *<location>* element. To prevent the preceding authentication settings from being overridden, you would modify the Web.config file as follows:

```
<configuration>
    <location allowOverride="false">
        <system.web>
            <authorization>
                <allow users="Andrew" />
                <deny users="*" />
            </authorization>
        </system.web>
    </location>
</configuration>
```

Note that the *<location>* element also has a *path* attribute that allows you to specify the path to which the settings contained between the *<location>* tags apply. This can be a very convenient way to specify the authorization settings for multiple files or directories in an application from a single Web.config file, allowing the developer or administrator to decide which settings can or cannot be overridden by child Web.config files. This is an especially useful feature in shared server or shared hosting situations. A server administrator can place master permissions in the Machine.config file for the server and use the *<location>* element to prevent overriding of these permissions.

Allowing or Denying Specific HTTP Methods

In addition to the *users* attribute, the *<allow>* and *<deny>* elements also expose a *verbs* attribute, which allows you to specify the HTTP verb type to allow or deny for the specified user(s) or role(s). The following example shows how you could prevent all users from making *POST* requests, while still allowing them other access. Modify your Web.config file as follows:

```
<configuration>
   <location allowOverride="false">
      <system.web>
         <authorization>
            <allow users="Andrew" />
            <deny verbs="POST" users="*" />
         </authorization>
      </system.web>
   </location>
</configuration>
```

Limiting the request types to those necessary for a page or pages in your application can be an important way to prevent hackers from compromising your site. If a hacker is unable to make a *POST* request, it is that much more difficult for him to take advantage of a vulnerability that requires sending data in an HTTP *POST* request. You can restrict or allow HTTP verb access for a page or set of pages by adding the *path* attribute to the *<location>* element, as described in the previous section. The Forms authentication example demonstrates the use of the *path* attribute of the *<location>* element.

Using Impersonation

Impersonation is the process by which ASP.NET takes on the security context of the user making the request. This allows ASP.NET (and components called by ASP.NET) to gain access to resources that the user is authorized to access.

In classic ASP, impersonation was used by default. If the user making the request had not been authenticated by IIS using basic or NTLM authentication, ASP requests ran with the security context of the IUSR_MACHINENAME built-in account. In ASP.NET, impersonation must be turned on explicitly by using the *impersonation* attribute of the *<identity>* element. Without impersonation, ASP.NET runs as the built-in ASPNET account. (You can use the *<processModel>* configuration section to configure ASP.NET to run as a different account that has more privileges, such as the SYSTEM built-in account, but this carries some increased security risks because of the higher privilege level of the SYSTEM account.)

▶ **Note** As mentioned earlier in this chapter, IIS 6.0, when running in native mode, ignores the <processModel> configuration element in favor of its own process model settings. The default identity for ASP.NET applications running under IIS 6.0 is Network Service.

For example, you might want to take advantage of impersonation to use trusted connections with SQL Server. Trusted connections use Windows security to connect to a SQL Server database without the need for a SQL Server username and password. As discussed earlier in this chapter, one of the challenges facing ASP.NET developers is where to store database login information to reduce the risk of it being compromised. With trusted connections, this is not a problem because the login information is never stored by the application.

Enable trusted connections to SQL Server

1 Configure your application to use Windows authentication, as described earlier in this chapter.

2 Add the *<identity>* element to your configuration file to make ASP.NET impersonate the identity of the client making the request.

```
<identity impersonate="true">
```

3 Add the desired Windows accounts to the SQL Server security database.

4 In the connection string used to connect to the database, specify *Trusted_Connection=yes*. The full connection string would look similar to the following:

```
"server=(local)\VSdotNET;database=pubs;Trusted_Connection=yes"
```

5 Using one of the accounts that you added to the SQL Server security database, log in to the ASP.NET application. You should be able to access the data on the SQL Server database.

▶ **Note**   If you cannot use Windows authentication in your ASP.NET application, you might still be able to take advantage of trusted connections by configuring the default ASPNET (or Network Service, in IIS 6.0) account (used to run the ASP.NET worker processes) as a SQL Server login account. Keep in mind, though, that this will allow anyone who can access any ASP.NET application to access the database according to the SQL Server permissions you have set up for the ASPNET account. The process of setting up the ASPNET account as a SQL Server login is described in Chapter 9.

Understanding Code Access Security

Another new security feature in ASP.NET is code access security. A full discussion of code access security is beyond the scope of this book, but here's an overview.

Code access security is Microsoft's answer to the challenge of preventing untrusted code from performing actions on your system that might result in the damage or compromise of data. It allows ASP.NET developers and/or server administrators to specify the level of trust a given application should have, using the *<securityPolicy>* and *<trust>* elements in Web.config. (See Appendix B for more information on these elements.) ASP.NET comes preconfigured with a set of code access security templates that are mapped to trust levels in machine.config. Depending on the level of trust specified in the *<trust>* element, the proper set of code access security permissions are applied to the application. This can include such permissions as whether the application can read from parts of the file system outside its Web space, can write to its file space, is restricted to read-only, or is allowed only to execute.

Like the *<location>* element that allows the lockdown of configuration settings at a machine level, code access security and the templates used to apply its permissions are ideal in shared server environments in which you want to allow users to create their own ASP.NET applications, but want to be able to choose which actions can be taken by code written by different users.

Security Resources

Keep the following URLs handy when securing your application:

- *http://www.microsoft.com/technet/security*   This is the starting point for finding security-related information for Windows, IIS, and other Microsoft products. You'll find a host of good information on improving the security of your servers and applications here.

- *http://www.microsoft.com/technet/security/iis5chk.asp*   This is the Secure Internet Information Services 5 Checklist. Prepared by Michael Howard of the Windows 2000 and IIS security teams, this document provides recommendations and best practices for securing IIS 5.

- *http://www.microsoft.com/technet/itsolutions/security/tools/tools.asp*   This is a list of security tools available through the Microsoft Technet Web site.

- *http://nsa2.www.conxion.com/win2k/download.htm*   This is the download site for the Windows 2000 Security Recommendation Guides prepared by the National Security Agency (NSA).

- *http://www.microsoft.com/technet/columns/security/10imlaws.asp*   This is the 10 Immutable Laws of Security, a list of the many ways to lose control of your computer.

- *http://www.microsoft.com/technet/columns/security/10salaws.asp*
  This is the 10 Immutable Laws of Security Administration, a list of sage advice for those who have the dubious pleasure of being responsible for securing their systems.

- *http://www.cert.org/advisories/CA-2000-02.html*   This advisory provides a detailed description of cross-site scripting (XSS) and the problems it can cause.

- *http://www.cert.org/tech_tips/malicious_code_mitigation.html*
  This provides mitigation strategies for preventing XSS attacks.

Chapter 6 Quick Reference

To	Do this
Remove unused services	Open the Control Panel, double-click the Add/Remove Programs icon, and then click the Add/Remove Windows Components button.
Create a security template	Open the Security Templates MMC snap-in, right-click the folder for the new template, and select New Template.
Apply a security template	Open the Security Configuration and Analysis MMC snap-in, import the desired template by right-clicking the Security Configuration and Analysis node and selecting Import Template. Apply the imported template by right-clicking the Security Configuration and Analysis node and selecting Configure Computer Now.
Change the blank *sa* password of a default install of MSDE	Use the osql command-line utility to run the *sp_password* stored procedure. You can also add logins, remove logins, and perform many other tasks with osql and the system stored procedures.
Enable logging for a Web site	Open the Internet Services Manager, navigate to the site you want to configure, right-click, and then select Properties. In the Properties dialog box, click the Web Site tab and ensure that the Enable Logging check box is checked.

To	Do this
Enable SSL communications for a site	Use the Web Server Certificate Wizard to create a certificate request (or follow the procedures recommended by the certification authority of your choice). Once you have received and installed your certificate, open the Internet Services Manager, navigate to the site to be configured for SSL, and access the Properties dialog box for the site. On the Directory Security tab, click the Server Certificate button and use the Assign An Existing Certificate option in the Web Server Certificate Wizard to assign the newly installed certificate to the site. You can require SSL communications by using the Edit button on the Directory Security tab.
Enable ASP.NET to use Windows authentication	Set the *mode* attribute of the *<authentication>* element in Web.config to *Windows*.
Enable ASP.NET to use Passport authentication	Set the *mode* attribute of the *<authentication>* element in Web.config to *Passport*. Install the Passport SDK and follow the instructions to configure. You must also acquire a license to use Passport authentication.
Enable ASP.NET to use Forms authentication	Set the *mode* attribute of the *<authentication>* element in Web.config to *Forms*. Add the *<forms>* element with the desired attributes, such as *loginURL* and *timeout*.
Lock down authorization settings	Wrap the *<authentication>* tags in a *<location>* element pair with the *allowOverride* attribute set to *false*.

ASP.NET Web Forms

Chapter

7

Creating Web Forms

In previous chapters, you've seen examples of both very simple and more complicated ASP.NET pages. The simplest ASP.NET page consists of plain HTML and is named with the .aspx extension. While that's perfectly valid, it's also missing a lot of the elements that make Web Forms so useful.

Web Forms go beyond what classic ASP pages offered, adding new directives, new reusability options in the form of user controls and server controls, and a new server-side data-binding syntax. This section will explore how a page is put together and how you can use these new features in your Web Forms.

Anatomy of an ASP.NET Web Form

The following listing shows an example of a relatively simple Web Forms page.

HelloSimple.aspx

```
<%-- Example of the @ Page directive --%>
<%@ Page Language="c#" ClassName="Hello" %>
<html>
<head>
   <script runat="server">
   // this is a script code declaration block
   private string name = "Andrew";
   public string Name
   {
```

```
          get
          {
           return name;
          }
          set
          {
           name = value;
          }
        }
        public void SayHello()
        {
          Label1.Text = "Hello, " + name + "!";
        }

        public void Page_Load(object sender, System.EventArgs e)
        {
          if ( IsPostBack )
          {
           if ( NameTextBox.Text != "" )
           {
             Name = NameTextBox.Text;
           }
           SayHello();
          }
        }
      </script>
</head>
<body>
    <!-- this is a server side form -->
    <form runat="server">
       <!-- a Server Control -->
       <asp:Label id="NameLabel" runat="server">Name: </asp:Label>
       <!-- a Server Control -->
       <asp:textbox id="NameTextBox" runat="server"/>
       <!-- a Server Control -->
       <asp:button id="NameButton" text="Submit" runat="server"/>
    </form>
    <!-- a Server Control -->
    <asp:Label id=Label1 runat="server"/>
</body>
</html>
```

The following sections describe the elements used in HelloSimple.aspx, as well as other elements that you can use in a Web Form page.

Understanding Page Elements

HelloSimple.aspx (the preceding listing) shows examples of many of the elements that you can use in an ASP.NET Web Form, including server-side comments, the @ *Page* directive, static HTML, a server-side *<script>* code-declaration block containing both event handlers and methods, and several ASP.NET server controls. Table 7-1 describes these elements.

Table 7-1. ASP.NET Page Elements

Element	Description
Static HTML tags	These standard HTML elements are treated by ASP.NET as literal controls, and are rendered to the client browser as represented in the source file.
HTML comments	Syntax: <!-- -->. HTML comments allow descriptive text to be added to a page. This text is sent to the client but is not rendered by the browser.
Directives	Directives, such as the @ *Page* directive, provide the ASP.NET runtime with information about how to process the page. Using directives, you can control such ASP.NET features as session state, wiring up of events, and output caching, as well as importing namespaces and registering custom controls for use within a page.
Server-side code	Code can be contained in either server-side *<script>* code declaration blocks or <% %> render blocks. See "Writing Code in Web Forms" on page 211 for information on using code declaration and render blocks. ASP.NET supports server-side code in any language that targets the runtime.
Event handlers	Event handlers are procedures in *<script>* code declaration blocks that handle page or server control events, such as *Page_Load* or *control Click* events. Most ASP.NET code should be written in or called from event handlers, rather than being written in render blocks.
<script> code declaration blocks	These blocks are used to contain page-level procedures and to declare variables that are global to the page. Executable code, other than global variable declarations in code declaration blocks, must be contained within a procedure declaration. Server-side code declaration blocks must have the *runat="server"* attribute, as shown in Hello-Simple.aspx.
<% %> render blocks	These blocks are used to contain executable code not contained within procedures. Overuse of render blocks can result in code that is difficult to read and maintain.
Client-side *<script>* blocks	These blocks are used to contain script code to be executed on the client, usually in response to a client-side event. Choice of language (set by the language attribute) is dictated by the languages supported by the target browser. JavaScript is the most common choice for cross-browser compatibility in client scripts.
Server-side comments	Syntax: <%-- --%>. Server-side comments allow descriptive text to be added to a page. Unlike HTML comments, this text is not sent to the client.

Table 7-1. ASP.NET Page Elements

Element	Description
User controls	These are custom controls that are defined declaratively in files with the .ascx extension. They provide a simple and straightforward mechanism for reuse of UI and UI-related code, and can contain most of the same elements as Web Forms pages.
ASP.NET server controls	This set of built-in controls provides ASP.NET developers with a programming model that mimics that of Microsoft Visual Basic. Controls are added to a page, and programmers write code to handle events raised by users' interaction with the controls at runtime. ASP.NET provides two sets of built-in controls: the HTML controls, which provide a 1-to-1 mapping of server-side controls for most HTML elements; and the Web controls, which provide a set of controls that are very similar to the Visual Basic UI controls. Note that some server controls, such as the *TextBox* and *Button* controls, must be placed within a server-side *<form>*, or an exception will be raised.
Custom server controls	Custom server controls are another mechanism for reuse in ASP.NET. They're defined in class files (.cs or .vb files) and are precompiled into managed assemblies before use.

Understanding Page Lifetime

The goal of the ASP.NET Web Forms programming model is to provide an experience similar to that of a Visual Basic rich-client event-driven application, in which user actions, such as selecting an item from a list or clicking a button, cause server-side code to be executed. This is accomplished through *postbacks*.

The first time that an ASP.NET Web Forms page is executed, the code contained within the page (and any code-behind class module associated with the page) is compiled into a class that inherits from the *Page* base class (actually, the code-behind class inherits from the *Page* class, and then the .aspx file inherits from the code-behind class via the *Inherits* attribute of the @ *Page* directive). The following illustration shows the relationship between the page, its code-behind class (if any), and the compiled assembly. Once compiled, the class is executed, the resulting HTML is rendered to the browser, and the class is removed from memory.

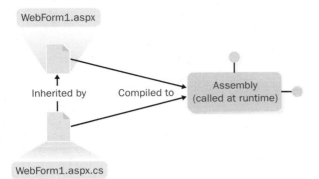

WebForm1.aspx

Inherited by   Compiled to

Assembly
(called at runtime)

WebForm1.aspx.cs

Each ASP.NET Web Forms page contains a server-side *<form>* tag that directs the page to post back to itself when the form is submitted by the user. Many ASP.NET server controls also render JavaScript to the client, allowing actions such as selecting an item in a drop-down list to cause a postback. The ASP.NET runtime also renders a hidden form field to the page that allows the page to maintain its state between requests.

The postback and the hidden field are key, because when the client is interacting with the page, no code is running on the server at all. The postback and the hidden field allow the page to be reconstituted on the server. Also, they allow code to be executed in response to the event raised by the user action, and based on any changes to the form fields. Once the page has been processed and the output rendered to the browser, the page and its controls are again discarded. The steps in this process are as follows:

1   The user requests the page from the browser.

2   The page and controls are loaded and initialized at the server.

3   If the page request is the result of a postback, the control state is loaded from the viewstate (hidden form field), and any changes submitted by the user are applied. (Note that both the original values in the viewstate and the updated values are available to server-side code.)

4   Page event handlers and event handlers for events triggered by user actions are executed.

5   Control state is saved to viewstate (hidden form field).

6   HTML output from the page is rendered to the browser.

7   The page and controls are unloaded on the server.

It's important to note that while most server controls save their state to view-state automatically, the same is not true for properties that you define in your pages, or in user controls or custom server controls. You'll learn how to use viewstate for storing custom control state in Chapter 10.

Using Directives

If you've developed a classic ASP page, you've worked with directives. There were few directives in classic ASP, but they were important. Most prominent were the @ *Language* directive and the *#Include* directive. The @ *Language* directive, which appeared at the top of every classic ASP page, told the ASP runtime which language engine to use in interpreting script found in <% %> render blocks in the page. The *#Include* directive told the ASP interpreter to include a particular file inline with the current ASP page.

Directives are simply ways for developers to declaratively determine how certain aspects of a program will operate. In classic ASP, this was somewhat limited. In fact, classic ASP had only four @ directives, in addition to the @ *Language* directive:

- @ *Codepage*   Used in globalization to set the code page for an ASP page
- @ *EnableSessionState*   Used to disable session state for a page
- @ *LCID*   Used to set the locale identifier for a page
- @ *Transaction*   Used to specify whether and how the page participates in COM+ transactions

ASP.NET greatly expands the use of directives, adding a number of useful directives for everything from controlling page behavior and configuration to caching page output. In addition, @ directives in ASP.NET have attributes, thereby increasing their power and flexibility. The four classic ASP directives listed previously are represented in ASP.NET as attributes of the @ *Page* directive, which is described in the next section.

@ Page

The @ *Page* directive, which is allowed in .aspx files only, defines page-specific attributes used by ASP.NET language compilers and the runtime to determine how the page will behave. The default values for a few of these attributes are set in the *Pages* configuration section in machine.config. Some of the attributes, including *AutoEventWireup*, are set or overridden in pages created by Microsoft Visual Studio .NET. The attributes available for the @ *Page* directive are listed in Table 7-2.

Table 7-2. @ *Page* Attributes

Attribute	Value	Purpose
AspCompat	*true/false*	Provides compatibility with COM components created with Visual Basic 6.0 (or earlier) by forcing the page to be run in an STA (Single Threaded Apartment). Also provides the component with access to unmanaged instances of the ASP intrinsics (*Session*, *Application*, *Request*, and so on). This setting will likely degrade performance, so use it only when necessary. Default is *false*.
AutoEventWireup	*true/false* Default is set in the *<pages>* section of machine.config or Web.config.	Determines whether handlers for events such as *Page_Load* are set up automatically. See "Event Handling" on page 220 for more information. Default is *true*.
Buffer	*true/false* Default is set in the *<pages>* section of machine.config or Web.config.	Determines whether rendered output is buffered before being sent to the client or is sent as it is rendered. Default is *true*.
ClassName	Any valid class name.	Determines the name of the page generated by dynamically compiling the page. This attribute works with or without *Codebehind*, and with either the *Src* or *Codebehind* attributes. The default behavior if this attribute is omitted is for the page name to be in the form *filename*_aspx.
ClientTarget	Any valid *UserAgent* string. Available values are set in the *<clientTarget>* section of machine.config or Web.config.	Determines the target browser for which server controls should render output. The *UserAgent* string should be one recognized by the server controls being used.
Codebehind	Filename of code-behind class.	This attribute is used in Visual Studio .NET to locate *code-behind* classes to be compiled during a build operation. It is not used by the ASP.NET runtime.
CodePage	Any valid code page value.	Used in globalization to set the code page for a Web Forms page.
CompilerOptions	String containing valid compiler options.	Allows developers to pass compiler options for the page to the compiler. For Visual Basic .NET and C#, this can be any valid sequence of command-line switches for the compiler.

Table 7-2. @ *Page* Attributes

Attribute	Value	Purpose
ContentType	Any valid MIME type (such as "*text/html*" or "*application/ vnd.ms-excel*").	Sets the MIME type for the page output. This attribute is useful when returning binary content (such as images) to the client.
Culture	Any valid culture string (such as *en-US* for US English).	Determines the culture setting for the page.
Debug	*true/false* Default is set by the *debug* attribute of the *<compilation>* section of machine.config or Web.config.	Determines whether pages are compiled with debug symbols or without. This setting affects performance, so production applications should have this set to *false*. The default is *false*.
Description	Any string.	Provides a text description of the page. This attribute is ignored by the ASP.NET runtime.
EnableSessionState	*true/false/readonly* Default is set in the *<pages>* section of machine.config or Web.config.	Determines whether a request to the page will initiate a new session, and whether the page can access or modify data stored in an existing session. Default is *true*.
EnableViewState	*true/false* Default is set in the *<pages>* section of machine.config or Web.config.	Determines whether viewstate is enabled for the page. *ViewState* allows server controls to save their current state from request to request. Default is *true*.
EnableViewStateMac	*true/false* Default is set in the *<pages>* section of machine.config or Web.config.	Determines whether ASP.NET runs a Machine Authentication Check (MAC) on the content of the hidden form field that is used to store viewstate, to ensure that it has not been altered on the client. Default is *false*.
ErrorPage	Any valid URL.	Specifies a page to which the client is redirected if there is an unhandled exception in the page.
Explicit	*true/false* Default is set in the *<compilation>* section of machine.config or Web.config.	Determines whether code written in Visual Basic is subject to the *Option Explicit* rule when compiled. Default is *true*.

Table 7-2.   @ *Page* Attributes

Attribute	Value	Purpose
Inherits	Any class derived from the *Page* class. Format is "*namespacename. classname*" or "*class-name*".	Specifies a code-behind class for the page. Any code contained in the page is combined with the code in the code-behind class into a single class.
Language	Any valid string for an installed .NET lan-guage (such as "*vb*"/ "*visualbasic*", "*c#*"/ "*cs*"/ "*csharp*", and so on) Default is set in the *<compilation>* section of machine.config or Web.config.	Specifies the language compiler to be used to compile the page. Default is *c#*.
LCID	Any valid locale identifier.	Used to set the locale identifier for a page.
ResponseEncoding	Any valid encoding string. Default is set in the *<globalization>* section of machine.config or Web.config.	Used in globalization to set the charac-ter encoding for the HTTP response. Default is *utf-8*.
SmartNavigation	*true/false*	Determines whether SmartNaviga-tion, which uses IFrame elements for clients running Microsoft Internet Explorer 5.0 or above to reduce the flash of navigation when repeatedly posting back to the same page, among other enhancements, is enabled or dis-abled. Default is *false*
Src	Filename of code-behind class	Specifies the name of a code-behind class file to be compiled dynamically at runtime.
Strict	*true/false*	Determines whether code written in Visual Basic is subject to the *Option Strict* rule when compiled. Default is *false*.

Table 7-2. @ *Page* **Attributes**

Attribute	Value	Purpose
Trace	*true/false* Default is set in the *<trace>* section of machine.config or Web.config.	Determines whether the page includes trace output. Default is *false*. Note: Leaving tracing enabled on production systems can cause both performance and security issues. Ensure that tracing is disabled before deploying an application.
TraceMode	*SortByTime/ SortByCategory* Default is set in the *<trace>* section of machine.config or Web.config.	Determines how the trace output is sorted when tracing is enabled. Default is *SortByTime*.
Transaction	One of the following: *Disabled* *NotSupported* *Supported* *Required* *RequiresNew*	Determines whether and how the page will participate in COM+ transactions. Default is *Disabled*.
UICulture	Any valid UI culture value.	Specifies the UI culture setting for a Web Forms page.
ValidateRequest	*true/false*	Specifies whether request validation will be performed on input data such as querystring values, form fields, and so on. If *true*, and if any potentially dangerous content such as HTML tags or script is found, an exception of type *HttpRequestValidationException* will be thrown. The default is *true*. Important: You should *not* disable this feature unless you are certain that you have adequately provided for filtering or validating that any input that the page accepts is safe for processing or display.
WarningLevel	0–4	Specifies the warning level at which the compiler should abort page compilation. Lower numbers allow compilation to continue through warnings of greater severity. Levels 2–4 apply to C# only.

@ *Page* Examples

In this section, we'll take a look at a couple of examples of using the @ *Page* directive. The first example will show how to enable debugging of ASP.NET pages, and the second will show how to enable page-level tracing.

Enabling Debug Information

By default, ASP.NET pages created as a part of a Visual Studio .NET Web application project are compiled with debug symbols. This is good for development, since it offers much richer error information than was available in classic ASP, as shown in the following illustration.

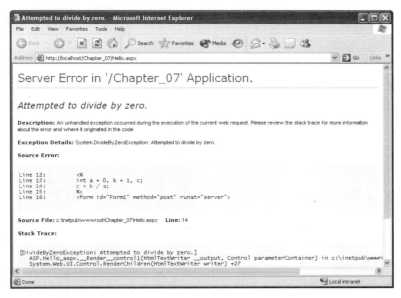

This functionality, however, exacts a performance penalty, so you should usually turn this option off when you deploy your application. Debug symbols are enabled in two specific places in Visual Studio .NET: in Web.config (which enables debug symbols for .aspx pages) and in the Configuration Manager properties for the project/solution (which enables debug symbols for code-behind classes and other compiled classes in the project). The following procedures describe how to turn off debug symbols in both places.

Disable debug symbols in Web.config

1   Open the Web.config for the desired project in Visual Studio .NET.

2   Change the *debug* attribute of the *<compilation>* element to *false*:

```
<compilation defaultLanguage="c#" debug="false" />
```

3   Save and close the file.

Now if you encounter an unhandled error in code contained within the .aspx page, ASP.NET will provide you with an error page without the specific error information made possible by the use of debug symbols, as shown in the following illustration.

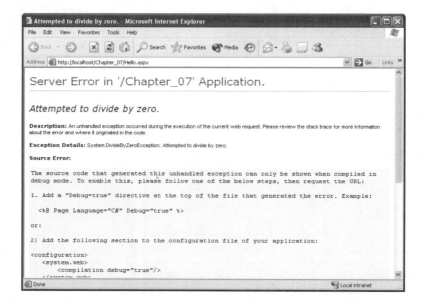

▶   **Important**   Debugging carries some performance penalty, but, more important, if you do not configure the *<customErrors>* configuration element properly, enabling debugging can result in information being displayed to the user that could present a security risk. You should always disable debugging in production applications to minimize the amount of exploitable information your application provides when an exception occurs, as well as to improve performance.

Disable debug symbols using the Configuration Manager

1   Right-click the solution containing the desired project in Solution Explorer, and select Configuration Manager. The dialog box shown in the following illustration is displayed.

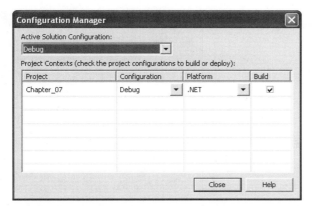

2   To disable debug symbols for a single project, select that project in the dialog box and change the value in the Configuration drop-down list from Debug to Release, as shown in the following illustration.

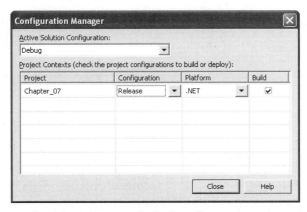

3   To disable debug symbols for all projects, change the Active Solution Configuration from Debug to Release, as shown in the illustration on the next page.

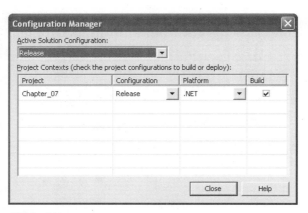

4   Click Close.

Enabling Tracing

By default, the *trace* functionality is not enabled for ASP.NET pages. As with the *debug* attribute, disabling tracing in production applications is good for performance, since there is overhead associated with tracing. Disabling tracing in production applications is also important for security because tracing provides a large amount of information about each request, information that could potentially assist a malicious user in attacking your site, if tracing isn't configured properly. Tracing enables you to view information about the current request, including the collections (cookies, forms, headers, querystrings, and server variables) associated with the request.

Enable tracing

1   Open the desired page in Visual Studio .NET and switch to HTML view.

2   Add the *trace* attribute to the @ *Page* directive, with a value of *true*.

```
<%@ Page trace="true" %>
```

3   Save the file. When you request the file from a browser, you'll be able to see the trace information appended to the page output, as shown in the illustration on the following page.

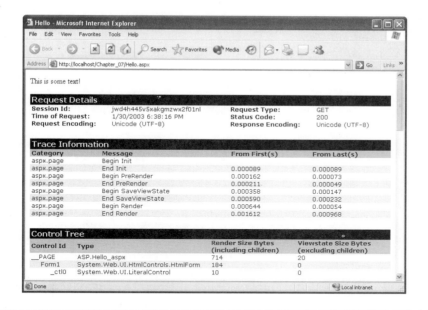

For more information on tracing and its uses in debugging ASP.NET applications, refer to Chapter 14.

▶ **Tip**   In addition to manually adding (or modifying) the attributes of the @ *Page* directive, you can enable or disable these features on a per-page basis by using the Properties window in Visual Studio .NET to set the *Debug* or *Trace* properties of the *DOCUMENT* object.

@ *Control*

The @ *Control* directive, which is allowed in .ascx files only, performs the same function as the @ *Page* directive. However, instead of setting attributes for pages, it sets the attributes for user controls, which are reusable snippets of code named with the .ascx file extension. The attributes exposed by the @ *Control* directive are a subset of the attributes exposed by the @ *Page* directive, and their purpose and values are the same as in the table of @ *Page* attributes table beginning on page 195. The following attributes are available for the @ *Control* directive:

- *AutoEventWireup*
- *ClassName*
- *Codebehind*
- *CompilerOptions*
- *Debug*

- *Description*
- *EnableViewState*
- *Explicit*
- *Inherits*
- *Language*
- *Strict*
- *Src*
- *WarningLevel*

@ Import

The @ *Import* directive is used to import either a Microsoft .NET Framework namespace or a custom namespace into a page. Importing a namespace allows you to write code against the members of that namespace without explicitly specifying the namespace each time. The @ *Import* directive has only one attribute, *Namespace*, which specifies the namespace to import. Each @ *Import* directive can have only one *Namespace* attribute, so you must use a separate @ *Import* directive for each namespace you want to import. For example, to use the .NET Framework *SmtpMail* and *MailMessage* classes to send e-mail from an ASP.NET page, you need to add the *System.Web.Mail* namespace to your page, as follows:

```
<%@ Import namespace="System.Web.Mail" %>
```

Then, to create an instance of the *MailMessage* class, you use the following:

```
MailMessage myMail = new MailMessage();
```

Without the @ *Import* directive, you need to use the following:

```
MailMessage myMail = new System.Web.Mail.MailMessage();
```

@ Implements

The @ *Implements* directive is used to implement a defined interface from within an ASP.NET page. An interface provides an abstract definition of a set of methods and properties. When you implement an interface, you commit to supporting the methods and properties defined by the interface, and you must create matching method and property definitions in your .aspx file, using *<script>* blocks. The @ *Implements* directive can't be used to implement interfaces in a code-behind file. It has one attribute, *interface*, which specifies the interface being implemented.

@ Register

The @ *Register* directive is used with both user controls and custom server controls to register them for use within a page. The @ *Register* directive's attributes are listed in Table 7-3.

Table 7-3. @ *Register* Attributes

Attribute	Value	Purpose
Assembly	Any valid assembly name. The assembly name should not contain a file extension.	Specifies the precompiled assembly for a custom server control. Used with the *Namespace* and *TagPrefix* attributes. The assembly named needs to be available to the application, either by being placed in the bin subdirectory of the application or by being installed into the global assembly cache.
Namespace	Any valid namespace name.	Specifies the namespace to be associated with the tag prefix specified by the *TagPrefix* attribute.
Src	Any valid path to a user control (.ascx) file. Accepts either relative or absolute URLs.	Specifies the location of a user control associated with a *TagName/TagPrefix* pair.
TagName	Any string (must be valid for XML).	Specifies an alias for a user control to be used in implementing the user control within the page. Must be used with the *TagPrefix* attribute.
TagPrefix	Any string (must be valid for XML).	Specifies an alias for a tag prefix for a user control or custom server control to be used in implementing the control within the page. If used without the *TagName* attribute, as with a custom server control, the tag name is the same as the class name defined in the server control assembly specified by the *Assembly* and *Namespace* attributes.

For examples of the use of the @ *Register* directive, see "Creating and Using User Controls" on page 213 and "Using Server Controls" in Chapter 8.

@ Assembly

The @ *Assembly* directive is used to link an assembly into a page at compilation time. This allows developers to use all of the classes, methods, and so forth exposed by the assembly as if they were part of the page. The @ *Assembly* directive's attributes are listed in Table 7-4. Only one of the *Name* and *Src* attributes of the @ *Assembly* directive can be used at a time.

Table 7-4. *@ Assembly* **Attributes**

Attribute	Value	Purpose
Name	Any valid assembly name.	Specifies the name of a compiled assembly to be linked to when the page is compiled.
Src	Any valid path to a class source file (.vb, .cs, and so on).	Specifies the path to a source file to be dynamically compiled and linked to the current page.

Note that it is not necessary to use the *@ Assembly* directive to link in assemblies residing in the bin subdirectory of your application. These assemblies are automatically linked in by default, based on the *<assemblies>* subsection of the *<compilation>* section of the machine.config configuration file, which contains the following tag:

```
<add assembly="*"/>
```

This specifies that ASP.NET should link in any assemblies in the bin subdirectory. Note also that any other assemblies specified by an *<add>* tag in the *<assemblies>* subsection do not require linking with the *@ Assembly* directive.

@ OutputCache

The *@ OutputCache* directive is used to specify that the rendered output of the page or user control in which it appears should be cached. This directive also specifies the attributes that determine the duration of caching, the location of the cached output, and the attributes that determine when a client will receive freshly rendered content rather than the cached content. Output caching in user controls can be especially useful when some of the content in a page is relatively static, but other content is frequently updated, making it a poor candidate for caching. In a case like this, you could move the static content into a user control and use the *@ OutputCache* directive to cache its content, while leaving the rest of the page to be dynamically generated with each request.

The *@ OutputCache* directive's attributes are listed in Table 7-5.

Table 7-5. @ *OutputCache* **Attributes**

Attribute	Value	Purpose
Duration	Number of seconds. (Required.)	Specifies the time, in seconds, for the page or control to be cached.
Location	One of the following: *Any* *Client* *Downstream* *None* *Server*	Specifies the location where cached output should be stored. (This attribute is not supported for user controls.)
Shared	*true/false*	New in ASP.NET 1.1, this attribute specifies whether a cached user control can be shared across multiple pages. If set to *true*, a single cached copy of the user control is shared among multiple pages within the application. If set to *false*, a separate copy of the user control will be cached for each page that uses the control. The default is *false*. This attribute is valid for user controls only.
VaryByCustom	Any valid text string.	Specifies a custom string by which to vary the output cache. If *browser* is used, output caching will vary based on the browser name and major version. If you want to vary by HTTP request data other than the requesting browser, you will need to override the *GetVaryByCustom-String* method of the *HttpApplication* class in Global.asax in order to implement your custom string.
VaryByHeader	List of valid HTTP headers, separated by semicolons.	Specifies one or more HTTP headers to be used to vary the output cache. When a request is received with a value for the specified HTTP header(s) that does not match that of any of the cached pages, a new version of the page will be rendered and cached. This attribute cannot be used with user controls.

Table 7-5.   @ *OutputCache* Attributes

Attribute	Value	Purpose
VaryByParam	List of querystring keys or form field names, separated by semicolons, or one of the following: *None* * (Required in ASP.NET pages and in user controls that don't have a *VaryByControl* attribute specified.)	Specifies one or more names of either querystring keys passed with a *GET* request, or form field names passed with a *POST* request to be used to vary the output cache. When a request is received with a value for one of the specified parameters that does not match that of any of the cached pages, a new version of the page will be rendered and cached. If the value of this attribute is set to *none*, the output cache will not vary based on *GET* and *POST* parameters. If the value is set to *, the output cache will vary by all *GET* and *POST* parameters. (Required in a user control if you don't specify a VaryByParam attribute.)
VaryByControl	List of properties exposed by a user control, separated by semicolons.	Specifies one or more properties exposed by a user control to be used to vary the output cache. When a request is received with a value that does not match the specified property of any of the cached pages, a new version of the page will be rendered and cached. This attribute can be used only for output caching with user controls, not with ASP.NET pages.

Enabling Output Caching

For pages or user controls whose content does not change frequently, output caching can provide a simple and powerful way to improve the performance of your application. With output caching enabled, requests that match the parameters of the cached pages will be served from the cache, which is much faster than rendering the page again.

Enable output caching on a Web Forms page

1   Open the desired Web Forms page in Visual Studio .NET. Switch to HTML view.

2   Add the @ *OutputCache* directive with, minimally, the required *Duration* and *VaryByParam* attributes. This directive should go at the top of the .aspx page, just below the @ *Page* directive.

```
<%@ OutputCache duration="60" location="Any" VaryByParam="*" %>
```

3   Save the file. With these values for the attributes, the output of the page
will be cached for 60 seconds. Any *GET/POST* requests with parameters that do not match an existing cached version of the page will be
served a freshly rendered version of the page, which will then be cached.

For more information on output caching and using the ASP.NET cache engine
to store arbitrary data, see Chapter 12.

@ Reference

The @ Reference directive allows you to dynamically load user controls by ref-
erencing the filename of the desired control and then using the Page.LoadCon-
trol method to load the control at runtime. The @ Reference directive directs
the ASP.NET runtime to compile and link the specified control to the page in
which it is declared. You'll see an example of using the @ Reference directive in
the section on user controls later in this chapter.

The *Page* Class

The *Page* class provides much of the functionality of an ASP.NET page. Pages
can take advantage of this functionality because every page derives from the
Page class and inherits all of the methods and properties that it exposes. Some
of the more notable members of the *Page* class, which resides in the *Sys-
tem.Web.UI* namespace, are included in the following list.

- **ASP *Intrinsic* objects**   These objects (*Application, Session, Request,
  Response, Server,* and *Context*) are implemented in ASP.NET as class
  instances, which are exposed as properties of the *page* object. For example, the *Server* functionality is provided by a class called *HttpServerUtility*. Because the instance of *HttpServerUtility* is exposed as the *Server*
  property of the *Page* class, you can call its methods (*Server.Transfer,* for
  example) just as you could in classic ASP.

- ***Controls* collection**   Provides access to the collection of controls
  defined for the page. As you'll see later in this chapter, you can use
  this collection to add or modify controls on a page.

- ***IsPostBack* property**   Allows you to determine whether the current
  request is a *GET* request or a *POST* request resulting from the current page being posted back to itself. This property is very useful in
  deciding what to do when loading a Web Forms page, as you'll see
  later in this chapter.

- ***User* property**   Provides access to information about the currently
  logged-in user.

- *Cache* **property**   Provides access to the ASP.NET cache engine, allowing data to be cached for later retrieval.
- *FindControl* **method**   Allows you to locate a control contained in the page's *Controls* collection by specifying its *ID* property.
- *ViewState* **property**   Provides access to a state dictionary (based on the *StateBag* class) that allows you to store information in *Key/Value* pairs. This information is passed with each request as a hidden HTML form field.
- *ClearChildViewState* **method**   Allows you to delete all viewstate information for any child controls on the page. This is useful if you want these controls to maintain their state most of the time, but you want to clear the state programmatically under specific circumstances.

Many other properties and methods are exposed by the *Page* class. A substantial number of these are inherited from the *Control* class, from which the *Page* class is derived, or the *Object* class, from which the *Control* class (and ultimately, every other class) is derived. This is an example of how inheritance allows you to build a very rich object model.

There are two ways to indicate that an ASP.NET page is inherited from the *Page* class. The first is adding the @ *Page* directive to an .aspx file, which automatically makes all of the properties and methods of the *Page* class available to any code written in the page. The second, which is discussed in more detail later in this chapter, is inheriting from the *Page* class in a code-behind class that is associated with the page by either the *Src* or *Inherits* attribute. This not only makes all of the members of the *Page* class available to the code-behind class, but also allows ASP.NET to combine the code in the Web Form's .aspx file with the code in the code-behind class file into a single compiled class at compile time. This single compiled class contains all of the methods and properties exposed by the *Page* class, as well as any methods and properties implemented by your code.

Any of the members of the *Page* class can be called within code in a page without explicitly using the page name. For example, to write text to the browser using the *Write* method of the *Response* object, you would use the following code:

```
<%
    Response.Write("Hello, World!");
%>
```

You could also use

```
<%
    Page.Response.Write("Hello, World!");
%>
```

However, it is not necessary to add the *Page* property because the *Response* property and the other *Page* members are exposed directly when inheriting from the *Page* class.

Writing Code in Web Forms

One of the strengths of classic ASP was that it gave you a lot of flexibility in writing your code. You could write your code inline with the HTML markup, as a part of <% %> render blocks. You could write your code in subroutines in render blocks. And you could write your code in *<script>* declaration blocks, either as arbitrary code or as subroutines.

While this flexibility made it very easy to create ASP pages, it was also a major weakness of classic ASP because it allowed for some sloppy coding. It was far too easy to write unmanageable spaghetti code, with some code inline, some code in subroutines, and so on. In addition, although code in render blocks in classic ASP was executed in a linear fashion, arbitrary code (code not contained in a subroutine) in a *<script>* block was not. This often resulted in confusion, because sometimes this code was executed out of sequence with what developers expected.

ASP.NET solves these problems by imposing limitations on what types of code you can write and where you can write it. While many of the examples in this book use the default technique of writing UI-specific code in a code-behind module (rather than in the Web Forms page itself), it's worth looking at these limitations for those times when you want to work without code-behind. As with classic ASP, there are still two ways to write code within a Web Forms page: *<script>* blocks and <% %> render blocks.

Using *<script>* Code Declaration Blocks

As I mentioned, in classic ASP you could write pretty much any code you wanted (property and method definitions, arbitrary code, and so on) in a *<script>* block using the *runat="server"* attribute. The problem was that you couldn't be sure when any arbitrary code in the *<script>* block would execute, relative to the code in the rest of the page. For this reason, ASP.NET does not allow you to use arbitrary code within *<script>* blocks—now referred to as *code declaration blocks*—to emphasize their purpose of declaring properties and methods.

In ASP.NET, if you want to call *Response.Write* within a code declaration block, you need to wrap that call within a method declaration. The following code will work:

```
<script language="c#" runat="server">
  public void SayHello()
  {
```

```
        Response.Write("Hello, World!");
    }
</script>
```

The following code will cause a compiler error, since the compiler expects to see either a variable or method declaration:

```
<script language="c#" runat="server">
    Response.Write("Hello, World!");
</script>
```

Likewise, you can declare a local member variable in a declaration block, but you cannot assign to it outside of a defined method. So the following code will work:

```
<script language="c#" runat="server">
    string Name;
    public void SetName()
    {
     Name = "Andrew";
    }
</script>
```

But the following will cause a compiler error:

```
<script language="c#" runat="server">
    string Name;
    Name = "Andrew";
</script>
```

There is one exception to the variable assignment rule. You can initialize the value of a variable by assigning a value as part of the variable declaration, as follows:

```
<script language="c#" runat="server">
    string Name = "Andrew";
</script>
```

The *language* attribute of the *<script>* block is optional. If it is omitted, the value will default to the language specified by the @ *Page* directive's *language* attribute. If no *language* attribute has been specified for the @ *Page* directive, the value will default to C# (this value is set in the *<compiler>* element of the web.config configuration file for C# projects created with Visual Studio .NET).

Using ASP <% %> Code Render Blocks

Like *<script>* blocks, <% %> render blocks in classic ASP were pretty much "anything goes." In many cases, this led to sloppy programming habits and hard-to-maintain code. ASP.NET solves these problems by not allowing anything other than inline code and expressions in render blocks. This means that you can no longer place method definitions in a render block. So the following code will cause a compiler error:

```
<%
public void SayHello()
{
  Response.Write("Hello, World!");
}
%>
```

whereas the following code will work fine:

```
<%
    Response.Write("Hello, World!");
%>
```

Compatibility with Classic ASP

Clearly, one of the issues that arises from these changes is that a good deal of code written in classic ASP will not be compatible with the restrictions on the use of code declaration and render blocks. For this reason, it is a good idea to examine any classic ASP code that you are considering migrating to ASP.NET for these incompatibilities, so that you can address them before making the migration (and discovering too late that the code won't work!).

Creating and Using User Controls

User controls are a new feature of ASP.NET that provides a simple and fast method for getting reuse out of your presentation code. User controls can also dramatically increase performance when used in conjunction with the *OutputCache* directive described earlier. User controls are sometimes referred to as *declarative* controls (as opposed to server controls, which are *compiled* controls).

At their simplest, user controls consist of HTML markup and/or ASP.NET code persisted in a file with the .ascx file extension. As you saw earlier in this chapter, developers of user controls can also add the @ *Control* directive to specify aspects of how the user control will behave. Unlike Web Forms pages, user controls cannot be called directly. Instead, they must be used in an existing page.

User controls can contain most, but not all, of the same elements that you can use in Web Forms pages. For example, user controls should not contain *<html>*, *<body>*, or *<form>* elements because presumably these elements already exist in the page in which the user control is used. It's also a good idea to at least add the @ *Control* directive, along with its *ClassName* attribute, as follows:

```
<%@ Control ClassName="MyClass" %>
```

Adding the *ClassName* attribute allows the user control to be strongly typed when added to a page programmatically (as opposed to declaratively). Creating a user control is fairly straightforward. In the following example, you'll create a user control that calculates compounding interest. (Don't worry about the math—it's provided as part of the example.)

Create a user control

1   Create a new Web Application project in Visual Studio .NET. Type the name the the project as **Chapter_07**. (If you've installed the practice files, make sure to create the project in a location other than *http://localhost/aspnetsbs/Chapter_07* to avoid conflicts.)

2   Add a User Control to the project by right-clicking the project in Solution Explorer, selecting Add, and then selecting Add Web User Control. Type the name of the user control as **Compound.ascx**.

3   Add six *Label* controls, three *TextBox* controls, a *DropDownList* control, and a *Button* control to the user control design surface. When you're finished, the control should look like the following illustration.

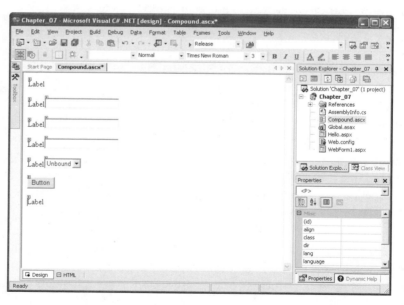

Since user controls start out in FlowLayout mode by default, you'll need to use the Enter key to move a control to a new line. It's important to name or number the controls in the order in which they appear on the page. (For example, the first label is *Label1*, the second, *Label2*, and so on.) This guarantees that the code in later steps will work.

4 Set the properties of the controls as follows:

Control	Property	Value
Label1	Text	Compound Interest Calculator
Label1	Font-Bold	True
Label1	Font-Size	Large
Label2	Text	Principal ($):
Label3	Text	Rate (%):
Label4	Text	Years:
Label5	Text	Compounding Frequency:
Button1	Text	Calculate
Label6	Text	(blank)

5 Click the *DropDownList1* control to select it, and then select the *Items* property and click the ellipsis (...) button to open the Collection Editor. Add four items, set the following text and values, and then click OK:

Item	Text	Value
0	Annually	1
1	Quarterly	4
2	Monthly	12
3	Daily	365

When you have finished modifying the properties, the design view of Compound.ascx should look like the illustration on the next page.

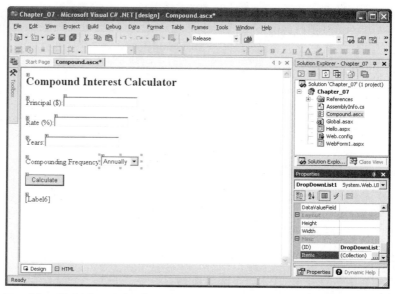

6   Double-click the Calculate button. This will switch to the code-behind for the user control and add the *Button1_Click* event handler. Add the following code, which calls the function to calculate the compounded interest, to the event handler.

```
Label6.Text = "Final Balance: $" +
    CalcBalance(Convert.ToInt32(TextBox1.Text),
    (Convert.ToInt32(TextBox2.Text) / 100),
    Convert.ToInt32(TextBox3.Text),
    Convert.ToInt16(DropDownList1.SelectedItem.Value)).ToString();
```

7   Immediately following the *End Sub* of the *Button1_Click* event handler, add the following code, which defines the function for calculating the compound interest:

```
private string CalculateBalance(int Principal,
    double Rate,

    int Years,
    int Period)
{
    double result;
    double NumToBeRaised = (1 + Rate / Period);
    result=Principal * System.Math.Pow(NumToBeRaised, (Years *
Period));
    return(result.ToString("C"));
}
```

8   Save the control and code-behind module, and then build the Chapter_07 project.

This control takes a dollar amount representing the principal to be invested (or borrowed), an interest rate, a period in years, and a compounding frequency, and uses these values to calculate the ending balance. This control encapsulates all of the controls and methods necessary for doing the calculation, so the only way to access them is through the user interface defined by the control. It is also possible, if desired, to expose the controls and/or their values publicly, so that they can be manipulated at runtime from the containing page.

To use this control, you need to add it to a Web Forms page. You can do this two ways: declaratively and programmatically. The declarative technique is simpler, but the programmatic technique gives you better runtime control.

Adding a User Control to a Page Declaratively

To use a user control in a Web Forms page, you need to make the control available to the page, and then implement the control on the page. As described in "Using Directives" on page 194, user controls can be made available to a page using either the @ *Register* directive or the @ *Reference* directive, depending on whether you are adding the control declaratively or programmatically. If you want to add the control declaratively, you need to use the @ *Register* directive to set up the tag syntax for the control. Fortunately, the Visual Studio .NET environment makes this a simple matter of drag and drop.

Add a control to a Web Form declaratively

1   Open the Chapter_07 project created in the previous example if it is not already open.

2   Add a new Web Forms page to the project and type its name as **CompoundContainer.aspx.**

3   Drag the Compound.ascx user control from the Solution Explorer onto the design surface of CompoundContainer.aspx. The result should look like the illustration on the next page.

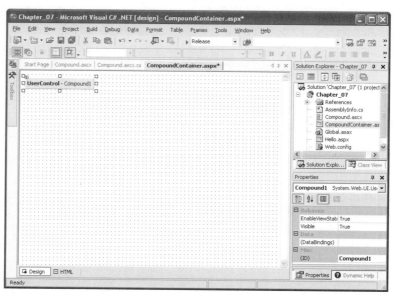

4   Save CompoundContainer.aspx, and then browse it using Internet Explorer by right-clicking the file in Solution Explorer and selecting Browse With. Enter amounts for the principal, rate, and years, then choose a compounding frequency, and then click Calculate. The result should look similar to the following illustration. Note that if you enter any non-integer value in the textboxes, an exception will occur when you click Calculate. You could prevent this by adding validator controls to ensure that only integer values are entered.

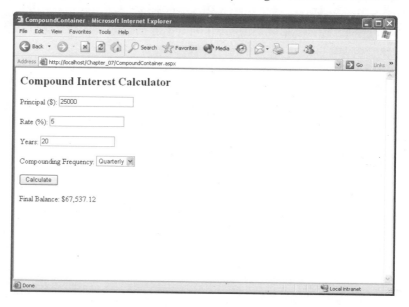

If you take a look at the HTML view for CompoundContainer.aspx, you'll see that Visual Studio .NET takes care of adding both the @ *Register* directive that makes the user control available to the page, and the tag that represents the user control. This greatly simplifies the process of adding a user control to the page, and should probably be your preferred method for adding user controls in Visual Studio .NET. You can, however, also add a user control to the page programmatically, as you'll see in the next section.

Adding a User Control to a Page Programmatically

The steps for adding a control to a page programmatically are somewhat similar to—but a bit more involved than—adding a control declaratively. You still need to make the control available to the page. For controls that are to be added programmatically, you can either use the @ *Register* directive, as in the previous example, or the @ *Reference* directive. Since the @ *Register* directive is more commonly used for declarative controls, use the @ *Reference* directive.

Add an @ *Reference* directive

1   Add a new Web Form to the Chapter_07 project. Type the name of the file as **CompoundProgrammatic.aspx**.

2   Switch to HTML view, and add the following code to the page, just below the @ *Page* directive:

```
<%@ Reference Control="Compound.ascx" %>
```

3   Save the file, but don't close it.

The @ *Reference* directive tells ASP.NET to compile and link the user control Compound.ascx with the page when it is compiled. This makes the control available for you to add to the page. Since you're not going to be adding a tag within the HTML markup for the control's output, take advantage of a special server control called the *Placeholder* control. As the name suggests, this allows you to put a placeholder in the HTML markup to which you can add controls later. In this way, you can decide precisely where you want the output from the control to appear.

Add the *Placeholder* control

1   Add a *PlaceHolder* control to CompoundProgrammatic.aspx by editing the <form> element to look like the following code:

```
<form id="Form1" method="post" runat="server">
   <asp:PlaceHolder ID="CompoundHolder" Runat="server"/>
</form>
```

2   Save the file, but don't close it yet.

Finally, we need to add the control to the page, and to the *Controls* collection of the *Placeholder* control, which will place the output of the control where we want it. Then the control will take care of the rest, just as in the previous example.

Add the user control to the page

1 Switch to Design view and double-click an empty area of the page. This will open the code-behind module for the page and place the cursor in the *Page_Load* event handler. Add the following code to the event handler:

```
Control CalcCompound = LoadControl("Compound.ascx");

CompoundHolder.Controls.Add(CalcCompound);
```

2 Save the page and code-behind module, and then build the Chapter_07 project.

3 Browse CompoundProgrammatic.aspx, using the Browse With dialog box. The output of the page should be the same as in the previous illustration.

Comparing User Controls to Include Files

User controls perform a similar function to server-side includes in classic ASP, but they're considerably more powerful because of the level of integration with the page model. A user control can have its own controls, and it can save the view-state of its controls or its own viewstate. This allows the user control to maintain its state across multiple calls without any effort on the part of the page containing the user control. User controls can expose both properties and methods, making them easy to understand for developers who are used to components.

Include files are still available in ASP.NET, mainly for backward compatibility with classic ASP. Given the advantages of user controls, it makes sense to use them for new applications.

Event Handling

One of the biggest differences between classic ASP and ASP.NET is the execution model. In classic ASP, pages were executed in a top-to-bottom fashion. In other words, with the exception of detours to execute functions defined in the page, classic ASP pages were procedural rather than event-driven, like Visual Basic programs.

ASP.NET changes that by bringing event-driven programming to Web development through server controls and postbacks. At runtime, the code in a Web Form, as well as in any code-behind class associated with that Web Form, is compiled into an assembly. When executed, the code in that assembly fires events that you can handle—both those exposed by the *Page* class and those that are fired by server controls that have been added to the page.

Page Processing Stages

A Web Forms page goes through the following processing stages:

- **Init**   Page and control settings are initialized as necessary for the request.
- **LoadViewState**   Server control state that was saved to viewstate in an earlier request is restored.
- **LoadPostData**   Any data returned in server control form fields is processed, and the relevant control properties are updated.
- **Load**   Controls are created and loaded, and control state matches the data entered by the client.
- **RaisePostDataChangedEvent**   Events are raised in response to changes in control data from the previous request to the current request.
- **RaisePostBackEvent**   The event that caused the postback is handled, and the appropriate server-side events are raised.
- **PreRender**   Any changes that need to be made prior to rendering the page are processed. Any processing after this point will not be rendered to the page.
- **SaveViewState**   Server control state is saved back to the page's viewstate prior to tearing down the controls.
- **Render**   Control and page output is rendered to the client.
- **UnLoad**   The page and its constituent controls are removed from memory on the server.

Of these stages, you can add page-level event handlers for the *Init, Load, PreRender,* and *UnLoad* events. These handlers are typically named *Page_Init, Page_Load, Page_PreRender,* and *Page_UnLoad.* For other stages, such as the *LoadViewState, SaveViewState,* and *Render* stages, you can override the appropriate method to customize the processing of these stages. Overriding these methods is discussed in Chapter 10.

Some events, such as those fired by the page, are fired automatically as certain stages of page processing occur. Others, such as those associated with server controls, are actually triggered on the client (such as a user clicking a button server control) but are fired and handled on the server when the page is posted back to the server. Because the page is reloaded and the control state is restored with each postback, to the client it appears as though the page is there throughout the client's interaction with it, and the application appears to operate much like a Visual Basic form–based application.

Handling Page Events

Each stage in the processing of a Web Forms page fires an event that allows you to perform processing of your own during that stage. While you might not have realized it, you've already learned how to take advantage of these event handlers in your own pages. When you double-click an empty area of a Web Form in Design view, the IDE opens the code-behind module for the Web Form and places the cursor in the *Page_Load* event handler, which is added to the code-behind module when the Web Form (and its associated code-behind module) is added to the project. By default, Visual Studio .NET also adds a handler for the *Page_Init* event to the code-behind module, but this event handler is hidden using the *# Region...#End Region* keywords. The following illustration shows the code contained within the *Web Form Designer Generated Code* region in CompoundProgrammatic.aspx.cs:

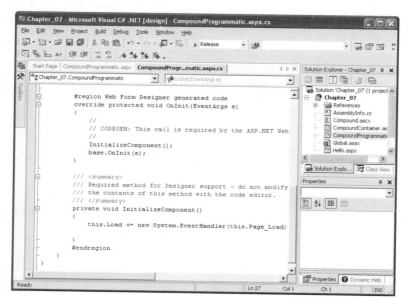

You can handle other page events, such as the *Page_Unload* event, by adding the appropriate handler code to the code-behind module.

```
private void Page_UnLoad(object sender,
  System.EventArgs e)
{
  // Event handling code
}
```

Of course, you can also handle events if you're not using code-behind by adding the appropriate event handler to a server-side script block within the .aspx page:

```
<script runat="server">
    public void Page_Load(object sender, System.EventArgs e)
    {
        // Event handling code
    }
</script>
```

▶ **Important**   The preceding code assumes that the *AutoEventWireup* attribute of the page has been set to *true*. For pages created outside of Visual Studio .NET, you won't need to set this attribute manually, since *true* is the default setting inherited from the *<pages>* configuration section in Machine.config. However, pages created in Visual Studio .NET have the *AutoEventWireup* attribute in their @ *Page* directive set to *false*. This means that all event handlers in these pages must be manually wired to the events that they are to handle. You'll learn more about manually wiring events in Chapter 8.

Handling Control Events

As with events exposed by the *Page* class, you've already seen many examples of handling control events in this and other chapters. Handling the default event for a given control is as simple as double-clicking the control in Visual Studio .NET's Design view. Visual Studio .NET then takes care of adding the appropriate event handler to the code-behind module for the page, and wiring it up using the *Handles* keyword. For example, if you were to double-click the *DropDownList* control in the Compound.ascx control in Design view, Visual Studio .NET would add the following code to Compound.aspx.cs:

```
private void DropDownList1_SelectedIndexChanged(object sender,
  System.EventArgs e)
{

}
```

You can add handlers for other events associated with a control by using similar syntax. When writing the event handler in code-behind, it doesn't matter what you name the event-handling procedure, as long as you properly add the event handler, like Visual Studio .NET does when it adds the *Page_Load* handler to the *InitializeComponent* event handler, as in this example:

```
this.Load += new System.EventHandler(this.Page_Load);
```

Still, it's a good idea to stick with the naming convention of *ControlName_EventName*, as this makes it easy to tell at a glance which control and event a given procedure is handling.

> ▶ **Tip**   When adding event handlers in a code-behind module, an easy way to make sure that your code is correct is to use the drop-down list boxes at the top of the code editor window. Simply select the control whose event you want to handle in the left-hand drop-down list, and then select the event you want to handle from the right-hand drop-down list (events are denoted by a lightning-bolt icon). Visual Studio .NET will automatically insert the code for the event handler into your code-behind module.

Handling control events in pages that do not use code-behind is fairly straightforward. There are two steps: First, add an event handler procedure to a server-side script block in the page. Then, map the event raised by the control to the event handler using an attribute on the control tag.

For example, if you wanted to handle the *Click* event of a *Button* control named *Button1*, you would add the following code to the *<script>* block in ServerControls.aspx:

```
public void Button1_Click(object Sender,System.EventArgs e)
{
    // Event handler code
}
```

And then you would add the following attribute to the *Button1* server control tag:

```
<asp:Button id="Button1" onClick="Button1_Click" runat="server"/>
```

Again, you are not required to name the event handler procedure with the *ControlName_EventName* naming convention, but using this convention will make your code easier to read.

Handling Page Errors

While using structured exception handling might be useful for catching exceptions that are expected (see Chapter 3), at times you'll want to handle errors at the page level. This is possible through a special event handler called *Page_Error*. The *Page_Error* event is raised whenever a page encounters an unhandled exception. Within the *Page_Error* event handler, you can examine the exception that occurred by using the *Server.GetLastError* method and take appropriate action or display a friendly message to the user.

Page Runtime Structure

As discussed earlier, at runtime ASP.NET combines the code in the page and any associated code-behind class into a single class, and then it compiles that class and executes it on the server. In the process, ASP.NET builds a control tree containing all of the controls on the page, including *LiteralControl* server controls for each section of HTML text.

▶ **Important** When compiling a page, ASP.NET automatically creates controls that represent the HTML markup in the page, using the *LiteralControl* server control class. This allows you to easily manipulate the HTML markup at runtime, and also allows greater flexibility in adding controls at runtime. If the page contains <% %> render blocks, however, ASP.NET will not create controls to encapsulate the HTML markup. If you want to be able to manipulate the markup as *LiteralControls*, don't use <% %> render blocks.

At the top of the control tree is the control that represents the page, which has the ID __*PAGE*. Beneath that control are any child controls that belong to the page's *Controls* collection. Each child control, depending on the type of control, can in turn have its own *Controls* collection containing child controls, and so on. This structure makes it much easier to find and manipulate controls at runtime.

Viewing the Page Control Tree

The easiest way to view the control tree for a page is to turn on tracing for the page.

View the control tree for ServerControls.aspx

1 Open ServerControls.aspx in a text editor.

2 Add the *Trace* attribute to the @ *Page* directive and set its value to *true*. The completed directive is as follows:

```
<%@ Page Language="cs" Trace="true" %>
```

3 Save the file and browse the page. The control tree section of the CompoundContainer.aspx trace output is shown in the illustration on the next page. Notice that where a control has been given an explicit ID through its *id tag* attribute, that ID is used in the control tree.

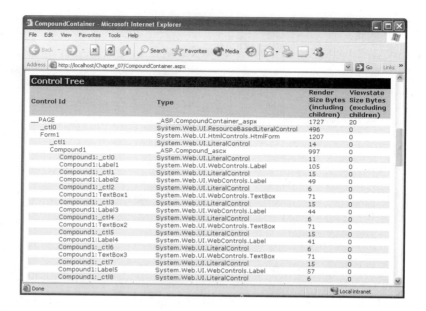

Adding and Manipulating Controls at Runtime

Thanks to the control tree built by ASP.NET at runtime, you can easily add, remove, or manipulate controls at runtime, even if you don't know the name o fa control. For example, you can use the *Add* method of the page's *Controls* collection to add a new control to the page at runtime:

```
TextBox MyTextBox = new TextBox();
Page.Controls.Add(MyTextBox);
```

If you want to place the new control at a particular position in the control tree, you can use the *AddAt* method instead:

```
TextBox MyTextBox = new TextBox();
Page.Controls.AddAt(2, MyTextBox);
```

To remove a control by name, you can use the *Remove* method:

```
Page.Controls.Remove(MyTextBox);
```

To remove a control by index, you can use *RemoveAt*:

```
Page.Controls.RemoveAt(2);
```

To locate a particular control by ID, you can use the *FindControl* method of the page or control containing the control you're looking for:

```
MyControl = Page.FindControl("MyTextBox");
```

Note that because *FindControl* returns an object of type *Control* (rather than of the specific type of control found), you will need to cast to the appropriate control type before using properties or methods that are specific to that control type.

Chapter 7 Quick Reference

To	Do this
Modify the runtime behavior of an ASP.NET Web Form	Add the @ *Page* directive to the page and set the desired attributes.
Use classes by name without explicitly specifying their namespace	In a Web Form, add the @ *Import* directive, with the namespace attribute specifying the namespace to import. In a C# .NET code-behind file, add the *using* statement with the desired namespace.
Make a user control or custom server control available for use on a Web Form	Drag and drop the user control from the Solution Explorer window onto the design surface of a Web Form.
Enable output caching	Add the @ *OutputCache* directive to the page, and set the desired attributes.
Create a user control	Right-click the project in Solution Explorer, select Add, and then select Add Web User Control. Add the desired controls to the user control, and write any code necessary, and then save the files and build the project.
Write server-side functions in a Web Forms page	Create a *<script>* block with the *runat="server"* attribute and place the functions within it.
Handle page-level events	Add an event handler with the appropriate signature (such as *Page_eventname*) to the code-behind module for the page (or the server *<script>* block for pages that do not use code-behind).

Using Server Controls

In this chapter, you will learn how to:

■ Use the two main types of server controls: HTML controls and Web controls.

■ Use specialized Web controls, such as the *Calendar* control and the *Validation* server controls.

■ Manipulate server controls programmatically at runtime.

■ Handle server control events.

Chapter 7 looked at how Web Forms pages are constructed, including some simple uses of server controls. This chapter will take an in-depth look at using server controls in your application.

Types of Controls

As discussed briefly in Chapter 7, the built-in server controls in ASP.NET are divided into two groups, HTML controls and Web controls, each of which is contained in its own namespace. In this section, I'll discuss the available controls in each group and show examples of when and how to use each type of control. I'll also discuss some of the specialized Web controls, including the *Calendar* and *AdRotator* controls, as well as the *Validation* server controls.

HTML Controls

The HTML controls map 1-to-1 with the standard HTML elements. However, some HTML elements don't map directly to a specific HTML control. Why would you want to use an HTML control instead of just coding HTML? Because you can easily manipulate the look and functionality of the page at runtime by changing the control's attributes programmatically.

The HTML controls reside in the *System.Web.UI.HtmlControls* namespace, which is available to Web Forms pages automatically. Table 8-1 describes how HTML elements map to HTML controls.

Table 8-1. Mapping of HTML Elements to HTML Controls

HTML Element	Control Type	Purpose
<a> Defines a hyper-text link.	*HtmlAnchor*	Provides programmatic access to an HTML anchor element. Exposes a *ServerClick* event.
<button> Renders an HTML button.	*HtmlButton*	Provides programmatic access to an HTML button element. This element is defined in the HTML 4.0 spec and is supported only by Microsoft Internet Explorer 4.0 and higher. Exposes a *ServerClick* event.
<form> Denotes an HTML form container.	*HtmlForm*	Provides programmatic access to an HTML form element. Acts as a container for other server controls. Any controls that need to participate in postbacks should be contained within an *HtmlForm* control.
<img> Embeds an image or video clip.	*HtmlImage*	Provides programmatic access to an HTML image element.
<input type="button"> *<input type="submit">* *<input type="reset">* Specifies a form input control.	*HtmlInputButton*	Provides programmatic access to an HTML input element for the *button*, *submit*, and *reset* input types. Exposes a *ServerClick* event.
<input type="checkbox"> Specifies a form input control.	*HtmlInputCheckBox*	Provides programmatic access to an HTML input element for the *checkbox* input type. Exposes a *Server-Change* event.
<input type="file"> Specifies a form input control.	*HtmlInputFile*	Provides programmatic access to an HTML input element for the *file* input type.
<input type="hidden"> Specifies a form input control.	*HtmlInputHidden*	Provides programmatic access to an HTML input element for the *hidden* input type. Exposes a *ServerChange* event.
<input type="image"> Specifies a form input control.	*HtmlInputImage*	Provides programmatic access to an HTML input element for the *image* input type. Exposes a *ServerClick* event.

Table 8-1. Mapping of HTML Elements to HTML Controls

HTML Element	Control Type	Purpose
<input type="radio"> Specifies a form input type.	*HtmlInputRadioButton*	Provides programmatic access to an HTML input element input control for the *radio* input type. Exposes a *ServerChange* event.
<input type="text"> *<input type= "password">* Specifies a form input control.	*HtmlInputText*	Provides programmatic access to an HTML input element for the *text* and *password* input types. Exposes a *ServerChange* event.
<select> Defines a list box or drop down list.	*HtmlSelect*	Provides programmatic access to an HTML select element. Exposes a *ServerChange* event.
<table> Denotes a section of tags organized into rows and columns.	*HtmlTable*	Provides programmatic access to an HTML table element. Note that some table subelements (such as *<col>*, *<tbody>*, *<thead>*, and *<tfoot>*) are not supported by the *HtmlTable* control.
<td> and *<th>* Denote table cells and header rows.	*HtmlTableCell*	Provides programmatic access to HTML table cell elements.
<tr> Denotes a table row.	*HtmlTableRow*	Provides programmatic access to HTML table row elements.
<textarea> Specifies a multi-line text input control.	*HtmlTextArea*	Provides programmatic access to an HTML text area element. Exposes a *ServerChange* event.
<body>, *<div>*, *<span>*, *<font>*, etc.	*HtmlGenericControl*	Provides programmatic access to any HTML element not specifically represented by its own HTML control class.

Each HTML control class is derived from the generic *HtmlControl* class. This class provides methods and properties common to all HTML controls, such as the *Attributes* collection, which provides a collection of name/value pairs for any attributes contained in the tag definition for the control (such as *id="myControl"* or *border="1"*). The individual control classes then expose additional methods and properties that are specific to the HTML element that they represent. For example, the *HtmlAnchor* control exposes an *Href* property that allows you to programmatically modify the URL to which the anchor tag is linked, as well as a *Target* property, which allows you to modify the target of the anchor tag.

> ▶ **Note** Because the HTML controls do not expose a strongly typed control equivalent for every HTML element, you can use the *Attributes* collection to programmatically add tag attributes to any HTML control. This allows you to programmatically set tag attributes that are not exposed as properties by the HTML control classes:
>
> ```
> HtmlInputText myTB = new HtmlInputText();
> myTB.Attributes("onBlur") = "javascript:alert('Lost focus!');";
> ```

Many of the HTML controls also expose events to which you can respond (above and beyond the standard events inherited from *HtmlControl*). Some HTML controls expose a *ServerClick* event and some expose a *ServerChange* event. The table starting on page 230 lists which controls support which event.

> ▶ **Note** Unlike the server controls in the Web control namespace, which handle only server-side events, HTML controls can handle both server-side events and any client-side events that exist for the HTML element to which they map. For example, the *HtmlInputButton* control supports both the server-side *ServerClick* event and the client-side *Click* event.
>
> To handle both events, you'd use the following tag declaration:
>
> ```
> <input type="submit" onclick="client_handler"
>     onserverclick="server_handler" runat="server"/>
> ```
>
> This allows you to perform actions on the client before the page is posted back to the server, if desired.

Because of their close mapping to individual HTML elements, HTML controls provide the fastest and easiest path for moving from static HTML to the power of ASP.NET server controls.

In Web Forms pages, there are three basic rules of the game when it comes to case sensitivity.

- Namespaces and class names are case sensitive. For example, namespaces imported using the @ *Import* directive will cause an error if the correct case is not used. This is a common cause of errors for those just getting started with ASP.NET.
- Tag names and attributes are not case sensitive. This also applies to server control properties expressed as tag attributes.
- Control names used in *<script>* blocks or in code-behind classes might or might not be case sensitive, depending on whether the language you're using is case sensitive. C# is case sensitive, for example, so using the incorrect case for a control name or property in C# code can lead to errors. Though Visual Basic .NET is not case-sensitive, you should still use case consistently, to ensure that your code is easy to read and maintain.

▶ **Note**   When you're working with a case-sensitive language, or when you receive errors such as "The Namespace or type *<namespace>* for the Import 'System.*<namespace>*' cannot be found," it's usually a good idea to check for incorrect case in control, class, or namespace names.

HTML Control Examples

To demonstrate the simplicity and power of HTML controls, let's take a look at some examples. Let's say you have the following static HTML page:

```
<html>
<body>
<p>This is some simple HTML text.</p>
</body>
</html>
```

By simply adding the *runat="server"* attribute and an *id* attribute to the *<body>* and *<p>* elements, you can turn these elements into *HtmlGenericControls*:

```
<html>
<body id="Body" runat="server">
<p id="TextPara" runat="server">This is some simple HTML text.</p>
</body>
</html>
```

Once you've converted the elements to HTML controls, it is fairly simple to manipulate them in server-side code:

```
<html>
<head>
<script language="cs" runat="server">
    void Page_Load(Object sender, EventArgs e)

    {

        Body.Attributes["bgcolor"] = "Gray";

        TextPara.Attributes["style"] = "color:Red;font-size:large;";

    }
</script>
</head>
<body id="Body" runat="server">
    <p id="TextPara" runat="server">This is some simple HTML text.</p>
</body>
</html>
```

If you save this code in a file with the .aspx extension to a directory set up as a virtual directory in IIS and browse the page, the output should look like the illustration on the next page.

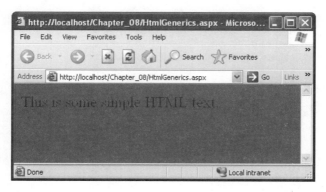

HTML controls are useful for dynamically adding and removing HTML table rows or *<select>* items. In the following example, you'll see how to dynamically add and remove items in a drop-down list created by an *HtmlSelect* control.

Add and remove list items dynamically

1   Create a new project in Visual Studio .NET. Name the project Chapter_08. (To avoid conflicting with the practice files—if they're installed—do not create this project under *http://localhost/aspnetsbs*.)

2   Add a new Web Form to the project and type its name as **HtmlSelect.aspx**.

3   Switch to HTML view and add the following HTML markup to the page between the *<form>* and *</form>* tags:

```
What's your favorite ice cream?<br/>
<select id="IceCream" size="1">
    <option>Chocolate</option>
    <option>Strawberry</option>
    <option>Vanilla</option>
</select>
<input id="Enter" type="button" value="Enter">
<h3><span id="Fave"></span></h3>
```

4   Switch back to design view. The page should look similar to the illustration on the following page.

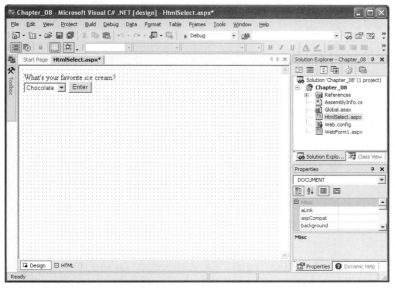

5 Right-click the drop-down list representing the *<select>* element, and select Run As Server Control. Repeat for the *button* element. Note the glyphs that Visual Studio .NET adds to these elements, indicating that they are now server controls. The glyphs are shown in the following illustration.

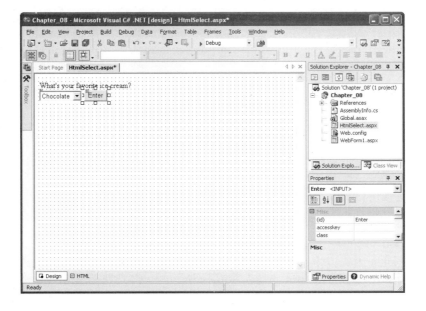

Because the *<span>* element has no representation in design view, you'll need to add the *runat="server"* attribute to this element manually.

6   Switch to HTML view, and then add the *runat="server"* attribute to the *<span>* element to transform it into a server control.

7   Switch back to design view and double-click in an open area of the page. This will open the code-behind module for the page, and place the cursor in the *Page_Load* event handler. Add the following code—which adds two items to the *HtmlSelect* control and removes one from it—to the *Page_Load* event handler:

```
if (!IsPostBack)
{
    IceCream.Items.Add("Pistachio");
    IceCream.Items.Add("Rocky Road");
    // We don't like Strawberry
    IceCream.Items.Remove("Strawberry");
}
```

8   Using the tabs at the top of the editor window, switch back to HtmlSelect.aspx. Double-click the button. This will add the *Enter_ServerClick* event handler to the code-behind module, and switch you back to the code-behind module. Add the following code to the *Enter_ServerClick* event handler:

```
Fave.InnerHtml = "Your favorite is " + IceCream.Value + "!";
```

9   Save the page and code-behind module, build the project, and then browse the page. The output should look similar to the following illustration.

10 Select Rocky Road from the drop-down list, and then press the Enter button. The output should look similar to the illustration on the following page.

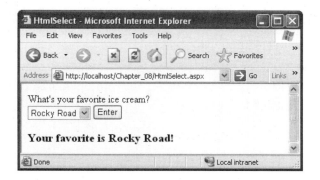

Web Controls

Web controls are truly the gem in the crown of ASP.NET. These server controls give you an unprecedented level of productivity by providing a rich, event-driven programming model, similar to that of Microsoft Visual Basic. The Web controls reside in the *System.Web.UI.WebControls* namespace, which is available to all Web Forms pages automatically.

The Web controls run the gamut of functionality, from simple controls such as the *Button*, *TextBox*, and *Label* controls, to the richer *ListBox* and *DropDownList* controls, to the even richer *Calendar* and *AdRotator* controls. There are even controls especially designed for data binding, including the *DataGrid*, *DataList*, and *Repeater* controls. You'll see examples of these controls in later sections.

▶ **Note**   Although the *System.Web.UI.WebControls* and *System.Web.UI.HtmlControls* namespaces are available to Web Forms pages automatically, the same is not true of code-behind pages associated with Web Forms pages. If you want to use controls in either of these namespaces without using the fully qualified class name, you need to add the appropriate *Using* statement to your code-behind class to import the namespace.

Adding Server Controls to a Page

As you saw in Chapter 7, adding server controls to a page is fairly easy. There are two different ways to add controls to a page, declaratively and programmatically. Either way allows you to set properties of the control as desired, and either one can be used to place a control where you want it on the page.

Adding Controls Declaratively

As you saw earlier in this chapter, the ASP.NET HTML controls use essentially the same syntax as standard HTML elements, with the exception of the *runat* attribute, which is always set to *server*. Web controls also use a tag-based syntax, but are prefaced with *asp:*. So, you'd declare an *HtmlInputButton* server control with the following syntax:

```
<input id="Enter" type="button" value="Enter"
    OnServerClick="Enter_Click" runat="server">
```

You would declare an ASP.NET Button server control with the following syntax:

```
<asp:button id="Enter" Text="Enter" OnClick="Enter_Click"
    runat="server" />
```

Notice that in the second example, a forward slash character (/) is added before the closing angle bracket (>). This is required when you do not use a complete closing tag. Here's an example of when you'd use a closing tag:

```
<asp:label id="myLabel" runat="server">Hi there!</asp:label>
```

You enclose the literal text *Hi there!* between opening and closing tags. The literal text becomes the *Text* property of the *Label* control. The *Label* control, which renders as a *<span>* on the client side, is one of a number of controls that allow you to enclose literal text for the *Text* property (or some other property of the control) between the opening and closing tags. Other controls include the *Literal*, *Panel*, *PlaceHolder*, and *TextBox* controls.

You could also accomplish the same result by using a single-tag syntax:

```
<asp:label id="myLabel" text="Hi there! " runat="server"/>
```

Choosing the Right Control

Because there are two distinct sets of server controls to choose from, you might wonder how to choose the right control for a given application. In general, if you are interested in handling client-side events or are converting HTML elements to server controls, you should look at the HTML controls. If you're familiar with the Visual Basic programming model, the Web controls map very closely to that model. The Web controls also provide additional functionality, such as validation, and provide a strong basis for customization.

When you add a control to the page declaratively, you are doing two things: giving the control enough information to be created and initialized properly, and setting the properties for the control. The first part is accomplished by the *asp:* prefix and the tag name, plus the *id* and *runat* attributes. Only the prefix/

tag name and the *runat* attribute are required to create a server control, but the *id* attribute is required if you want to refer to the control in server-side code.

Once you've provided this minimum information, you can set additional properties by adding attributes to the tag declaration corresponding to the property you want to set. For example, if you wanted to set the *Visible* property of a *Label* control to false (to set up a message declaratively and show it by making it visible later in server-side code), you would modify the declaration as follows:

```
<asp:label id="myLabel" text="Hi there! " visible="false"
   runat="server"/>
```

Some of the more feature-filled controls, such as the *DataGrid* control, use a combination of attributes in the main tag definition and subtags that declare additional controls or set properties (such as the *ItemStyle* and *AlternatingItemStyle* tags that can be used with the *DataGrid* or *DataList* controls) to define the properties for the control. You'll see examples of these controls later in this chapter.

Adding and Manipulating Controls Programmatically

Although adding controls to the page declaratively is probably the most straightforward approach, you can also add controls to the page and manipulate them programmatically. This gives you greater control because you can choose how and whether to add controls at run time.

Adding a control programmatically is as simple as declaring a new instance of the control class and adding it to the page's *Controls* collection, as follows:

```
Label myLabel = new Label();
// You can also just use Controls, but the Page reference makes it
// clear what you intend, which is always a good idea.
Page.Controls.Add(myLabel);
myLabel.Text = "Hi there! ";
```

The preceding code creates the *Label* control and sets its text property to *Hi there!*. There's just one problem. As written, the code adds the control to the end of the page's Controls collection, which is actually after the closing *<body>* and *<html>* tags, which ASP.NET treats as Literal controls on the server. The code that is sent to the browser is shown here:

```
<html>
<head>
</head>
<body>
</body>
</html>
<span>Hi there!</span>
```

While this output will still be rendered in most browsers, the incorrect HTML syntax makes it less than ideal. This presents even more of a problem when you are dealing with both declarative and programmatically created controls. Creating controls out of order can produce unintended results. So what do you do?

One option is to call the *AddAt* method of the *Controls* collection, instead of *Add*. *AddAt* takes two arguments: an integer representing the location in the collection where the control should be added, and the name of the control to add.

```
Page.Controls.AddAt(3, myLabel);
```

The only problem is that in order to render the control where you want it in the page, you have to know exactly where the control should appear in the collection. This is not always practical.

An easier way to ensure that programmatically created controls appear where you want them to is to use a *PlaceHolder* control to locate the control in the page. The *PlaceHolder* control has no UI of its own. All of the content within a *PlaceHolder* control is rendered based on the controls in its *Controls* collection. So, to make sure that the control in the previous example is displayed within the body of the HTML document sent to the browser, you can use the following code:

```
<%@ Page Language="cs" %>
<html>
<head>
<script runat="server">
   void Page_Load()

   {
      Label myLabel = new Label();
      myPH.Controls.Add(myLabel);
      myLabel.Text = "Hi there!";
   }
</script>
</head>
<body>
   <asp:placeholder id="myPH" runat="server" />
</body>
</html>
```

This produces the following HTML output:

```
<html>
<head>
</head>
<body>
   <span>Hi there!</span>
</body>
</html>
```

You can add multiple controls to the same placeholder, and you can use multiple placeholders in the same page.

Adding Controls with Visual Studio .NET

Of course, the easiest way to add ASP.NET server controls to a Web Forms page (and to discover all of the properties available for a control) is to use the Visual Studio .NET Toolbox. The Web Forms tab of the Toolbox is shown in the following illustration.

Add server controls using Visual Studio .NET

1   Open Visual Studio .NET and then open the Chapter_08 project created earlier in this chapter.

2   Add a new Web Form to the project. Type the name of the file as **DropDownList.aspx**.

3   Open the Toolbox window by moving the mouse pointer over the Toolbox tab in the IDE. If necessary, select the Web Forms tab of the Toolbox by clicking it.

    To add a control to the page, you can simply double-click the desired server control. The control will be inserted into the page at the location of the cursor if the page is in FlowLayout mode, or at the top-left corner of the page if the page is in GridLayout mode. In GridLayout mode, you can also select a control from the Toolbox and draw it on the form as you would a Visual Basic–style control. In either

FlowLayout or GridLayout mode, you can also drag and drop controls from the Toolbox onto the page at the desired location.

4   Using one of the techniques described in the previous step, add a *Label* control, a *DropDownList* control, a *Button* control, and another *Label* control to the page. Once the controls have been added, the page should look similar to the following illustration.

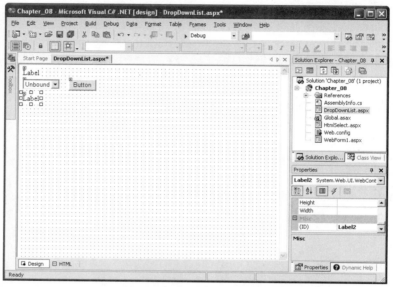

5   Set the properties of the added controls as follows, using the Properties window:

Control	Property	Value
Label1	*Text*	What's your favorite ice cream?
Button1	*Text*	Enter
Label2	*Text*	(blank)
Label2	*Font-Bold*	True
Label2	*Font-Size*	Larger

6   Select DropDownList1 by clicking it in the designer window, and then select its *Items* property in the Properties window. Click the ellipsis button (...) to open the ListItem Collection Editor and edit the *Items* property.

7   Use the Add button to add three items to the collection. Set their *Text* and *Value* properties by typing **Chocolate**, **Strawberry**, and **Vanilla**, respectively. The result should look similar to the illustration on the following page. When you are done adding items, click OK.

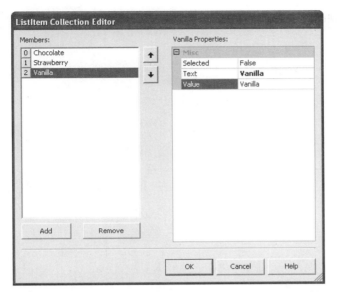

8   Double-click in an open area of the page. This will open the code-behind module for the page, and place the cursor in the *Page_Load* event handler. Add the following code, which adds two items to the *DropDownList* control and removes one, to the *Page_Load* event handler. (This code is almost identical to the code used in the HTML controls example; only the control name has been changed.)

```
if (!IsPostBack)

{

    DropDownList1.Items.Add("Pistachio");

    DropDownList1.Items.Add("Rocky Road");

    // We don't like Strawberry

    DropDownList1.Items.Remove("Strawberry");

}
```

9   Using the tabs at the top of the editor window, switch back to Drop-DownList.aspx. Double-click the button. This will add the *Button1_Click* event handler to the code-behind module, and switch you back to the code-behind module. Add the following code to the *Button1_Click* event handler:

```
Label2.Text = "Your favorite is " + _
    DropDownList1.SelectedItem.Value + "!";
```

10   Save the page and code-behind module, build the project, and then browse the page. The output should look similar to the illustration on the next page.

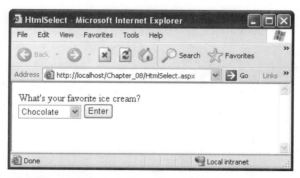

11 Select Rocky Road from the drop-down list, and then click the Enter button. The output should look similar to the following illustration.

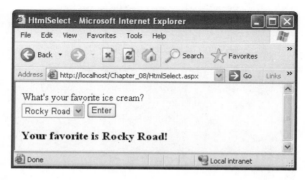

Applying Styles to Controls

Once you've added your controls to the page, eventually you'll probably want to make changes to how those controls are displayed. For example, you might want to make the text of a *Label* control red. Simply set the *ForeColor* property of the control to *Red*, as follows:

```
<asp:label id="myLabel" forecolor="red" runat="server">
   Hi there!
</asp:label>
```

What if you want to do something more complicated? While controls such as the *Label* control expose properties like *ForeColor* and *BackColor*, at times these properties will not be sufficient. Let's say you want to apply a cascading style sheet (CSS) class defined elsewhere (either in a *Style* block at the top of the page or in a linked style sheet) to a server control. Or maybe you just want to use CSS styles directly in your control tag.

For these occasions, the *CssClass* and *Style* properties defined in the *WebControl* base class (and inherited by all *WebControl* classes) come in handy. With the *CssClass* property, you can set up a CSS class such as the following:

```
<style type="text/css">
.mylabel { font-size:24pt; font-weight:bold; color:red;}
</style>
```

You can use this to format your control as follows:

```
<asp:label id="myLabel" cssclass="mylabel" runat="server">
   Hi there!
</asp:label>
```

This technique works fine for linked style sheets as well.

You can use the *Style* property to specify CSS styles directly, as follows:

```
<asp:label id="myLabel"
   style="font-size:24pt; font-weight:bold; color:red;"
   runat="server">
   Hi there!
</asp:label>
```

Note that whether you set the color of a Label control with the ForeColor property or use the CssClass or Style properties declaratively, the result is rendered as a class or style attribute on the resulting <span> tag, which is the client-side representation of the WebControl control.

▶ **Note**   Although you can set most control properties declaratively by using the property name as an attribute of the tag used to declare the control, some compound properties (properties that are represented by another class) require that you use a slightly different attribute syntax.

A good example of this is the *Font* property (defined in the *WebControl* base class), which returns an instance of the *FontInfo* class. To modify the font of a control that inherits from *WebControl* (such as the *Label* control), you use attributes in the form *font-<propertyname>*, as follows:

```
<asp:label id="myLabel" font-name="arial"
   runat="server">
```

You can also access these properties programmatically, using the form *<controlname>.Font.<propertyname>*, as follows:

```
myLabel.Font.Name = "Arial";
```

Finally, you can also apply styles to your controls based on the client-side representation of the control. As noted, *Label* controls are rendered on the client as *<span>* tags, so if you define a style that applies to all *<span>* elements, your

Label controls will also use this style. As long as you know the client-side representation of a particular control (which you can get by viewing the source of the page from the browser), you can create a style sheet to format that control.

Additional Web Control Examples

Web controls are quite easy to use and provide a great deal of flexibility. So far, you've used only simple examples. This section will look at a few more complex examples to demonstrate the use of various Web controls. The first example will show you how to use server controls to set up a form for sending e-mail from an ASP.NET Web Form via the Simple Mail Transport Protocol (SMTP). The second example will show you how to use *Panel* controls to simulate a wizard-style multipage interface within a single Web Forms page.

Sending Mail

A common task for many Web applications is sending e-mail to customers or visitors. Often, this e-mail is generated automatically, without the need for specific data entry. But site operators might also want a way to send a quick e-mail through the site. Web controls, in combination with the .NET *SmtpMail* and *MailMessage* classes, can make adding this functionality to a Web application quick and easy.

▶ **Note** This example assumes that you have access to an SMTP server from which to send your e-mail. Microsoft Windows 2000, Microsoft Windows XP Professional, and Microsoft Windows Server 2003 come with an SMTP service that is part of the services provided by IIS. The SMTP service is relatively easy to install and configure. You can find details for setting up the SMTP service at *http://msdn.microsoft.com/library/en-us/dnduwon/html/d5smtp.asp*.

Add e-mail sending functionality to a Web application

1 Open the Chapter_08 project created earlier in this chapter (if it is not already open) and add a new Web Form to the project. Type the name of the Web Form as **SmtpEmail.aspx**.

2 Use the Visual Studio .NET Table editor to add an HTML table to the page (click the Table menu, then select Insert, and then select Table) to ensure that your controls line up nicely on the page. The table should have 6 rows and 2 columns, as shown in the illustration on the following page. Click OK to insert the table.

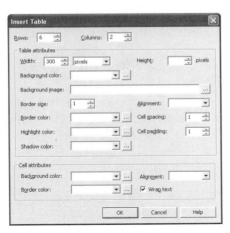

3   Add a *Label* control and a *TextBox* control to each of the first five rows of the table, as shown in the following illustration. Note that in addition to dragging controls from the toolbox to the page, you can create new controls by clicking an existing control of the desired type (such as a *Label* control) and dragging it to the new location while holding down the Ctrl key. (Click first, then press control and drag.) This technique has the advantage of creating a copy of the existing controls including its properties (with the exception of the *ID* property).

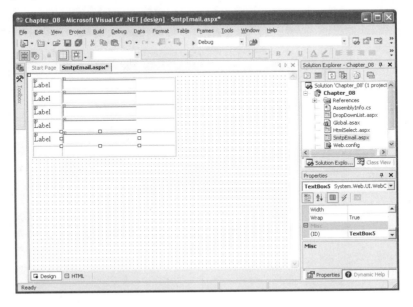

4 Add a *Button* control and an *HtmlInputButton* control with the type set to *reset* to the last row of the table. To add the HTML Reset button, you will need to switch to the HTML tab of the toolbox, drag the Reset Button to the appropriate table cell, and then right-click the Reset Button and select Run As Server Control.

Using an *HtmlInputButton* control allows you to reset the form fields on the client without a round-trip to the server, while allowing you to manipulate the control on the server side as well, as you'll do in a later step.

5 Set the properties of the added controls as follows:

Control	Property	Value
Label1	*Text*	*To:*
Label2	*Text*	*CC:*
Label3	*Text*	*BCC:*
Label4	*Text*	*Subject:*
Label5	*Text*	*Body:*
TextBox5	*TextMode*	*MultiLine*
TextBox5	*Columns*	*60*
TextBox5	*Rows*	*10*
Button1	*Text*	*Send*

When you've finished, the page should look like the following illustration.

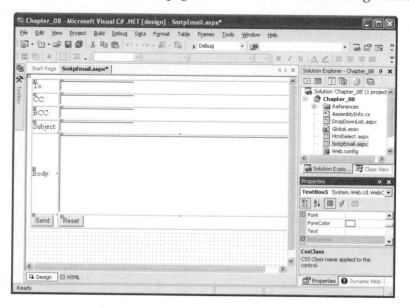

6   Switch to the code-behind module by double-clicking an empty area of the page. Add an *using* directive to import the *System.Web.Mail* namespace so you can refer to its classes without using the namespace name each time. This directive should go at the top of the code-behind module, before the class definition:

```
using System.Web.Mail;
```

7   Now you need to add code to send the mail when the Send button is clicked. Switch back to SmtpEmail.aspx, and double-click the Send button, which will open the code-behind module for the page and insert a *Click* event handler for the button, and then add the following code, which creates an instance of the *MailMessage* class, sets the necessary properties, and then sends the message using the *Send* method of the *SmtpMail* class. (Because the *Send* method is a *Static* method, it is not necessary to create an instance of *SmtpMail* to use the method.)

```
// Create MailMessage instance, set properties, and send
MailMessage Mail = new MailMessage();

Mail.To = TextBox1.Text;
Mail.Cc = TextBox2.Text;
Mail.Bcc = TextBox3.Text;
Mail.Subject = TextBox4.Text;
Mail.Body = TextBox5.Text;

// Set the property below to a valid email address
Mail.From = "feedback@aspnetsbs.com";
SmtpMail.SmtpServer = "localhost";
SmtpMail.Send(Mail);
// Use the first label to display status
Label1.Text = "Mail Sent";

// Hide the rest of the controls
TextBox1.Visible = false;
Label2.Visible = false;
TextBox2.Visible = false;
Label3.Visible = false;
TextBox3.Visible = false;
Label4.Visible = false;
TextBox4.Visible = false;
Label5.Visible = false;
TextBox5.Visible = false;
Button1.Visible = false;
Reset1.Visible = false;
```

8

Using Server Controls

```
// Add a Hyperlink control to allow sending another email
HyperLink Link = new HyperLink();
Link.Text = "Click here to send another email.";
Link.NavigateUrl = "SmtpEmail.aspx";

// This line is only necessary if the page is in GridLayout mode
Link.Attributes["Style"] = "LEFT: 8px; POSITION: absolute; TOP: 50px";
Page.Controls.Add(Link);
```

Once the mail has been sent, the code hides all of the form controls by setting the *Visible* property for each control to *false* and adds a *HyperLink* control to link back to the original page to send another e-mail, if desired. Note that you need to set *Mail.From* to a valid e-mail address and change *SmtpMail.SmtpServer* to the name of an available server running SMTP if the local machine is not running an SMTP service.

8   Save the page and code-behind module, and then build the project. Browse the page by right-clicking SmtpEmail.aspx in Solution Explorer, selecting Browse With, and then selecting Internet Explorer. The output should look something like the following illustration. Once you've sent e-mail, the link should take you back to the original page.

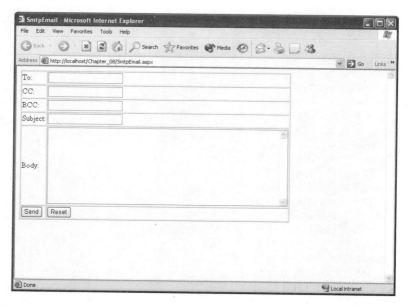

This example shows how simple it can be to send e-mail using server controls on a Web Form, but it does have a couple of shortcomings. One is that if you don't enter an address in the To, CC, or BCC field, you'll get an error. Another is that it takes a fair amount of code to hide all the controls once you've sent the e-mail. You can fix this second shortcoming by adding another *Label* control outside the table, and then turning the table into an *HtmlTable* control by adding the *runat="server"* attribute. You can then hide all of the controls in the table by setting the *Visible* property of *HtmlTable* to *false*.

Registration Wizard

Another common need in Web applications is providing users with an easy way to register. Registration allows you to provide your visitors with personalized services, saved shopping carts, and other valuable assistance. To make registration as simple as possible, you might want to use a multipage format similar to a Windows Wizard interface. This type of interface will be immediately familiar to Windows users. The following listing shows the code for a simple registration wizard implemented as an ASP.NET Web Form. This listing also shows how you can use a single-page structure for controls and code, as opposed to the code-behind structure of Visual Studio .NET. Unlike Web Forms created in Visual Studio .NET, the code in the following listing does not need to be precompiled. However, since the code is included in the page (which must be deployed to the Web server on which it will run), anyone with file access to the Web server can read the code (assuming they have the correct permissions). By contrast, using code-behind modules allows you to deploy just the .aspx files and compiled assembly (or assemblies) without deploying the code-behind modules that contain the UI-related code.

RegWiz.aspx

```
<%@ Page Language="cs" %>
<html>
<head>
<script runat="server">
   void Page_Load()
   {
      if (!IsPostBack)
      {
         Step1.Font.Bold = true;
      }
   }
   private void Next_Click(object sender, System.EventArgs e)
   {
      switch (((Button)sender).Parent.ID)
      {
         case "Page1":
```

```
                    Page1.Visible = false;
                    Step1.Font.Bold = false;
                    Page2.Visible = true;
                    Step2.Font.Bold = true;
                    break;
                case "Page2":
                    Page2.Visible = false;
                    Step2.Font.Bold = false;
                    Page3.Visible = true;
                    Step3.Font.Bold = true;
                    ReviewFName.Text   = "First Name: " + FirstName.Text;
                    ReviewMName.Text   = "Middle Name: " + MiddleName.Text;
                    ReviewLName.Text   = "Last Name: " + LastName.Text;
                    ReviewEmail.Text   = "Email: " + Email.Text;
                    ReviewAddress.Text = "Address: " + Address.Text;
                    ReviewCity.Text    = "City: " + City.Text;
                    ReviewState.Text   = "State: " + State.Text;
                    ReviewZip.Text     = "Zip: " + Zip.Text;
                    break;
            }
        }
        private void Previous_Click(object sender, System.EventArgs e)
        {
            switch (((Button)sender).Parent.ID)
            {
                case "Page2":
                    Page2.Visible = false;
                    Step2.Font.Bold = false;
                    Page1.Visible = true;
                    Step1.Font.Bold = true;
                    break;
                case "Page3":
                    Page3.Visible = false;
                    Step3.Font.Bold = false;
                    Page2.Visible = true;
                    Step2.Font.Bold = true;
                    break;
            }
        }
    </script>
    <style type="text/css">
    div
    {
        background:silver;
        width:400px;
        border:2px outset;
        margin:5px;
        padding:5px;
    }
    </style>
</head>
```

```
<body>
    <form runat="server">
        <asp:label id="RegWiz" text="Registration Wizard"
            font-bold="true" font-size="16" font-name="verdana"
            runat="server"/>
        <br/>
        <asp:label id="Step1" text="Step 1: Enter Personal Info"
            font-name="verdana" runat="server"/>
        <br/>
        <asp:label id="Step2" text="Step 2: Enter Address Info"
            font-name="verdana" runat="server"/>
        <br/>
        <asp:label id="Step3" text="Step 3: Review"
            font-name="verdana"
            runat="server"/>
        <br/>
        <asp:panel id="Page1" runat="server">
            <table align="center">
                <tr>

                    <td>
                        <asp:label id="FirstNameLabel" text="First Name:"
                            runat="server"/>
                    </td>
                    <td>
                        <asp:textbox id="FirstName" runat="server"/>
                    </td>
                </tr>
                <tr>
                    <td>
                        <asp:label id="MiddleNameLabel" text="Middle Name:"
                            runat="server"/>
                    </td>
                    <td>
                        <asp:textbox id="MiddleName" runat="server"/>
                    </td>
                </tr>
                <tr>
                    <td>
                        <asp:label id="LastNameLabel" text="Last Name:"
                            runat="server"/>
                    </td>
                    <td>
                        <asp:textbox id="LastName" runat="server"/>
                    </td>
                </tr>
                <tr>
                    <td>
                        <asp:label id="EmailLabel" text="Email:"
```

```
                    runat="server"/>
                </td>
                <td>
                   <asp:textbox id="Email" runat="server"/>
                </td>
            </tr>
            <tr>
                <td colspan="2" align="center">
                   <asp:button id="P1Previous" Text="Previous"
                      enabled="false" onclick="Previous_Click"

                      runat="server"/>
                   <asp:button id="P1Next" Text="Next"
                      onclick="Next_Click" runat="server"/>
                   <input id="P1Reset" type="reset" runat="server"/>
                </td>
            </tr>
        </table>
</asp:panel>
<asp:panel id="Page2" visible="false" runat="server">
    <table align="center">
        <tr>
            <td>
               <asp:label id="AddressLabel" text="Street Address:"
                   runat="server"/>
            </td>
            <td>
                <asp:textbox id="Address" runat="server"/>
            </td>
        </tr>
        <tr>
            <td>
               <asp:label id="CityLabel" text="City:"
                   runat="server"/>
            </td>
            <td>
               <asp:textbox id="City" runat="server"/>
            </td>
        </tr>
        <tr>
            <td>
               <asp:label id="StateLabel" text="State:"
                   runat="server"/>
            </td>
            <td>
               <asp:textbox id="State" runat="server"/>
            </td>
        </tr>
        <tr>
```

```
        <td>
            <asp:label id="ZipLabel" text="Zip Code:"
                runat="server"/>
        </td>
        <td>
            <asp:textbox id="Zip" runat="server"/>
        </td>
    </tr>
    <tr>
        <td colspan="2" align="center">
            <asp:button id="P2Previous" Text="Previous"
                onclick="Previous_Click" runat="server"/>
            <asp:button id="P2Next" Text="Next"
                onclick="Next_Click" runat="server"/>
            <input id="P2Reset" type="reset" runat="server"/>
        </td>
    </tr>
    </table>
</asp:panel>
<asp:panel id="Page3" visible="false" runat="server">
    <table align="center">
        <tr>
            <td colspan="2">
                <asp:label id="ReviewFName" runat="server"/>
            </td>
        </tr>
        <tr>
            <td colspan="2">
                <asp:label id="ReviewMName" runat="server"/>
            </td>
        </tr>
        <tr>
            <td colspan="2">
                <asp:label id="ReviewLName" runat="server"/>
            </td>
        </tr>

        <tr>
            <td colspan="2">
                <asp:label id="ReviewEmail" runat="server"/>
            </td>
        </tr>
        <tr>
            <td colspan="2">
                <asp:label id="ReviewAddress" runat="server"/>
            </td>
        </tr>
        <tr>
```

```
                    <td colspan="2">
                        <asp:label id="ReviewCity" runat="server"/>
                    </td>
                </tr>
                <tr>
                    <td colspan="2">
                        <asp:label id="ReviewState" runat="server"/>
                    </td>
                </tr>
                <tr>
                    <td colspan="2">
                        <asp:label id="ReviewZip" runat="server"/>
                    </td>
                </tr>
                <tr>
                    <td colspan="2">
                        <asp:button id="P3Previous" Text="Previous"
                            onclick="Previous_Click" runat="server"/>
                        <asp:button id="P3Next" Text="Next" enabled="false"
                            onclick="Next_Click" runat="server"/>
                        <input id="P3Reset" type="reset" disabled="true"
                            runat="server"/>
                    </td>
                    </td>
                </tr>
            </table>
        </asp:panel>
    </form>
</body>
</html>
```

The keys to the functionality of the registration wizard are the three *Panel* controls and the *Next_Click* and *Previous_Click* event handlers. The *Panel* controls contain *Label*, *TextBox*, and *Button* Web controls (as well as an *HtmlInputButton* control for resetting the form fields), which are formatted using standard HTML table elements. When the user clicks the Next button or the Previous button (depending on which one is enabled for that page), the event handlers hide the currently visible panel, show the next (or previous) panel, and update the *Label* controls that tell the user which step in the process they are on currently.

Since ASP.NET takes care of maintaining the state of the controls from request to request (using ViewState), it is simple to display the data entered by the user on the third panel by simply accessing the *Text* property of the *TextBox* controls on the other panels. Notice that the caption text of the controls on the third panel is set declaratively in the tag, and then the text that the user entered is appended to this text programmatically in the event handler using the & operator. The first page of the registration wizard is shown in the illustration on the following page.

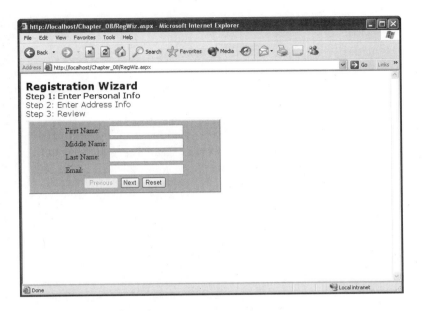

> ▶ **Note**   The *<style>* block defined in RegWiz.aspx takes care of formatting for
> the *Panel* controls by defining the desired style for the *<div>* HTML element.
> Note that since the *Panel* control is rendered as a *<div>* on Internet Explorer
> and as a *<table>* element on Netscape and other non–Internet Explorer brows-
> ers, you might need to find another way to do the formatting if you want cross-
> browser compatibility.
>
> One way to accomplish this is through browser sniffing. The *Request* object
> exposed by the *Page* class has a *Browser* property that provides information on
> the browser making the current request. By querying the *Browser* property (and
> its subproperties), you can perform a simple *if* statement that links to one style
> sheet if the browser is Internet Explorer and to another style sheet if it is
> another browser.

Specialty Controls

In addition to the standard suite of Web controls that provide functionality
much like that provided by the Visual Basic GUI controls, ASP.NET offers a
set of richer specialty controls that reside in the *System. Web. UI. WebControls*
namespace. Currently these controls include the *AdRotator*, *Calendar*, and *Xml*
controls. In this section I'll describe the purposes of these controls and show
some examples.

AdRotator

The *AdRotator* control is used to display a random selection from a collection
of banner advertisements specified in an XML-based advertisement file. The

advertisement file contains an *<Ad>* element for each specified advertisement. This element contains sub-elements that configure the path to the image to display for the ad, the URL to navigate to when the ad is clicked, the text to be displayed when and if the image is not available, the percentage of time the ad should come up in rotation, and any keyword associated with the ad. (You can use keywords to filter ads, allowing the use of a single advertisement file with multiple *AdRotator* controls and providing each control with different content.)

▶   **Note**   The random selection for the *AdRotator* control will be identical for any *AdRotator controls* on the page that have identical attributes. You can take advantage of this by using the *AdRotator* control to display a random selection of header/footer information that you want to be the same for both header and footer.

Use the *AdRotator* control from a Web Form

1   Open the Chapter_08 project that you created earlier in this chapter (if it is not already open) and then add a new Web Form to the project. Type the name of the Web Form as **AdRotator.aspx**.

2   Change the *pageLayout* property from GridLayout to FlowLayout.

3   Switch to HTML view, then add three *Label* controls and two *AdRotator* controls between the *<form>* tags, with the attributes shown in the following code, and then save AdRotator.aspx:

```
<asp:label id="title" font-name="Verdana" font-size="18"
    text="AdRotator Example" runat="server"/>
<br/><br/>
<asp:label id="DevLabel" font-name="Verdana" font-size="16"
    text="Ad 1" runat="server"/>
<br/>
<asp:AdRotator id="AdRotDev" target="_blank" runat="server"
    advertisementfile="Ads.xml" keywordfilter="Developers"/>
<br/><br/>
<asp:label id="UserLabel" font-name="Verdana" font-size="16"
    text="Ad 2" runat="server"/>
<br/>
<asp:AdRotator id="AdRotUsr" target="_blank" runat="server"
    advertisementfile="Ads.xml" keywordfilter="Users"/>
```

4   Create a new XML file by right-clicking the Chapter_08 project in Solution Explorer, selecting Add, then Add New Item, and then choosing XML File as shown in the illustration on the following page. Type the name of the file as **Ads.xml**.

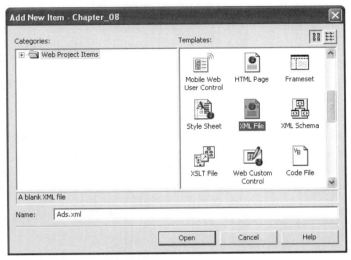

5 Add the following XML to the file, and then save Ads.xml:

```xml
<Advertisements>
    <Ad>
        <ImageUrl>images/image1.gif</ImageUrl>
        <NavigateUrl>http://www.microsoft.com</NavigateUrl>
        <AlternateText>Microsoft Main Site</AlternateText>
        <Impressions>60</Impressions>
        <Keyword>Users</Keyword>
    </Ad>
    <Ad>
        <ImageUrl>images/image2.gif</ImageUrl>
        <NavigateUrl>http://msdn.microsoft.com/net</NavigateUrl>


        <AlternateText>Microsoft .NET on MSDN</AlternateText>
        <Impressions>80</Impressions>
        <Keyword>Developers</Keyword>
    </Ad>
    <Ad>
        <ImageUrl>images/image3.gif</ImageUrl>
        <NavigateUrl>http://www.microsoft.com</NavigateUrl>
        <AlternateText>Microsoft Main Site</AlternateText>
        <Impressions>40</Impressions>
        <Keyword>Users</Keyword>
    </Ad>
    <Ad>
        <ImageUrl>images/image4.gif</ImageUrl>
        <NavigateUrl>http://msdn.microsoft.com/net</NavigateUrl>
```

```
            <AlternateText>Microsoft .NET on MSDN</AlternateText>
            <Impressions>20</Impressions>
            <Keyword>Developers</Keyword>
        </Ad>
    </Advertisements>
```

6 Create a new folder in the project, typing its name as **images**. Copy the images contained in the images directory of the practice files for Chapter 8 to this new folder.

7 Save and build the project, and then browse AdRotator.aspx. The output should look similar to the following illustration. When you refresh the page, you should see the ads change randomly, based on the weightings set in the XML file.

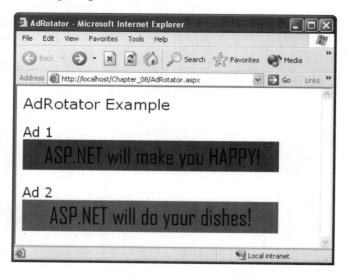

Calendar

The *Calendar* control is one of the richest and most flexible of the specialized controls, providing nearly 30 properties for controlling the appearance of the calendar. The *Calendar* control allows you to provide a calendar-based interface for choosing dates or for viewing date-related data.

For example, you could query date data for a series of events or appointments and then use a *Calendar* control to display them by adding the dates to the calendar's *SelectedDates* collection. When a user clicks on a selected date on the calendar, you could then display additional information about the event on that date.

You could also allow users to specify one or more dates for data entry by providing a *Calendar* control for them to click. The *Calendar* control supports selection of both single dates and date ranges (by week or month). Using a *Calendar* control instead of a text box for date entry can help prevent errors in converting the date entered by the user into a *Date* data type for storage or manipulation.

Create a Web Forms page that uses a *Calendar* control

1   Open the Chapter_08 project created earlier in this chapter if it is not already open. Add a new Web Form to the project and type its name as **Calendar.aspx**.

2   Change the *pageLayout* property from GridLayout to FlowLayout.

3   Switch to HTML view, and use the following code to add three *Label* controls, two *RadioButton* controls, two *Textbox* controls, and a *Calendar* control between the *<form>* tags. Note that the *Group-Name* property is used to make the radio buttons mutually exclusive.

```
<asp:label id="title" text="Calendar Example"
    font-name="Verdana" font-size="18" runat="server"/>
<br/>
<asp:calendar id="Calendar1" runat="server"/>
<br/>
<asp:radiobutton id="StartRadio" text="Start Date"
    groupname="Chooser" runat="server"/>
<asp:radiobutton id="EndRadio" text="End Date"
    groupname="Chooser" runat="server"/>


<br/>
<asp:label id="StartDateLabel" text="Start Date" runat="server"/>
<asp:textbox id="StartDate" runat="server"/>
<br/>
<asp:label id="EndDateLabel" text="End Date" runat="server"/>
<asp:textbox id="EndDate" runat="server"/>
```

4   Save the page, then build the project, and then browse the page. The output should look similar to the illustration on the next page.

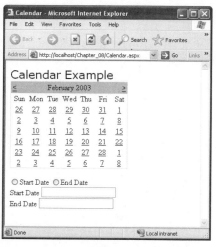

5   Now you need to relate clicking on a date on the calendar to setting the text in the text boxes. Switch back to design view, and then double-click the *Calendar* control. This will switch to the code-behind module for Calendar.aspx and will add the *Calendar1_SelectionChanged* event handler. Add the following code to the event handler:

```
if (StartRadio.Checked)
{
    StartDate.Text = Calendar1.SelectedDate.ToShortDateString();
}
else // EndRadio must be checked
{
    EndDate.Text = Calendar1.SelectedDate.ToShortDateString();
}
```

6   Add the following code to the *Page_Load* event handler in the code-behind module to take care of initializing the controls:

```
if (!IsPostBack)
{
    StartRadio.Checked = true;
    Calendar1.SelectedDate = DateTime.Now;
    StartDate.Text = Calendar1.SelectedDate.ToShortDateString();
    Calendar1.TodaysDate = Calendar1.SelectedDate;
}
```

7   Save the page and code-behind module, and then build the project and browse Calendar.aspx. At this point, you should be able to use the calendar to set the value of both text boxes. Which text box is set depends on which radio button is checked.

8   At this point the calendar is fairly plain, so let's use some of the available properties to liven it up a bit. Switch back to Calendar.aspx and

modify the *<asp:calendar>* tag to match the following code. Notice that you need to add a closing *</asp:calendar>* tag so that you can use the child *<titlestyle>* tag to set attributes of the calendar's *Title-Style* property.

```
<asp:calendar id="Calendar1"
    backcolor="lightgray"
    borderstyle="groove"
    borderwidth="5"
    bordercolor="blue"
    runat="server">
    <titlestyle backcolor="blue" forecolor="silver"
        font-bold="true"/>
</asp:calendar>
```

9   Save and browse the page again. (Because you only changed the .aspx file, you don't need to rebuild the project.) The output should look similar to the following illustration.

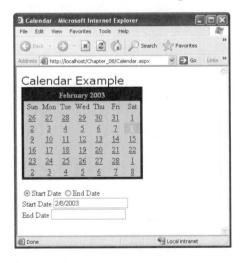

Xml

The *Xml* control is a specialty control that lets you display XML code in Web Forms pages. This is important because raw XML within an ASP.NET Web Form will not be displayed predictably. The *Xml* control can read XML from a string, from a provided URL, or from an object of type *System.Xml.XmlDocument*.

In addition to simply displaying XML from a given source, the *Xml* control can apply an XSL *Transform* document to the XML to perform formatting on the document. The XSL Transform can come from a URL, or it can be provided by an object of type *System.Xml.Xsl.XslTransform*. The files Xml.aspx and Xml.xslt, included with the practice files for this chapter, show how you can use the *Xml* control to display the contents of the Ads.xml document in an HTML table.

Validation Controls

Another specialized set of controls that reside in the *System.Web.UI.WebControls* namespace are the *Validation* controls, which perform various kinds of validation on other controls. You can use *Validation* controls to do the following:

- Ensure that required fields are filled out
- Ensure that data entered by the user falls within a given range
- Ensure that data entered by the user matches a specific pattern
- Compare the values of two controls for a given condition (equality, greater than, and so on) or compare the value of a control to a specified value
- Ensure that all controls on a page are valid before submitting the page

Shared Members

All *Validation* controls share a number of important properties and methods. These properties and methods are inherited from the *BaseValidator* class and include the following:

- *ControlToValidate*   This property sets or retrieves a value of type *String* that specifies the input control to validate.
- *Display*   This property sets or retrieves a value that determines how the error message for a *Validation* control will be displayed. The value must be one of the values specified by the *ValidatorDisplay* enumeration. The default is *Static*.
- *EnableClientScript*   This property sets or retrieves a Boolean value that determines whether client-side validation will be performed. Server-side validation is always performed with the Validation controls, regardless of this setting. The default is true.
- *Enabled*   This property sets or retrieves a Boolean value that determines whether the control is enabled. The default is *true*.
- *ErrorMessage*   This property sets or retrieves a value of type *String* that specifies the error message to be displayed if the input from the user is not valid.
- *ForeColor*   This property sets or retrieves a value of type *Color* that represents the color of the error message specified in the *ErrorMessage* property. The default is *Color.Red*.
- *IsValid*   This property sets or retrieves a Boolean value that signifies whether the control specified by the *ControlToValidate* property passes validation.

- *Validate*   This method causes the control on which it is called to perform validation, and it updates the *IsValid* property with the result.

Table 8-2 lists the *Validation* controls available in ASP.NET.

Table 8-2. Validation Controls

Control Type	Purpose	Important Members
CompareValidator	Performs validation of a user-entered field with either a constant or another user-entered field. The *ControlToCompare* and *ValueToCompare* properties are mutually exclusive. If both are set, the *ControlToCompare* property takes precedence.	*ControlToCompare* This property sets or retrieves a value of type *String* containing the name of the control whose value will be compared to the value of the control specified by the *ControlToValidate* property. *Operator* This property sets or retrieves a value that represents the type of comparison to be performed. The value must be one of the values specified by the *ValidationCompareOperator* enumeration. The default is *Equal*. *ValueToCompare* This property sets or retrieves a value of type *String* containing a constant value to which the value of the control specified by the *ControlToValidate* property will be compared.
CustomValidator	Performs customized validation based on developer-specified logic.	*ServerValidate* This event is raised when server-side validation is to be performed. Map the *OnServerValidate* method in the *Validation* control tag to the desired server-side event handler to perform custom validation. *ClientValidationFunction* This property sets or retrieves a value of type *String* containing the name of a client-side function with which to perform client-side validation, if desired.
RangeValidator	Performs validation of a user-entered field to ensure that the value entered is within a specified range.	*MaximumValue* This property sets or retrieves a value of type *String* containing the maximum value of the range to validate against. *MinimumValue* This property sets or retrieves a value of type *String* containing the minimum value of the range to validate against.

Table 8-2.   Validation Controls

Control Type	Purpose	Important Members
RegularExpressionValidator	Performs validation of a user-entered field to ensure that the value entered matches a specified pattern.	*ValidationExpression* This property sets or retrieves a value of type *String* containing the regular expression to validate against.
RequiredFieldValidator	Performs validation of a user-entered field to ensure that a value is entered for the specified field.	*InitialValue* This property sets or retrieves a value of type *String* containing the initial value of the control to validate against. The default is an empty string. If this property is set to a string value, validation will fail for the control only if the user-entered value matches the value of this property.
ValidationSummary	Provides a summary of validation errors in a given Web Form, either in the Web Form page, a message box, or both.	*DisplayMode* This property sets or retrieves a value that determines the way the control will be displayed. The value must be one of the values specified by the *ValidationSummaryDisplayMode* enumeration. The default is *BulletList*. *HeaderText* This property sets or retrieves a value of type *String* containing the header text to be displayed for the validation summary. *ShowMessageBox* This property sets or retrieves a Boolean value that determines whether the validation summary is displayed in a client-side message box. The default is *false*. This property has no effect if the *EnableClientScript* property is set to *false*. *ShowSummary* This property sets or retrieves a Boolean value that determines whether the validation summary is displayed in the Web Form page. The default is *true*.

Validating Required Fields

To see how the *Validation* controls operate, let's return to one of the earlier examples, the Web Form named SmtpEmail.aspx. One of the problems that you had with the page was that if it was submitted without a To, CC, or BCC address, it would throw an exception. You can prevent this problem by requiring at least one To address.

Require data entry with the *RequiredFieldValidator* control

1   Open the file SmtpEmail.aspx created earlier in this chapter.

2   Add a *RequiredFieldValidator control* to the same table cell as the *TextBox1* textbox control and set its properties as follows:

Control	Property	Value
RequiredFieldValidator1	ControlToValidate	TextBox1
RequiredFieldValidator1	Display	Dynamic
RequiredFieldValidator1	ErrorMessage	Required!

3   Save the page and browse it with Internet Explorer using the Browse With option. (Again, since you have changed only the .aspx file, the project does not need to be rebuilt.) If you do not enter a To address, the output will look something like the following illustration, and you will not be able to submit the page.

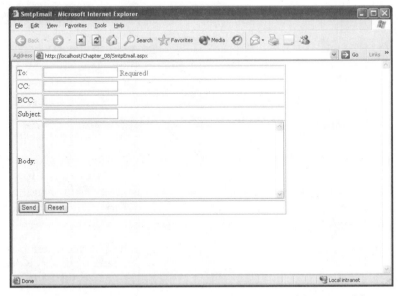

One problem with this setup is that once you add a To address and submit the page, you might get a JavaScript error. This is because the newly added *Validation* control is looking for the text box on the client, but since you hid the control in the event handler by setting its

Visible property to *false*, the control no longer exists on the client. You can solve this by modifying how you hide the elements on the page, as you'll see in the steps that complete this example.

4   Add a new *Label* control for your status message. (In the original page, the first label in the table was used for this purpose.) This control should go just before the HTML *<table>* element.

```
<asp:label id="Status" text="" runat="server"/>
```

5   Turn the HTML *<table>* element into an *HtmlTable* control by adding an *id* attribute (if necessary, otherwise, just modify the *id* attribute to match the code snippet that follows) and then switch to design view, right-click the table border, and select Run As Server Control:

```
<table id="MailTable" runat="server">
```

6   Switch to code view and take out the line of code in the *Button1_Click* event handler that sets the status message and replace it with the following code:

```
// Use the first label to display status
Status.Text = "Mail Sent";
```

7   Replace the lines of code in the *Button1_Click* event handler that set the *Visible* property of the controls to *false* with the following lines:

```
// Hide the table
MailTable.Visible = false;
```

8   Save the page, browse it, and submit an e-mail. You should no longer get the JavaScript error (and your code's a lot cleaner to boot).

In addition to using the *RequiredFieldValidator* to ensure that an e-mail address is entered, you could add a *RegularExpressionValidator* to each of the address-fields to ensure that the data entered by the user matches the pattern for a valid e-mail address. This prevents delivery errors that are due to malformed e-mail addresses and helps prevent the mail server's resources from being wasted attempting to deliver such mail. A good place to find regular expressions for use with the RegularExpressionValidator control is *http://www.regexlib.com/*.

Validating by Comparison

Another one of the previous examples with the potential for trouble is the *Calendar* control example. As coded in the example, the *Calendar* control can be used to set a start date that is later than the end date. Clearly, if you're storing these dates or using them to drive some programmatic logic, this is not something you want to allow. Fortunately, the *CompareValidator* control can help prevent this problem, as illustrated by the following example.

Use the *CompareValidator* control

1   Open the file Calendar.aspx created earlier in this chapter.

2   Add a *CompareValidator* control below the *EndDate TextBox* control and set its properties as follows:

Control	Property	Value
CompareValidator1	*ControlToValidate*	*StartDate*
CompareValidator1	*ControlToCompare*	*EndDate*
CompareValidator1	*Type*	*Date*
CompareValidator1	*Operator*	*LessThan*
CompareValidator1	*Display*	*Dynamic*
CompareValidator1	*ErrorMessage*	*Start Date must be before End Date!*

3   Right-click an empty area of the page and select View Code to switch to the code-behind module, and then add a line of code to the *Calendar1_SelectionChanged* event handler to cause the *Validation* control to validate each time the event handler is fired. The *Page.Validate* call should go just before the closing curly brace of the *Calendar1_SelectionChanged* function:

```
Page.Validate();
```

4   Save the file and code-behind module, and then rebuild the project. Browse the page and set the end date to a date earlier than the start date. The validation error message will appear, as shown in the following illustration. Additionally, the *IsValid* property of the page will be set to *false*. You can test this property before saving the date values to ensure that they are valid.

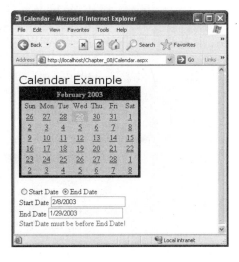

Validation controls can also improve the security of your application. For example, you can use the *RegularExpressionValidator* control to ensure that passwords entered by users (such as when establishing account information) meet minimum length and complexity requirements. This can make it more difficult for the bad guys to crack your application.

Data-Bound Controls

One of the most significant advances in ASP.NET is in the area of data binding. The *System.Web.UI.WebControls* namespace contains a set of data-bound controls that offer substantial functionality and flexibility, without the necessity of tying front-end UI logic into back-end database logic, as was the case with the data-bound Design-Time Controls available in classic ASP through the Microsoft Visual InterDev 6.0 development environment. The data-bound controls also allow you to provide data binding regardless of the browser that your clients are using. This is because the controls run on the server and return plain HTML to the client, unlike some of the data-binding techniques that were possible with Internet Explorer versions 4.0 and later.

Another major improvement is that the data-bound controls can use a variety of sources, not just data from a database. Data-bound controls in ASP.NET can be bound to data from an array, an ADO.NET DataSet, a DataView, or any data source that implements the ICollection or IList interfaces. The data-bound controls include the *DataGrid*, *DataList*, and *Repeater* controls. In Chapter 9 you'll learn more about these controls.

ASP.NET Mobile Web Applications and Controls

Starting with version 1.1 of the Microsoft Windows .NET Framework, a new set of controls (formerly available as a separate download) have been added to facilitate developing Web applications for mobile devices such as cell phones and Personal Digital Assistants (PDAs). In addition to the new controls, a new project type, the ASP.NET Mobile Web Application project, has been added to Microsoft Visual Studio .NET 2003 to make it easy to take advantage of these controls.

ASP.NET Mobile Controls

The controls available for developing mobile Web applications using ASP.NET include many that you're already familiar with, plus a few new controls that have functionality geared towards smaller devices.

The Mobile Web Forms control toolbox pane, shown in the following illustration, contains the controls you'll want to use in your ASP.NET mobile Web application development. The toolbox contains familiar controls, such as the Panel, Label, and TextBox controls, as well as some new ones that we'll discuss next. In addition to the new controls, some of the existing controls have added functionality specific to mobile development, such as the ability to have more than one form per mobile Web Form page, and the ability to render differently depending on the device accessing the application.

The new controls included specifically for mobile include the following:

- **Form**   The *Form* control acts as a container for other mobile controls. You can have multiple forms on a mobile Web Forms page, but forms cannot be nested. Use the *Panel* control for nesting content or controls.

- **TextView**   Similar to a *Label* control, the *TextView* control is used to display larger amounts of text, and supports markup tags within the text content.

- **Command**   The *Command* control is the mobile equivalent of a *Button* control, and it renders a device-appropriate UI element to allow posting back of a mobile Web Forms page.

- **Link**   The *Link* control, which is similar to the ASP.NET *Hyperlink* control, provides a link to another *Form* control on the page, or to a URL.

- *List*   The *List* control is a control that renders a list of items and may be databound.

- *SelectionList*   The *SelectionList* control is similar to the *List* control but provides the ability to select one or more items from the list.

- *ObjectList*   The *ObjectList* control displays multiple fields per item in a given list of objects. This control may be databound to a *DataSet* or *DataView*, as well as to collections or arrays.

- *DeviceSpecific*   The *DeviceSpecific* control provides a means of specifying multiple content alternatives. The content displayed is dependent on the device profiles specified within the *DeviceSpecific* control.

To see how the ASP.NET mobile controls work, let's re-create the "Favorite Ice Cream" page using the mobile controls.

Create a Mobile Web Forms Page

1   Create a new project in Visual Studio .NET, using the ASP.NET Mobile Web Application template, as shown in the following illustration. Type the name of the project as **Chapter_08_Mobile**.

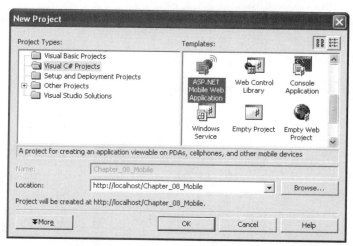

When the project is created, the default page, MobileWebForm1.aspx, will be opened in the Visual Studio editor. The page will contain one *Form* control, as shown in the illustration on the following page.

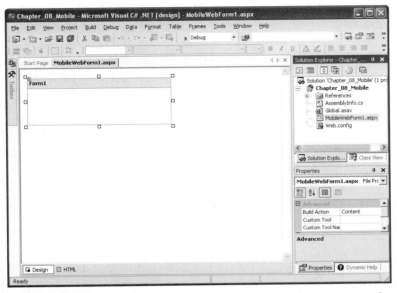

2   Add a *Label* control, a *SelectionList* control, and a *Command* con-
    trol (in that order) to the existing form.

3   Set the *Text* property of the *Label* control to **What's your favorite ice
    cream?**, and the *Text* property of the *Command* control to **Enter**.
    When finished, the form should look like the following illustration.

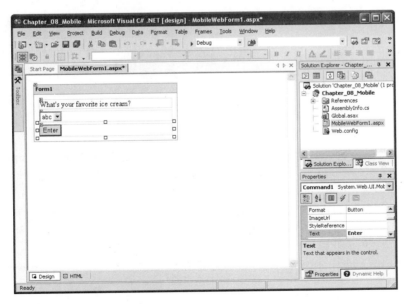

4   Select the *SelectList* control, then scroll down in the Properties window to find its *Items* property and highlight it. Click the ellipsis button to open the Properties dialog box for the control. Using the Create New Item button, create three items, and set the text and value of each by typing **Chocolate**, **Strawberry**, and **Vanilla**, respectively. When finished, the dialog box should look like the following illustration. Click OK to close the dialog box.

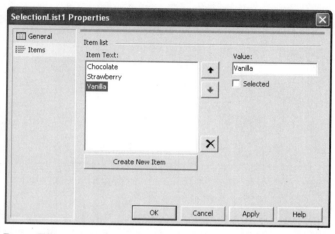

5   Press F7 to switch to the code-behind module for the page. Add the following code to the *Page_Load* event handler:

```
if (!IsPostBack)
{
    SelectionList1.Items.Add("Pistachio");
    SelectionList1.Items.Add("Rocky Road");
    // We don't like Strawberry
    SelectionList1.Items.Remove("Strawberry");
}
```

6   Switch back to MobileWebForm1.aspx, and double-click the *Command* control. This will add the *Command1_Click* event handler to the code-behind module. Add the following code to the event handler:

```
Label1.Text = "Your favorite is " + _
    SelectionList1.Selection.Text + "!";
```

7   Save the open files and build the project.

You can test your work using the standard built-in browser, but that's not terribly useful in telling you how it will look on a cell phone or PDA. A better bet is to use either the actual device you're developing for, or an emulator for that device. Emulators are often available from the manufacturer of the device you're developing for. The following illustration shows the initial output of the previous example on the PocketPC 2002 Emulator.

If you selected Rocky Road from the list box, and then press Enter, the output would look like the following illustration.

The following screen shots show how the same Mobile Web Form would appear on a mobile phone (or, in this case, the OpenWave phone emulator, available at *http://www/openwave.com/*). The illustration below shows the initial output.

Image courtesy of Openwave Systems Inc.

If you selected Rocky Road from the list, the output would look like the following illustration.

Image courtesy of Openwave Systems Inc.

Chapter 8 Quick Reference

To	Do this
Create a control that can handle both client- and server-side events	Modify an HTML control by right-clicking the control in Design view and selecting Run As Server Control (or by adding an *id* attribute and the *runat="server"* attribute to the desired HTML element). Note that the element must support the desired client-side event. You can then add attributes to map the events to the appropriate client- and server-side event handlers.
Show or hide an ASP.NET server control	Modify the *Visible* property of the control.
Add (or modify) an HTML attribute to an HTML control or Web control that is not exposed as a property of the control	Add or modify the attribute by its name using the *Attributes* collection of the control: *MyControl.Attributes("Attribute")*. Note that all attributes, including those exposed as properties on a control, are available via the *Attributes* collection.
Apply styles to a control	Set the *Style* or *CssClass* (Web controls only) of the control to the desired CSS style or class string.
Validate user input	Add a *Validator* server control to the page, and set its *ControlToValidate* property to the ID of the control the user will use to enter input. The type of control to use depends on what you want to validate.

Chapter

9

Accessing and Binding Data

In this chapter, you will learn how to:

■ Connect to a database using ADO.NET.

■ Use ASP.NET data-bound controls to display and edit data.

■ Use the *DataGrid*, *DataList*, and *Repeater* controls.

In the previous two chapters, you learned about creating Web Forms and taking advantage of ASP.NET server controls in your Web Forms applications. With that overview of these two important technologies under your belt, let's look at data access. The ability to store and access data is central to most Web applications, and this is an area that classic ASP made very simple for developers through the ActiveX Data Objects (ADO) COM components. The Microsoft .NET platform provides a set of classes called ADO.NET that is the logical successor to ADO, although the underlying object model has undergone significant changes. ASP.NET, meanwhile, exposes a set of data-bound controls (which I touched on briefly in Chapter 8) that integrate seamlessly with ADO.NET to provide data-binding services.

▶ **Important**　ADO.NET is a large enough topic to merit a book of its own, so at best this chapter will provide an overview. I strongly encourage you to use the available resources, such as the ASP.NET and HowTo QuickStart tutorials (installed with the Microsoft .NET Framework SDK samples), which have numerous ADO.NET examples. Other resources include the .NET Framework SDK and Microsoft Visual Studio .NET documentation, and of course other books, such as *ADO.NET Step by Step* by Rebecca M. Riordan (Microsoft Press, 2002), and *Building Web Solutions with ASP.NET and ADO.NET* (Microsoft Press, 2002) by Dino Esposito, a noted expert on ADO and ADO.NET.

Understanding ADO.NET

In classic ASP, the most common way to access data was through ADO. Developers used ADO *Connection* objects to connect to a database, and then used ADO *Command* and *Recordset* objects to retrieve, manipulate, and update data. When designing applications, particularly those with high scalability requirements or those whose back-end datasource might change at some point, developers needed to be careful not to tie in their front-end presentation code with their back-end database. Otherwise, they'd end up having to rewrite everything if there was a change in the back-end database.

The ADO.NET class architecture is factored somewhat differently from classic ADO. ADO.NET classes are separated into two major categories: datasource-specific and non-datasource-specific.

Understanding .NET Data Providers

Classes specific to a particular datasource are said to work with a specific .NET Data Provider, which is a set of classes that allow managed code to interact with a specific datasource to retrieve, update, and manipulate data. ADO.NET comes with two .NET Data Providers: the SQL Server .NET Data Provider, which provides optimized access to Microsoft SQL Server databases, and the OLE DB .NET Data Provider, which lets you connect to any datasource for which you have an OLE DB provider installed.

▶ **Important** The OLE DB .NET Data Provider does not support the OLE DB 2.5 interfaces. This means that you cannot use the Microsoft OLE DB Provider for Exchange and the Microsoft OLE DB Provider for Internet Publishing with the OLE DB .NET Data Provider. Additionally, the OLE DB .NET Data Provider is incompatible with the OLE DB Provider for ODBC. For accessing data via ODBC, use the .NET Framework Data Provider for OCBD, which is integrated into the Microsoft Windows .NET Framework version 1.1.

Also new in version 1.1 of the Framework is the .NET Framework Data Provider for Oracle.

The following illustration shows the major classes of the SQL Server .NET Data Provider and how they relate to one another.

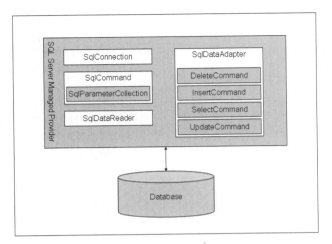

The *SqlConnection* class is used to establish a connection to a SQL Server database. Unlike the ADO *Connection* object, the *SqlConnection* class (or its OLE DB equivalent, the *OleDbConnection* class) cannot be used to execute SQL statements against a datasource. The *SqlConnection* class is used solely for opening connections, setting or retrieving properties of a connection, or handling connection-related events. You'll learn how to use the *SqlConnection* class to connect to a database later in this chapter.

The *SqlCommand* class is used to execute SQL statements or stored procedures against a SQL Server database. The *SqlCommand* class (and its OLE DB equivalent, the *OleDbCommand* class) can execute statements or stored procedures that do not return values, or that return single values, XML, or datareaders.

The *SqlDataReader* class provides forward-only, read-only access to a set of rows returned from a SQL Server database. Datareaders (including both the *SqlDataReader* and *OleDbDataReader*) provide lightweight, high-performance access to read-only data and are the best choice for accessing data to be displayed in ASP.NET.

The *SqlDataAdapter* class is used as a bridge between the *DataSet* class and SQL Server. You can use the *SqlDataAdapter* class to create a dataset from a given SQL statement or stored procedure represented by a *SqlCommand* instance, to update the back-end SQL Server database based on the contents of a dataset, or to insert rows into or delete rows from a SQL Server database. The *OleDbAdapter* class performs the same tasks for OLE DB datasources.

▶ **Important**   You may have noticed that in the discussion of the classes that make up the SQL Server .NET Data Provider, the names of the classes start with *Sql* rather than *SQL*. This is because the names of the classes in the .NET Framework use Pascal casing (after the style of the Pascal language), in which the first character of each distinct word in a given class is capitalized. This naming convention is especially important because you must declare class and namespace names with the proper case when using a case-sensitive language such as C#. Using the incorrect case name (for example, *SQLConnection* instead of *SqlConnection*) will result in a compiler error. So if you get an error complaining that the type isn't defined or the namespace doesn't exist, you're probably dealing with a capitalization problem. But even in a language that isn't case sensitive, such as Visual Basic .NET, using the proper case for namespaces and classes will result in code that's easier to read and maintain.

Understanding Datasets

The main class not specific to a datasource is the *DataSet* class. This is essentially an in-memory representation of one or more tables of data. This data can be read from an XML file or stream, or it can be the result of a query against a datasource.

One important thing about the *DataSet* class is that it doesn't know anything about the datasource from which it receives its data, other than what that data is and sometimes the types of the data columns. (See the section on typed datasets later in this chapter.) The following illustration shows the major classes associated with the *DataSet* class and how they relate to one another. Note that the *Rows*, *Columns*, and *Constraints* objects are properties of the *DataTable* class.

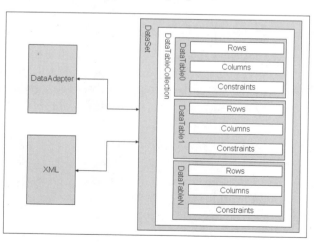

The fact that a dataset knows nothing about the source of its data means that it's abstracted from the back-end datasource. This is important because it means that if you pass a dataset from a component used for data retrieval to your Web Forms page to be used for data-binding, your Web Forms page neither knows nor cares where the data comes from, as long as the dataset structure remains the same. You can change the back-end database without necessitating any changes in the Web Forms page, making it much easier to maintain a Web application.

Datasets contain a collection of tables, each of which contains a collection of rows, a collection of columns, and a collection of constraints. You can use these collections to get information on the objects contained within them, as well as to access and update individual data values. The dataset can also contain a collection of relationships between the tables it contains, allowing hierarchical data to be represented. You'll learn about the *DataSet* class and related classes in detail later in this chapter.

XML in ADO.NET

Unlike classic ADO, in which XML support was added after the initial object model had been created, XML support has been designed into the ADO.NET model from the ground up. Classes such as *SqlCommand*, *OleDbCommand*, and *DataSet* have built-in support for reading and writing XML data. Datasets in particular can be built from or saved as XML, making them ideal for transporting data between tiers in a multi-tier application or for temporarily storing data to disk for later retrieval.

Creating and Opening Connections

The first step in accessing data from a database is, of course, creating the connection. ADO.NET provides two classes for creating connections to a database: *SqlConnection* and *OleDbConnection*. The class you use depends on the type of database you will be connecting to and the needs of your application.

SqlConnection

For applications that use SQL Server as the back-end database and are unlikely to change to a different database in the future, the *SqlConnection* class is the appropriate choice. This class is optimized for the best performance when connecting to a SQL Server database. The *SqlConnection* class will also provide superior performance when accessing data in an MSDE database, since MSDE uses the same database engine and protocols as SQL Server.

Creating a *SqlConnection* class is simple and can be done in one line of code:

```
SqlConnection mySqlConn=new SqlConnection(ConnectionString);
```

This creates a connection called mySqlConn to the SQL Server specified by the MyConnectionString parameter passed to the constructor of the SqlConnection class. Opening the connection is as simple as calling the following:

```
mySqlConn.Open();
```

Closing the connection is just as easy:

```
mySqlConn.Close();
```

▶ **Important**   As with classic ADO, it is very important that you close any connection you open when you are finished with it. Connections are not closed automatically when they go out of scope. Open connections are not returned to the connection pool, where they would be available to other clients. Leaving connections open can prevent your application from effectively handling larger numbers of users without unacceptable performance degradation.

In addition to setting the connection string by passing it to the constructor of the *SqlConnection* instance, you can also create the *SqlConnection* instance with no constructor argument and set the connection string later through the *ConnectionString* property.

The connection string for *SqlConnection* consists of key/value pairs separated by semicolons. You can delimit values by using either single or double quotes, but you cannot use both for the same value. (For example, key='value's' should be key="value's".) All spaces except those appearing in quotes are ignored.

▶ **Important**   When you're creating connection strings dynamically based on user input, make sure to validate user input so that additional keys are not intentionally added to the connection string by the user. For example, a malicious user could add the database key to his password in an attempt to connect to a different database. Since the last key with the same name will be used to set the value for a connection string, failure to validate input can result in inappropriate access.

Table 9-1 lists the valid keys for a *SqlConnection* connection string.

Table 9-1. *SqlConnection* Connection String Keys

Key	Description
Application Name	The name of the application from which the connection is being made.
AttachDBFilename	The filename and full path to the primary file of an attachable database. This key requires the *Database* key to specify the database name.
Connect Timeout or *Connection Timeout*	The number of seconds before an attempted connection is aborted and an error is raised. The default is *15*.

Table 9-1. *SqlConnection* **Connection String Keys**

Key	Description
Connection Lifetime	The time, in seconds, that a pooled connection should remain alive. When a connection is returned to the connection pool, it is destroyed if the current time is more than this many seconds past its creation time. The default is *0*, meaning that the connection will not be destroyed.
Connection Reset	A Boolean value that determines whether the connection state is reset when a connection is retrieved from the pool. If this key is set to *false*, the connection state will not be reset, which saves a trip to the server. But the programmer must then manually take any steps necessary to ensure that the connection state is appropriate for the application's use. The default is *true*.
Current Language	The SQL Server language name.
Data Source or *Server* or *Address* or *Addr* or *Network Address*	The server name or network address of the SQL Server instance to connect to.
Enlist	Determines whether the connection is automatically enlisted in the creator's current transaction context. The default is *true*.
Initial Catalog or *Database*	The name of the database to connect to.
Integrated Security or *Trusted Connection*	Determines whether the connection uses the Windows authentication credentials of the caller to authenticate against SQL Server. Setting this to *true* alleviates the need for authenticating a user ID and password, which means that you don't need to worry about storing these values. The default is *false*.
Max Pool Size	Determines the maximum number of connections to be pooled. The default is *100*.
Min Pool Size	Determines the minimum number of connections that should be in the pool. The default is *0*.
Network Library or *Net*	Specifies the network library to use when connecting to the specified SQL Server. The default is *dbmssocn*, which specifies the TCP/IP sockets library. Other valid values are *dbnmpntw* Named pipes *dbmsrpcn* Multiprotocol *dbmsadsn* Apple Talk *dbmsgnet* VIA *dbmsipcn* Shared memory *dbmsspxn* IPX/SPX. The server must have the appropriate DLL for the specified network library.

Table 9-1. *SqlConnection* **Connection String Keys**

Key	Description
Packet Size	Specifies the number of bytes per network packet to use in communicating with SQL Server. The default is *8192*.
Password or *Pwd*	Specifies the password to use to log into the SQL Server database.
Persist Security Info	If set to *false*, this key prevents sensitive information, such as passwords, from being returned as a part of the connection if the connection is open. The default is *false*.
Pooling	Determines whether pooling is enabled for this connection. When *true*, a requested connection will be pulled from the appropriate pool. If no connections are available from the pool, the requested connection is created and then returned to the pool when closed. The default is *true*.
User ID	The name of the SQL Server user account with which to log into the server.
Workstation ID	The name of the machine connecting to SQL Server. The default is the local machine name.

OleDbConnection

For applications that need to be able to query databases other than SQL Server, such as Microsoft Access or Oracle, the *OleDbConnection* class is the appropriate choice. This class uses a standard OLE DB Provider string to connect to any OLE DB datasource through the OLE DB provider for that datasource.

Creating an *OleDbConnection* class is simple and can be done in one line of code:

```
OleDbConnection myOleDbConn = new OleDbConnection (ConnectionString);
```

This creates a connection called myOleDbConn to the database specified by the MyConnectionString parameter passed to the constructor of the OleDbConnection class. The ConnectionString argument is a standard OLE DB provider string. The following, from the MSDN .NET Framework Class Library Reference, shows some examples of OLE DB Provider strings for connecting to Oracle, Access, and SQL Server datasources, respectively:

```
Provider=MSDAORA; Data Source=ORACLE8i7; User ID=OLEDB;Password=OLEDB;

Provider=Microsoft.Jet.OLEDB.4.0;Data Source=c:\bin\LocalAccess40.mdb;

Provider=SQLOLEDB;Data Source=MySQLServer;Integrated Security=SSPI;
```

The *Provider=* clause is required. You can also use other clauses supported by the particular OLE DB provider to set other properties for the provider. For example, the *Initial Catalog=* clause is used by the SQL Server OLE DB Provider to indicate the database against which queries will be run.

> ▶ **Note**   With the integration of data providers for Oracle and ODBC data sources into the .NET Framework, you should use those data providers, rather than the OLE DB data provider, when accessing Oracle or ODBC data, as these providers are optimized for this purpose, and will be more efficient than attempting to use the .NET Framework Data Provider for OLE DB along with the OLE DB provider for the specific database type.

You open the connection by calling the following:

```
myOleDbConn.Open();
```

And you close it by calling the following:

```
myOleDbConn.Close();
```

Later in this chapter, you'll see examples of using connections to perform data access.

> ▶ **Note**   Most of the discussion and examples in this chapter will use either the .NET Framework Data Provider for SQL Server, or the .NET Framework Data Provider for OLE DB. Using other data providers will be similar, although there may be minor differences in the SQL syntax used to query a given database. For more information on the specifics of a given data provider, refer to the MSDN documentation for Visual Studio .NET 2003, which contains detailed documentation and examples for all of the .NET Framework Data Providers.

Using Trusted Connections

As mentioned in Chapter 6, ASP.NET is configured by default to use the unprivileged ASPNET account to run ASP.NET worker processes. This means that unlike in beta versions of ASP.NET, you must now employ one of the following two techniques to use a trusted connection:

- Use Windows authentication and impersonation to connect to the database using the credentials of the logged-in user.
- Set up the ASPNET account as a login in SQL Server (or any other data source that supports trusted connections).

In this section you'll learn how to use the latter technique to enable the use of trusted connections without the need for Windows authentication.

▶ **Important**   Setting up the ASPNET account in SQL Server will allow any
ASP.NET application on the Web server to access the database with whatever
privileges have been granted to the ASPNET account. For this reason, you
should use this technique only on development systems or production systems
on which you are in control of all ASP.NET applications. This technique should
generally not be considered for shared server applications.

There are a couple of ways to provide access to a database for the ASPNET
account, depending on the software you have installed. If you have the full version of SQL Server installed, you can use the graphical tool SQL Enterprise
Manager to add the ASPNET account as a SQL Server login. If you have only
MSDE installed, you will need to use the oSQL command-line utility to perform
these tasks. You'll learn both techniques in the following two sections.

Use SQL Enterprise Manager to set up the ASPNET account

1   Open SQL Enterprise Manager by clicking Start, All Programs,
Microsoft SQL Server, and then Enterprise Manager.

2   Expand the tree and locate the desired SQL Server or MSDE
instance. Expand this instance and locate the Security node.

3   Expand the Security node, right-click the Logins node, and then
select New Login.

4   In the General tab, in the Authentication section, select the desired
domain (or local machine name) from the Domain drop-down list,
and then click the ellipsis (...) button next to the Name text box.

5   Locate and select the account named ASPNET (aspnet_wp account),
click Add, and then click OK.

6   Also in the General tab, change the Database default to pubs (or the
desired database). Click the Database Access tab.

7   Scroll to the pubs database (or the desired database), check the Permit check box, and then add the db_datareader and db_datawriter
roles to the ASPNET login account by checking the check boxes for
these roles.

8   Click OK. You can now use a trusted connection to read from and
write to the pubs sample database (or the database you selected in
Steps 6 and 7).

If you do not have SQL Enterprise Manager available, you can still take advantage of the oSQL command-line utility to add the ASPNET account, as shown
in the following exercise.

▶ **Note**   You must be logged in as an administrator or use an account with appropriate rights to the MSDE database to successfully complete the steps in the following procedure.

Use the oSql command-line tool to set up the ASPNET account

1   Start the oSql command-line utility by entering the following code at a command prompt. (If you're using a SQL Server database other than a local version of the VSdotNET MSDE instance, enter that server or instance name as the *-S* parameter.)

```
oSql -S(local)\VSdotNET -E
```

You should see a 1> prompt if the command completes successfully.

2   Call the sp_grantlogin system stored procedure to grant login access to the ASPNET account.

The syntax should look like the following, with *<domain>* replaced by your domain or local machine name. The *go* command entered at the 2> prompt tells oSql to execute the stored procedure.

```
1> sp_grantlogin '<domain>\ASPNET'
2> go
```

3   Call the sp_defaultdb system stored procedure to change the default database for the ASPNET account to pubs.

▶ **Note**   The VSdotNET MSDE instance that ships with Visual Studio .NET does not automatically install sample databases, including the Pubs database. See Appendix C for instructions on manually adding the Pubs database to the VSdot-NET MSDE instance.

The syntax should look like the following, with *<domain>* replaced by your domain or local machine name.

```
1> sp_defaultdb '<domain>\ASPNET', 'pubs'
2> go
```

4   Call the sp_adduser system stored procedure to add the ASPNET login account to the pubs database, passing the *db_datareader* argument to add the account to the db_datareader role.

The syntax should look like the following, with *<domain>* replaced by your domain or local machine name.

```
1> sp_adduser '<domain>\ASPNET', 'ASPNET', 'db_datareader'
2> go
```

9

Accessing and Binding Data

5   If desired, call the sp_addrolemember system stored procedure to add the ASPNET account to the db_datawriter role. In this step, ASP-NET is the username added to the pubs database in the previous step. The syntax should look like the following:

```
1> sp_addrolemember 'db_datawriter', 'ASPNET'
2> go
```

6   Type **exit** and press the Enter key to exit the oSql utility.

Once you've set up the ASPNET account as described in the preceding steps, you should be able to access the desired database using a trusted connection, as shown in the connection strings used in the samples later in this chapter.

Reading and Updating Data with Commands

The *Command* classes—*SqlCommand* and *OleDbCommand*—are the ADO.NET equivalents of the ADO *Command* object. You can use these classes to retrieve read-only data through a datareader (as you'll see later in this chapter), execute *Insert*, *Update*, *Delete*, and other statements that don't return records, retrieve aggregate results, or retrieve an XML representation of data. You can also use *SqlCommand* and *OleDbCommand* in conjunction with a related datareader to populate a dataset with data or to update a back-end database with updated data from a dataset. The *SqlCommand* and the *OleDb-Command* classes can work with either SQL statements or stored procedures (for datasources that support them).

SqlCommand

The *SqlCommand* class is the appropriate class to use when you want to run commands against a SQL Server database. Each of the following steps outlines one or more ways to initialize or use the *SqlCommand* class.

Use the *SqlCommand* class

1   Create the *SqlCommand* object.

Note that the constructor of the *SqlCommand* object is overloaded, so you can save steps by passing arguments (such as the query for the *Command* and/or the *SqlConnection* object to use for the command) to its constructor, rather than setting the properties after the object is created. The following examples demonstrate several of the arguments that can be passed to the *SqlConnection* constructor.

```
// Default constructor
SqlCommand mySqlCmd = new SqlCommand();

//Passing in a query
string SQL = "SELECT au_id FROM authors";
SqlCommand mySqlCmd2 = new SqlCommand(SQL);

//Passing in a query and a connection
string ConnStr = "datasource=localhost\VSdotNET;"
   + "database=pubs;integratedsecurity=true";
SqlConnection mySqlConn = new SqlConnection(ConnStr);
string SQL = "SELECT au_id FROM authors";
SqlCommand mySqlCmd3 = new SqlCommand(SQL, mySqlConn);

//Passing in a query, a connection, and a transaction
string ConnStr = "datasource=localhost\VSdotNET;"
   + "database=pubs;integratedsecurity=true";
SqlConnection mySqlConn = new SqlConnection(ConnStr);
SqlTransaction mySqlTrans = mySqlConn.BeginTransaction();
string SQL = "SELECT au_id FROM authors";
SqlCommand mySqlCmd4 = new SqlCommand(SQL, mySqlConn, mySqlTrans);
```

2 If you haven't set them in the constructor, set the *CommandText* property to the desired SQL query or stored procedure name and set the *Connection* property to an open *SqlConnection* object.

```
mySqlCommand.CommandText = "SELECT au_id FROM authors";
// Assumes that mySqlConn has already been created and opened
mySqlCommand.Connection = mySqlConn;
```

3 Call one of the following four methods that execute the command. (Note that the value of the *CommandText* property will vary depending on the method you call.)

```
//Use ExecuteNonQuery to execute an INSERT, UPDATE or
//DELETE query where that query type has been set using the
//CommandText property
mySqlCmd.ExecuteNonQuery();

//Use ExecuteReader to execute a SELECT command and
//return a datareader
SqlDataReader mySqlReader = mySqlCmd.ExecuteReader
```

```
//Use ExecuteScalar to execute a command and return the value of
//the first column of the first row. Any additional results
//are ignored.
Object Result;
Result = mySqlCmd.ExecuteScalar();

//Use ExecuteXmlReader to execute a SELECT command and
//fill a DataSet using the returned XmlReader
string SQL = "SELECT * FROM authors FOR XML AUTO, XMLDATA";
SqlCommand mySqlCmd = new SqlCommand(SQL, mySqlConn);
DataSet myDS = new DataSet();
MyDS.ReadXml(mySqlCmd.ExecuteXmlReader(), XmlReadMode.Fragment);
```

4   Make sure to close the connection when you're finished with it.

The following example walks you through creating the code necessary to retrieve the contents of the Authors table of the Pubs sample SQL Server database as XML and to display that data in a Web Forms page.

▶   **Note**   The data access samples in this book are written to run against the MSDE sample database included with Microsoft Visual Studio .NET. For information on installing MSDE, see Appendix C. If you want to run the data access samples against a SQL Server database other than the VSdotNET MSDE database, or if you are unable to use a trusted connection to SQL Server or MSDE, you must modify the connection string in the examples to match the appropriate server name and login credentials.

Display XML Data in a Web Page

1   Open Visual Studio and create a new project called **Chapter_09**. Rename the default Web Page created by Visual Studio from WebPage1.aspx to **ExecuteXmlReader.aspx** by selecting WebForm1.aspx in the Solution Explorer and then selecting File, then Save WebForm1.aspx As.

2   Copy the file Authors.xsl from the practice files for this chapter into the folder where you just created the project. (If you have not downloaded and installed the practice files, you can add a new XSL file to the project, and then add the code from the Authors.xsl listing that follows this example.)

3 Drag an *Xml* control from the toolbox onto the form. Use the Properties window to change the ID to XmlDisplay. Set the Transform-Source to Authors.xsl.

4 Switch to the source code window by using F7 or by selecting View, and then Code.

5 Add the following *using* clause to the top of the source file:

```
using System.Data.SqlClient;
```

6 Scroll down to the *Page_Load* event handler and add the following code:

```
string ConnStr;
// You may want to adjust this string...
ConnStr = "data source=(local)\\VSdotNET;" +
  "database=pubs;integrated security=true";
// Create and open the connection
SqlConnection MySqlConn = new SqlConnection(ConnStr);
MySqlConn.Open();
try
{
   string SQL = "SELECT * FROM authors FOR XML AUTO, XMLDATA";
   SqlCommand mySqlCmd = new SqlCommand(SQL, MySqlConn);
   DataSet MyDS = new DataSet();
   // Fill the DataSet, using the XML read from MSDE/SQL Server
   MyDS.ReadXml(mySqlCmd.ExecuteXmlReader(), XmlReadMode.Fragment);
   XmlDisplay.DocumentContent = MyDS.GetXml();
}
finally
{
   MySqlConn.Close();
}
```

7 Save the project and both open files.

8 Build the project.

9 Test the page by right-clicking ExecuteXmlReader.aspx, selecting Browse With, and then selecting Microsoft Internet Explorer. The resulting screen should look like the illustration on the following page.

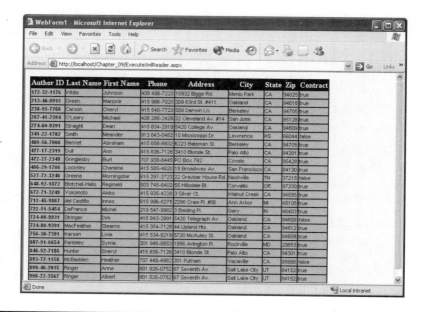

This example creates a *SqlConnection* object that opens a connection to the Pubs database, creates a SQL query string to retrieve the contents of the Authors table as XML, and creates a new *SqlCommand* object, passing in the SQL query and *SqlConnection* object. Then it creates a dataset and uses the *ExecuteXmlReader* method of the *SqlCommand* object to pass an *XmlReader* object to the dataset's *ReadXml* method, which allows the dataset to populate itself from the *XmlReader*. Finally, the code sets the *DocumentContent* property of the declared *Xml* server control to the result of the *GetXml* method of the dataset. The *Xml* control uses the XSL Transformation document authors.xsl to format the Xml content displayed by the *Xml* control.

▶ **Important**   The code in Step 6 in the previous example shows an important pattern when using database connections. Immediately after the call to *Open*, you enter a *try* block. In the *finally* section, you close the connection. This ensures that the connection is closed, even if an exception occurs in the code after the call to *Open*.

It's also not a bad idea to add *catch* blocks for exceptions that might occur in connecting to and reading from the database. This will make your database code more robust, which will make your users happier!

The following listing shows the content of authors.xsl.

Authors.xsl

```
<xsl:stylesheet version='1.0'
   xmlns:xsl='http://www.w3.org/1999/XSL/Transform'>
   <xsl:template match="/">
   <style>
      .header{font-weight:bold;color:white;background-color:black;}
      .value{font-family:arial;font-size:.7em;background-color:silver}
   </style>
   <table border="1" cellspacing="0" cellpadding="1"
      bordercolor="black">
      <tr class="header">
         <th>Author ID</th>
         <th>Last Name</th>
         <th>First Name</th>
         <th>Phone</th>
         <th>Address</th>
         <th>City</th>
         <th>State</th>
         <th>Zip</th>
         <th>Contract</th>
      </tr>
   <xsl:for-each select='Schema1/authors'>
      <tr>
         <td nowrap="true" class="value">
            <b>
               <xsl:value-of select='@au_id' />
            </b>
         </td>
         <td nowrap="true" class="value">
            <xsl:value-of select='@au_lname' />

         </td>
         <td nowrap="true" class="value">
            <xsl:value-of select='@au_fname' />
         </td>
         <td nowrap="true" class="value">
            <xsl:value-of select='@phone' />
         </td>
         <td nowrap="true" class="value">
            <xsl:value-of select='@address' />
         </td>
         <td nowrap="true" class="value">
            <xsl:value-of select='@city' />
         </td>
         <td nowrap="true" class="value">
            <xsl:value-of select='@state' />
         </td>
```

```
                    <td nowrap="true" class="value">
                        <xsl:value-of select='@zip' />
                    </td>
                    <td nowrap="true" class="value">
                        <xsl:value-of select='@contract' />
                    </td>
                </tr>
            </xsl:for-each>
        </table>
    </xsl:template>
</xsl:stylesheet>
```

OleDbCommand

For most purposes, using the *OleDbCommand* class is effectively the same as using the *SqlCommand* class. Instead of connecting with the *SqlConnection* class, you can just use the *OleDbConnection* class. One significant difference, however, is that the *OleDbCommand* class does not have an *ExecuteXmlReader* method.

The following example assumes that you have the Northwind.mdb database installed locally.

1   Create and open an *OleDbCommand* object with the appropriate connection string for connecting to the Northwind database, where *<filepath>* is the path to Northwind.mdb on your machine.

```
string ConnStr;
ConnStr = "Provider=Microsoft.Jet.OLEDB.4.0;";
ConnStr += "Data Source=<filepath>\northwind.mdb;";
OleDbConnection myOleDbConn = new OleDbConnection(ConnStr);
myOleDbConn.Open;
```

2   Create a variable to contain the SQL query. (Note that the query can also be passed as a literal string to the constructor of the *OleDb-Command* class.)

```
string SQL  = "SELECT Count(*) FROM products";
```

3   Create an *OleDbCommand* object, passing the SQL query and the connection object to the constructor.

```
OleDbCommand myOleDbCmd = new OleDbCommand(SQL, myOleDbConn);
```

4   Create a variable to receive the return value from the command. This variable is declared as type *Object* because that is the return type of the *ExecuteScalar* method of the *OleDbCommand* object.

```
object Result;
```

5   Call the *ExecuteScalar* method of the *OleDbCommand* object, and use the returned value. Note that you must cast the value to the correct type before using it because the returned type is *Object*. This is

especially important if you need to use methods of a particular type that are not implemented by *Object*.

```
Result = myOleDbCmd.ExecuteScalar();
Value.Text += Result.ToString;
```

The following example shows how you would use the objects in the *OleDb* namespace to display the returned result in a Web Forms page.

Display a single query result from Microsoft Access

1   Open Visual Studio, and then open the project created in the previous example.

2   Add a new Web Form to the project and name it **ExecuteScalar.aspx**.

3   Add a label to the form. Use the Properties window to change the ID of the label to Value.

4   Switch to code view by pressing the F7 key or by selecting View, and then Code.

5   Add the following *using* clause to the *using* clauses at the top of the file:

```
using System.Data.OleDb;
```

6   Scroll down to the *Page_Load* event handler and add the following code. This code assumes that a copy of the Northwind Microsoft Access sample database exists in the same directory as ExecuteScalar.aspx:

```
string DbPath  = Server.MapPath("Northwind.mdb");
string ConnStr;
string SQL;
ConnStr = "Provider=Microsoft.Jet.OLEDB.4.0; " +
  @"Data Source=" + DbPath +";";
OleDbConnection MyOleDbConn = new OleDbConnection(ConnStr);
MyOleDbConn.Open();
try
{
  SQL = "SELECT Count(*) FROM products";
  OleDbCommand MyOleDbCommand = new OleDbCommand(SQL,MyOleDbConn);
  object Result;
  Result = MyOleDbCommand.ExecuteScalar();
  Value.Text = "There are " + Result.ToString() +
               " products in the Northwind database.";
}
finally
{
  MyOleDbConn.Close();
}
```

7   Save the page and code-behind module, and then build the project.

8 Test the page by right-clicking ExecuteScalar.aspx, selecting Browse With, and then selecting Microsoft Internet Explorer. The resulting screen should look like the following illustration.

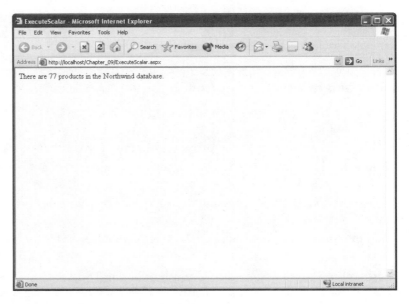

> ▶ **Note** Although the previous example uses Microsoft Access to demonstrate the ability of the *OleDbCommand* object to connect to non–SQL Server databases, you should generally avoid using Access for ASP.NET applications. For initial prototyping and development, or for applications with minimal scalability requirements (up to 100 or so concurrent users, depending on the activity generated by each user), MSDE is the better choice.
>
> MSDE is a SQL Server–compatible database that is available with a number of Microsoft products, including SQL Server, Microsoft Office, and Visual Studio. A version of MSDE also comes with Visual Studio .NET, as well as with the .NET Framework SDK, and it's installed with and used to run the SDK samples, if you choose to install them. (Please refer to Chapter 6 for important guidance about installing sample applications.) MSDE is built on the same database engine as SQL Server, but it's tuned for approximately five concurrent users.
>
> The advantage of using MSDE is that all of your development tasks are then identical to developing against SQL Server, without the licensing expense of a full-blown SQL Server. (The license to use and distribute MSDE is included in the aforementioned products. Check the end-user license agreement to ensure that your use is within the terms of the agreement.) And if your application's scalability needs to grow, you can simply move your database to SQL Server for increased performance and scalability, with no code or data changes required.

Using Stored Procedures

In addition to using SQL text queries, you can also use stored procedures as the basis of a *SqlCommand* or *OleDbCommand* object. This is as simple as setting the *CommandText* property of the object to the name of the stored procedure that you want to execute, and setting *CommandType* to *CommandType.StoredProcedure*. If you're familiar with the execution of stored procedures under classic ADO, this isn't so different from what you would have done with the ADO *Command* object.

Calling Stored Procedures with Parameters

Calling stored procedures with input or output parameters is a little more involved, but it's still pretty straightforward. You simply create parameters (either *SqlParameter* or *OleDbParameter* objects); set the appropriate properties, such as *ParameterName*, *Direction*, type (*SqlType* or *OleDbType*), and *Value*; and then add the parameter object to the *Parameters* collection of the *Command* object. The following example shows the code required to execute the *byroyalty* stored procedure in the Pubs sample SQL Server database, and it returns a *SqlDataReader* object, which is then bound to an ASP.NET *DataGrid* control. (You'll learn more about data binding later in this chapter.)

Read data using a stored procedure and *SqlDataReader*

1 Open Visual Studio and then open the Chapter_09 project created earlier in the chapter.

2 Add a new Web Form to the project. Name the form **ExecuteReader.aspx**.

3 Drag a *DataGrid* from the toolbox and drop it onto the form. Use the Properties window to change the ID of the *DataGrid* to *MyGrid*.

4 Switch to code view by pressing the F7 key or by selecting View, and then Code.

5 Add the following *using* clause to the *using* clauses at the top of the file:

```
using System.Data.SqlClient;
```

6 Scroll down to the *Page_Load* event handler and add the following code:

```
string ConnStr;
string SQL;
ConnStr = @"Data Source=(local)\VSdotNET;" +
    "database=pubs;integrated security=true";
SqlConnection MySqlConn = new SqlConnection(ConnStr);
MySqlConn.Open();
try
{
```

```
SQL = "byroyalty";
SqlCommand MySqlCmd = new SqlCommand(SQL,MySqlConn);

MySqlCmd.CommandType = CommandType.StoredProcedure;
SqlParameter MySqlParam =
    new SqlParameter("@ percentage", SqlDbType.Int);
MySqlParam.Value = 40;
MySqlCmd.Parameters.Add(MySqlParam);
SqlDataReader Reader;
Reader = MySqlCmd.ExecuteReader();
if (Reader.HasRows)
{
    MyGrid.DataSource=Reader;
    MyGrid.DataBind();
}
else
{
    Label Message = new Label();
    Message.Text = "No rows to display";
    Page.Controls.Add(Message);
}
}
finally
{
    MySqlConn.Close();
}
```

7   Save the page and code-behind module.

8   Build the project.

9   Test the page by right-clicking ExecuteReader.aspx, selecting Browse With, and then selecting Microsoft Internet Explorer. The resulting screen should look like the following illustration.

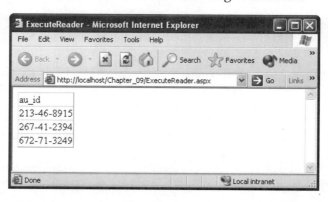

The previous example creates and opens a connection to the Pubs database, creates a *SqlCommand* object and sets its *CommandType* property to *Command-Type.StoredProcedure*, and then creates a *SqlParameter* object, passing the parameter name and data type to the parameter's constructor.

▶ **Important**   Unlike in ADO, when you specify a parameter name to ADO.NET you must use the exact name the stored procedure expects, including the at symbol (@).

The code then sets the value of the parameter, adds it to the *Parameters* collection of the *SqlCommand* object, and executes the command. The code then checks the datareader's *HasRows* property, and if the query returned one or more rows, the *SqlDataReader* object is then bound to a *DataGrid* control, which displays the results.

Using Datasets

Datasets are one of the two main ways of working with data in ADO.NET. (The other way is with DataReaders, which you've been using already and will learn about in more detail later in this chapter.) Unlike most other objects we have looked at, in which there is one version in the *SqlClient* namespace and a similar object in the *OleDb* namespace, there is a single *DataSet* class, found in the *System.Data* namespace. Dataset objects provide a database-independent in-memory representation of data. This data can be used for display or to update a back-end database through the appropriate *DataAdapter* object. A dataset can also read data from and write data to an XML file or a *Stream* object.

Dataset objects can be constructed and manipulated programmatically by adding, modifying, or deleting *DataTable*, *DataColumn*, and *DataRow* objects in the dataset. You can also use such datasets to update a back-end database (assuming that the schema of the tables you've constructed is compatible) by calling the *Update* method of the dataset object.

You can work with typed datasets to make your code easier to read and your ADO.NET code less error prone. Also, you can use a *DataView* object to filter the contents of a dataset for use in display (such as for data binding) or calculations.

Using *DataAdapter* Objects

DataAdapter objects allow you to get data from a back-end database into a dataset and to update a back-end database from a dataset. Several *DataAdapters* are installed with the .NET Framework—the *SqlDataAdapter* and the *OleDbDataAdapter* are the ones you'll use most frequently, as well as the *OdbcDataAdapter* and *OracleDataAdapter*, which are new in version 1.1

of the Framework. Each of the *DataAdapter* classes uses the appropriate *Connection* and *Command* classes to either retrieve or update data.

You can use the *Fill* method of the *SqlDataAdapter* and *OleDbAdapter* classes to populate a dataset with results from a back-end database, using the *Command* object specified by the *SelectCommand* property of the *DataAdapter*. The following code creates and opens a connection to the database specified by the *ConnStr* argument. Then it creates a new *SqlDataAdapter* and sets its *SelectCommand* property to a newly created *SqlCommand* object that uses the query specified by the SQL argument. Finally the code creates a new dataset, populates it using the *Fill* method of the *SqlDataAdapter*, and closes the connection.

```
SqlConnection mySqlConn = new SqlConnection(ConnStr);
mySqlConn.Open();
SqlDataAdapter mySqlAdapter = new SqlDataAdapter();
mySqlAdapter.SelectCommand = new SqlCommand(SQL, mySqlConn);
DataSet myDS = new DataSet();
mySqlAdapter.Fill(myDS);
mySqlConn.Close();
```

At this point, the data in the dataset can be updated or deleted, new rows can be added, or the entire dataset can be passed to another component because it no longer has a connection to the back-end database. It's important to understand that updating the dataset does not automatically update the back-end database (or other data source) from which the dataset was filled. To update the back-end database, you need to call the *Update* method of the data adapter used to fill the dataset. You'll learn how to do this later in this chapter.

Reading XML Data

In addition to populating a dataset from a database using a *DataAdapter*, you can also read the data for a dataset from an XML file or stream using the *ReadXml* method of the dataset. Since you can also save a dataset as XML using the *WriteXml* method, the two techniques together can be a convenient way of serializing and deserializing the data in a dataset. The ExecuteXml-Reader.aspx example earlier in the chapter shows an example of using the *ReadXml* method to populate a dataset with XML data retrieved from SQL Server using the FOR XML AUTO query syntax.

Using *DataTable*, *DataColumn*, and *DataRow* Objects

Another way of populating a dataset object is to create its table, column, and row objects programmatically. This allows you to create a dataset without connecting to a back-end database. Assuming that the schema of the created table(s) matches your database (which is handled in the following code by using an XSD schema file, shown in the listing AddTitle.xsd later in the chapter, created from the Pubs Titles table), you can then connect to the database and update it based on the row(s) you've added to the dataset programmatically.

The following example shows how to create a program to add a new row to the Titles table of the Pubs sample SQL Server database. Note that the *Select-Command* property of the *SqlDataAdapter* is set by passing the SQL string variable to the constructor of the *SqlDataAdapter*. This is necessary to allow the *UpdateCommand* (the command that is called when the *Update* method of the *SqlDataAdapter* is called) to be built automatically, using the *SqlCommand-Builder* object. The call to *SqlAdapter.Update* updates the database, and then the call to *SqlAdapter.Fill* refreshes the data in the dataset with the current data from the database table.

Add a new row to a table

1   Open Visual Studio, and then open the Chapter_09 project you created earlier in the chapter.

2   Add a new Web Form to the project. Name the form **AddTitle.aspx**.

3   Copy AddTitle.xsd from the practice files to the folder the project resides in.

4   Unlike previous examples, this example will use an HTML table to format the output. To make this easier, use the Properties window to change the *pageLayout* property from *GridLayout* to *FlowLayout*. (Click an empty area of the page to make sure the properties for the page are displayed.)

5   Change to HTML mode by clicking on the HTML tab at the bottom of the design window. Insert the following HTML between the beginning and ending *form* tags. (If you've downloaded and installed the practice files, you can copy the code from the AddTitle.aspx sample to save typing.) The HTML code sets up a table to be used to display captions and textboxes.

```
<h3>Inserting a Title</h3>
<table width="300">
  <tr>
    <td colspan="2" bgcolor="silver">Add a New Title:</td>
  </tr>
  <tr>
    <td nowrap>Title ID: </td>
    <td>
    <asp:textbox id="title_id" text="XX0000" runat="server"/>
    </td>
  </tr>
```

```html
<tr>
  <td nowrap>Title: </td>
  <td>
    <asp:textbox id="title" text="The Tao of ASP.NET"
        runat="server"/>
  </td>
</tr>
<tr>

  <td  nowrap >Type: </td>
  <td>
    <asp:textbox id="type" text="popular_comp"
        runat="server"/>
  </td>
</tr>
<tr>
  <td>Publisher ID: </td>
  <td>
      <asp:textbox id="pub_id" text="1389" runat="server"/>
  </td>
</tr>
<tr>
  <td>Price: </td>
  <td>
    <asp:textbox id="price" text="39.99" runat="server"/>
  </td>
</tr>
<tr>
  <td>Advance: </td>
  <td>
    <asp:textbox id="advance" text="2000" runat="server"/>
  </td>
</tr>
<tr>
  <td>Royalty: </td>
  <td>
    <asp:textbox id="royalty" text="5" runat="server"/>
  </td>
</tr>
<tr>
  <td nowrap>Year-to-Date Sales: </td>
  <td>
    <asp:textbox id="ytd_sales" text="0" runat="server"/>
  </td>
</tr>
<tr>
```

```
        <td>Notes: </td>
        <td>
            <asp:textbox id="notes" textmode="multiline"
                text="Philosophy and Code...a perfect mix. "
                rows="3" columns="30" runat="server"/>
        </td>
    </tr>
    <tr>
        <td nowrap>Publication Date: </td>
        <td>
            <asp:textbox id="pubdate" text="12/01/01"
                runat="server"/>
        </td>
    </tr>
    <tr>
        <td></td>
        <td style="padding-top:15">
            <asp:button text="Add Title" runat="server"/>
        </td>
    </tr>
    <tr>
        <td colspan="2">
            <asp:datagrid id="titlegrid" runat="server"
                BorderColor="#999999"
                BorderStyle="None"
                BorderWidth="1px"
                BackColor="White"
                CellPadding="3"
                GridLines="Vertical">
            <SelectedItemStyle Font-Bold="True"
                ForeColor="White" BackColor="#008A8C">
             </SelectedItemStyle>
            <AlternatingItemStyle BackColor="#DCDCDC">
            </AlternatingItemStyle>
            <ItemStyle ForeColor="Black"
                  BackColor="#EEEEEE">
             </ItemStyle>
            <HeaderStyle Font-Bold="True"
                ForeColor="White" BackColor="#000084">
             </HeaderStyle>

            <FooterStyle ForeColor="Black"
                BackColor="#CCCCCC">
             </FooterStyle>
            <PagerStyle HorizontalAlign="Center"
                ForeColor="Black" BackColor="#999999"
                Mode="NumericPages">
```

```
                </PagerStyle>
            </asp:datagrid>
        </td>
    </tr>
</table>
```

After inserting this code, switch back to design mode by clicking in the Design tab at the bottom of the editor window. In the designer, the screen should look similar to the following illustration.

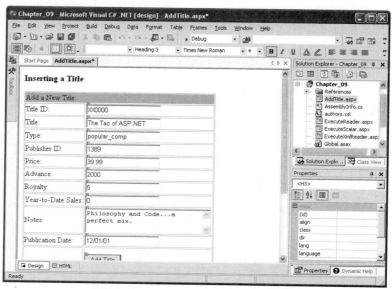

6   Switch to the code window by pressing F7, or by selecting View, and then Code. At the top of the file, add the following *using* clause:

```
using System.Data.SqlClient;
```

7   Scroll down to the Page_Load event handler and add the following code:

```
DataSet MyDS = new DataSet();
DataTable TitleTable;
DataRow TitleRow;
string ConnStr;
ConnStr = @"server=(local)\VSdotNET;database=pubs; " +
    "Trusted_Connection=yes";
string SQL;
SQL = "SELECT * FROM Titles";
SqlConnection MySqlConn = new SqlConnection(ConnStr);
SqlDataAdapter MySqlAdapter = new SqlDataAdapter(SQL,ConnStr);
SqlCommandBuilder MySqlCB = new SqlCommandBuilder(MySqlAdapter);

MyDS.ReadXmlSchema(Server.MapPath("AddTitle.xsd"));
```

```csharp
if ( this.IsPostBack )
{
   TitleTable = MyDS.Tables[0];
   TitleRow = TitleTable.NewRow();

   TitleRow["title_id"] = title_id.Text;
   TitleRow["title"] = title.Text;
   TitleRow["type"] = type.Text;
   TitleRow["pub_id"] = pub_id.Text;
   TitleRow["price"] = double.Parse(price.Text);
   TitleRow["advance"] = double.Parse(advance.Text);
   TitleRow["royalty"] = int.Parse(royalty.Text);
   TitleRow["ytd_sales"] = int.Parse(ytd_sales.Text);
   TitleRow["notes"] = notes.Text;
   TitleRow["pubdate"] = DateTime.Parse(pubdate.Text);
   TitleTable.Rows.Add(TitleRow);

   //Update back-end table based on new row
   MySqlAdapter.Update(MyDS);
   //Reset dataset before filling with data from DB
   MyDS.Reset();
   //Fill dataset with data from the Titles table
   MySqlAdapter.Fill(MyDS);

   titlegrid.DataSource = MyDS.Tables[0].DefaultView;
   titlegrid.DataBind();
}
else
{
   //To prevent conflicts on multiple inserts, we can
   //generate a random value for title_id
   Random RandomNum = new Random();
   title_id.Text = "XX" + String.Format("{0:000#}",
      RandomNum.Next(9999));
}
```

8 Save the page and code-behind module.

9 Build the project.

10 Test the page by right-clicking AddTitle.aspx, selecting Browse With, and then selecting Microsoft Internet Explorer. The resulting screen should look like the illustration on the following page. After you click the Add Title button, a DataGrid will be displayed below the form fields with the current data in the Titles table, including the added row.

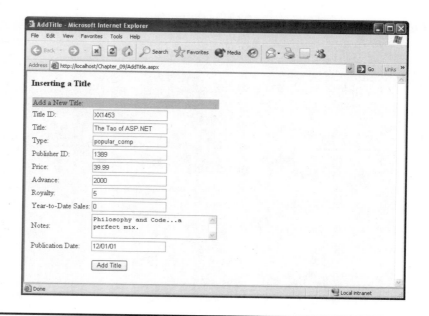

Setting Up Relationships

Since datasets can contain multiple tables of data, it only makes sense that you might want the dataset object to contain information about the relationships between these tables. This would allow you to treat them as true relational data and to maintain any hierarchy and foreign key relationships inherent in the data. The *DataSet* class fulfills this need with its *Relations* collection, which contains a collection of *DataRelation* objects, each of which describes a parent/child relationship between two matching columns in different tables in the dataset.

You can add *DataRelation* objects to a dataset programmatically, or they can be inferred from a supplied XSD schema.

Accessing Values

Values in a dataset are accessed by referring to the *DataTable* and *DataRow* objects containing the data. The *DataTables* are available via the *Tables* collection of the dataset, and you can reference a particular table either by index (zero-based) or by table name (key) as follows:

```
DataTable MyTable = myDS.Tables[0];
DataTable MyTable = myDS.Tables["tablename"];
```

You can also iterate over the *DataTableCollection* (returned by the *Tables* property of the dataset), *DataRowCollection* (returned by the *Rows* property of a *DataTable*), or the *DataColumnCollection* (returned by the *Columns* property of a *DataTable*). The code in the following example iterates over all of the tables in a dataset and all of the rows in each table. Then it displays the value of each column in the row, using an ASP.NET *Literal* control as a placeholder for the text.

Iterate over a *DataTable* collection

1   Open Visual Studio, and then open the Chapter_09 project you created earlier in the chapter.

2   Add a new Web Form to the project. Name the form **DisplayDataSetItems.aspx**.

3   Add an ASP.NET *Literal* server control to the form. Change the ID of the *Literal* control to *Value*.

4   Switch to the code window by pressing F7, or by selecting View, then Code. At the top of the file, add the following *using* clauses:

```
using System.Data.SqlClient;
```

5   Scroll down to the *Page_Load* event handler and add the following code:

```
DataSet MyDS = new DataSet();
string ConnStr;
string SQL;
ConnStr = @"server=(local)\VSdotNET;database=pubs; " +
    "Trusted_Connection=yes";
SQL = "SELECT * FROM Titles " + "SELECT * FROM Publishers ";
SqlConnection MySqlConn = new SqlConnection(ConnStr);
SqlDataAdapter MySqlAdapter = new SqlDataAdapter(SQL,ConnStr);

MySqlAdapter.Fill(MyDS);
```

Most of this should look somewhat familiar by now. One difference is that the SQL command contains two distinct *SELECT* statements. This is to cause two tables to be retrieved into the *DataSet*.

6   Add code to iterate over the *DataTables*, *DataRows* and *DataColumns*. Just below the code added in the previous step, add the following code:

```
// Get each DataTable in the DataTable Collection
// and display each row value by appending it to
// the Text property of the Literal control.
```

```
foreach ( DataTable CurrentTable in MyDS.Tables )
{
    Value.Text += "Table: " +
        CurrentTable.TableName.ToString() + "<br/>";
    Value.Text += "------------------<br/>";
    foreach ( DataRow CurrentRow in CurrentTable.Rows )
    {
        Value.Text += "<br/>    ";
        foreach ( DataColumn CurrentColumn in CurrentTable.Columns )
        {
            if ( CurrentRow[CurrentColumn] != null )
            {
                if ( CurrentRow[CurrentColumn] != DBNull.Value )
                {
                    Value.Text += CurrentRow[CurrentColumn].ToString();
                }
                else
                {
                    Value.Text += "NULL";
                }
                Value.Text += "<br/>    ";
            }
        }
    }
}
```

7   Save the page and code-behind module.

8   Build the project.

9   Test the page by right-clicking DisplayDataSetItems.aspx, selecting Browse With, and then selecting Microsoft Internet Explorer. The resulting screen should look like the following illustration.

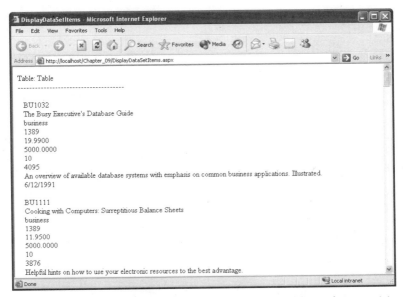

10 Scroll toward the bottom of the screen. You should see the transition between the titles and publishers tables, as the following illustration shows:

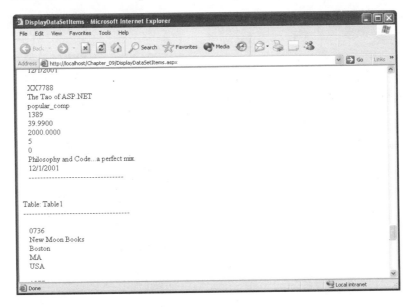

Updating Datasets

Once you've populated a dataset with data—either by using a *DataAdapter* or by calling the *ReadXml* method of the dataset—you might want to update that data. You can edit an individual value by specifying the table, row, and column of the item you want to edit and then supplying a new value.

```
myDS.Tables[0].Rows[0].Columns[2] = " popular_comp";
```

But what if you edit several values, and then you realize that you want to roll back one or more of the changes? Fortunately, the dataset provides robust support for accepting and rejecting changes in its data by maintaining multiple versions of the data for each row. Each row contains the following versions:

- *Original*   Contains the data originally loaded into the row.
- *Default*   Contains the default values for the row (specified by the *DefaultValue* property of the row's columns). If no defaults have been specified, this contains the same data as *Original*.
- *Current*   Contains updated data for any columns that have been updated, and the same data as *Original* for columns that have not been updated.
- *Proposed*   Valid after calling *BeginEdit* on a row and before calling the *EndEdit* or *CancelEdit* methods of the *DataRow*, the *Proposed* version contains changes to data that have not yet been applied to the *Current* version. If *CancelEdit* is called, the *Proposed* version is deleted. If *EndEdit* is called, the changes in the *Proposed* version are applied to the *Current* version.

You can determine whether changes have been made to an item in a row by comparing the item's *Original* or *Default* version with the *Current* version:

```
if ( CurrentRow[1, DataRowVersion.Current] ==
     CurrentRow[1, DataRowversion.Proposed] )
{
    // Take appropriate action
}
```

You can accept or reject changes to data on a row-by-row basis:

```
if ( CurrentRow[0, DataRowVersion.Current] == "" )
// Blank field not allowed
{
    CurrentRow.RejectChanges();
}
else
{
    CurrentRow.AcceptChanges();
}
```

Finally, you can check the current state of a row by checking the row's RowState property:

```
string CurrentState;
CurrentState = CurrentRow.RowState;
if ( CurrentState == DataRowState.Modified )
{
    // Take appropriate action
}
```

There are five possible row states.

- **Added** Represents a row that has been added to the table prior to *AcceptChanges* being called. Once *AcceptChanges* is called, this row's *RowState* will be set to *Unchanged*.
- **Deleted** Represents a row whose *Delete* method has been called.
- **Detached** Represents a newly created row that has not yet been added to a *DataRowCollection*, or a row that has been removed from a *DataRowCollection* but not destroyed.
- **Modified** Represents a row whose data has changed, but whose *AcceptChanges* method has not been called.
- **Unchanged** Represents a row whose data has not changed since the last call to *AcceptChanges*.

Once you've called *AcceptChanges* on the dataset, you would call the *Update* method of the *DataAdapter* used to load data into the dataset to update the underlying database with the new values.

Typed Datasets

One of the coolest new features of ADO.NET is the ability to create strongly typed datasets. Typed datasets are special classes, generated by the xsd.exe command-line utility, that inherit from the *DataSet* class. They use an XSD schema to create additional public properties and methods that allow you to access the columns of the dataset's tables directly by name, rather than having to use either an index or a late-bound key. This can improve run time performance and reduce the likelihood of errors in coding against the dataset.

You can create typed datasets two ways: you can create them using Visual Studio .NET, or, if you find the auto-generated code more than you need or you want finer control, you can create them manually. Let's look at the manual procedure first.

Creating a typed dataset manually for the AddTitles example shown earlier requires just a few steps. The following example assumes that you've already created an XSD schema for the table or tables in the dataset (you can use the AddTitle.xsd schema included with the practice files), which you can do with the *WriteXmlSchema* method of a dataset that's been loaded with data from the table or tables.

Create a typed dataset manually

1   Open a command prompt at the location of the XSD schema file.

2   Create the class for the typed dataset using the xsd.exe utility, located by default in the folder C:\Program Files\Microsoft Visual Studio .NET 2003\SDK\v1.1\Bin\:

```
xsd.exe /d /l:cs AddTitle.xsd /n:AddTitle
```

The /d option specifies that we want to create a dataset, the /l option sets the language as Visual C#, and the /n option specifies that the class should use the namespace *AddTitle*. AddTitle.xsd is the name of your XSD schema file, which is shown in the AddTitle.xsd listing that follows this section. The output of xsd.exe with these arguments is a .cs class file (in this case, AddTitle.cs).

3   Compile the class using the csc.exe command-line compiler, located by default in the folder *%windir%\Microsoft.NET\Framework\ %version%*, where *windir* is the Windows directory, and *version* is the version of the framework that is installed). Note that the three lines that follow should be entered as a single command:

```
csc.exe /t:library AddTitle.cs /r:System.dll
/r:System.Data.dll /r:System.XML.dll
/out:bin/AddTitle.dll
```

The /t option specifies that you want to compile as a library component (DLL), the /r options specify assemblies that you need to reference, and the /out option directs the compiler to save the compiled assembly in the bin subdirectory of the current directory.

▶   **Tip**   Note that to use xsd.exe and csc.exe without specifying the entire path to the executable, the paths to these programs must be registered in the PATH environment variable for the machine you're working on. The steps necessary to do this are detailed in Appendix C.

AddTitle.xsd

```
<?xml version="1.0" standalone="yes"?>
<xsd:schema id="TitleDataSet"
xmlns=""
xmlns:xsd="http://www.w3.org/2001/XMLSchema"
```

```
   xmlns:msdata="urn:schemas-microsoft-com:xml-msdata">
    <xsd:element name="TitleDataSet" msdata:IsDataSet="true">
     <xsd:complexType>
      <xsd:choice maxOccurs="unbounded">
       <xsd:element name="Titles">
       <xsd:complexType>
       <xsd:sequence>
       <xsd:element name="title_id" type="xsd:string" minOccurs="0" />
       <xsd:element name="title" type="xsd:string" minOccurs="0" />
       <xsd:element name="type" type="xsd:string" minOccurs="0" />
       <xsd:element name="pub_id" type="xsd:string" minOccurs="0" />
       <xsd:element name="price" type="xsd:decimal" minOccurs="0" />
       <xsd:element name="advance" type="xsd:decimal" minOccurs="0" />
       <xsd:element name="royalty" type="xsd:int" minOccurs="0" />
       <xsd:element name="ytd_sales" type="xsd:int" minOccurs="0" />
       <xsd:element name="notes" type="xsd:string" minOccurs="0" />
       <xsd:element name="pubdate" type="xsd:dateTime" minOccurs="0" />
       </xsd:sequence>
       </xsd:complexType>
       </xsd:element>
      </xsd:choice>
     </xsd:complexType>
    </xsd:element>
   </xsd:schema>
```

You can also create a typed dataset using Visual Studio .NET. The following steps walk you through doing just that on a new form modeled after AddTitle.aspx, the form you created in a previous example.

Create and use a typed dataset in Visual Studio .NET

1   Open Visual Studio, and then open the Chapter_09 project created earlier in the chapter.

2   Add a new Web Form to the project. Name the form **AddTitle_TypedDS.aspx.**

3   Copy the HTML code used in step 5 of the AddTitle.aspx example (see page 303) and paste it into the HTML view of AddTitle_TypedDS.aspx. Change the heading (between the <h3> tags) from Inserting a Title to **Inserting a Title with a Typed DataSet.**

4   Switch back to Design view and add a DataAdapter to the page. In the past examples, these have been created programmatically. Visual Studio .NET allows you to create them interactively. Open the Toolbox, click the Data tab, and then drag a *SqlDataAdapter* from the Toolbox onto the form.

The Data Adapter Configuration Wizard, shown in the following illustration, will appear:

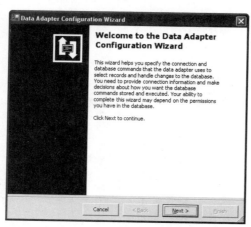

5   Click Next. You will be asked to select or create a connection.

6   Create a connection by clicking the New Connection button and the Data Link Properties dialog box will appear. Select the (local)\VSdot-NET instance of SQL Server, set the login information to use NT Integrated security and the database to pubs.

The Data Link Properties dialog box, when filled in, should look like the following illustration (assuming you are logged into a Windows account that has rights to connect to the VSdotNET MSDE instance). You can click the Test Connection button to ensure that the connection settings are correct:

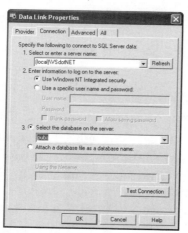

7   Click OK in the Data Link Properties dialog box, and then click Next in the Data Adapter Configuration Wizard. The Choose A Query Type page will appear, as shown in the following illustration.

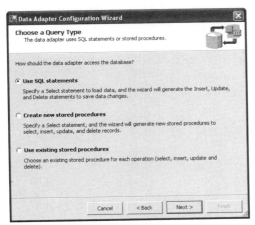

You will proceed to the Generate The SQL Statements page allowing you to generate the *Select* statement to use. While you can just type in commands (for instance, SELECT * FROM Titles), the Query Builder provides the means to create a query visually.

8   Click the Query Builder button. The Add Table dialog box will appear.

9   Select the Titles table from the list and click Add, and then click Close to close the Add Tables dialog box, which will return you to the Query Builder. You can click the (All Columns) check box to select all columns, or you can select the columns individually. Selecting explicitly the columns you want can often be more efficient. In this example, check each column individually, as shown in the following illustration. Click OK to close the Query Builder dialog box.

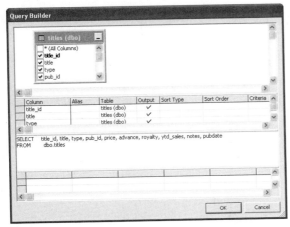

10   Click next on the Generate The SQL Statements page.

The final screen of the Data Adapter Configuration Wizard should appear, as shown in the following illustration.

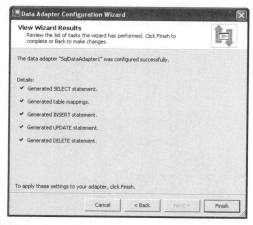

11 Click Finish.

A new window should appear at the bottom of the main editing window in Visual Studio .NET. It will have two components, sqlDataAdapter1 and sqlConnection1. Use the Properties windows to change the names to **daTitles** and **cnPubs**, respectively. When you've renamed the components, the screen should look like the following illustration.

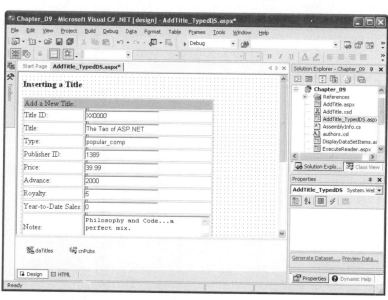

12 Click on the daTitles component. From the Data menu, select Generate DataSet. The Generate DataSet dialog box will appear, as shown in the following illustration. The default name for the typed dataset will be DataSet1. Change the dataset name to **TitleDataSet** and click OK.

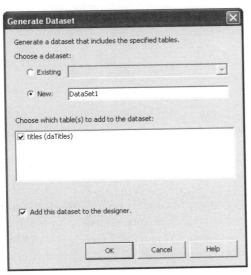

13 Switch to the code window by pressing F7, or by selecting View, and then Code. At the top of the file, add the following *using* clause:

```
using System.Data.SqlClient;
```

14 Add the following code to the *Page_Load* event handler:

```
if ( this.IsPostBack )
{
    cnPubs.Open();
    try
    {
        TitleDataSet.titlesRow MyTitleRow;
        MyTitleRow = titleDataSet1.titles.NewtitlesRow();
        MyTitleRow.title_id = title_id.Text;
        MyTitleRow.title = title.Text;
        MyTitleRow.type = type.Text;
        MyTitleRow.pub_id = pub_id.Text;
        MyTitleRow.price = decimal.Parse(price.Text);
        MyTitleRow.advance = decimal.Parse(advance.Text);
        MyTitleRow.royalty = int.Parse(royalty.Text);
        MyTitleRow.ytd_sales = int.Parse(ytd_sales.Text);
        MyTitleRow.notes = notes.Text;
        MyTitleRow.pubdate = DateTime.Parse(pubdate.Text);
        titleDataSet1.titles.AddtitlesRow(MyTitleRow);
        this.daTitles.Update(titleDataSet1);
```

```
        titlegrid.DataSource = titleDataSet1.Tables[0];
        titlegrid.DataBind();
    }
    finally
    {
        cnPubs.Close();
    }
}
else
{
    //To prevent conflicts on multiple inserts, we can
    //generate a random value for title_id
    Random RandomNum = new Random();
    title_id.Text = "XX" + String.Format("{0:000#}",
        RandomNum.Next(9999));
}
```

15 Save the page and code-behind module.

16 Build the project.

17 Test the page by right-clicking AddTitle_TypedDS.aspx, selecting Browse With, and then selecting Microsoft Internet Explorer. The resulting screen should look almost exactly like the previous AddTitles.aspx example, with a different heading.

Now when you create the dataset, you create an instance of *TitleDataSet*—the class that implements the typed dataset—instead of *DataSet*. When you look at the code Visual Studio .NET adds to the code-behind module, you will see the following declaration (note that in Visual Studio .NET 2003, this declaration is hidden in the region marked Web Form Designer Generated Code):

```
protected Chapter_09.TitleDataSet titleDataSet1;
```

Similarly, you'll see strong types for the table and row. The code that you added to the *Page_Load* event handler, for example, includes a strongly typed declaration for a row in the Titles table:

```
TitleDataSet.titlesRow MyTitleRow;
```

Another useful feature of typed datasets is that when you use them with Visual Studio .NET, you automatically get IntelliSense code completion for all the members of the *TitleDataSet*. This makes coding against a typed dataset much easier and considerably less error prone. The following illustration shows how easy it is to choose the correct field from a typed dataset using IntelliSense.

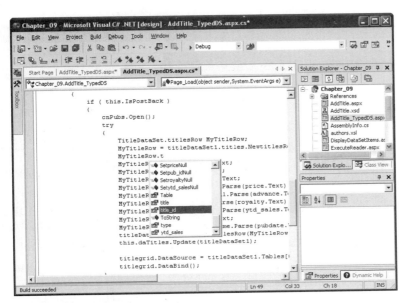

It's important to note that when you're programming against a typed dataset (rather than a standard dataset), the fields of the typed dataset are exposed as strongly typed properties. This means that if you try to assign data of an incompatible type to a property, you'll get an error at compile time (allowing you to fix the problem before your users find it). Therefore, typed datasets make it easier to create error-free data access code.

Using *DataView* Objects

The *DataView* class provides a means for sorting, searching, editing, filtering, and navigating *DataTable* objects. *DataViews* can also be data-bound, as you'll see in later examples. Data binding allows ASP.NET server controls to display bound data automatically, even when multiple rows or columns of data are contained in the datasource. This greatly simplifies the display of data in ASP.NET. You can access an unfiltered view of the data in a table in a dataset as follows:

```
DataView MyDV;
MyDV = MyDS.Tables[0].DefaultView;
```

Once you have a reference to the *DataView*, filter it by adding an expression to the *RowFilter* property:

```
myDV.RowFilter = "type='business'";
```

Search the DataView using the Find method:

```
Dim RowNum As Integer = myDV.Find("BU1032");
```

Sort the DataView by adding an expression to the Sort property:

```
myDV.Sort = "type, title_id DESC";
```

You've already seen some basic examples of binding to a *DataView*. You'll look at data binding in more detail later in this chapter.

Reading Data with *DataReader* Objects

Datasets are great when you need really rich control over your data—updates, rollbacks, reading and writing schemas, and so on. But when all you need to do is display some data quickly and efficiently, the *DataSet* object (and the *DataAdapter* used to fill it) has a fair amount of overhead that you might not want to incur. Enter the *DataReader* object.

A *DataReader* object provides the equivalent of a forward-only, read-only cursor on your data. It is both faster and more lightweight than a dataset object, making it ideal when you need to retrieve a set of rows and iterate over them just once (to display them, for example). Unlike datasets, datareaders can also be data-bound to directly, without the need for a *DataView*.

SqlDataReader

SqlDataReader is the class to use when accessing data from a SQL Server database. You create this class by calling the *ExecuteReader* method on a *SqlCommand* object.

```
SqlDataReader MySqlDR = MySqlCmd.ExecuteReader();
```

To access the rows in a SqlDataReader instance, call the Read method of the instance, usually in a loop:

```
while ( MySqlDR.Read() )
{
    Response.Write(MySqlDR.Item[0]);
}
```

▶ **Tip**   If you want a simple way to check if a datareader contains data before performing any operations on it, you can check the HasRows property (new for version 1.1 of the Framework), which returns a *true* if the datareader contains one or more rows of data.

Once you're finished with *SqlDataReader*, you should always call its *Close* method, as well as calling the *Close* method on the associated *Connection* object: *mySqlDR.Close();*

> ▶ **Note** To avoid having to explicitly close the connection associated with the Command object used to create either a *SqlDataReader* or an *OleDbData-Reader*, pass the *CommandBehavior.CloseConnection* argument to the *ExecuteReader* method of the Command:
>
> ```
> mySqlDR = mySqlCmd.ExecuteReader(CommandBehavior.CloseConnection);
> ```
>
> The connection associated with the Command object will be closed automatically when the *Close* method of the datareader is called. This makes it all the more important to always remember to call *Close* on your DataReader objects!

OleDbDataReader

Creating and using an *OleDbDataReader* object is essentially the same as for the *SqlDataReader*, with one notable exception. The *OleDbDataReader* can handle hierarchical recordsets retrieved using the *MSDataShape* OLE DB Provider (also known as the Data Shaping Service for OLE DB). When you create an *OleDbDataReader* based on an *OleDbCommand* that returns a hierarchical recordset, the OLE DB chapter is returned as a column in the *OleDbDataReader*. The value of the column is an *OleDbDataReader* representing the child records. See *http://msdn.microsoft.com/library/en-us/wp/htm/wpmdac_tf_shaping_service.asp* for more information on the Data Shaping Service for OLE DB.

Data Binding

One exciting advance in the move from classic ASP to ASP.NET is the availability of server-side data binding, which is the process of declaratively tying elements (such as controls) of the UI for a page to data in an underlying datastore. Data binding on the client has been available in Internet Explorer for a number of years, but it requires all of your users to use the same browser, or else you need to do a massive amount of testing to ensure compatibility with different browser versions. Server-side data binding solves this problem by binding and rendering data on the server and returning cross-browser-compatible HTML.

ASP.NET allows you to bind against a variety of sources, including properties and method call results, arrays and collections, and DataReader and DataView objects. Typically, binding is done either declaratively, using the *<%#expression%>* syntax, or by programmatically setting the *DataSource* property of a control to the desired datasource. The data is bound by calling the *DataBind* method, either at the *Page* level (which binds all controls on the page) or on the control being bound (which binds the control and any child controls). The *DataBind* method causes the control and its children to evaluate any data-binding expression(s) associated with the control and assign the resulting values to the appropriate control attribute. Data binding allows controls such as the

DataGrid control, which can handle multiple rows and columns, to iterate over and format the data specified by their *DataSource* property for display.

Simple Data Binding

The simplest type of data binding uses the <%#*expression*%> syntax to replace the <%#*expression*%> construct with the value represented by the expression. This is different than, for instance, the <%=*expression*%> syntax, which simply writes the result of the expression to the browser. With the <%#*expression*%> syntax the substitution takes place only when *DataBind()* is called. For example, the following listing shows a simple page that binds to a page-level property.

SimpleDataBinding.aspx

```
<%@ Page Language="cs" %>
<html>
  <head>
    <script runat="server">
      string Name;
      void btnSubmit_Click(object sender, EventArgs e)
      {
        Name = txtHello.Text;
        lblHello.Visible = true;
        DataBind();
      }
  </script>
  </head>
  <body>
    <asp:label id="lblHello" visible="false" runat="server">
      Hello, <%# Name %>!
    </asp:label>
    <form runat="server">
      <asp:textbox text="" id="txtHello" runat="server"/>
      <br>
      <asp:button text="Submit" id="btnSubmit"
        OnClick="btnSubmit_Click" runat="server" />
    </form>
  </body>
</html>
```

The output of this listing after entering a value and clicking the button is shown in the following illustration.

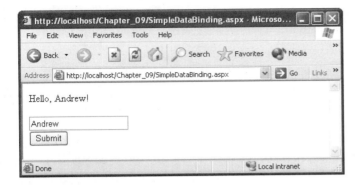

Binding to Controls

You can use the same syntax to bind to controls. For example, you can bind the selected item of a *DropDownList* control to the *Text* property of an ASP.NET *Label* control, as shown in the following example.

Bind data to a *Label* control

1 Open Visual Studio, and then open the Chapter_09 project created earlier in the chapter.

2 Add a new Web Form to the project. Name the form **ControlBinding.aspx**.

3 Add a DropDownList, a Label, and a Button to the form.

4 Change the *ID* property of the Label to **Flavor**, its *Visible* property to **False**, and its *Text* property to **Favorite Ice Cream: <%# MyList.SelectedItem.Text %>!**

5 Change the *ID* property of the DropDownList to **MyList**.

6 Change the *ID* property of the button to **Submit** and the *Text* property of the Button to **Submit**. The resulting screen should look similar to the illustration on the following page.

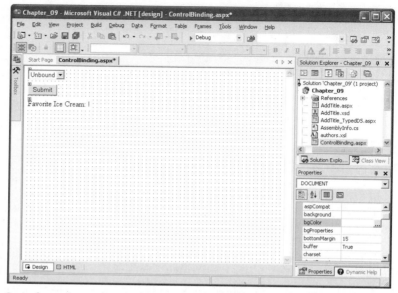

7   Switch to the code window by pressing F7, or by selecting View, then Code.

8   Add the following code to the *Page_Load* event handler:

```
if ( this.IsPostBack != true )
{
    ArrayList MyArrayList = new ArrayList();
    MyArrayList.Add("Chocolate");
    MyArrayList.Add("Vanilla");
    MyArrayList.Add("Strawberry");
    MyList.DataSource=MyArrayList;
    MyList.DataBind();
}
else
{
    Flavor.Visible = true;
}
DataBind();
```

9   Save the page and code-behind module.

10   Build the project.

11   Test the page by right-clicking ControlBinding.aspx, selecting
     Browse With, and then selecting Microsoft Internet Explorer. After
     you select a flavor from the drop-down list and click Submit, the
     resulting screen should look like the following illustration.

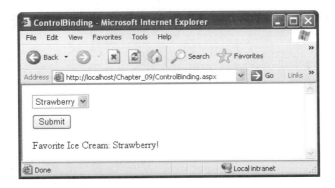

Using *DataBinder.Eval*

DataBinder.Eval is a static method used to evaluate a data-binding expression at run time. This can simplify the process of casting various data types to be displayed as text. The basic syntax of *DataBinder.Eval* is

```
<%# DataBinder.Eval(Container, EvalExpression, FormatExpression) %>
```

Container is the object that contains the expression to be evaluated. (For *DataGrid*, *DataList*, or *Repeater* controls, this expression is always *Container.DataItem.*) *EvalExpression* is the full name of the property or item to be evaluated. *FormatExpression* is a string formatting expression (such as *{0:c}*) to be used to format the string result. Note that if no format expression argument is passed, *DataBinder.Eval* will return an object instead of a string.

▶ **Important**   Because *DataBinder.Eval* uses late binding and reflection (which allows managed code to interrogate other managed code at run time), it can be significantly slower than the other data-binding techniques. For this reason, you should use *DataBinder.Eval* only when you need to, such as for performing string formatting on numeric data.

Using the *Data-Bound* Controls

Chapter 8 looked at the ASP.NET server controls and mentioned briefly one very important group of controls. The *DataBound* controls, which include the *DataGrid* control (and its constituent controls), the *DataList* control, and the *Repeater* control, allow you to set a data source programmatically. Then they iterate over that data source and display the data based on formatting that you define, either through properties of the control or by adding template definitions. The neat thing about this is that you define the formatting for a single row; the data-bound controls take care of applying that formatting to all rows of data.

Choosing which control to use rests largely on the format you want your data in and how much control you want over the formatting of the data. The *Data-Grid* control is the simplest to use and displays data in a table format. The *DataList* control is a little more involved in terms of implementation, but it provides a greater degree of control over formatting through the use of templates. Finally, for the control freak in all of us, the *Repeater* control, which has no built-in formatting of its own, provides ultimate control over formatting through templates.

Using *DataGrids*

The *DataGrid* control presents bound data in a tabular format and provides a number of properties that you can use to format the data. This control can automatically generate all columns in the table from its *DataSource* property, or you can use specialized column controls to provide additional functionality or formatting for a given column or columns.

At its simplest, there are three basic steps to using a *DataGrid* control.

1 Add the *DataGrid* control to the page.

2 Set the *DataSource* property of the *DataGrid* to an appropriate data source. This data source can be defined in the page, or you can call a method in an external object to supply the data.

3 Call the *DataBind* method of the control to automatically bind the data to the control. You can also call the *DataBind* method of the *Page* object, which will bind (or rebind) all of the data-bound controls on the page by calling *DataBind* on each control in turn.

Let's look at an example. In "HTML Controls" in Chapter 8, you saw an example that used a drop-down list box to list flavors of ice cream for a user to choose from. Suppose that you want to show similar information in a table format. The problem with this approach is that the data is explicitly added to the control in the code (or declaratively by adding items to the control in its tag declaration). Thus, any time the data changes you have to explicitly change the code that creates the control. Additionally, because the creation of the data and the creation of the control are tightly coupled, it's not possible to reuse this data, either elsewhere on the page or elsewhere in the application.

So in this first example, you'll create the data that you want to use in a custom procedure in a *<script>* block, and then call that procedure in order to populate the data source of your *DataGrid* control. Start with a very simple *DataGrid* that has no formatting whatsoever.

Bind an array to a *DataGrid*

1 Open Visual Studio, and then open the Chapter_09 project created earlier in the chapter.

2 Add a new Web Form to the project. Name the form **DataGrid.aspx**.

3 Add a *Label* control and a *DataGrid* control to the form.

4 Change the *ID* property of the datagrid to **MyGrid**, change the *ID* property of the label to **Title**, and then set the *Text* property of the label to **DataGrid Example**.

5 Switch to the code window by pressing F7, or by selecting View, and then Code.

6 Add the *CreateData* function inside the *DataGrid* class:

```
private ICollection CreateData()
{
    ArrayList DataArray = new ArrayList();

    DataArray.Add("Chocolate");
    DataArray.Add("Vanilla");
    DataArray.Add("Strawberry");
    DataArray.Add("Pistachio");
    DataArray.Add("Rocky Road");

    return DataArray;
}
```

This function simply creates an *ArrayList* named *DataArray*, adds a few items, and then returns the *ArrayList* to the caller.

7 Add the following code to the *Page_Load* event handler:

```
MyGrid.DataSource = CreateData();
MyGrid.DataBind();
```

Because *CreateData* returns an *ArrayList* (which implements the *ICollection* interface), you can actually use the function itself for the *DataSource* property of the *DataGrid* control.

8 Save the page and code-behind module.

9 Build the project.

10 Test the page by right-clicking DataGrid.aspx, selecting Browse With, and then selecting Microsoft Internet Explorer. The resulting screen should look like the illustration on the following page.

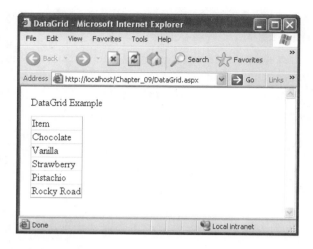

Although this is a very simple example, you used two lines of code (setting the *DataSource* and calling *DataBind*) to accomplish what would have taken considerably more code in classic ASP. Now let's jazz things up a bit by binding to live data with multiple columns per row in a grid.

Bind live data to a *DataGrid*

1   Open Visual Studio, and then open the Chapter_09 project created earlier in the chapter.

2   Add a new Web Form to the project and name the form **DataGridEdit.aspx**.

3   Add a *DataGrid* control to the form and change the *ID* property of the datagrid to **MyGrid**.

4   Drag a *SqlDataAdapter* onto the page from the Data tab of the Toolbox, and use the techniques you learned in the typed dataset example earlier in the chapter to configure the data adapter to query the Publishers table of the Pubs database in the VSdotNET MSDE instance. (You can use "SELECT * FROM Publishers" as the SQL statement for the data adapter.) Change the name of the resulting data adapter to **PubAdapter**, and change the name of the *SqlConnection* to **PubsConn**.

5   Generate a *DataSet* based on *PubAdapter* by selecting it on the design surface, and then clicking the Generate DataSet link in the Properties window. Name the generated dataset **PublisherDataSet**.

6   Select the *DataGrid* control, and set its *DataSource* property to *publisherDataSet1*, and its *DataMember* property to *publishers*. At the end of this step, the IDE should look similar to the following illustration.

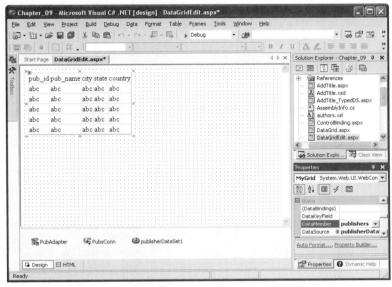

7   Switch to the code-behind module for the page and add the following code to the Page_Load event handler:

```
PubAdapter.Fill(publisherDataSet1);
MyGrid.DataBind();
```

8   Save the page and code-behind module.

9   Build the project.

10   Test the page by right-clicking DataGridEdit.aspx, selecting Browse With, and then selecting Microsoft Internet Explorer. The resulting screen should look like the illustration on the next page. Leave DataGridEdit.aspx open in the IDE because you'll be working on it again in the next example.

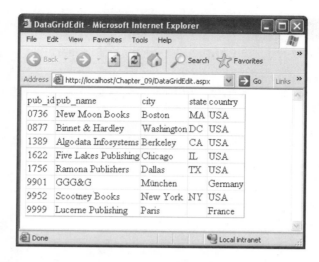

But wait! There's more. In addition to autogenerating columns from the bound data, *DataGrids* also support creating columns declaratively. This gives you greater control over both the formatting and the behavior of individual columns. For example, you can use a *BoundColumn* control to provide customized header text for a column, or to apply special formatting to the bound text in each row. You can also use a *ButtonColumn* control to display a command button in each row of a column, an *EditButtonColumn* control to provide in-place editing for a row, or a *HyperlinkColumn* control to provide a hyperlink for each row of the grid, with the text caption, the URL, or both being data-bound. Finally, you use a *TemplateColumn* control to apply complex formatting to each row of a specific column. In addition to manually creating and modifying the various controls within the grid, you can also use Visual Studio .NET to control the behavior and look of the *DataGrid*. Let's see how we can improve this example's appearance using Visual Studio .NET.

Use Visual Studio .NET to format a *DataGrid*

1   Switch to DataGridEdit.aspx and then click on the *DataGrid* control. Look at the Properties window. Near the bottom of the Properties window you will see two links, AutoFormat and Property Builder, which invoke tools specially designed for working with the *DataGrid* control.

2   Click on AutoFormat. The Auto Format dialog box will appear. Select "Professional 1" from the scheme list, as shown in the following illustration, and then click OK.

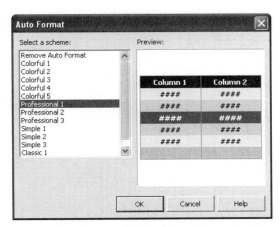

Simply by selecting the scheme from the Auto Format dialog, the HTML declaration for the *DataGrid* will change from a very simple declaration to something similar to the following code. Using schemes helps you quickly create a consistent look for all your datagrids.

```
<asp:DataGrid id="MyGrid"
    style="ZINDEX: 101; LEFT: 19px; POSITION: absolute;
           TOP: 22px" runat="server"
    BorderColor="#999999" BorderStyle="None" BorderWidth="1px"
    BackColor="White" CellPadding="3" GridLines="Vertical">
    <SelectedItemStyle Font-Bold="True" ForeColor="White"
                       BackColor="#008A8C">
    </SelectedItemStyle>
    <AlternatingItemStyle BackColor="#DCDCDC">
    </AlternatingItemStyle>
    <ItemStyle ForeColor="Black" BackColor="#EEEEEE">
    </ItemStyle>
    <HeaderStyle Font-Bold="True" ForeColor="White"
                 BackColor="#000084">
    </HeaderStyle>
    <FooterStyle ForeColor="Black" BackColor="#CCCCCC">
    </FooterStyle>
    <PagerStyle HorizontalAlign="Center" ForeColor="Black"
                BackColor="#999999" Mode="NumericPages">
    </PagerStyle>
</asp:DataGrid>
```

3   Click on the Property Builder link at the bottom of the Properties window. The Properties dialog box appears, as shown in the illustration on the next page.

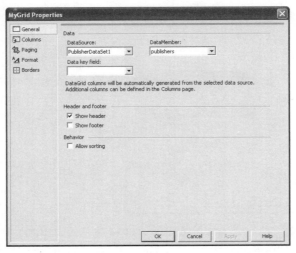

4   Click the Columns item in the left side of the dialog box. Uncheck Create Columns Automatically At Run Time. Use the Add (>) button to add a column to the Selected Columns list box for each data field in the Available Columns list box, changing the Header text to a friendlier name for each column, as shown in the following illustration.

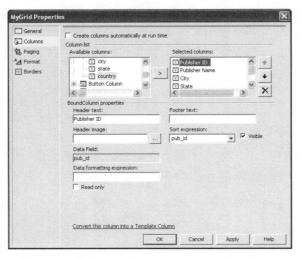

5   Click the Format item on the left side of the dialog box, and you can select several options from a tree view on the resulting dialog box. Click on Header and change the Horizontal Alignment to Center. When finished, the dialog box should look like the following illustration.

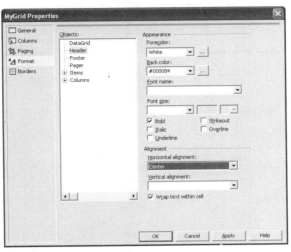

6 Click OK to apply the changes and close the dialog box.

7 Save the page. Because you didn't change anything in the code-behind module, you don't need to rebuild the project.

8 Test the page by right-clicking DataGridEdit.aspx, selecting Browse With, and then selecting Microsoft Internet Explorer. The resulting screen should look like the following illustration. Leave DataGrid-Edit.aspx open in the IDE, as you'll be working on it again in the next example:

This looks much better, but there is still more we can do to improve this example. We might want to add the ability to sort by one or more of the columns.

Sort a DataGrid

1   With the DataGrid control selected in DataGridEdit.aspx, click on the Property Builder link. The Property Builder dialog box will appear.

2   Click on Columns on the left side of the dialog box, and note that the Sort Expression for each column is set to the name of the field the column is based upon. This is because in the previous example, you used bound columns to create the columns for the grid, which automatically set a default Sort Expression based on the typed dataset to which the datagrid is bound.

3   To enable sorting, click the General item on the left side of the dialog box, and then check the Allow Sorting check box.

4   To make sorting work, you'll also add code to perform the sort and re-bind the grid in a later step, so change the DataSource drop-down list from PublisherDataSet1 to (Unbound). Click OK to close the dialog box when you're finished.

5   Click the DataGrid, and click the lightning bolt in the Properties pane to show the events available in the grid. Double-click the field to the right of SortCommand. This will insert an event handler for the event. The result should look similar to the following illustration.

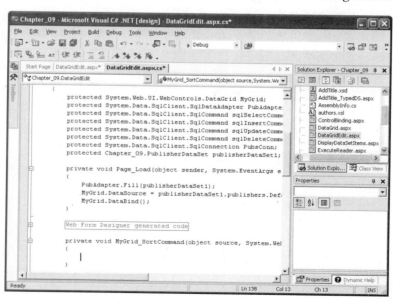

6 Add the following code to the event handler:

```
DataView SortView = publisherDataSet1.publishers.DefaultView;
SortView.Sort = e.SortExpression;
MyGrid.DataSource = SortView;
MyGrid.DataBind();
```

This code creates a new *DataView* based on the publishers table from the typed dataset, sets the sort expression of the dataview to the one passed from the column whose header is clicked at run time, and then re-binds the grid.

7 Since you removed the design-time binding of the datagrid in Step 2, you'll also need to change the code in the *Page_Load* event handler to the following code:

```
PubAdapter.Fill(publisherDataSet1);
if (!IsPostBack)
{
    MyGrid.DataSource = publisherDataSet1.publishers.DefaultView;
    MyGrid.DataBind();
}
```

This code fills the dataset and, if the request is not the result of a postback, sets the *DataSource* of the datagrid to the default dataview of the publishers table, and then databinds the grid.

8 Save the page and code-behind module.

9 Build the project.

10 Test the page by right-clicking DataGridEdit.aspx, selecting Browse With, and then selecting Microsoft Internet Explorer. The resulting screen should look like the following illustration. Leave DataGridEdit.aspx open in the IDE, as you'll be working on it again in the next example.

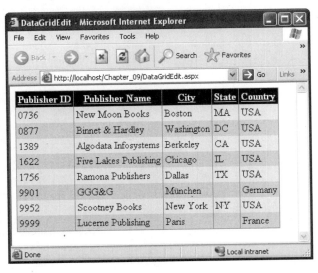

You can click on any of the column headers to sort the data by the selected column. Because you can specify the exact sort expression, you can also choose to make the sort more complex, perhaps sorting by State and City when you click on the State header.

▶ **Tip**   The preceding example of sorting only implements sorting in one direction. That is, if you click a given heading more than once, the second (and subsequent) clicks have no effect. If you want to enable both ascending and descending sorts for a datagrid, you will need to track the current sort order. An easy way to do this is to save the current sort order to the ViewState field after setting the *Sort* property of the dataview, then compare that value to the *SortExpression* property the next time the *SortCommand* event is fired, adding "DESC" to the *Sort* property if the same column is clicked twice in a row (and setting the *Sort* property to e.*SortExpression* normally otherwise). The code required to perform a two-way sort follows:

```
private void MyGrid_SortCommand(object source,
    System.Web.UI.WebControls.DataGridSortCommandEventArgs e)
{
    DataView SortView = publisherDataSet1.publishers.DefaultView;
    string CurrentSort = "";
    if (ViewState["Sort"] != null)
    {
        CurrentSort = (string)ViewState["Sort"];
    }
    if (CurrentSort.StartsWith(e.SortExpression))
    {
        if (CurrentSort.EndsWith("DESC"))
        {
            SortView.Sort = e.SortExpression;
        }
        else
        {
            SortView.Sort = e.SortExpression + " DESC";
        }
    }
    else
    {
        SortView.Sort = e.SortExpression;
    }
    ViewState["Sort"] = SortView.Sort;
    MyGrid.DataSource = SortView;
    MyGrid.DataBind();
}
```

Now that you've seen how to sort data in a *DataGrid*, you might want to allow in-place editing, as shown in the following example.

Edit and delete data in a *DataGrid*

1   Click on the *DataGrid* and then click on the link to the Property Builder. Click on Columns on the left side and then click on Button Column label to expand the types of buttons. Using the Add (>) button, add an Edit, Update, Cancel button column, and a Delete button column. Rearrange the columns so that the Edit, Update, Cancel button is first in the list and Delete is second, as shown in the following illustration.

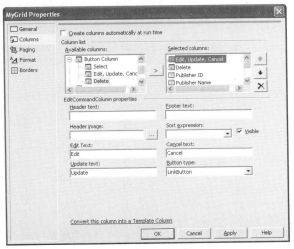

2   To keep the example simple, disable sorting for this example by clicking the General item and then unchecking the Allow Sorting check box. Click OK to apply the changes and close the dialog box.

3   Switch to the code-behind module, and add the following line to *Page_Load*, just before the call to *DataBind()*. The *DataKeyField* property controls which field is used as the primary key for editing, to allow you to identify the selected record:

```
MyGrid.DataKeyField = "pub_id";
```

4   Using the same techniques you used to add the *SortCommand* event handler in the last example, add an event handler for the *EditCommand* event. Add the following code to the event handler:

```
MyGrid.DataSource = publisherDataSet1.publishers.DefaultView;
MyGrid.DataKeyField = "pub_id";
MyGrid.EditItemIndex = e.Item.ItemIndex;
MyGrid.DataBind();
```

This code sets the *EditItemIndex* to the index passed in as a member of the *DataGridCommandEventArgs* object and re-binds the grid.

5   Add an event handler for the *CancelCommand* event, using the same techniques as in Step 4. Add the following code to the event handler:

```
MyGrid.DataSource = publisherDataSet1.publishers.DefaultView;
MyGrid.DataKeyField = "pub_id";
MyGrid.EditItemIndex = -1;
MyGrid.DataBind();
```

This code sets the *EditItemIndex* to -1, indicating that no row should be selected as an edit row.

6   Add an event handler for the *UpdateCommand* event. Add the following code to the event handler:

```
TextBox m_pub_name, m_city, m_state, m_country;
m_pub_name = (TextBox)e.Item.Cells[3].Controls[0];
m_city = (TextBox)e.Item.Cells[4].Controls[0];
m_state = (TextBox)e.Item.Cells[5].Controls[0];
m_country = (TextBox)e.Item.Cells[6].Controls[0];
PublisherDataSet.publishersDataTable pubTable =
publisherDataSet1.publishers;
PublisherDataSet.publishersRow rowToUpdate =
    (PublisherDataSet.publishersRow)pubTable.Rows[e.Item.ItemIndex];
rowToUpdate.pub_name = m_pub_name.Text;
rowToUpdate.city = m_city.Text;
rowToUpdate.state = m_state.Text;
rowToUpdate.country = m_country.Text;
PubAdapter.Update(publisherDataSet1);
MyGrid.DataSource = publisherDataSet1.publishers.DefaultView;
MyGrid.EditItemIndex = -1;
MyGrid.DataBind();
```

This code updates the typed dataset with the values from the datagrid and then calls the *SqlDataAdapter.Update* method to update the back-end database. Because the code gets the values from the item passed in as part of the *DataGridCommandEventArgs*, you have to cast the control to the appropriate type (in this case, *TextBox*) to get its *Text* property, which contains the updated value.

7   Add an event handler for the *DeleteCommand* event. Add the following code to the event handler:

```
publisherDataSet1.publishers.Rows.Item(e.Item.ItemIndex).Delete();
PubAdapter.Update(publisherDataSet1);
MyGrid.DataSource = publisherDataSet1.publishers.DefaultView;
MyGrid.EditItemIndex = -1;
MyGrid.DataBind();
```

This code deletes the appropriate row from the dataset and then calls *Update* on the data adapter. Note that if, as in the Publishers table, foreign key relationships are associated with a given table, you might not be able to delete a row if a row in a related table is dependent on that row.

8 Save the page and code-behind module.

9 Build the project.

10 Test the page by right-clicking DataGridEdit.aspx, selecting Browse With, and then selecting Microsoft Internet Explorer. The resulting screen should look like the following illustration.

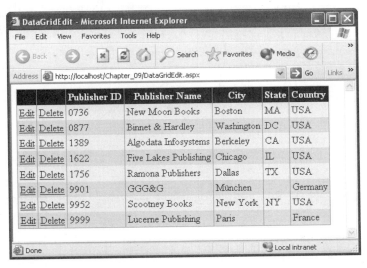

You should now be able to edit, update, and delete rows (assuming there are no foreign key constraints that would prevent deletion, as there are in the case of the Publishers table) from the table.

▶ **Important** In-place editing in a *DataGrid* is not always the best solution to providing editing. Alternatively, especially when there are a number of columns, you could insert a link column to an edit form, or even use the *EditCommand* to link to a different view of the data for editing.

Using *DataLists*

DataLists provide an excellent mix of built-in functionality and control over display formatting. Unlike the *DataGrid* control, in which the rows are displayed one after the other in a table format, the *DataList* can display its items in multiple columns and can display rows horizontally or vertically.

Bind to a *DataList* control

1 Open Visual Studio, and then open the Chapter_09 project created earlier in the chapter.

2   Add a new Web Form to the project. Name the form
    TitlesDataList1.aspx.

3   Add a Label and a DataList to the form. Change the *Text* property of
    the Label to **Binding to a DataList control**. Change the ID of the
    DataList to **TitleList**, RepeatColumns to **3**, and GridLines to **Both**.

4   While Visual Studio .NET also has a Property Builder for DataList
    controls, sometimes it is useful to manually create the code to be dis-
    played for each row in the DataList. In this case, you will start with a
    simple bit of code for the Item Template, but it will become more
    complex as the example becomes more complex. To do this, switch
    to HTML mode, and find the *<asp:DataList>* opening tag, and then
    insert the following code between the opening and closing
    <asp:DataList> tags:

```
<ItemTemplate>
    <h5><%# DataBinder.Eval(Container.DataItem,"title")%></h5>
    <br/>
</ItemTemplate>
```

5   Switch to the code window by pressing F7, or by selecting View, then
    Code. Add the following *using* clause at the top of the code file:

```
using System.Data.SqlClient;
```

6   Scroll down to the *Page_Load* event handler. In this example, you
    will use a *DataAdapter* and a *DataSet* to fill the *DataList*. Insert the
    following code:

```
string ConnStr;
DataSet MyDS = new DataSet();
ConnStr = @"server=(local)\VSdotNET;database=pubs;" +
    "Trusted_Connection=yes";
string SQL;
SQL = "SELECT * FROM Titles ORDER BY Title";
SqlConnection MySqlConn = new SqlConnection(ConnStr);
SqlDataAdapter MySqlAdapter = new SqlDataAdapter(SQL,MySqlConn);
MySqlConn.Open();
try
{
    MySqlAdapter.Fill(MyDS);
    TitleList.DataSource = MyDS.Tables[0].DefaultView;
    TitleList.DataBind();
}
finally
{
    MySqlConn.Close();
}
```

7   Save the page and code-behind module.

8 Build the project.

9 Test the page by right-clicking TitlesDataList1.aspx, selecting Browse With, and then selecting Microsoft Internet Explorer. The resulting screen should look like the following illustration.

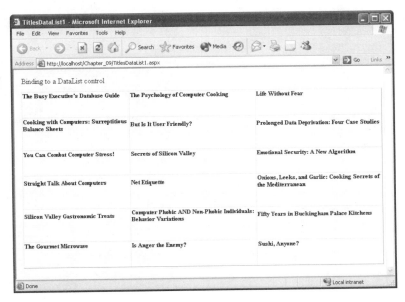

The *<ItemTemplate>* is but one of the templates that you can use with the *DataList* control, but they all work similarly. Other templates that you can define include the following:

- *AlternatingItemTemplate* Sets the formatting for alternating items.
- *EditItemTemplate* Formats the fields used when an item in the *DataList* is switched to Edit mode.
- *FooterTemplate* Sets formatting for the footer of the *DataList*.
- *HeaderTemplate* Sets formatting for the header of the *DataList*.
- *SelectedItemTemplate* Sets the formatting for the item in the *DataList* that has been selected by the user.
- *SeparatorTemplate* Sets the format of the divider between items in the *DataList*.

Like a *DataGrid*, a *DataList* can be set up for in-place editing of values. This requires adding a *LinkButton* or *Button* control to the *ItemTemplate* with the *CommandName* set to "edit"; implementing an *EditItemTemplate*; setting up the event handlers for the *EditCommand*, *DeleteCommand*, *CancelCommand*, and

UpdateCommand events; and mapping the event handlers to the events. When the Edit button for an item is clicked, the event handler should set the *EditItem-Index* to the number of the item that was clicked, which can be retrieved from the *DataListCommandEventArgs* passed to the event handler. The *EditItemTemplate* should include *LinkButton* or *Button* controls for the *DeleteCommand*, *Cancel-Command*, and *UpdateCommand*, and event handlers should be added for each.

Using Repeaters

The *Repeater* control lets you go hog-wild with templates. If you can write it in HTML and/or server controls, you can put it into a template.

▶ **Important**   Because of the way that you add HTML code to a *Repeater* control, it is possible to create a perfectly valid page that will not display properly in the Visual Studio .NET Designer window.

The following listing shows how you can update the previous example to work with a *Repeater* instead of a *DataList*. It adds a *HeaderTemplate* and a *SeparatorTemplate* to improve the look of the page.

Use a *Repeater* with headers and separators

1   Open Visual Studio, and then open the Chapter_09 project created earlier in the chapter.

2   Add a new Web Form to the project. Name the form **TitlesRepeater.aspx**.

3   When using a *Repeater* control, you will want to use flow layout rather than the default grid layout. The *Repeater* control does not allow for placement using the grid layout, and will move to the upper left of the page even in Grid Layout mode. Change to Flow Layout by right-clicking on the page, selecting Properties from the context menu, and then setting the page layout to Flow Layout.

4   Add a Label and a Repeater to the form. Change the *Text* property of the Label to **Binding to a Repeater control**. Change the ID of the Repeater to **TitleRepeater**.

5   Switch to HTML mode, find the *<asp:Repeater>* opening tag, and then insert the following code between the opening and closing *<asp:Repeater>* tags:

```
<ItemTemplate>
    <table>
        <tr>
            <td rowspan="4">
                <img align="top"
```

```
                     src='<%# DataBinder.Eval(Container.DataItem,
    "title_id", "/quickstart/aspplus/images/title-{0}.gif") %>' >
              </td>
           </tr>
           <tr>
              <td>
                 <em>Title: </em>
              </td>
              <td nowrap>
              <%# DataBinder.Eval(Container.DataItem, "title")%>
                 <br/>
              </td>
           </tr>
           <tr>
              <td>
                 <em>Price: </em>
              </td>
              <td nowrap>
              <%# DataBinder.Eval(Container.DataItem, "price",
   "{0:c}")%>
                 <br/>
              </td>
           </tr>
           <tr>
              <td>
                 <em>Category: </em>
              </td>
              <td nowrap>
               <%# DataBinder.Eval(Container.DataItem, "type")%>
                 <br/>
              </td>
           </tr>
        </table>
     </ItemTemplate>
     <HeaderTemplate>
        <h4 style="background-color:silver;">Titles</h4>
     </HeaderTemplate>
     <SeparatorTemplate>
        <hr>
     </SeparatorTemplate>
```

6   Switch to the code window by pressing F7, or by selecting View, and
    then Code. Add the following *using* clauses at the top of the code file:

    ```
    using System.Data.SqlClient;
    ```

7   Scroll down to the *Page_Load* event handler. In this example, you
    will use a *DataAdapter* and a *DataSet* to fill the *DataList*. This code
    is identical to the code in the previous example, except that a

Repeater is bound to a *DataSet* rather than a *DataList*. Insert the following code:

```
string ConnStr;
DataSet MyDS = new DataSet();
ConnStr = @"server=(local)\VSdotNET;database=pubs; " +
    "Trusted_Connection=yes";
string SQL;
SQL = "SELECT * FROM Titles";
SqlConnection MySqlConn = new SqlConnection(ConnStr);
SqlDataAdapter MySqlAdapter = new SqlDataAdapter(SQL,MySqlConn);
MySqlConn.Open();
try
{
  MySqlAdapter.Fill(MyDS);
  TitleRepeater.DataSource = MyDS.Tables[0].DefaultView;
  TitleRepeater.DataBind();
}
finally
{
  MySqlConn.Close();
}
```

8 Save the page and code-behind module.

9 Build the project.

10 Test the page by right-clicking TitlesRepeater.aspx, selecting Browse With, and then selecting Microsoft Internet Explorer. The resulting screen should look like the following illustration.

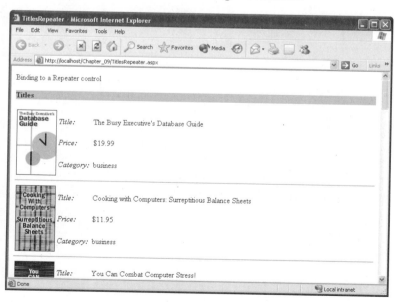

For the images in this example to be displayed, the ASP.NET QuickStart samples must be installed on the machine on which the example is run.

All templates available to the DataList control can be used with the Repeater control, and editing is handled the same with a Repeater as with a DataList.

Chapter 9 Quick Reference

To	Do this
Connect to a SQL Server database	Create and open an instance of the SqlConnection class from the System.Data.SqlClient namespace.
Connect to an OLE DB datasource	Create and open an instance of the OleDbConnection class from the System.Data.OleDb namespace.
Execute SELECT, UPDATE, INSERT, or DELETE statements against a database	Create an instance of the SqlCommand or OleDbCommand class, define a query, and call one of its Execute methods.
Use an in-memory cache of hierarchical data	Create an instance of the DataSet class from the System.Data namespace. Populate the dataset by calling the Fill method of the SqlDataAdapter or OleDbDataAdapter class.
Display read-only data in a bound control	Bind the control to a SqlDataReader or an OleDbDataReader. Be sure to pass the CommandBehavior.*CloseConnection* argument to the *ExecuteReader* method when creating the datareader. This ensures that the underlying connection is closed when the datareader is closed.
Bind data to a control	Set the *DataSource* property of the control to the *DataReader*, *DataView*, or other data source, and then call the *DataBind* method of the control (or call the page's *DataBind* method).
Edit bound data in a *DataGrid*	Add an Edit, Update, Cancel button column using the Property Builder, and add event handlers for Edit, Update, and Cancel in code.
Delete bound data in a *DataGrid*	Add a Delete button column using the Property Builder, and add a *Delete* event handler in code.
Display bound data in multiple columns	Use a *DataList* control and set the *RepeatColumns* attribute to the number of columns desired.
Display bound data with the greatest possible flexibility	Use a *Repeater* control, and manually add HTML code, along with data-binding directives.

Part

4

Beyond the Basics

10

Creating Custom Server Controls

In this chapter, you will learn how to:
■ Choose a base class for your control.
■ Create a namespace for your control.
■ Register and use your control in a page.
■ Extend and aggregate existing controls.
■ Maintain state in custom server controls.
■ Handle postbacks.

You've spent the last two chapters studying ASP.NET server controls, Microsoft ADO.NET, and data-binding. By now you're probably thinking, "These server controls sure are cool, but I wish I could create my own." Well, wish no longer! In this chapter, you'll learn how to create custom ASP.NET server controls.

There are nearly as many reasons for developing custom server controls as there are developers, but generally these reasons fall into three main categories: reuse, specialization, and maintenance.

Custom server controls make reuse easy. You can wrap up a bunch of related functionality and UI elements into a control, and then reuse that control where you need that functionality. For example, you could create a server control that encapsulates all of the fields and validation logic necessary for user registration. Then, instead of rewriting that code every time you need a user registration screen, you simply add your control to the page.

Specialization refers to taking an existing piece of functionality, such as a server control, and adding your own customized functionality to it. Specialization in ASP.NET server controls is typically done through inheritance. You specialize through inheritance by inheriting from a class that provides most of the functionality you want, and then adding additional functions or overriding existing ones and adding your own implementation of those functions. The *TextBox-Plus* control sample later in this chapter provides an example of specialization.

Finally, custom ASP.NET server controls simplify the maintenance of your applications. Once you have developed and tested a server control, you can reliably use it in many places. If you find a bug in your control, you can fix it in a single place (the source class for your control), and all you need to do to distribute the fix is replace the assembly containing the fixed control. This is a major improvement over reuse through include files (or having no reuse at all).

Creating Your First Control

Creating custom server controls with ASP.NET is fairly straightforward. A custom ASP.NET server control is any class that inherits from the *Control* class of the *System.Web.UI* namespace, or one that inherits from any of the controls derived from *Control*. Choosing the control from which to derive your custom control is largely a matter of how much functionality you want to build into your control. You'll learn how to choose a control to inherit from later in this section.

All server controls that send output directly to the browser do so by overriding the *Render* method of the control from which they're derived. Controls derived from a control with its own UI rendering (such as the *TextBox* server control) should also call the *Render* method on the base class in order to have the base control render its own output. Note that the location in your code at which you call the *Render* method of the base class is important. That's where the rendered output of the base control will appear. The *Render* method of the sample file TextBoxPlus.cs, included with the sample code for this chapter, demonstrates this concept.

In addition to sending output to the browser directly through the *Render* method, some custom controls (compositional controls in particular) send output to the browser indirectly by overriding the *CreateChildControls* method of the base *Control* class, which is used to add controls to a custom control at runtime. Some custom controls also call the *RenderChildren* method, which causes all of the child controls of a given control to execute their *Render* methods.

▶ **Tip**   While there is no inherent difference in the resulting HTML on the browser between rendering controls using the *Render* method and composing controls using the *CreateChildControls* method, there are differences in terms of performance and ease of programming. Using composition is somewhat easier for the developer, and it does not require any knowledge of HTML. Rendering offers better performance and reduced overhead, but to take advantage of it you do need to know HTML. Additionally, if you want to create a control that contains two distinct server controls (such as a text box with a built-in validation control), a composite control is really the only way to go.

Creating a Namespace

Each custom control must belong to a namespace. The @ *Register* directive, which makes custom controls available for use in a page, has a *Namespace* attribute that is used to locate the control class to instantiate at runtime.

You create a namespace using the *namespace* keyword. In C#, you use the *namespace* keyword and a bracketed block of code following it to define the scope of the namespace.

```
namespace myNS
{
  // Class definitions, etc. go inside the namespace
}
```

Note that if you are creating your custom control using Microsoft Visual Studio .NET, the IDE will create the namespace for you automatically.

▶ **Important**   Although Visual Studio .NET creates a namespace for each new project automatically, this is implemented differently depending on the language you choose. For example, in a Microsoft Visual C# project, the *namespace* keyword is added to class files and code-behind files automatically.

In a Visual Basic .NET Web application, the namespace for the project is defined by the *Root Namespace* option set in the Project Properties dialog box for the project. This means that although you will not actually see the *Namespace* keyword in your class files, a namespace will be created when the class is compiled during the build process for the project.

In both languages, the default name for the namespace is the name of the project.

Creating a Class

Each custom server control is defined in a class. You can have more than one class defined in a single namespace within a file, but the class is what defines the boundary of the control. You can put multiple controls within a single file, if you want. When you compile this file, all of the classes (and the controls they represent) are compiled into a single assembly. When you have multiple related controls, having them all in a single assembly can make deploying your controls simpler.

Similar to namespaces, classes in Visual C# .NET are defined with the *class* keyword and a pair of curly braces that together define the scope of the class.

```
class myControl
{
  // Variables, procedures, etc.
}
```

As with namespaces, Visual Studio .NET automatically takes care of creating a class for you when you create a new Web Control Library project. This default class, which inherits from the WebControl class in the System.Web.UI.WebControls namespace, contains a property declaration for a default Text property, as well as an overridden Render method that renders the contents of the Text property to the browser. These default members are provided to give you a head start in creating your own control functionality.

> ▶ **Important**   The Standard Edition of Visual C# .NET does not support the Web Control Library project type. You can, however, still add a Web Custom Control to a Web Project. If you want to create a standalone assembly for your custom control for reuse in other projects, you can simply remove the default Web Form (WebForm1.aspx) from the Web Project, and then add one or more Web Custom Control classes to the project for the control or controls you want to create.

Inheriting from a Base Class

One of the most important steps in creating a custom server control is choosing the class from which your control will inherit. This can be a more difficult decision than you might think, because you have so many choices.

You need to consider both how the control will be used and who will use it. Since one of the reasons for creating custom controls in the first place is to reuse controls that have most (but not quite all) of the functionality you need, you might be tempted to simply jump right into inheriting a very rich control to get the most bang for your buck. But keep in mind that any public property, method, or event exposed by the base control will be exposed by a derived control automatically. If you don't plan for this, your control might do something unexpected, or you might unwittingly introduce bugs when someone uses the control in a way that you didn't anticipate.

This might not be a problem if you are creating the control for your own use. If you plan to share it with others, however, just remember that people can be very creative in finding ways to break software, and developers are more creative than most. By making available a lot of public methods that you didn't write, you increase the chances that another developer will break your code. To avoid this problem, you should generally inherit from the class that provides the fewest public members while still providing the desired functionality.

For example, let's say you want basic UI plumbing code but don't want the additional functionality of a *TextBox* or *Label* control. You can inherit from the *WebControl* class, which implements such basic UI features as the *Back-Color* and *ForeColor* properties and the *ApplyStyle* method. As noted earlier, this is the default for a Web Custom Control class added with Visual Studio .NET. If you don't even need the UI plumbing, you can inherit from the *Control* class, which has no UI-related members. Of course, this means that you have to implement all UI-related code yourself.

Rendering Output from a Control

Another important consideration in the implementation of a control is rendering its output. To do this, you override the *Render* method of the base class. Remember that, as when you choose a base class to inherit from, this step is handled for you automatically when you add a Web Custom Control class to a Visual Studio .NET project.

```
protected override void Render(HtmlTextWriter output)
{
    // custom rendering code
}
```

As mentioned earlier, you can also call the *Render* method of the base class in order to send its rendered output to the browser. This is useful mainly for controls that inherit from classes that define their own UI, such as the *TextBox* class. Note that the call to the *Render* method of the base class can appear anywhere within the *Render* method of the derived control, allowing you to determine where in your custom control the rendered output of the base class will appear. The *MyBase* keyword in the following snippet provides access to the members of the class from which the current class is inherited:

```
protected override void Render(HtmlTextWriter output)
{
    // custom rendering code
    base.Render(output);
    // additional custom rendering code, if desired
}
```

Note that since the ASP.NET runtime calls the overridden *Render* method automatically when the containing page is requested, passing in the necessary *HtmlTextWriter* instance (the *output* variable in the previous code snippet), you can simply pass that instance as the argument to the *Render* method in the base class.

Building Your First Control in Visual Studio .NET

Once you understand the basics of writing a control, the next step is to actually write one. There are several ways to create a control. Of course, you can use the tools provided with the .NET SDK and create the control in Notepad or a similar editor, or you can use Visual Studio .NET. Depending upon the version of Visual Studio .NET you use, you can create your controls two ways. Using the Professional version or greater, you can create a separate Web Control Library project to house your Web control. Using the Standard or Deluxe Learning Edition, you can create Web controls only as part of an ASP.NET Web Application project. In the examples that follow, we'll build the controls using the former method.

In the first example, you'll create a control that adds a built-in label to a simple *TextBox* control.

Create an enhanced *TextBox* control

1   Open Visual Studio .NET and create a new Web Control Library project. Name the project **Chapter_10_Controls**. When project creation is complete, delete the default class, WebCustomControl1.cs.

2   Right-click the project in Solution Explorer, select Add, and then select Add Component. The dialog box that appears has quite a few likely sounding options (including *Component Class*). Select the Web Custom Control entry toward the bottom of the list of options. Name the control **TextBoxPlus.cs**, as shown in the following illustration.

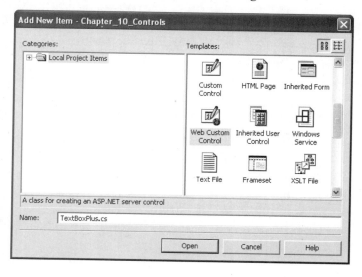

The default class added by Visual Studio .NET is a completely functional (though otherwise uninteresting) example control. It inherits from the *WebControl* class, and it contains a string property named *Text*. The *Render* method simply writes the *Text* property to the HTML stream being written. Once compiled, the control will reside in the *Chapter_10_Controls* namespace. Visual Studio .NET also automatically adds metadata attributes to the class to provide design-time support for the control. You'll learn about these attributes later in this chapter.

3   Begin customizing the control by changing the class that the control inherits from to the *TextBox* class (which also resides in the *System.Web.UI.WebControls* namespace) in order to reuse its functionality. Change the *Inherits* statement that immediately follows the class declaration from

```
public class TextBoxPlus : System.Web.UI.WebControls.WebControl
```

to

```
public class TextBoxPlus : System.Web.UI.WebControls.Textbox
```

4   Change all occurrences of *Text* (the property definition) to **LabelText,** and all occurrences of *text* (the name of the private instance variable that contains the value of the property) to **_labelText**. The *LabelText* property will allow users of the control to set the text to be displayed with the text box.

5   Add a call to render the base control. Within the *Render* method, add the following line immediately after the call to *output.Write*:

```
base.Render(output);
```

This will cause the output of the base *TextBox* control to be rendered immediately following the text of the *LabelText* property. The complete code for the class is shown here. (The attributes have been removed for clarity.)

```
public class TextBoxPlus : System.Web.UI.WebControls.TextBox
{
    private string _labelText;

    [Bindable(true),
        Category("Appearance"),
        DefaultValue("")]
    public string LabelText
    {
        get
        {
            return _labelText;
        }
```

```
        set
        {
            _labelText = value;
        }
    }

    protected override void Render(HtmlTextWriter output)
    {
        output.Write(LabelText);
        base.Render(output);
    }
}
```

6   Save the class file, and build the project. The control is now ready for use.

The next step is to actually use the control. To make using the control as easy as possible, you can add your custom control to the Visual Studio .NET Toolbox, as described in the following steps.

Add a custom Web control to the Toolbox

1   Without closing the Chapter_10_Controls project, from the File menu, select Add Project then New Project. Choose the ASP.NET Web Application type, and name the project **Chapter_10**. The IDE should automatically load the WebForm1.aspx file of the new project.

2   Open the Toolbox, right-click inside the Toolbox, and then select Add/Remove Items from the drop-down menu. The dialog box shown in the following illustration will appear.

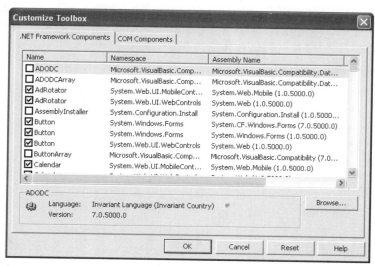

3 Click the Browse button. In the resulting dialog box, navigate to the bin folder under the Chapter_10_Controls project folder, select Chapter_10_Controls.dll, and then click OK. You will be returned to the previous dialog box with the *TextBoxPlus* control highlighted, as shown in the following illustration.

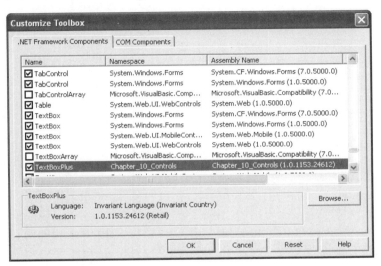

4 Click OK to close the Customize Toolbox dialog box. The *TextBox-Plus* control will be added to the Web Forms tab of the Toolbox (or whichever tab was active when you selected Customize Toolbox).

Of course, adding the control to the toolbox is only part of the process. Next you'll learn how to use the custom control on a Web Forms page.

Add a custom server control to a Web Form

1 Use the Properties window to change the *pageLayout* property of the WebForm1.aspx to **FlowLayout**. (Because of the way the *TextBox-Plus* control is rendered, it will not display correctly if the page is in GridLayout mode.)

2 Open the Toolbox if it's not already open, select the Web Forms tab, and then scroll to the bottom of the tab. You should see the *TextBox-Plus* control at the bottom of the list, as shown in the illustration on the next page.

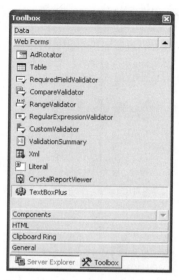

3   Double-click the *TextBoxPlus* control. This will add a copy of the
control to WebForm1.aspx. Select the control, and then use the Properties window to change the *LabelText* property to **Name:**. The page
with the control should look like the following illustration.

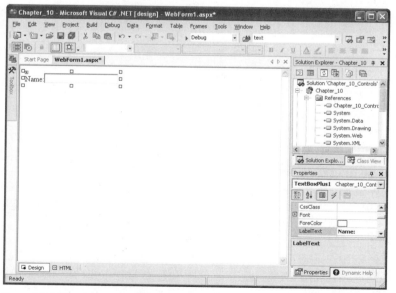

4   Save WebForm1.aspx, and then build the project.

5   Right-click WebForm1.aspx, select Browse With, and then select
Microsoft Internet Explorer. The output should look similar to the
following illustration.

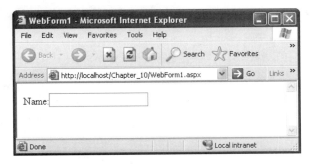

While Visual Studio .NET makes it easy to add a control to a page, there is no
magic involved. All of the things that Visual Studio .NET does while adding a
component could be done without Visual Studio .NET. It is important to understand some of the things that Visual Studio .NET is doing. When you add a control by double-clicking the control or by dragging it from the toolbox to the page,
an *@ Register* directive is added at the top of the .aspx file, just below the *@ Page*
directive. In this example, the *@ Register* directive looks like the following line:

```
<%@ Register TagPrefix="cc1" Namespace="Chapter_10_Controls"
    Assembly="Chapter_10_Controls" %>
```

Additionally, the tag to create the control is added wherever the control has
been dropped (or at the cursor location, in the case of double-clicking the control in the Toolbox):

```
<cc1:TextBoxPlus id="TextBoxPlus1" runat="server"
                 LabelText="Name:"></cc1:TextBoxPlus>
```

▶ **Note**   The default *TagPrefix* used by Visual Studio .NET is *cc1*, *cc2* and so on.
You can manually change the *TagPrefix* and then change the beginning namespace part of the opening and closing tag from *cc1*: to whatever you would like
to use. Alternatively, you can use the *TagPrefix* attribute in the control to specify
a *TagPrefix* to be used when the control is dropped onto a form in Visual Studio
.NET. Add the following line to the AssemblyInfo.cs file in the control project,

```
[assembly: TagPrefix("Chapter_10_Controls","MyControls ")]
```

and then rebuild the project. You might have to remove the custom control from
the toolbox and add it again as described earlier for the changes to take effect
in the Toolbox.

Using the preceding line, *TextBoxPlus* would have a *TagPrefix* of *MyControls*
rather than *cc1*.

Private vs. Shared Assemblies

By default, all custom assemblies that you create are private. You make them available to a Web application by placing them in the bin directory of the application, where they are loaded by ASP.NET automatically. You can also share assemblies across all clients on a machine by placing them in the Global Assembly Cache (GAC). Barring any security configuration in the assembly that prevents it, assemblies in the GAC can be used by any managed application on that machine.

Private assemblies allow you to limit the use of an assembly to the application in whose bin subdirectory the assembly resides. Shared assemblies allow you to reuse your assemblies in multiple applications without needing to maintain a copy of an assembly for each application that uses it.

To install an assembly into the GAC, give the assembly a strong name (signing it with a public key, which you can generate with the sn.exe .NET Framework utility). Then add it to the GAC either by using the gacutil.exe .NET Framework utility or by dragging and dropping the assembly into the %windir%\assembly folder, which will add the assembly to the GAC automatically. Note that when you deploy assemblies to the GAC for production applications, Microsoft recommends using Microsoft Windows Installer 2.0 to install the assembly to the GAC, which provides rollback protection, as well as automated uninstall. The Web Setup project type, available in Visual Studio .NET Professional and later, will create a Windows Installer package for your Web application to which you can add a Global Assembly Cache folder containing any controls you want to install in the GAC.

The GAC supports versioning of assemblies, so you can install multiple versions of the same assembly by setting its *AssemblyVersionAttribute* attribute. Clients can then specify which version of an assembly to load at runtime. This attribute is added to the AssemblyInfo.cs (or AssemblyInfo.vb, for Visual Basic .NET projects) file automatically by Visual Studio .NET, with the value *1.0.**, which automatically increments the build number of the assembly each time the project is built.

Adding Custom Controls Programmatically

In addition to adding the control to the page declaratively as shown earlier, you can add custom controls to the page programmatically, just as you can with the standard ASP.NET server controls. Adding controls programmatically does not require the @ *Register* directive. If you created the control in a separate project from the project in which it will be used, you might want to add a *using* directive to the *codebehind* class to avoid the need to use the fully qualified name to refer to the controls in your assembly.

Add a control programmatically

1   Open the Chapter_10_Controls solution you created earlier if it's not already open. The solution should contain both the Chapter_10_Controls and Chapter_10 projects. If not, add the missing project to the solution by right-clicking the solution name, selecting Add and then Existing Project.

2   Add a new Web Form to the Chapter_10 project. Name the form **AddControl.aspx,** and change its *pageLayout* property to **FlowLayout.**

3   Double-click anywhere on the page and you will be brought to the *Page_Load* event handler in the code-behind module for AddControl.aspx. Add the following code to the event handler:

```
Chapter_10_Controls.TextBoxPlus TBP =
    new Chapter_10_Controls.TextBoxPlus();
TBP.LabelText = "Programmatic Control Label: ";
this.Controls.Add(TBP);
```

4   Save the changes, and then build the project. Browse AddControl.aspx. The result will be an error informing you that "Control '_ctl0' of type 'TextBoxPlus' must be placed inside a form tag with runat=server." The reason for this error is that the *Add* method of the *Controls* collection actually places the added control at the end of the controls collection. In this case, that means the control is placed after the last HTML tag in the page (which is represented in the *Controls* collection as an ASP.NET Literal control). Because the *TextBox* control from which *TextBoxPlus* is derived must be placed between the *<form runat="server">* and *</form>* tags, this code generates an exception. There are a couple of solutions for this. You could use the *AddAt* method rather than the *Add* method to add the control to the *Controls* collection. *AddAt* takes an additional parameter, an index into the array of controls. This is not an ideal solution, since you need to know which index to use. A better solution is to add an ASP.NET Placeholder control.

5   Switch back to AddControl.aspx by clicking on its tab in the editor or by double-clicking on AddControl.aspx in the Solution Explorer. Drag a *PlaceHolder* control from the Toolbox onto the page.

6   Switch back to the *Page_Load* event handler by double-clicking anywhere on the page. Change the following line

```
this.Controls.Add(TBP);
```

to

```
PlaceHolder1.Controls.Add(TBP);
```

Dragging the *PlaceHolder* control onto the page inserted it between the *<form runat="server">* and *</form>* tags. Adding the *TextBox-Plus* control to the placeholder's *Controls* collection ensures that the control will be rendered in the desired location (and one that won't generate an exception!).

7 Save the changes, and then build the project. When you browse AddControl.aspx, the output should look similar to the following illustration.

Adding Functionality

As cool as it can be to create and consume a custom server control in a very few lines of code (including both the control and the Web Forms page that consumes it), the control you just created provides minimal functionality. Clearly, for this control to be truly useful, you need to add to the control.

The next several sections will look at how to add properties and methods to a control; create, raise and handle events; handle postbacks; maintain state in a control; and create templated controls. By the end of this section, you'll be able to add a significant amount of functionality to what is now a very simple control.

Adding Properties and Methods

To make the control more functional, you're going to provide a property that determines the type of data entered into the text box. You'll also define a method to format text entered into the text box based on this property.

Let's start with adding a property by following these steps.

Add a property

1 Open TextBoxPlus.cs in the Chapter_10_Controls project.

2   Add the following code to the top of the file, just below the curly brace below the *namespace* keyword. The code creates an enumeration that defines the allowable values of the property you're going to add:

```
public enum TextTypes
{
    CurrencyText,
    DecimalText,
    PlainText
}
```

3   Copy the *_labelText* variable definition and paste a copy below the original. Modify the variable name of the copy to **_textType**, change the type from String to **TextTypes**, and then set its default value to **TextTypes.PlainText**. Using *TextTypes* as the datatype will restrict the allowable values for this property to those defined by the *TextTypes* enumeration:

```
private TextTypes _textType = TextTypes.PlainText;
```

4   Copy the *LabelText Property* procedure and paste a copy below the original. Change the *DefaultValue* attribute of this property to **TextTypes.PlainText,** and then modify the property procedure so that it looks like the following code. (The attributes have been omitted for clarity.)

```
public TextTypes TextType
{
    get
    {
        return _textType;
    }

    set
    {
        _textType = value;
    }
}
```

5   Save the file, but don't close it yet.

▶ **Note**   Contrary to what you might think, the *DefaultValue* attribute you set in Step 4 does not actually initialize the value of the variable it is applied to. This attribute is actually intended to allow developers to query the metadata for a component to determine the default value of a property programmatically, and reset it to that value if desired. Thus, if you want the value of a variable to be initialized to a particular value, you should do so by initializing the value of the private member associated with the property, as shown in Step 3 of the preceding example. You can find out more about this attribute at *http://msdn.microsoft.com/library/en-us/cpref/html/frlrfsystemcomponentmodeldefaultvalueattributeclasstopic.asp* and *http://support.microsoft.com/default.aspx?scid=kb;en-us;Q311339.*

Now let's look at adding a method.

Add a method

1   Add the following code directly below the closing curly brace of the *Render* method:

```
protected void FormatText()
{
    switch(_textType)
    {
        case TextTypes.CurrencyText:
            this.Text=(double.Parse(this.Text)).ToString("C");
            break;
        case TextTypes.DecimalText:
            this.Text=(Convert.ToInt32(this.Text)).ToString("F");
            break;
    }
}
```

Using the *FormatCurrency* and *Format* methods ensures that the currency and decimal formatting will work for multiple locales, based on the *LCID* attribute of the @ *Page* directive.

2   Add the following code to the *Render* method, before the call to *base.Render*:

```
if ( Page.IsPostBack )
{
    if ( _textType != TextTypes.PlainText )
    {
        this.FormatText();
    }
}
```

Checking the *IsPostBack* method prevents the text property from being formatted at design time, since the *Render* method of the control is called at design time each time a property of the control is altered, in order to display the design-time rendering of the control.

3   Save the class file and rebuild the project.

4   Add a new Web Form to the Chapter_10 project. (Not the Chapter_10_ Controls project.) Name it **TBP_Client.aspx**.

5   Change the *pageLayout* property of the page to **FlowLayout**.

6   Using the Toolbox, add an instance of the *TextBoxPlus* control to the page, and then add a Button control to the page.

7   Set the *TextType* property of the *TextBoxPlus* control to *Currency-Text*, and the *LabelText* property to **Enter a whole number:**. (Note: If you don't see the *TextType* property listed, then, in the Solution

Explorer, expand the References node under the Chapter_10 project and delete the reference for Chapter_10_Controls. Delete the *TextBox-Plus* control you just added to the form and add a fresh one. The reference for Chapter_10_Controls will be updated within the project.)

8   Save TBP_Client.aspx, build the project, and then browse the page. The output should look similar to the following illustration.

9   Enter **250** in the text box, and then click the button. The resulting output should look similar to the following illustration.

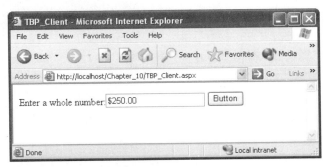

If you add the LCID attribute to the @ *Page* directive, and set its value to that of a country other than the United States (such as 2057 for the United Kingdom), the output of the *TextBoxPlus* control will automatically reflect the change, with no changes to the control necessary.

Creating More Advanced Controls

As you have seen in the previous sections, ASP.NET makes it very easy to create useful controls by inheriting from an existing control and adding properties and methods to create a specialized version of that control by extending its functionality. But the fun doesn't stop there. You can override control methods to allow your control to participate in the postback process, and also create custom events for your control. In this section, you'll learn about these techniques, including building a registration and login control that implements them.

Handling Postbacks

As discussed previously, a *postback* is the process by which a Web Forms page submits an HTTP *POST* request to itself in response to some user action, such as clicking a button. The postback itself is initiated by a control that causes the HTML form to be submitted, such as a client-side button element, the *Button* server control, or a server control that emits JavaScript code to submit the page, such as the *DropDownList* control. (Note that the *DropDownList* control emits JavaScript code for posting back the page only if its *AutoPostBack* property is set to true.) In this section we'll be focusing on the processing of postbacks, which occurs on the server after the postback has been initiated by the user's action. At some point, it is likely that you will want to develop a control that handles postback data and/or events. In this section, you'll learn how to handle both.

You have the opportunity to work with postback information during three phases in the execution of an ASP.NET Web Forms page: the *LoadPostData* phase, the *RaisePostDataChangedEvent* phase, and the *RaisePostBackEvent* phase. To work with the associated data or events, you override the associated method for the desired phase. To override the methods, you need to implement the *IPostBackDataHandler* interface, the *IPostBackEventHandler* interface, or both. *IPostBackDataHandler* defines the *LoadPostData* method and the *RaisePostDataChangedEvent* method. *IPostBackEventHandler* defines the *RaisePostBackEvent* method.

▶ **Note** You implement interfaces in the fashion specified by the language you're using. As shown earlier, interfaces are implemented in Visual C# .NET using the same syntax used to inherit from a base class:

```
class MyClass : System.Web.UI.Control, IPostBackDataHandler,
    IPostBackEventHandler
```

Unlike inheritance, which allows inheriting only from a single base class, you can implement as many interfaces as you'd like. The first name following the colon above indicates a class, while the next two are interfaces. Separate each interface name with a comma, as shown above.

Table 10-1 summarizes what the postback methods are typically used for.

Table 10-1.   Postback-related Methods

Method	Purpose
LoadPostData	Loads data posted in form fields into local variables for later processing. Returns a Boolean indicating whether form values have changed since the last postback.
RaisePostBackDataChangedEvent	Called if *LoadPostData* returns *true*. Used to respond to changes in posted data.
RaisePostBackEvent	Used to process data posted back from form fields, and raise any related events from the control.

You'll see examples of how to work with postback data in the registration and login control example that follows the next section.

Creating, Raising, and Handling Events

Another important aspect of creating a custom server control is dealing with events. While the event model in ASP.NET is designed to closely emulate event handling in a desktop application, such as a Visual Basic forms-based application, there are some significant differences in the models.

The most significant difference is that control events are raised and handled only on the server. Only after a Web Forms page has been posted back to the server can the state of each control be examined and appropriate events raised and handled.

Another difference is that custom ASP.NET server controls do not directly handle client events, such as clicks, mouseovers, and key presses, because these events occur on the client (although controls can emit client-side code to handle such events). To communicate an event that occurs on the client to the server, the page must be posted back to the server.

There are three parts to dealing with custom events in a custom server control: creating the event, raising the event, and handling the event. (Handling the event is typically done outside the control, but the plumbing to make it work is set up in the control.)

Creating and Raising Events

Events in ASP.NET use two important objects: *EventHandler* and *EventArgs*. *EventHandler* is a *delegate* used as the basis for creating a new event, while the *EventArgs* class is used to pass data with an event, or to signify that no event data was passed.

You create events using the *event* keyword as follows:

```
public event EventHandler EventName;
```

EventName is the name of the event being created. Notice that the event is declared as type EventHandler.

> ► **Note**   The *EventHandler* delegate is the basis for all event handler delegates. A *delegate* defines the signature for the event—that is, it specifies the arguments that an event handler for that event must accept—and acts as a type-safe function pointer to link the event to its event handler routine. The signature for *EventHandler* is as follows:
>
> ```
> public delegate void EventHandler(object sender, EventArgs e);
> ```
>
> This means that any event defined using the *EventHandler* delegate must accept both an *Object* and an *EventArgs* argument:
>
> ```
> void Control_Event(object sender,EventArgs e)
> {
>     // event handling code
> }
> ```
>
> You can create your own events that pass data to their event handlers by creating a custom class derived from *EventArgs*, then creating a new delegate for your event that specifies your custom class instead of *EventArgs* as one of its arguments.

Next, you raise the event (based on the criteria you set up within your control to determine if the event should be called) by calling the event name as follows:

```
public void RaisePostBackEvent(string eventArgument)
{
    if ( EventName != null )
    {
        EventName(this, EventArgs.Empty);
    }
}
```

This code is executed when the *RaisePostBackEvent* method is called during page execution. It tests whether *SomeExpression* is *true*. If it is, it raises the *EventName* event, which is typically handled outside of the control.

Handling Custom Events

Once you've created the event and the code to raise the event, you (or the developer consuming the event) will need to write code to handle the event. This consists of two steps: creating an event handler and wiring the event to it. Although Chapter 7 covered event handlers, it's worth reviewing those steps here.

An event handler is a page-level procedure that typically accepts two arguments: the source of the event and an *EventArgs* instance (or an instance of a class derived from *EventArgs*) representing any data passed with the event. An event handler for the *EventName* event would look like this:

```
void ControlName_EventName(object source, EventArgs e)
{
    // Event handling code
}
```

In the preceding code, *ControlName* represents the name of the control in which the event is defined, and *EventName* represents the name of the event. This syntax is not required, but it's the naming convention typically followed for event handlers. You can call your event handlers whatever you want, but following the *ControlName_EventName* naming standard will make your code easier to read and maintain. A good example of this is the *Page_Load* event handler found in the code-behind module for every new Web Form created in Visual Studio .NET. Since the *Page* class is derived from the *Control* base class, it exposes the *Load* event defined by the base class. Because *Page_Load* is the most common event for adding logic to a Web Form, the template for a Web Form in Visual Studio .NET creates the handler for you by default.

To wire the event handler to your control, you need to do one of two things, depending on whether you're dealing with a declarative control or a control added programmatically. For declarative controls (those defined using a tag in the .aspx file), add an *OnEventName* attribute to the tag in which you declare the control, with the value set to the name of the event handler routine:

```
<ASPNETSBS:MyControl id="MC1" OnEventName="MC1_EventName"
    runat="server">
```

The good news is that Visual Studio provides support for handling and wiring up events, including custom events through the code editor and IntelliSense statement completion.

Overriding Inherited Events

In addition to creating custom events from scratch, you can also override events that are defined on the base control from which your control is derived. The following standard events are defined by the control class:

- **Init**   Initialize settings for the current request
- **Load**   Perform actions that need to be performed for each request once child controls have been created and initialized
- **DataBinding**   Perform actions needed to evaluate data-binding expressions associated with a control

- **PreRender**   Perform any modifications to the control or data necessary before rendering the control
- **UnLoad**   Perform cleanup tasks before the control is removed from memory

To override an event exposed by an inherited class, you override its associated *OnEventName* method. For example, to override the *PreRender* event, you would use the following code in your control. (Note that the *OnPreRender* method takes only one argument, of type *EventArgs*.)

```
protected override void OnPreRender(EventArgs e)
{
    // Event handling code
    base.OnPreRender(e);
}
```

Event Execution Order

When you're handling events, it's important to understand that the standard control events and methods occur in a consistent order, including events and methods related to postbacks. This is important because if you write code in an event handler that occurs before the objects manipulated by that code have been created and initialized, the results will be unpredictable at best. One of the most common problems relating to event execution order occurs when you add controls to the page programmatically. If you add those controls in the *Page_Load* event handler, the controls will not maintain their *ViewState* during postbacks, because the *LoadViewState* event, which takes care of repopulating the state of controls on the page, occurs *before* the *Load* event. Because the controls have not yet been created when the *LoadViewState* event is fired, the state for controls created in *Page_Load* is discarded. If you want controls added programmatically to maintain *ViewState*, you should add those controls in the *Page_Init* event handler instead.

The following is the order of the standard events and methods for controls.

- **Initialize**   During this phase, the *Init* event is raised.
- **LoadViewState**   During this phase, controls that use *ViewState* are populated with data from the hidden *__VIEWSTATE* field submitted with the request. The *LoadViewState* method can be overridden to customize this process.
- **LoadPostData**   During this phase, data posted back with the request is evaluated and appropriate action is taken. Override the *LoadPostData* method to write code for this phase.

- **Load** During this phase, the *Load* event is raised.
- **RaisePostDataChangedEvent** During this phase, change events are raised in response to differences between the current state of a control's members and the values submitted with the request. Override the *RaisePostDataChangedEvent* method to write code for this phase.
- **RaisePostBackEvent** During this phase, event handlers for server-side events are called. Override the *RaisePostBackEvent* method to write code for this phase.
- **PreRender** During this phase, any modifications necessary before rendering are made. Changes made after this phase will not be saved to *ViewState*.
- **SaveViewState** During this phase, controls that use *ViewState* save their data to the hidden __*VIEWSTATE* field. The *ViewState* method can be overridden to customize this process.
- **Render** During this phase, the control and its children are rendered to the browser.
- **Dispose** During this phase, any cleanup of expensive resources—file handles, database connections, and so on—is performed. Override the *Dispose* method to write code for this phase.

When overriding methods for inherited events (*Init*, *Load*, *PreRender*, and so on), it's usually a good idea to call the base implementation of the event's method from within your overridden version. This ensures that any handlers associated with those events are called. The syntax for calling the base handler is as follows:

```
protected override void OnLoad(EventArgs e )
    // Event handling code
    base.OnLoad(e);
}
```

A Registration and Login Control

To demonstrate event handling and postback handling, you're going to build a control that can handle user registration and logins. This control will integrate with ASP.NET Forms authentication, and can be used to prevent content in your application from being viewed or downloaded by users who have not registered on your site. (Note that any content you want to protect must be registered to ASP.NET in the IIS App Mappings.)

The control will have two modes: Login and Register. In Login mode, the control will render two text boxes—one for the username and another for the password—a Submit button, and a reset button. In Register Mode, the control will render three text boxes—one for the username, one for the password, and one for the user to confirm a desired password. The control will expose four custom events—*AuthSuccess*, *AuthFailure*, *RegSuccess*, and *RegFailure*—that the client can use to determine whether the user entered the correct credentials, or whether there was a problem with the user's registration information. To raise these events, you'll use some of the postback methods that were described earlier. This example is more involved than others you've seen previously, so let's break it up into sections to make it easier to follow.

Create the basic control

1   Open the Chapter_10_Controls solution and add a new Web Custom Control class to the Chapter_10_Controls project. Name the class **RegLogin.cs**.

2   Add the following *using* statements to the list of using directives at the top of the RegLogin.cs file.

```
using System.Collections.Specialized;
using System.Data;
using System.Web.Security;
using System.Web;
```

3   Add a reference to both System.Data.dll (required for the second *using* statement above) and System.Xml.dll by right-clicking the references folder under Chapter_10_Controls in Solution Explorer and selecting Add Reference. In the Add Reference dialog box, highlight the desired DLLs (you can hold down the Control key to select multiple items), then click the Select button, and then click OK.

4   Change the class's *Inherits* statement so that the control inherits from the *System.Web.UI.Control* class, rather than *System.Web.UI.WebControl*. (Attributes have been omitted for clarity.)

```
public class RegLogin : System.Web.UI.Control
```

5   Delete the *DefaultProperty("Text")* attribute that precedes the class definition, since we won't be using a *Text* property in the control:

```
[ToolboxData("<{0}:RegLogin runat=server></{0}:RegLogin>")]
public class RegLogin : System.Web.UI.Control
```

6   Save RegLogin.cs.

Now that you've got the control class created, let's continue by adding member variables for storing the username, password, and other important information for the control, including a *Mode* property that will use an *Enumeration* as its type.

Add member variables and properties

1 Just below the class declaration, add private *string* variables for the username, password, password confirmation, and status message (which will contain read-only information about the status of the control). Note that variables declared at the class level with the *private* keyword are private to that class. You can delete the text member variable that was created when you created the control class—we won't be using it.

```
private string _userName;
private string _password;
private string _passwordConfirm;
private string _statusMessage;
```

2 Add a Boolean member variable called *_displayRegLink*. This variable will be used to determine whether to display a hyperlink that will allow the user to switch the control to Register mode. The default is *false*.

```
private bool _displayRegLink = false;
```

3 Between the namespace declaration and the class definition, add the following code, which creates an *enum* for the *_mode* member variable:

```
public enum RegLoginMode
{
    Register,
    Login
}
```

An *enumeration* allows you to specify the valid values for a given property or argument that uses the enumeration as its type. The enumeration is also used by Visual Studio .NET to provide IntelliSense statement completion for members of that type. Enumerations can make working with variables and properties less error-prone by limiting input to only valid values.

4 Add a new member variable called *_mode*, with the type *RegLoginMode*. Set the value of the member to *RegLoginMode.Login*:

```
private RegLoginMode _mode = RegLoginMode.Login;
```

5   Modify the default *Text* property procedure (which was added automatically when the file was created) to look like this:

```
[Bindable(false), Browsable(false)]
public string StatusMessage
{
    get
    {
        return _statusMessage;
    }
}
```

This exposes *_statusMessage* as a public property, so that the consuming page can read it. The property exposes only a *get* accessor
because it is used only to communicate information from the control
to the page. Because the property value cannot be set, we add the
Bindable and *Browsable* attributes to the property declaration and
set the value of each to *false*. This prevents the property from being
available for databinding, and from showing up in the property
browser.

6   Save RegLogin.cs.

The next part of the process is displaying a UI for the control. As with the *Text-
BoxPlus* control, you'll do this by overriding the *Render* method. But in this case,
the actual rendering will be passed off to specialized methods for the two modes:
Login and Register. Two different rendering techniques will be demonstrated.

The first rendering technique, which will be used for rendering the login UI, will
make use of the methods and properties exposed by the *HtmlTextWriter* class,
an instance of which is passed to the *Render* method by the ASP.NET runtime.
These include the *WriteLine*, *WriteBeginTag*, *WriteEndTag*, and *WriteAttribute*
methods, which allow you to construct HTML elements programmatically,
piece by piece, as well as the *DefaultTabString* and *SelfClosingTagEnd* properties. Using these methods and properties allows you to render code that will be
more readable (hence, easier to troubleshoot) on the client end of the request,
without having to remember a language-specific escape character for tabs or
linefeeds. The code produced using this technique is a little heftier than that
produced using the second technique.

The second rendering technique, which will be used for rendering the registration UI, will make use of the *StringBuilder* utility class in the *System.Text*
namespace. Use the *StringBuilder* class whenever you need to do a significant
number (generally 5 or more) of string concatenations. Since string concatenation results in a new *String* object being created based on the string and/or

literals being concatenated, it can carry significant performance overhead. Using a *StringBuilder* can significantly improve performance by allowing you to manipulate string data without having to create and allocate space for a new *String* object with each manipulation. With this technique, we create a *StringBuilder* instance and call its *Append* method to add to the output string. Unlike the technique using the *HtmlTextWriter* class, this technique requires using constants like \t (tab) and \n (newline), or their literal equivalents, for formatting the rendered code.

Create the user interface

1   Since the default Web Custom Control code already has an override for the *Render* method of the *Control* class, simply modify the existing method to look like this:

```
protected override void Render(HtmlTextWriter output)
{
    switch (_mode)
    {
        case RegLoginMode.Register:
            DisplayRegUI(output);
            break;
        case RegLoginMode.Login:
            DisplayLoginUI(output);
            break;
    }
}
```

Note that you use the *_mode* member variable to decide which UI to display. If the control is in Login mode (the default), the login UI will be displayed. If the control is in Register mode, the registration UI will be displayed. Note also that both UI rendering functions (which you'll add next) accept the *HtmlTextWriter* instance passed into the *Render* method as an argument. This will be used in these functions to render output to the browser.

2   Create two private functions, *DisplayLoginUI*, and *DisplayRegUI*:

```
private void DisplayLoginUI(HtmlTextWriter output)
{

}

private void DisplayRegUI(HtmlTextWriter output)
{

}
```

3   Add the following code to *DisplayLoginUI*.

```
output.WriteLine(HtmlTextWriter.DefaultTabString +
    "<table>");
output.WriteLine(HtmlTextWriter.DefaultTabString +
    HtmlTextWriter.DefaultTabString + "<tr>");
output.WriteLine(HtmlTextWriter.DefaultTabString +
    HtmlTextWriter.DefaultTabString +
    HtmlTextWriter.DefaultTabString + "<td>");
output.WriteLine(HtmlTextWriter.DefaultTabString +
    HtmlTextWriter.DefaultTabString +
    HtmlTextWriter.DefaultTabString +
    HtmlTextWriter.DefaultTabString + "Username: ");
output.WriteLine(HtmlTextWriter.DefaultTabString +
    HtmlTextWriter.DefaultTabString +
    HtmlTextWriter.DefaultTabString + "</td>");
output.WriteLine(HtmlTextWriter.DefaultTabString +
    HtmlTextWriter.DefaultTabString +
    HtmlTextWriter.DefaultTabString + "<td>");
output.Write(HtmlTextWriter.DefaultTabString +
    HtmlTextWriter.DefaultTabString +
    HtmlTextWriter.DefaultTabString +
    HtmlTextWriter.DefaultTabString);
output.WriteBeginTag("input");
output.WriteAttribute("name", this.UniqueID);
output.WriteAttribute("type", "text");
output.WriteAttribute("value", userName);
output.WriteLineNoTabs(HtmlTextWriter.SelfClosingTagEnd);
output.WriteLine(HtmlTextWriter.DefaultTabString +
    HtmlTextWriter.DefaultTabString +
    HtmlTextWriter.DefaultTabString + "</td>");
output.WriteLine(HtmlTextWriter.DefaultTabString +
    HtmlTextWriter.DefaultTabString + "</tr>");
output.WriteLine(HtmlTextWriter.DefaultTabString +
    HtmlTextWriter.DefaultTabString + "<tr>");
output.WriteLine(HtmlTextWriter.DefaultTabString +
    HtmlTextWriter.DefaultTabString +
    HtmlTextWriter.DefaultTabString + "<td>");
output.WriteLine(HtmlTextWriter.DefaultTabString +
    HtmlTextWriter.DefaultTabString +
    HtmlTextWriter.DefaultTabString +
    HtmlTextWriter.DefaultTabString + "Password: ");
output.WriteLine(HtmlTextWriter.DefaultTabString +
    HtmlTextWriter.DefaultTabString +
    HtmlTextWriter.DefaultTabString + "</td>");
output.WriteLine(HtmlTextWriter.DefaultTabString +
    HtmlTextWriter.DefaultTabString +
    HtmlTextWriter.DefaultTabString + "<td>");
output.Write(HtmlTextWriter.DefaultTabString +
```

```
            HtmlTextWriter.DefaultTabString +
            HtmlTextWriter.DefaultTabString +
            HtmlTextWriter.DefaultTabString);
output.WriteBeginTag("input");
output.WriteAttribute("name", this.UniqueID);
output.WriteAttribute("type", "password");
output.WriteLineNoTabs(HtmlTextWriter.SelfClosingTagEnd);
output.WriteLine(HtmlTextWriter.DefaultTabString +
    HtmlTextWriter.DefaultTabString +
    HtmlTextWriter.DefaultTabString + "</td>");
output.WriteLine(HtmlTextWriter.DefaultTabString +
    HtmlTextWriter.DefaultTabString + "</tr>");
output.WriteLine(HtmlTextWriter.DefaultTabString +
    HtmlTextWriter.DefaultTabString + "<tr>");
output.WriteLine(HtmlTextWriter.DefaultTabString +
    HtmlTextWriter.DefaultTabString +
    HtmlTextWriter.DefaultTabString + "<td>");
output.Write(HtmlTextWriter.DefaultTabString +
    HtmlTextWriter.DefaultTabString +
    HtmlTextWriter.DefaultTabString +
    HtmlTextWriter.DefaultTabString);
output.WriteBeginTag("input");
output.WriteAttribute("name", this.UniqueID);
output.WriteAttribute("type", "button");
output.WriteAttribute("value", "Submit");
output.WriteAttribute("OnClick", "javascript:" +
    Page.GetPostBackEventReference(this, "Login"));
output.WriteLineNoTabs(HtmlTextWriter.SelfClosingTagEnd);
output.WriteLine(HtmlTextWriter.DefaultTabString +
    HtmlTextWriter.DefaultTabString +
    HtmlTextWriter.DefaultTabString + "</td>");
output.WriteLine(HtmlTextWriter.DefaultTabString +
    HtmlTextWriter.DefaultTabString +
    HtmlTextWriter.DefaultTabString + "<td>");
output.Write(HtmlTextWriter.DefaultTabString +
    HtmlTextWriter.DefaultTabString +
    HtmlTextWriter.DefaultTabString +
    HtmlTextWriter.DefaultTabString);
output.WriteBeginTag("input");
output.WriteAttribute("name", this.UniqueID);
output.WriteAttribute("type", "reset");
output.WriteLineNoTabs(HtmlTextWriter.SelfClosingTagEnd);
output.WriteLine(HtmlTextWriter.DefaultTabString +
    HtmlTextWriter.DefaultTabString +
    HtmlTextWriter.DefaultTabString + "</td>");
output.WriteLine(HtmlTextWriter.DefaultTabString +
    HtmlTextWriter.DefaultTabString + "</tr>");
if ( displayRegLink == true )
```

```
     {
         output.WriteLine(HtmlTextWriter.DefaultTabString +
            HtmlTextWriter.DefaultTabString + "<tr>");
         output.WriteLine(HtmlTextWriter.DefaultTabString +
            HtmlTextWriter.DefaultTabString +
            HtmlTextWriter.DefaultTabString + "<td colspan='2'>");
         output.WriteBeginTag("a");
         output.WriteAttribute("name", "RegLink");
         output.WriteAttribute("href", "javascript:" +
            Page.GetPostBackEventReference(this, "DisplayRegUI"));
         output.Write(HtmlTextWriter.TagRightChar);
         output.Write("Register");
         output.WriteEndTag("a");
         output.WriteLine(HtmlTextWriter.DefaultTabString +
            HtmlTextWriter.DefaultTabString +
            HtmlTextWriter.DefaultTabString + "</td>");
         output.WriteLine(HtmlTextWriter.DefaultTabString +
            HtmlTextWriter.DefaultTabString + "</tr>");
     }
     output.WriteLine(HtmlTextWriter.DefaultTabString +
        "</table>");
     }
```

This code uses methods and properties exposed by the *HtmlText-Writer* class to write out the desired HTML output—in this case, an HTML table for formatting, with two text boxes for input, as well as an HTML button for posting back the control's contents, and a reset button. The code also uses these methods and properties to write white space (tabs and carriage returns) to the control output. While this is not strictly necessary from a functional standpoint, adding white space can make the rendered code easier to read, which can help in troubleshooting when something isn't working (not that that ever happens, right?).

Note the call to *GetPostBackEventReference* in the code for rendering the submit button. This allows a value ("*Login*") to be passed when the page is posted back, so that the code that processes the postback knows which button was clicked. Note also the *If* statement that checks the value of the *_displayRegUI* member variable. If the value of this variable is *true*, a hyperlink will be rendered to allow the user to switch to registration mode.

4   Add the following code to *DisplayRegUI*. This code creates a *String-Builder* object, concatenates the HTML output, and then writes the contents of the *StringBuilder* to the browser.

```
//Create StringBuilder for concatenating output string
System.Text.StringBuilder SBOut = new System.Text.StringBuilder();
```

```
SBOut.Append("\t" + "<table>" + "\n");
SBOut.Append("\t" + "\t" + "<tr>" + "\n");
SBOut.Append("\t" + "\t" + "\t" + "<td>" + "\n");
    SBOut.Append("\t" + "\t" + "\t" + "Username: " + "\n");
SBOut.Append("\t" + "\t" + "\t" + "</td>" + "\n");
SBOut.Append("\t" + "\t" + "\t" + "<td>" + "\n");
SBOut.Append("\t" + "\t" + "\t" + "<input type='text' " +
    "name='" + this.UniqueID + "' value='" +
    this._userName + "'/>" + "\n");
SBOut.Append("\t" + "\t" + "\t" + "</td>" + "\n");
SBOut.Append("\t" + "\t" + "</tr>" + "\n");

SBOut.Append("\t" + "\t" + "<tr>" + "\n");
SBOut.Append("\t" + "\t" + "\t" + "<td>" + "\n");
SBOut.Append("\t" + "\t" + "\t" + "Password: " + "\n");
SBOut.Append("\t" + "\t" + "\t" + "</td>" + "\n");
SBOut.Append("\t" + "\t" + "\t" + "<td>" + "\n");
SBOut.Append("\t" + "\t" + "\t" + "<input type='password' " +
    "name='" + this.UniqueID + "'/>" + "\n");
SBOut.Append("\t" + "\t" + "\t" + "</td>" + "\n");
SBOut.Append("\t" + "\t" + "</tr>" + "\n");
SBOut.Append("\t" + "\t" + "\t" + "<td>" + "\n");
SBOut.Append("\t" + "\t" + "\t" + "Confirm Password: " + "\n");
SBOut.Append("\t" + "\t" + "\t" + "</td>" + "\n");
SBOut.Append("\t" + "\t" + "\t" + "<td>" + "\n");
SBOut.Append("\t" + "\t" + "\t" + "<input type='password' " +
    "name='" + this.UniqueID + "'/>" + "\n");
SBOut.Append("\t" + "\t" + "\t" + "</td>" + "\n");
SBOut.Append("\t" + "\t" + "</tr>" + "\n");
SBOut.Append("\t" + "\t" + "<tr>" + "\n");
SBOut.Append("\t" + "\t" + "\t" + "<td>" + "\n");
SBOut.Append("\t" + "\t" + "\t" + "<input type='button' " +
    "value='Submit' OnClick=\"jscript:" +
    Page.GetPostBackEventReference(this, "Register") +
    "\">" + "\n");
SBOut.Append("\t" + "\t" + "\t" + "</td>" + "\n");
SBOut.Append("\t" + "\t" + "\t" + "<td>" + "\n");
SBOut.Append("\t" + "\t" + "\t" + "<input type='reset'/>" + "\n");
SBOut.Append("\t" + "\t" + "\t" + "</td>" + "\n");
SBOut.Append("\t" + "\t" + "</tr>" + "\n");
SBOut.Append("\t" + "</table>" + "\n");
// Send the output to the browser.
output.Write(SBOut);
```

Note that as with the *DisplayLoginUI* method, a call to *GetPost-BackEventReference* is used to generate the code necessary for initiating the postback, including indicating which button was clicked (in this case, "*Register*").

5   Save RegLogin.cs.

At this point, if you were to build the Chapter_10_Controls project and add the control to a page, it would render the login UI and could postback the data in its form fields, but that's about it. To take things further, you'll need to add postback handling and custom event code.

Handle postbacks and events

1   Define events for success and failure of both authentication and registration, using the base *EventHandler* delegate as the basis for the events. Place the event declarations just below the member variable declarations you added earlier:

```
public event EventHandler AuthSuccess;
public event EventHandler AuthFailure;
public event EventHandler RegSuccess;
public event EventHandler RegFailure;
```

2   Directly after the inherited class name, add the *IPostBackDataHandler* and *IPostBackEventHandler* interfaces, separated by commas:

```
public class RegLogin : System.Web.UI.Control,
    IPostBackDataHandler,
    IPostBackEventHandler
```

3   Implement the *LoadPostData* method defined in the *IPostBackDataHandler* interface to load the posted values into the local variables. Visual Studio .NET makes this pretty easy. When you finish typing the name of the interface, you will be prompted to press the Tab key to implement the methods in the interface, as shown in the following illustration. Press Tab when prompted after typing the name of each interface. The definition of the methods will be automatically inserted into the file. The methods will be in collapsed #region sections (used to hide/show regions of code in the IDE), so you will need to click the + sign next to each region to see the methods.

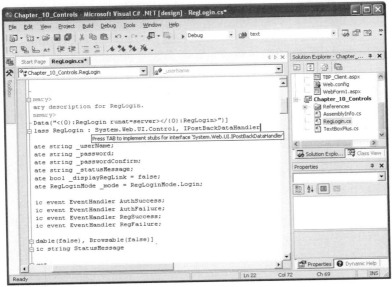

4   Replace the boilerplate code inserted in the *LoadPostData* method
    by the IDE with the following code:

```
string[] newValues = postCollection[postDataKey].Split('.');
bool Result = false;

switch (Page.Request.Form["__EVENTARGUMENT"])
{
   case "DisplayRegUI":
      _mode = RegLoginMode.Register;
      break;
   case "Login":
      Result = LoadLoginPostData(newValues);
      break;
   case "Register":
      _mode = RegLoginMode.Register;
      Result = LoadRegisterPostData(newValues);
      break;
}
return Result;
```

The code takes the collection of form field values posted from the
form and places them into the string array *newValues*. It then
declares a Boolean for the return value of the *LoadPostData* method.
Next, it uses the *__EVENTARGUMENT* form field, which is automatically sent with each postback (thanks to our use of *GetPost-
BackEventReference*), to decide how to process the loaded data (or,
in the case of the value *DisplayRegUI*, to display the registration UI
and forego further processing).

5   Add declarations for the *LoadLoginPostData* and *LoadRegisterPost-Data* methods below the *RaisePostBackEvent* method. These methods are custom methods we're using to load data depending on whether the control is in Login or Register mode:

```
private bool LoadLoginPostData(string[] newValues)
{

}

private bool LoadRegisterPostData(string[] newValues)
{

}
```

6   Add the following code to *LoadLoginPostData*:

```
string newUserName="";
string newPassword="";

// Get the username
newUserName = newValues[0];
// ...and the password
newPassword = newValues[1];

// return true if the values have changed
//  since last postback
if ( newUserName != _userName || newPassword != _password )
{
    _username = newUserName;
    _password = newPassword;
    return true;
}
else
{
    return false;
}
```

The preceding code retrieves the username and password entered by the user, checks to see if they've changed since the last postback, and then loads them into local variables for later processing. If the values have changed since the last postback, the code returns *true*, which will cause the *PostBackDataChangedEvent* method to be called later in the processing of the request.

7   Add the following code to *LoadRegisterPostData*:

```
// Get the user name
_userName = newValues[0];
// ...and the password
_password = newValues[1];
```

```
// ...and the password confirmation
_passwordConfirm = newValues[2];

// We don't expect the data to change from
//  request to request here, so we just
//  return false
return false;
```

8　Add the following code to *RaisePostBackEvent*:

```
switch (mode)
{
    case RegLoginMode.Register:
        if ( eventArgument != "DisplayRegUI" )
        {
            if ( !(SaveCredentials(_userName, _password,passwordConfirm)) )
            {
                if ( RegFailure != null )
                {
                    RegFailure(this, EventArgs.Empty);
                }
                _mode = RegLoginMode.Register;
            }
            else
            {
                if ( RegSuccess != null )
                {
                    RegSuccess(this, EventArgs.Empty);
                }
                _mode = RegLoginMode.Login;
            }
        }
        break;

    case RegLoginMode.Login:
        // If login is not valid, raise the AuthFailed event
        // and display the link for registration.
        if ( !(VerifyCredentials(_userName, _password)) )
        {
            if ( AuthFailure != null )
            {
                AuthFailure(this, EventArgs.Empty);
            }
        }
        else
        {
            if ( AuthSuccess != null )
            {
```

```
            AuthSuccess(this, EventArgs.Empty);
        }
        FormsAuthentication.SetAuthCookie(_userName, false);
    }
    break;
}
```

The preceding code uses the *_mode* variable to decide how to process the data that was loaded in the *LoadPostData* method, calling either *VerifyCredentials* or *SaveCredentials*. You'll add both of these methods in the next section. If the authentication or registration succeeds, the appropriate success event is raised. Likewise, if the authentication or registration processing fails, the appropriate failure event is raised. Note that if authentication succeeds, the code also calls the *Forms-Authentication.SetAuthCookie* method, passing in the username of the current user.

9 Save RegLogin.cs.

Now it's time to get down to the nitty gritty: verifying and saving user credentials. The technique the control will use to store credentials is a simple XML file. The XML file, which will be automatically created by the control the first time the control is used, will contain the date a user registered, a username, and an MD5 hashed value representing a password. Saving new registration information will be performed by the *SaveCredentials* method. Verifying the user's credentials against existing *credentials* will be performed by the *VerifyCredentials* method. Finally, the control will use a *CreateBlankUsersFile* utility method to create the initial XML file.

▶ **Important** You should not use this control for restricting access to critical information. This control is designed only to limit anonymous browsing of content. Because the control will allow users to register on their own, it provides only a means of limiting who can access content on your site. Note that you could further restrict access to content by adding a field to the XML file for whether the user is approved or enabled. By setting this field to *false* by default, you could choose whether someone who registered could access content *before* he or she logged in.

Save and validate user credentials as XML

1 Add the following code to RegLogin.cs after the *RaisePostBackEvent* method:

```
private bool SaveCredentials(string Username,
    string Password, string PasswordConfirm)
{
```

```
DataSet LoginDS = new DataSet();
LoginDS.ReadXml(Page.Server.MapPath("Users.xml"));
if ( !(LoginDS.Tables[0].Select("username='" +
   Username + "'").Length > 0 ))
{
    if ( _password != "" &&
        _password == _passwordConfirm )
    {
        DataRow NewLogin = LoginDS.Tables[0].NewRow();
        NewLogin["username"] = _userName;
        NewLogin["password"] =
          FormsAuthentication.HashPasswordForStoringInConfigFile
             (_password, "MD5");
        NewLogin["registerDate"] = DateTime.Today.ToShortDateString();
        LoginDS.Tables[0].Rows.Add(NewLogin);
        LoginDS.WriteXml(Page.Server.MapPath("Users.xml"));
        _statusMessage = "Registration succeeded. Please log in.";
        return true;
    }
    else
    {
        _statusMessage = "No password entered " +
           "or passwords do not match. Please re-enter.";
        return false;
    }
}
else
{
    _statusMessage =
        "An identical username exists. Please choose another.";
    return false;
}
}
```

The *SaveCredentials* method uses the *ReadXml* method of the *DataSet* class to read the current Users.xml file, then checks to see if there's already a user in the file with the same name as that entered by the user in the registration form. If not, the method then checks to make sure that both the password and confirmation password values are identical. If they are, the method creates a new row from the dataset, stores the username and a hashed version of the password, adds the row to the dataset, and then uses the *DataSet*'s *WriteXml* method to save the updated table to the file. Once all of this succeeds, the method sets the *statusMessage* property to indicate that registration succeeded, and returns *true* (which causes the *RegSuccess* event to be raised). If the username already exists, or if the passwords don't match, the *statusMessage* property is set to an appropriate message, and the method returns *false* (causing the *RegFailure* event to be raised).

2   Add the following code to RegLogin.cs, after the *SaveCredentials* method:

```
private bool VerifyCredentials(string Username,
   string Password )
{
   DataSet LoginDS = new DataSet();
   try
   {
      LoginDS.ReadXml(Page.Server.MapPath("Users.xml"));
   }
   catch ( System.IO.FileNotFoundException )
   {
      CreateBlankUsersFile();
      LoginDS.ReadXml(Page.Server.MapPath("Users.xml"));
   }

   if(LoginDS.Tables[0].Select("username='" +
                              Username + "'").Length > 0 )
   {
      DataRow[] LoginRow =
         LoginDS.Tables[0].Select("username='" + Username + "'");
      if(LoginRow[0]["password"].ToString() ==
         FormsAuthentication.HashPasswordForStoringInConfigFile
            (Password,"MD5") )
      {
         _statusMessage = "Credentials Validated.";
         return true;
      }
      else
      {
         _statusMessage = "Invalid Password.";
         return false;
      }
   }
   else
   {
      _statusMessage = "Username not found. Have you registered?";
      _displayRegLink = true;
      return false;
   }
}
```

The *VerifyCredentials* method also uses the *ReadXml* method to fill the dataset from Users.xml. Unlike *SaveCredentials*, however, the code in *VerifyCredentials* is wrapped in a *Try...Catch* block. This is because *VerifyCredentials* will always be called first, and if a *FileNot-FoundException* is thrown, the *CreateBlankUsersFile* method is called to create the Users.xml file. Once the dataset has been filled, the code selects the row that matches the provided username (if it exists) and checks the stored password hash against the hashed version of the password entered by the user. If the passwords match, the *statusMessage* property is set to indicate success, and the method returns *true* (which results in the *AuthSuccess* event being raised). If either the username does not exist in the XML file, or the passwords do not match, the *statusMessage* property is set to indicate these problems, and the method returns *false* (resulting in the *AuthFailure* method being raised).

3 Add the following code to RegLogin.cs, after the *VerifyCredentials* method:

```
public void CreateBlankUsersFile()
{
System.IO.StreamWriter NewXml =
   System.IO.File.CreateText(Page.Server.MapPath("Users.xml"));

   NewXml.WriteLine("<users>");
   // user field describes a single user
   NewXml.WriteLine("   <user>");
   // date field contains the Registration date
   NewXml.WriteLine("      <registerDate>" +
      DateTime.Today.ToShortDateString() + "</registerDate>");
   // username field
   NewXml.WriteLine("      <username>TempUser</username>");
   // password field contains MD5 hash value
   NewXml.WriteLine("      <password>" +
      FormsAuthentication.HashPasswordForStoringInConfigFile("password",
      "MD5") + "</password>");
   NewXml.WriteLine("   </user>");
   NewXml.WriteLine("</users>");
   NewXml.Close();
}
```

The *CreateBlankUsersFile* method allows the control to create its own storage file without requiring the intervention of the user. The method uses a *StreamWriter* to create and write to a text file. When finished writing the default elements, the method closes the *StreamWriter*.

> ▶ **Tip**   To create the Users.xml file, the ASPNET user account must have write access to the directory in which the page that uses the *RegLogin* control resides (in our case, the root of the Chapter_10 project). If, for security reasons, you do not wish to provide the ASPNET account with these permissions, you can create the file manually and provide the ASPNET account with write permissions to this file alone, rather than the entire directory. You can also provide the ASPNET account with write permissions to the directory temporarily, run a page containing the control, and then remove the write permissions. If you create the file manually, make sure the file extension is .xml, not .xml.txt (which can happen if you have file extensions hidden in Windows Explorer), or you will receive errors when the control attempts to write to the file.
>
> If the file is created by the ASP.NET process, by default it will have full permissions granted to the ASPNET user account under which ASP.NET is run, as well as to the SYSTEM account and the Administrators group. However, the Users group will have only Read & Execute and Read permissions on the file. This means that unless you are logged on as an Administrator, you will not be able to manually edit the Users.xml file.

4   Save RegLogin.cs, and build the Chapter_10_Controls project. If you entered all of the code correctly, the project should build correctly, and the control will be ready to use. If you have any problems, you can check your code against the finished example that is available with the practice files for this chapter.

The last part of the process is using the control in a page. To use the control, you'll need to create a new Web Forms page, create the control (either declaratively or programmatically), and set up handlers for its exposed events. You'll also need to configure your application to use Forms Authentication, create a sample page to be protected by Forms Authentication, and configure your application to prevent browsing of the Users.xml file created by the control.

Configure for Forms Authentication

1   Open the Web.config file for the Chapter_10 project.

2   Modify the *<authentication>* configuration element to look like the following:

```
<authentication mode="Forms">
   <forms
      loginUrl="Login.aspx"
      protection="All">
   </forms>
</authentication>
```

This forces any requests for content that require authentication to be redirected to Login.aspx if an authentication cookie is not present. It also specifies that the cookie is both encrypted and subject to validation to protect its contents.

3   Add a *<location>* section with an *<authorization>* configuration element that looks like the following. This code should go between the opening *<configuration>* tag and the opening *<system.web>* tag:

```
<location path="ProtectMe.aspx">
   <system.web>
      <authorization>
         <deny users="?"/>
      </authorization>
   </system.web>
</location>
```

This section disallows any requests for the file ProtectMe.aspx (which you'll add to the project shortly) by users who have not been authenticated. Thanks to the *<authentication>* section, such requests will be redirected to Login.aspx (which you'll also add to the project shortly, and which will make use of the RegLogin control).

4   Save Web.config, but don't close it yet.

The preceding steps will effectively protect the file ProtectMe.aspx from unauthorized access (once you've created it, anyway), but they leave out something very important: protecting the XML file that will contain the user information. By default, XML files are browsable from within a Web application. All someone needs to know is the name of the file to view its contents. While the *RegLogin* control does make use of MD5 hashing to protect passwords, it's still a good idea to prevent browsing of the Users.xml file. The next set of steps will show you how to do this.

Secure Users.xml

1   Open the Web.config file for the Chapter_10 project if it's not already open.

2   Add the following section between the *<system.web>* and *</system.web>* tags:

```
<httpHandlers>
   <add verb="*" path="Users.xml"
type="System.Web.HttpForbiddenHandler"/>
</httpHandlers>
```

This will prevent any requests for a file named Users.xml within the scope of the application from being fulfilled by passing the request to the *HttpForbiddenHandler HttpHandler* class. This is the same technique used by ASP.NET to protect the global.asax, web.config, and other non-browsable files.

3   Save Web.config.

4   Open the Internet Information Services administration tool (you must either be logged in as an administrator, or use the Run As feature to run the tool using an account with administrator rights), drill down to the Chapter_10 project application, right-click the application icon, and then select Properties. The properties dialog box for the Chapter_10 application will be displayed, as shown in the following illustration.

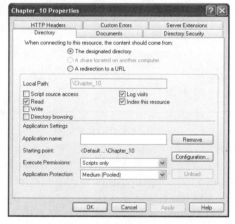

5   Click the Configuration button. The Application Configuration dialog box will be displayed, as shown in the following illustration.

6 In the Mappings tab, which is selected by default, click the Add button. The Add/Edit Application Extension Mapping dialog box will be displayed, as shown in the following illustration.

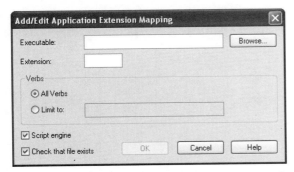

7 Click the Browse button, change the Files Of Type drop-down to **Dynamic Link Libraries** (*.dll), browse to the location of aspnet_isapi.dll (by default *%windir%*\Microsoft.NET\Framework*%version%*), select it, and click the Open button.

8 When you are returned to the Add/Edit Application Extension Mapping dialog box, click in the Executable: text box. (This step is required in Microsoft Windows XP to enable the OK button, as described in Microsoft Knowledge Base article Q317948.)

9 In the Extension: text box, type **.xml**.

10 Click the OK button to add the mapping. Once the mapping has been added, the Application Configuration dialog box will look similar to the illustration on the following page.

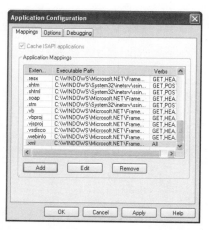

11 Click the OK button to close the Application Configuration dialog box, and then Click OK again to close the Properties dialog box. Now, anyone attempting to view Users.xml will see the message shown in the following illustration.

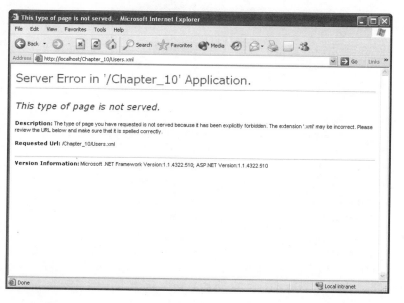

Note that if you want to protect any file named Users.xml in any application on the machine, add the *<add>* element in Step 2 to the *<httpHandlers>* element in machine.config rather than to Web.config, and you should add the mapping of the .xml extension to the ASP.NET ISAPI process using the Master Properties in IIS, and apply the changes to all Web sites when prompted. Keep in mind that there is some overhead in having ASP.NET process all requests for .xml files, so you should only do this on a machine-wide basis if you intend to use the *RegLogin* control across many applications or sites on a machine.

▶ **Important**   It's worth reiterating at this point that although this example uses hashed passwords, and you've added protection for the Users.xml file, this example should be used only for protecting content from casual anonymous browsing. If you have content for which security is critical, you should consider storing user credentials in a more secure location, such as a database, and implementing SSL encryption for the login page to ensure that usernames and passwords aren't captured in transit.

Create a page to protect

1   Add a new Web Form to the Chapter_10 project. Name the file **ProtectMe.aspx**.

2   Press F7 to view the code behind module and add the following *using* statement at the top of the ProtectMe.aspx.cs file.

```
using System.Web.Security;
```

3   Switch back to ProtectMe.aspx and add a Label and a Button to the page, and set the button's *Text* property to **Log Out**, as shown in the following illustration.

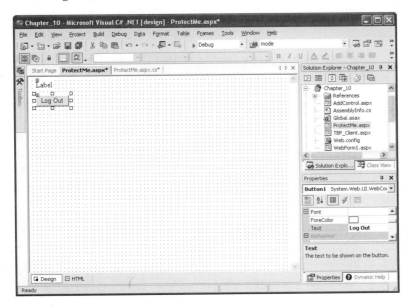

4   Double-click the button, and then add the following code to the
Button1_Click event handler:

```
FormsAuthentication.SignOut();
Response.Redirect(Request.RawUrl);
```

This code will remove the authentication cookie, and then redirect
the request to the same page, which will result in the user being redirected to the login page.

5   Add the following code, which displays the username of the currently
logged-in user, to the *Page_Load* event handler:

```
Label1.Text = "Logged in as " + User.Identity.Name + ".";
```

6   Save and close both the code-behind module and the Web Form.

Now you're finally ready to create your login page. In this next procedure,
you'll create a login page, add the RegLogin control to the Visual Studio .NET
Toolbox, add the control to the page, and add the necessary event handlers to
handle the control's events.

Use the *RegLogin* control

1   Add a new Web Form to the Chapter_10 project. Name the file
Login.aspx.

2   With Login.aspx open in Design View, expand the Toolbox, right-
click in the Web Forms tab, and select Add/Remove Items.

3   In the Customize Toolbox dialog box, click the Browse button.

4   Browse to the location of the Chapter_10_Controls assembly (the
/bin directory of the Chapter_10_Controls project), select the assembly, and then click the Open button.

5   Click the OK button to add the *RegLogin* control to the Toolbox.

6   Double-click the *RegLogin* control icon to add it to the page. At this
point, the page should look similar to the following illustration.

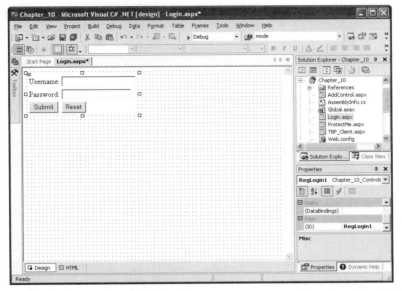

7   Add a *Label* control below the *RegLogin* control, and set its *Visible* property to *false*. Leave a little space vertically between the *RegLogin* control and the *Label* control.

8   Right-click in an empty area of the page and select View Code.

9   Just above the Page_Load declaration, add a declaration for a Boolean named *DoRedirect*. (You'll use this later when handling the *AuthSuccess* event handler.)

```
protected bool DoRedirect = false;
```

10 Go back to Login.aspx, and select the RegLogin control. In the Properties window, click the lightning bolt icon, and then double-click the AuthSuccess event from the list. This will add an event handler for the *AuthSuccess* event to the code-behind module for the page, as shown in the illustration on the next page.

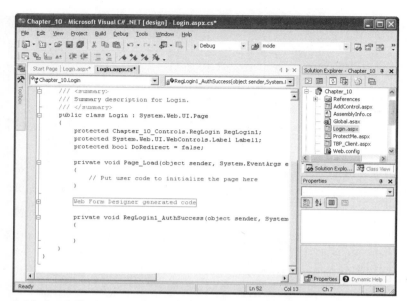

11 Add the following code to the *AuthSuccess* event handler:

```
if ( Request.QueryString("ReturnUrl") != null )
{
    DoRedirect = true;
}
```

This will signal that the page should redirect users to the page they originally requested. (You'll add the code for this in a few steps.) Because the *RegLogin* control automatically sets the Forms authentication cookie when authentication succeeds, this request will be allowed.

12 Using the same technique as in Step 10, add the *AuthFailure* event handler, and then add the following code to it:

```
Label1.ForeColor = System.Drawing.Color.Red;
Label1.Text = RegLogin1.StatusMessage;
Label1.Visible = true;
```

13 Using the same technique as in Step 10, add the *RegSuccess* event handler, and then add the following code to it:

```
Label1.ForeColor = System.Drawing.Color.Green;
Label1.Text = RegLogin1.StatusMessage;
Label1.Visible = true;
```

14 Using the same technique as in Step 10, add the *RegFailure* event handler, and then add the following code to it:

```
Label1.ForeColor = System.Drawing.Color.Red;
Label1.Text = RegLogin1.StatusMessage;
Label1.Visible = true;
```

15 Switch back to Login.aspx. Select Login System.Web.UI.Page from the drop-down list in the properties window, click the lightning bolt icon, and then double-click PreRender. Add the following code, which redirects the user if *DoRedirect* is *true*:

```
if ( DoRedirect )
{
    Response.Redirect(Request.QueryString["ReturnUrl"]);
}
```

16 To prevent the Label1 text from being displayed when you switch to Register mode, add the following to the *Page_Load* event handler:

```
Label1.Visible = false;
```

17 Save the Web Form and code-behind, and then build the Chapter_10 project.

Now that you've finished your login page, you'll test it by attempting to access ProtectMe.aspx, which is protected from anonymous access by the *<location>* section you added to Web.config earlier.

Test the page

1 Browse ProtectMe.aspx with Internet Explorer by right-clicking it in Solution Explorer, selecting Browse With, and then selecting Internet Explorer and clicking Browse. The initial output should look like the following illustration.

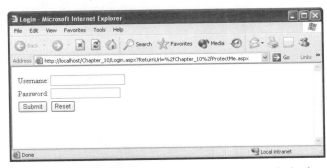

2 Without entering a username or password, click the Submit button. The output shown should look like the following illustration.

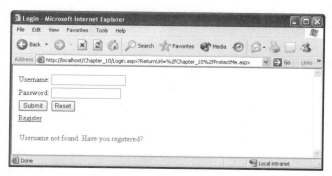

At this point, if it did not already exist, the Users.xml file has been created by the control.

3 Click the Register link. The output shown should look like the following illustration.

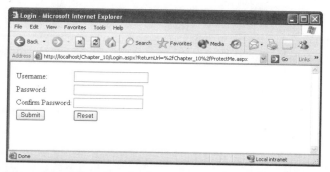

4 Enter **NewUser** for the Username and **password** (case sensitive) for the Password and Confirm Password fields, and then click Submit. The output shown should look like the following illustration.

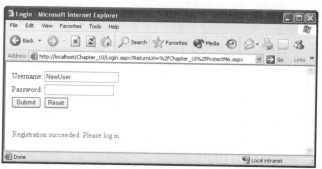

5 Enter **password** (case sensitive) for the Password field, and then click Submit. You will be redirected to ProtectMe.aspx, and the output shown should look like the following illustration.

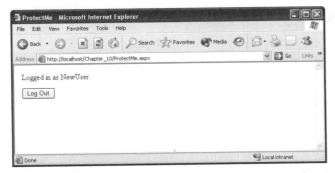

6   Click the Log Out button. You will be redirected to Login.aspx.

7   Experiment with the registration interface, such as entering an existing username or omitting the passwords, and see how the control responds.

Maintaining State

In the previous examples, data used by the controls has been stored in local variables. For many controls, this can work just fine. But unless you explicitly retrieve submitted values and repopulate the member controls with these values, as you did in the *LoadPostData* method of the previous example, the member controls will be blank when the page is posted back to the server and the results are returned. In many cases, you might want to maintain the state of the constituent controls of your custom server control, without explicitly having to write code to test for new values and repopulate the member controls with each postback.

To solve this problem, ASP.NET provides a state-management facility called *ViewState*. This is provided by an instance of the *StateBag* class of the *System.Web.UI* namespace. You store data in *ViewState* as key/value pairs, which makes working with it quite similar to working with session state. To add a value to *ViewState* or modify an existing value, you can simply specify the item's key and assign a value as follows:

```
ViewState["MyKey"] = MyValue;
```

▶ **Important**   For a control to use *ViewState*, it must be contained within a *<form>* block with the *runat="server"* attribute set.

Note that you can also add items to *ViewState* using the *Add* method of the *StateBag* class, and remove them using the *Remove* method. You can clear all *ViewState* values with the *Clear* method.

Retrieving values from *ViewState* is a bit more involved. Since the *Item* property of the *StateBag* class returns an object, you will need to cast the object to the proper type before performing any type-specific actions on it or passing it to another procedure that expects a particular type. The syntax for retrieving a string value is as follows:

```
string MyString;
MyString = (string)ViewState["MyKey"];
```

The simplest way to automate the process of saving control state to *ViewState* is to substitute *ViewState* items for the local member variables for storing the values of properties of the control.

▶ **Important**   Using *ViewState* has both performance and security implications, because all of the information stored in *ViewState* is round-tripped to the client as a base64 encoded string. The size of the *ViewState* hidden field can become quite large with controls that contain a lot of data, which can have a negative impact on performance. You might want to disable *ViewState* for these controls by setting their *EnableViewState* property to *false*.

Because the *ViewState* field is sent as a text string, you should never use *ViewState* to store information such as connection strings, server file paths, credit card information, or other sensitive data. Remember that once the *ViewState* has been sent to the client, it would be fairly simple for a hacker to decode the string and retrieve any data contained within. Don't count on base64 encoding to protect sensitive data sent to the client.

The designers of ASP.NET added a couple of features to help prevent a malicious user from capturing the *ViewState* of a page and attempting to use it to mount an attack by either modifying the *ViewState* on the client and resubmitting the page, or by attempting to replay a captured request (1-click attacks). The *EnableViewStateMac* attribute of the @ *Page* directive, which is set to *true* by default, runs a machine authentication check on the *ViewState* field when the page is resubmitted, to ensure that its contents were not changed on the client. To prevent 1-click attacks, a new Page-level property has been introduced in version 1.1 of the .NET Framework called *ViewStateUserKey*. You can set the *ViewStateUserKey* property (during *Page_Init*, attempts to set this property later will result in an error) to a string value that uniquely identifies the user to prevent these types of attacks. This value can be checked when the page is posted back. If it does not match the value you set, you should not process the request.

Finally, the *ViewState* of controls is saved between the firing of the *PreRender* and *Render* events, so any changes to control state that you want to save in *ViewState* must be made during the *PreRender* event. Changes made to control state after the *PreRender* event will not be saved to *ViewState*.

Creating Custom Controls Through Composition

The previous examples in this chapter overrode the *Render* method of the *Control* class to render its custom output, and called the *Render* method of the base class to reuse its UI. This method works fine, but it's difficult to make use of the functionality of more than one pre-existing control using this technique.

Compositional controls use a different technique to create the user interface for a custom control out of a number of preexisting or custom controls. A compositional control overrides the *CreateChildControls* method exposed by the *Control* class, and in that method, it programmatically instantiates and sets properties of the constituent controls that make up the user interface for the custom server control. Compositional controls should also implement the *INamingContainer* interface, which provides a new naming scope for the constituent controls, to ensure that their names are unique within the page.

Most often you'll want to inherit from the *Control* class for custom controls that use composition, rather than from a more functional class. Most of the functionality in a compositional control is provided by its constituent controls, allowing you to expose a minimum of functionality from the base class. Exposing less functionality from the base class can help avoid unexpected behavior in your control from superfluous base class members. For example, a control that inherits from *WebControl* exposes a number of UI-related members, such as *BackColor*, *BorderColor*, *Height*, and *Width*—members that might not be desirable in your custom control.

Overriding *CreateChildControls*

The *CreateChildControls* method is substituted for the *Render* method in compositional controls. A sample *CreateChildControls* method looks like this:

```
protected override void CreateChildControls()
{
    Label MyLabel = new Label();
    MyLabel.Text = "Label: ";
    Me.Controls.Add(MyLabel);
    MyText = new TextBox();
    this.Controls.Add(MyText);
    Button MyButton = new Button();
    MyButton.Text = "Submit";
    this.Controls.Add(MyButton);
}
```

It is not necessary in a compositional server control to call the Render method, because all of the individual controls added to the Controls collection will take care of rendering themselves during the Render stage of page processing.

If you want to manipulate controls after they've been added to the *Controls* collection, you can access them either by numeric index (casting to the appropriate type), as shown in the following code snippet, or by calling the *FindControl* method of the *Control* class and passing in the ID of the control you want to manipulate.

```
TextBox MyText = (TextBox)Controls[1];
```

Implementing *INamingContainer*

Compositional controls should always implement the *INamingContainer* interface. This interface does not contain any property or method declarations. It simply creates a new naming scope for the current control to ensure that the names of child controls are unique within the page. As with any interface in Visual C# .NET, inheriting the *INamingContainer* interface is done by adding the name of the interface to the comma-separated list of interfaces inherited, which appears as part of the class definition, separated from the class name by a colon. If you include a *using* statement for the *System.Web.UI* namespace, you can omit the namespace in the statements shown here:

```
public class CompControl : System.Web.UI.Control,
    System.Web.UI.INamingContainer
{
    // class code
}
```

In the following code listing, which replicates the functionality of the *TextBox-Plus* control, you'll see examples of both overriding the *CreateChildControls* method and implementing *INamingContainer*. The .cs file for this control—as well as a Web Form that uses the compositional version of the control—is available in the practice files for this chapter.

TextBoxPlus_Comp.cs

```
using System;
using System.Web.UI;
using System.Web.UI.WebControls;
using System.ComponentModel;

namespace Chapter_10_Controls
{
    /// <summary>
    /// Summary description for TextBoxPlus_Comp.
    /// </summary>
    [DefaultProperty("Text"),
    ToolboxData("<{0}:TextBoxPlus_Comp runat=server></{0}:TextBoxPlus_Comp>")]
    public class TextBoxPlus_Comp : System.Web.UI.WebControls.WebControl
    {
```

```
private TextTypes textType;
private Label label;
private TextBox textBox;

[Bindable(true), Category("Appearance"), DefaultValue("Label")]
public string LabelText
{
   get
   {
      EnsureChildControls();
      return label.Text;
   }

   set
   {
      EnsureChildControls();
      label.Text = value;
   }
}

[Bindable(true), Category("Appearance"), DefaultValue("PlainText")]
public TextTypes TextType
{
   get
   {
      EnsureChildControls();
      return textType;
   }

   set
   {
      EnsureChildControls();
      textType = value;
   }
}

[Bindable(true), Category("Appearance"), DefaultValue(" ")]
public string Text
{
   get
   {
      EnsureChildControls();
      return textBox.Text;
   }

   set
   {
      EnsureChildControls();
      textBox.Text = value;
```

```csharp
        }
    }

    protected override void CreateChildControls()
    {
        label = new Label();
        this.Controls.Add(label);

        textBox = new TextBox();
        this.Controls.Add(textBox);
    }

    protected override void OnPreRender(System.EventArgs e)
    {
        if ( Page.IsPostBack )
        {
            if ( textType != TextTypes.PlainText )
            {
                FormatText();
            }
        }
    }

    protected void FormatText()
    {
        EnsureChildControls();
        switch(textType)
        {
            case TextTypes.CurrencyText:
                this.Text = (double.Parse(this.Text)).ToString("C");
                break;
            case TextTypes.DecimalText:
                this.Text = (Convert.ToInt32(this.Text)).ToString("F");
                break;
        }
    }
  }
}
```

Chapter 10 Quick Reference

To	Do this
Inherit from a base class	Add a colon immediately following the class name, followed by the name of the base class. Interfaces (if any) to be inherited are added after the single base class, separated by commas.
Render output from a control	Override the *Render* method of the control class from which the custom control is derived. To take advantage of the rendered output of controls such as *TextBox* and *Label*, call the *Render* method of the base class when you are finished rendering custom output.
Handle postbacks	Implement the *IPostBackDataHandler* and/or *IPostBackEventHandler* interfaces, and implement the methods defined by the interfaces.
Maintain state in a custom control	Store state in and retrieve state from the *ViewState* object in your property procedures.

Creating and Using Web Services

In this chapter, you will learn how to:

■ Determine when to use a Web service.

■ Create a Web service.

■ Advertise and locate Web services.

■ Consume a Web service.

Previous chapters have focused on the creation of ASP.NET Web Forms, as well as the technologies that make ASP.NET development possible and the technologies that make it simple to quickly create robust, feature-rich Web applications. XML-based Web services are another important and useful part of ASP.NET.

Today, Web services are not a very well understood technology. This is partly because of inaccurate and superficial reporting from the media, who describe Web services as everything from subscription software to a proprietary plot by Microsoft to take over the Internet. These stories might sound great in print, but they are based on misunderstanding and ignorance of this potentially revolutionary technology.

Understanding XML-Based Web Services

For many years, developers have sought ways to reuse the products of their work and to bring together disparate systems that their organizations have already invested in to form a cohesive whole. This quest has been fraught with difficulties, ranging from dissimilar platforms and systems with no common standard for communication to security measures that prevented potential clients outside a corporate network from being able to use existing functionality.

Precursors to Web Services

Early on, remote procedure calls (RPC) were used as a way to allow one machine to use functionality on a remote machine. RPC involved calling a function on a client machine, and passing parameter information to the server, which in turn passed result and status information back to the client. While RPC did in fact work, it required at least one developer on the team who understood the somewhat arcane world of Interface Definition Language (IDL). Distributed COM (DCOM) offered a somewhat easier-to-use solution, but both RPC and DCOM required opening normally unopened ports in corporate firewalls, and the binary nature of the communications between client and server (also known as the *wire format*) caused problems when, for instance, integer sizes or internal byte ordering differed from machine to machine. Even with two Windows machines communicating using DCOM, configuration problems caused many a veteran programmer to give up on DCOM.

Some of the solutions for these difficulties have included creating custom Web front ends for existing functionality, or using proprietary communications and/or packaging technologies to bridge the gap between systems. The former solution worked well in some situations, but the organization hosting the application had to create and maintain a UI for the functionality that they made available, as well as creating a front end for any additional functionality added later. Moreover, this UI might or might not fully meet the needs of their existing and/or future clients. The use of proprietary communications or bridging software typically meant greater expense, reliance on a single vendor, and dependence on that vendor's maintenance and upgrades. XML-based Web services address both of these issues squarely, allowing programmatic functionality to be exposed without the need for a custom Web-based UI, and without the need for proprietary bridging software.

Web services are discrete units of programmatic functionality exposed to clients via standardized communication protocols and data formats, namely HTTP and XML. These protocols and formats are both well understood and widely accepted. (While XML is still a relatively immature technology, it has rapidly gained acceptance in the industry because of its promise as a bridging technology.) By communicating over HTTP, Web services overcome the problem of communicating across the Internet and across corporate firewalls without resorting to proprietary solutions that require additional communications ports to be opened to external access. Because Web services use XML for the formatting of requests and responses, they can be exposed from and consumed by any platform that can format and parse an XML message. This allows XML-based Web services to bring together disparate pieces of functionality—existing or new, internal or external to an organization—into a coherent whole. The following illustration shows how XML-based Web services can bring together a variety of applications and platforms. Note that because XML-based Web services can communicate over standard protocols such as HTTP, they can work over firewalls. In addition to the interactions shown here, server-to-server Web services calls are also possible.

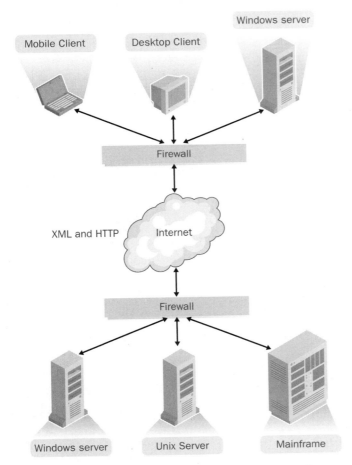

A client accesses Web services by calling into a listener that is able to provide a contract to describe the Web service and also processes incoming requests or passes them on to other application logic and passes any responses back to the client. The following illustration shows how a Web service application can be layered. You can also use Web services to access both legacy logic and new application logic, or to wrap legacy logic for access by a Web service.

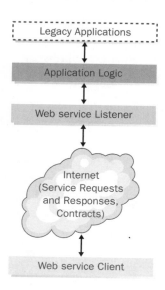

SOAP and Web Services

The SOAP is a key enabler of XML-based Web services as a strategy for application integration and Internet-based software services. SOAP is an XML-based messaging protocol that's being standardized by the World Wide Web Consortium (W3C) and has wide support from a variety of vendors. The SOAP specification provides a mandatory format for SOAP messages (referred to as *SOAP envelopes*), as well as optional standards for data encoding, request/response processing, and binding of SOAP messages to HTTP.

SOAP and XML-based Web services are too complicated to cover in a single chapter. Fortunately, one of the advantages of the ASP.NET programming model is that it abstracts the complexity of SOAP messaging from the development of Web services.

Additional Needs for Web Services

As mentioned earlier in this chapter, a Web service is nothing more than a way to provide discrete units of application functionality over standard Web protocols using a standardized message format. To be truly useful, however, Web services also need to provide the following:

■   A contract that specifies the parameters and data types it expects, as well as the return types (if any) that it sends to callers

11

Creating and Using Web Services

- A facility for locating the Web service or a means of discovering Web services offered by a given server or application, and the descriptions of those services

The next several sections will examine creating, advertising, locating, and consuming Web services from the standpoint of an ASP.NET Web developer.

Creating a Web Service

In ASP.NET, the complexities of SOAP messaging and HTTP transport are abstracted from developers, so creating XML-based Web services is actually quite simple. This abstraction is enabled through attributes that tell the common language runtime (CLR) to treat a specified class and its methods as Web services. Based on these attributes, the CLR provides all of the plumbing necessary to expose the class and methods as Web services, as well as providing a contract that clients can use to determine how to call the Web service and the return types to expect from it.

Declaring a Web Service

Web services in ASP.NET are defined in files with the .asmx file extension. The actual code for an ASP.NET Web service can reside either in the .asmx file or in a precompiled class. Either way, the Web service is declared in the .asmx file by adding the @ *WebService* directive to the file. The syntax for declaring a Web service in which the class will be defined within the .asmx files is

```
<%@ WebService Language="C#" Class="ClassName" %>
```

ClassName is the name of the class that contains the Web service methods. The syntax for declaring a Web service in which the code that defines the class and methods resides in a compiled class is

```
<%@ WebService Class="NamespaceName.ClassName,AssemblyName" %>
```

NamespaceName is the name of the namespace in which the class for the Web service resides, *ClassName* is the name of the class that contains the Web service methods, and *AssemblyName* is the name of the assembly that contains the compiled code for the Web service. This assembly should reside in the bin directory of the Web application in which the .asmx file resides. The *NamespaceName* portion of the *Class* attribute is optional if you have not specified a namespace for your class, but it is good practice to always specify a namespace for your classes. The *AssemblyName* portion of the *Class* attribute is also optional, since ASP.NET will search the bin directory for the assembly if no assembly name is provided. However, you should always provide an assembly name to avoid the performance impact of doing a search the first time the Web service is accessed.

▶ **Note**   Unlike using code-behind with ASP.NET Web Forms, you cannot use the *src* attribute with a Web service. This means that you must precompile the code-behind class that is to be used as the basis for the Web service, either manually using the command-line compiler or by building a Microsoft Visual Studio .NET Web Service application.

▶ **Important**   Visual Studio .NET provides a default framework for any Web service you create inside its IDE. The following section describes the specifics of creating a Web service class. In the section that follows, you'll create examples using Visual Studio .NET, and therefore many of the tasks required to get a basic Web service class will be in place with the default class created in the IDE. Nonetheless, it is important to understand the base classes and attributes used to create a Web service.

Creating the Web Service Class

Each .asmx file is associated with a single class, either inline in the .asmx file or in a code-behind class (the default in Visual Studio .NET). Either way, the syntax of a Web service class is as follows:

```
using System.Web.Services;

namespace NamespaceName
{
    public class ClassName : System.Web.Services.WebService
    {
        // Methods exposed by the Web service
    }
}
```

ClassName is the name of the Web service class.

Inheriting from *WebService*

In this syntax example, an *Imports* statement imports the *System.Web.Services* namespace. This namespace contains the classes and attributes that provide ASP.NET's built-in support for XML-based Web services. In this case, the class we care about is *WebService*, which is inherited in this example using the *Inherits* keyword.

Inheriting from the *WebService* class is not required for a class to function as a Web service, but the *WebService* class provides useful plumbing for Web services. This includes access to *Application*, *Session*, and other ASP.NET objects, including the *Context* object, which provides access to information about the HTTP request that invokes the Web service. Any Web service you create using Visual Studio .NET will use the *WebService* class as the base class.

Using the *<WebService()>* Attribute to Specify XML Namespace

XML-based Web services use XML namespaces to uniquely identify the end-point or listener to which a client sends requests. By default, ASP.NET sets the XML namespace for a Web service to *http://tempuri.org/projectname/class-name*. If you plan to make your Web service available publicly over the Internet, you might want to change the default namespace to avoid potential conflicts with other XML-based Web services using the same names as your Web service, and which also might use the default namespace. Using a domain name that you control can help ensure uniqueness.

You can modify the default namespace for a Web service class by adding the *WebService* metadata attribute to the class definition and setting its *Namespace* property to the desired value for the new namespace. This value can be any unique URI that you control, such as your organization's domain name. The namespace is used only for identification—the URI specified is not used in any other way, and need not be a valid, accessible Web site.

In Microsoft Visual C# .NET, metadata attributes use the syntax *[Attribute-Name(PropertyName=value)]* and are placed on the same line as the entity (class, method, and so on) that they modify:

```
[WebService(Namespace="http://www.aspnetsbs.com/webservices/")]
public class ClassName
```

Metadata Attributes

Prior to this chapter, the term *attributes* referred to the key/value pairs added to HTML or ASP.NET server control tags to define specific properties of those entities or controls. This chapter introduces the concept of *metadata* attributes.

ASP.NET and the Microsoft .NET Framework make extensive use of attributes to provide programmatic plumbing for classes, as well as to add descriptive information to managed assemblies. You can also use your own attributes (by creating classes derived from *System.Attribute*) to add your own descriptive information to your classes.

Attributes in ASP.NET Web services, in addition to providing access to the XML namespace used for the Web service, are used to tell ASP.NET that a given method is to be exposed as a *WebMethod*. ASP.NET then provides all of the run-time functionality necessary for clients of the Web service to access the *WebMethod* without requiring the programmer to write additional code.

You can set multiple properties in an attribute declaration and separate them by commas. Placing each property definition on a separate line can substantially improve code readability, particularly if you are using many properties in an attribute declaration.

Using the <WebMethod()> Attribute to Expose Methods

Once you've declared the class that implements the Web service, you will need to add one or more methods that provide functionality for the Web service. Each method will use the *WebMethod metadata* attribute to declare the method as one for which ASP.NET should provide the necessary plumbing to expose it to clients.

To add the *WebMethod* attribute to a Visual C# .NET method, use the following syntax:

```
[WebMethod()]
public <ReturnType> MethodName()
{
    // method code
}
```

MethodName is the name of the method to be exposed by the Web service; ReturnType is the type of the value (if any) to be returned by the method. Even if your method does not return a value that is a result of a calculation or other action, it is usually a good idea to at least return a value that indicates the success or failure of the method.

<WebMethod()> Attribute Properties

Like the *WebService* attribute, the *WebMethod* attribute has properties that you can use to alter the behavior of the Web method. Table 11-1 describes these properties.

Table 11-1. WebMethod Properties

Property	Description
BufferResponse	Determines whether output from the method is buffered in memory before being sent to the client. The default is *True*.
CacheDuration	Allows the output of a Web service method to be cached on the server for the specified duration, in seconds. The default is *0*, which turns off caching for the method.
Description	Sets a text description of the Web service method. This description is shown in the documentation pages autogenerated by ASP.NET, and it's included in the Web Service Description Language (WSDL) contract for the Web service.
EnableSession	Determines whether session support is enabled for the Web service method. Default is *False*. Enabling session state requires the Web service class to inherit from *WebService*. Note that enabling session state for a Web service can have a negative impact on performance.

Table 11-1.   WebMethod Properties

Property	Description
MessageName	Allows methods to be given alias names. This can be useful when you have an overloaded method, in which the same method name has multiple implementations that accept different input parameters. In this case, you can supply a different *Message-Name* for each overloaded method version, allowing you to uniquely identify each one. The default is the method name.
TransactionOption	Allows adding support for COM+ transactions in a Web service method. Allowable values are *Disabled*, *NotSupported*, *Supported*, *Required*, and *RequiresNew*. The default is *Disabled*. Note that this property requires the use of an @ *Assembly* directive to load the *System.EnterpriseServices* assembly into the Web service application.

Create a HelloWorld Web service

1   Create a new project in Visual Studio .NET. Unlike previous projects, this project should be an ASP.NET Web Service rather than an ASP.NET Web Application. Type the name of the project as **Chapter_11**, and click OK. The resulting screen should show the default Web Service, Service1.asmx.cs, in design view, as shown in the following illustration.

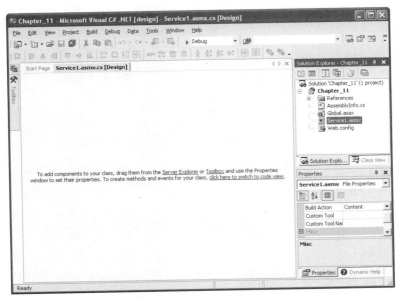

2   Switch to code view. You can click on the link provided in design view to switch to code view, or use the standard Visual Studio .NET key, F7. However you switch to code view, the screen should look similar to the following illustration:

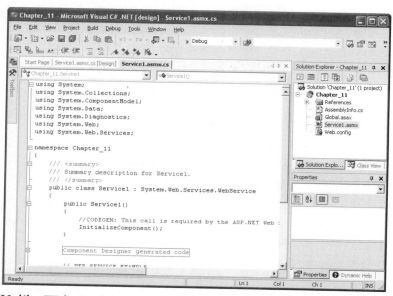

Unlike Web Applications, in which a great deal of the work of building the page is done in design view, Web services are generally modified using code directly.

3   Toward the bottom of the file, locate a comment titled WEB SERVICE EXAMPLE. The code will look similar to the following:

```
// WEB SERVICE EXAMPLE
// The HelloWorld() example service returns the string Hello World
// To build, uncomment the following lines then save and build the
// project
// To test this web service, press F5

//    [WebMethod]
//    public string HelloWorld()
//    {
//      return "Hello World";
//    }
```

4   Remove the comments from the beginning of each line from *[WebMethod()]* to the closing curly brace for the function. Rather than leave this example exactly as it is created by Visual Studio .NET, add a parameter to *HelloWorld*, and append the parameter to the value returned. The finished method should look like the following code:

```
[WebMethod]
public string HelloWorld(string name)
{
    return "Hello World, from " + name;
}
```

5   Save the file, and then build the project.

6   Right-click on Service1.asmx in Solution Explorer. Select Browse With from the drop-down menu. Select Microsoft Internet Explorer from the browser list, and then click Browse. The resulting screen should look similar to the following illustration.

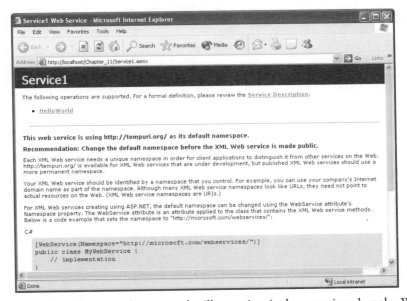

One thing that stands out on the illustration is the warning that the Web service is using the *http://tempuri.org/namespace*. There is a recommendation to change the namespace before the Web service is made public. Although it is unlikely this Web service will ever be made public, let's fix this now. Close the browser and return to the source code.

7   Add a line directly below the closing summary tag just above the top of the class declaration. Note that if you press Enter at the end of the line with the closing summary tag, you should see that Visual Studio .NET will insert three slashes (as a convenience, presuming you are adding more comments). Delete the three slashes if they appear. On the line just below the closing summary tag, add the following (you can substitute a different namespace value, if you like, as long as it is unique):

```
[WebService(Namespace="http://www.aspnetsbs.com/webservices/")]
```

8   Save the open files, and build the project again.

9   Browse the web service again using Internet Explorer, as described in
step 6. The result should look similar to the following illustration:

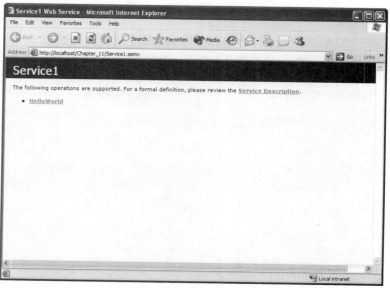

There are two links on this page. The first is Service Description. Click
this link, and a screen similar to the following illustration will appear:

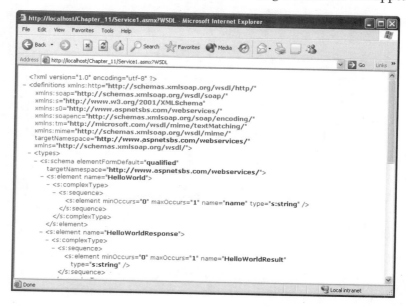

10 You can scroll through the entire document and see the complete Web Services Description Language (WSDL) contract for the Web service method. Click the Back button on the browser and select the other link on the page, *HelloWorld*. The screen should look similar to the following illustration.

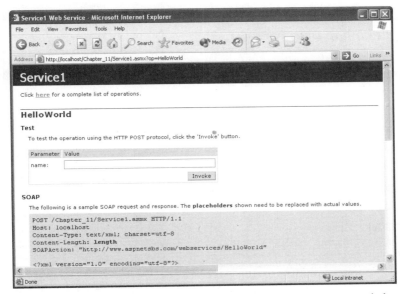

11 Enter your name in the text box provided for the name, and then click the Invoke button. The resulting screen should look similar to the following illustration, which shows the XML output returned by the Web service.

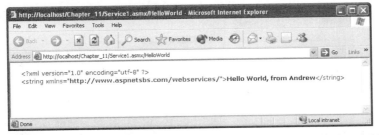

The complete source for the .asmx file and the code-behind file can be found in the practice files for the book.

▶ **Important**   The example Web services in this chapter all use the XML namespace *http://www.aspnetsbs.com/webservices/*. As with the default *http://tempuri.org* namespace, if you intend to make your XML-based Web services publicly available over the Internet, you should not use *http://www.aspnetsbs.com/webservices/* as the namespace for your Web service. Instead, use a URL that you control, and one that will allow you to be sure that your Web service can be uniquely identified.

Using Primitive Data Types

The *HelloWorld* example takes a single string as an input parameter, and returns a value of type *String*. But XML-based Web services are not limited to strings and can accept input parameters and return values of most types.

XML-based Web services in ASP.NET use the XML Schema Definition (XSD) draft specification to specify the datatypes that are supported by ASP.NET Web services. This includes primitive data types such as *string*, *int*, *boolean*, *long*, and so on, as well as more complex types such as classes or structs.

The definition for a Web service method that adds two numbers and returns the result would look like the following:

```
[WebMethod()]
public int Add(int Num1, int Num2)
{
    return (Num1 + Num2);
}
```

Accessing Data in a Web Service

In addition to primitive types, classes, and structs, ASP.NET Web services can also return or accept ADO.NET datasets as input parameters. This is possible because the *DataSet* class has built-in support for being serialized as XML, which can be easily sent over an HTTP connection.

Return data from a Web service

1   In Visual Studio .NET, open the Chapter_11 project if it is not already open.

2   Create a new Web service. Right-click on the root of the project, then select Add from the drop-down menu, and then select Add Web Service. In the resulting dialog box, type the name of the file as **AuthorsService.asmx**, and click Open. When the design view of the new Web service appears, click on the link provided on the design surface to switch to code view.

3   At the top of AuthorsService.asmx.cs, add the following line:

```
using System.Data.SqlClient;
```

4   Just above the class declaration for the *AuthorsService* class, add the following line. If you press Enter at the end of the line with the closing Summary tag, Visual Studio .NET will add a new line with three slashes. Delete these before adding the line.

```
[WebService(Namespace="http://www.aspnetsbs.com/webservices/")]
```

5   Scroll to the bottom of the code file, and uncomment the commented *HelloWorld* method. Change the name of the method to **GetAuthors**, and the return type of the method from *string* to **DataSet**. Modify the *WebMethod* attribute just before the *GetAuthors* method, adding the description so that it looks like the following line:

```
[WebMethod(Description="Returns the Pubs Authors table.")]
```

6   Modify the *GetAuthors* method so that it looks like the following code:

```
[WebMethod(Description="Returns the Pubs Authors table.")]
public DataSet GetAuthors()
{
    DataSet dsAuthors = new DataSet();
    SqlConnection cn = new SqlConnection();
    SqlDataAdapter da;
    string strCn;

    strCn=@"server=(local)\vsDotNet;database=pubs;" +
        "Trusted_Connection=yes";
    cn.ConnectionString=strCn;

    da=new SqlDataAdapter(
        "SELECT * FROM Authors ORDER BY au_LName,au_FName",cn);
    da.Fill(dsAuthors,"Authors");
    return dsAuthors;
}
```

Much of the database access code should look very familiar from previous examples. Note that the connection is neither opened nor closed in this example. This is because the *SqlDataAdapter* class takes care of opening, and closing the connection automatically, using the connection object passed to its constructor.

7   Save the file and build the application.

8   Browse the Web service with Internet Explorer. The screen should look similar to the illustration on the next page. (Note that the description specified is the same as the *Description* property of the *WebMethod* attribute.)

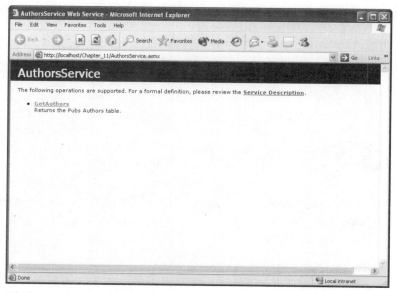

9. Click GetAuthors. The resulting page will look similar to the last example page that allowed you to invoke the Web service, except in this case, there will be an Invoke button, but no text box (because there are no parameters). Click Invoke, and a window similar to the following illustration will appear.

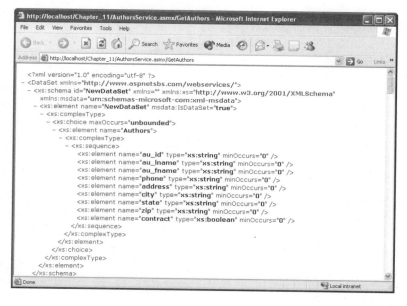

10 The schema for the resulting data is at the top of the result from invoking the Web service. Scroll down in the browser window, and you will see the actual data, as shown in the following illustration.

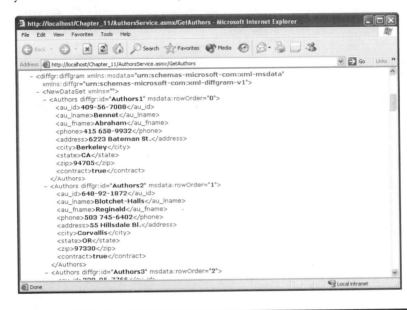

Advertising a Web Service

Once you've created a Web service using the techniques in the previous examples, the Web service is ready to be accessed by clients. The challenge at this point is how to give clients the information necessary to allow them to access your Web service.

In an intranet-based scenario, this is relatively simple. You can provide potential internal clients with the URL to your Web service directly, either by e-mailing it to those who need it or by creating a centrally located Web page that users within your organization can browse to find the appropriate URL. In an Internet-based scenario, however, you might not know who your potential clients are. This makes it much more difficult to ensure that they can find and use your Web services.

You have two solutions for this dilemma: Web services discovery, and Web services directories using Universal Description, Discovery, and Integration (UDDI).

Advertising Web Services Through a Discovery Document

A discovery document is an XML-based document containing references to Web services and/or other discovery documents. Through the use of discovery documents, you can easily catalog all of the available Web services on a Web server at a single location.

By publishing a discovery document to a publicly available URL, you can make it possible for clients to easily locate and consume Web services that you have made available. Clients can access the discovery document using tools such as the wsdl.exe command-line utility supplied with the .NET Framework, or with Visual Studio .NET's Add Web Reference dialog box, in order to create clients for the Web service. We'll discuss this process in greater detail in "Using a Web Service" on page 429.

A discovery file uses the extension .disco and contains two types of nodes: *contractRef* nodes and *discoveryRef* nodes. The *contractRef* nodes refer to WSDL files that you can use to create clients for a Web service, while *discoveryRef* nodes refer to additional discovery documents. The discovery document for the two example Web services created in this chapter is shown in the following listing, Chapter11.disco. The *ref* attribute of the *contractRef* node contains the URL to the WSDL contract for the Web service, in this case generated by ASP.NET by appending the ?WSDL argument to the URL for the .asmx file that implements the Web service. The *docRef* attribute contains the URL to the documentation for the Web service, in this case simply the URL to the .asmx file, since ASP.NET automatically generates documentation for Web services implemented in an .asmx file. The *xmlns* attributes in the *discoveryRef* and *contractRef* nodes establish the XML namespaces in which these nodes reside.

Chapter_11.disco

```xml
<?xml version="1.0" encoding="utf-8" ?>
<discovery xmlns="http://schemas.xmlsoap.org/disco/">
   <contractRef ref="AuthorsService.asmx?wsdl"
      docRef="AuthorsService.asmx"
      xmlns="http://schemas.xmlsoap.org/disco/scl/" />
   <contractRef ref="Service1.asmx?wsdl"
      docRef="Service1.asmx"
      xmlns="http://schemas.xmlsoap.org/disco/scl/" />
</discovery>
```

Note that for the sake of readability, this listing contains relative URLs. Discovery documents can contain either relative or absolute URLs. When relative URLs are used, they are assumed to be relative to the location of the URL of the discovery document. If you browse to the disco file, it will be displayed just as any other XML file. You can add a .disco file to your project by right-clicking the project in Solution Explorer, then highlighting Add, then selecting Add New Item. In the Add New Item dialog box, select the Static Discovery File icon, and give the file the desired name.

Advertising Web Services Through UDDI

Another option for advertising Web services to potential clients is UDDI. This is a multivendor initiative, spearheaded by Ariba, IBM, and Microsoft, and designed to provide an Internet-based business registry (or registries) in which creators of Web services can register their publicly available Web services. The UDDI specification describes how Web services can be registered in such a way as to allow clients to easily search for the type of Web service desired, or to discover all of the Web services offered by a particular partner or company.

> ▶ **Note** While the UDDI initiative is based on Web standards and proposed standards such as DNS, HTP, XML, and SOAP, UDDI itself is not a proposed standard. Rather, it's a multivendor specification, created and maintained by Ariba, IBM, and Microsoft, with input from other companies. It is the stated intent of the involved parties that the UDDI specification will eventually be transitioned to a standards body.

The model for UDDI is for multiple identical versions of the UDDI business registry to be hosted by multiple participants, providing redundancy and load balancing for the registry. Web service providers can register their Web services at any node and the information will be replicated to all registries daily, allowing potential clients to find these services from any registry.

Currently, both Microsoft and IBM provide online UDDI registries, and both can be reached from *http://www.uddi.org/*, where you can also find a number of helpful white papers on UDDI.

Securing a Web Service

One challenge of implementing a Web service comes when you need to limit who can access it. You might want to limit access to only those clients who ha v epaid a subscription fee, for example. Or, if your Web service stores and uses data specific to individual users, you might want to implement some sort of login process to allow clients to view and modify only data that is specific to them.

One potential issue here is that the SOAP protocol, on which Web services are based, does not provide any specifications for securing Web services. There are newly proposed standards for Web service security, such as WS-Security. (See *http://msdn.microsoft.com/library/en-us/dnglobspec/html/wssecurspecindex.asp* for more information.) However, until all or most Web Service vendors adopt these standards, their usefulness will be limited to situations in which you can control all parts of the application. This means that it's up to you to choose an existing means of securing your Web service that provides the level of security you need but that's also relatively easy to implement, both for you and your clients. The last thing you want is to make your Web service so difficult to use that potential clients go elsewhere. You should keep track, however, of new information as it becomes available, at sites such as *http://msdn.microsoft.com/webservices/default.aspx*. Keeping up on the latest information better allows you to determine when new specifications such as WS-security are widely accepted enough for use in your applications.

Exploring Authentication Options

The first choice you must make when securing your Web service is how to authenticate users of your Web service. There are a number of options, each with its own advantages and disadvantages.

While ASP.NET does not define any specific authentication and authorization method for Web services, you can take advantage of the authentication mechanisms that IIS offers. These mechanisms are described in detail in Chapter 6, in the section titled "Using Windows-Based Authentication."

The advantage of using one of the IIS authentication mechanisms is that the infrastructure for them already exists. You do not need to create your own credential store for user account information. One disadvantage is that each of the authentication methods offered by IIS requires the creation of NT accounts for each client of your application. This can be difficult to administer, depending on how your Web server is set up (whether it is part of an NT domain, whether it uses Microsoft Active Directory, and so on). Another disadvantage is that the Integrated Windows authentication method, while secure, requires the client to belong to the same domain (or a trusted domain) as the server, making it impractical for Internet use. Basic authentication is suitable for Internet use, but it sends username and password as clear text, making it easy for them to be compromised. You can use SSL encryption to prevent this problem, but this can add an unacceptable performance overhead if user credentials must be passed with each Web service request.

Another option for authenticating users is a third-party authentication mechanism such as Microsoft Passport. Unfortunately, the developer tool support for Passport is currently poor, and most available tools focus on allowing the use of Passport to authenticate users from Web sites, rather than Web services. While it is likely that Passport and other third-party authentication mechanisms will add support for simple implementation in Web services eventually, today these mechanisms likely will require too much effort on the part of your clients.

Finally, you can "roll your own" Web services authentication by implementing a login function in one or all of your Web services, with the login method returning a unique key (which should be hashed or encrypted) identifying the logged-in user. This key is then passed as a parameter of each Web service request, indicating that the user is an authenticated user. To protect the username and password, the login Web service method should be requested over an SSL connection. Subsequent requests can be made over a standard HTTP connection, however, so as to avoid the performance overhead of SSL encryption. To reduce the risk of a user being impersonated by someone who has intercepted the login key, these keys should be stored in such a way that they can be easily expired after a predetermined timeout value (in a back-end database, for example).

While this authentication method is more difficult to implement and maintain than some of the others, it's the simplest for your clients to use. Once you have given a client his account information (username and password), all he needs to do is make the request to the login Web service (over an SSL connection) and store his login key. With each subsequent request, he passes the key as one of the parameters of the Web service method he's calling. If the timeout value expires between one request and the next, the user must call the login method again to receive a new key. Therefore, the timeout value should be set to provide a balance between security and convenience. In addition to the login method, you could also implement a logout method in your Web service to explicitly expire the login key.

▶ **Important**   In addition to controlling access to a Web service with authentication, you should also use SSL to encrypt communications if you are passing sensitive data to or from the Web service. This includes usernames and passwords sent when authenticating users, as well as data such as patient information in the healthcare industry, where the requirement to protect personal data is not only common sense, it's the law!

You can find more information on Web services security, including information on the proposed WS-Security specification, in the Microsoft XML Web Services Developer Center at *http://msdn.microsoft.com/webservices/* and at *http://msdn.microsoft.com/ws-security/*.

Using a Web Service

So now that you've got a couple of nifty Web services, you'll probably want to know how to use them, beyond testing them by invoking them from a browser. While the formatting of SOAP requests and responses necessary to call a Web service can be somewhat complicated, the .NET Framework adds an abstraction layer that hides much of this complexity.

Nonetheless, you still need to know how to locate and use a Web service, including the following techniques:

- Locating a Web service, using either a discovery document or UDDI
- Using the WSDL.EXE utility to create a proxy class for the Web service
- Using the proxy class from an ASP.NET page or console application to access the Web service

Locating a Web Service

The first step in using an XML-based Web service is to locate it. If you're dealing with a Web service that you or someone in your organization created, you might already know the location of the Web service. If so, you can skip this step.

Locating a Web service is essentially the mirror image of advertising a Web service, so the same techniques apply here. There are two techniques for locating a Web service in ASP.NET: discovery documents and UDDI.

Locating a Web Service with a Discovery Document

To use a discovery document to locate Web services, you need the URL for the discovery document that describes the services in which you're interested. You might get the URL for the document from a listing on an organization's public Web site, from an e-mail promotion, or from a catalog.

Once you have the URL for a discovery document, you can use the disco.exe command-line utility to generate WSDL contracts for using the Web services described in the discovery document. The syntax for the disco.exe utility is

```
disco [options] URL
```

Here, options represents one or more command-line options for the utility, and URL represents the URL to the discovery document. Table 11-2 shows options for the disco.exe utility.

Table 11-2.   disco.exe Options

Option	Description
/d:*domain* or /domain:*domain*	Sets the domain to use when connecting to a site that requires authentication.
/nosave	Prevents disco.exe from saving files for the discovered WSDL and discovery documents.
/nologo	Prevents the start-up banner from being displayed.
/o:*directory* or /out:*directory*	Provides the directory name where output should be saved.
/p:*password* or /password:*password*	Sets the password to use when connecting to a site that requires authentication.
/proxy:*url*	Sets the proxy to use for HTTP requests.
/pd:*domain* or /proxydomain:*domain*	Sets the domain to use when connecting to a proxy server that requires authentication.
/pp:*password* or /proxypassword:*password*	Sets the password to use when connecting to a proxy server that requires authentication.
/pu:*username* or /proxyusername:*username*	Sets the username to use when connecting to a proxy server that requires authentication.
/u:*username* or /username:*username*	Sets the username to use when connecting to a site that requires authentication.
/?	Provides help for command-line options.

Locating a Web Service with UDDI

Unlike using a discovery document to locate a Web service, UDDI does not require you to know in advance the URL of a document describing the desired Web service. Any provider of a UDDI business registry usually will provide a tool for searching their instance of the registry for businesses or Web services that meet your needs. The criteria you can search on will depend on the organization hosting that instance. For example, Microsoft's UDDI registry at *http://uddi.microsoft.com* supports searching by business name, business location, discovery URL, keyword, and a variety of other criteria. The following illustration shows the list of available criteria for searching the Microsoft UDDI registry.

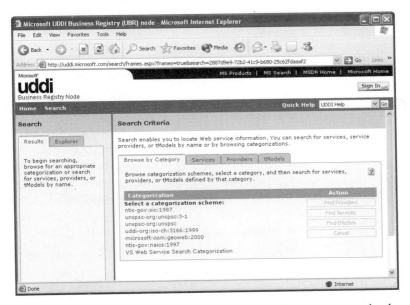

One effective technique for searching for Web services on the *http://uddi.microsoft.com* registry is to search by discovery URL and search for URLs that contain "wsdl." These URLs are the most likely to point to live WSDL contracts that you can use to access available Web services.

Understanding WSDL Files

WSDL is an XML-based standard for documents that describe the services exposed by a Web service. You can view the WSDL contract for any of the Web services you create with ASP.NET by calling up the URL for a Web service in a browser and appending ?WSDL to it.

WSDL contracts are similar to COM type libraries or .NET assembly metadata in that they are used to describe the public members of the Web service, including all publicly available methods, the parameters (and data types) those methods expect when called, and the data type of any return value. Because this information is encoded in a standard XML-based format, any client that can read XML and can understand WDSL and SOAP should be able to effectively consume the Web application that the WSDL contract describes.

> ▶   **Important**   The SOAP and WSDL specifications are still in the process of being standardized. In the short term, this means that there might be inconsistencies between different implementations of WSDL on different plat-forms, since these implementations can be based on different drafts of the proposed standard. Until SOAP and WSDL become settled standards (W3C Recommendations), you might need to tweak your WSDL contracts to achieve interoperability between different Web services implementations. This shouldn't be an issue once these specifications have received approval as W3C Recom-mendations. In the meantime, you can read an interesting article on interopera-bility between various Web services implementations on the MSDN Library Web site at *http://msdn.microsoft.com/library/en-us/dn_voices_webservice/html/service08152001.asp*.

Creating a Proxy Class

Consuming a Web service via SOAP is a fairly complex affair. It involves creating and formatting a SOAP envelope, a set of SOAP headers, and a SOAP body, all with the correct elements and attributes for the Web service you're targeting. Fortunately, thanks to the built-in support for Web services in the .NET Framework, all of the plumbing necessary for accessing a Web service is provided for you. The .NET Framework provides another command-line utility, wsdl.exe, to help you by creating a .NET proxy class for a Web service described by a WSDL contract.

Using the wsdl.exe Utility

The wsdl.exe utility generates a proxy class in C#, Visual Basic .NET, or JScript .NET for a WSDL contract specified by URL or path. This proxy class can be instantiated and its methods called by any client, just like any other .NET class. Visual Studio .NET provides an easier way to generate a proxy class, which the next example will cover. However, at times (especially when you have special requirements not met by the standard proxy classes) you might find it handy to manually create the proxy class.

The syntax for the wsdl.exe utility is as follows:

```
wsdl [options] {URL | path}
```

Here, options represents one or more command-line options for the utility, and URL represents the URL to the WSDL contract. Alternatively, a file path to the WSDL contract can be passed as the path argument. Table 11-3 shows options for the wsdl.exe utility.

Table 11-3. wsdl.exe Options

Option	Description
/appsettingurlkey:*key* or /urlkey:*key*	Sets the key of the configuration setting from which to read the default URL for generating code.
/appsettingbaseurl:*baseurl* or /baseurl:*baseurl*	Sets the base URL to use for calculating relative URLs when a URL fragment is specified for the *URL* argument.
/d:*domain* or /domain:*domain*	Sets the domain to use when connecting to a site that requires authentication.
/l:*language* or /language:*language*	Sets the language to use when generating the proxy class. Valid values include *CS*, *VB*, *JS*, or the fully qualified name of any class that implements the *System.CodeDom.Compiler.CodeDomProvider* class. Default is *CS* (C#).
/n:*namespace* or /namespace:*namespace*	Sets the namespace to be used when generating the proxy class.
/nologo	Prevents the start-up banner from being displayed.
/o:*filename* or /out:*filename*	Provides the file name (and path) to use for saved output.
/p:*password* or /password:*password*	Sets the password to use when connecting to a site that requires authentication.
/protocol:*protocol*	Sets the protocol (SOAP, *HttpGet*, or *HttpPost*) to use for requests. Default is SOAP.
/proxy:*url*	Sets the proxy to use for HTTP requests.
/pd:*domain* or /proxydomain:*domain*	Sets the domain to use when connecting to a proxy server that requires authentication.
/pp:*password* or /proxypassword:*password*	Sets the password to use when connecting to a proxy server that requires authentication.
/pu:*username* or /proxyusername:*username*	Sets the username to use when connecting to a proxy server that requires authentication.
/server	Creates an abstract base class with the same interfaces as specified in the WSDL contract.
/u:*username* or /username:*username*	Sets the username to use when connecting to a site that requires authentication.
/?	Provides help for command-line options.

Take the following steps to create proxy classes in Visual C# .NET for the *HelloService* and *AuthorsService* example Web services created earlier in this chapter.

Create proxy classes

1   Open a command line and navigate to the directory where you would like the proxy classes to be generated. (Or use the /o option to specify a path and filename for saving the proxy class.)

2   Execute the wsdl.exe utility, using the /l option to specify Visual C# .NET as the language and passing the URL to the HelloService.asmx file, including the ?WSDL parameter, which tells ASP.NET to return the WSDL contract for the .asmx file. (Both of the following lines should form a single command.) The URL you specify should match the location of the .asmx file on your Web server, and it might differ from the following URL.

```
wsdl /l:cs /n:ASPNETSBS_CS
http://localhost/Chapter11/Service1.asmx?WSDL
```

3   Execute the wsdl.exe utility again for AuthorsService.asmx, using the same syntax as shown in step 2 but modifying the URL to point to AuthorsService.asmx.

4   Optionally, you can create a batch file (with the .bat extension) containing both of the preceding commands. If you want to see the results of the batch execution before the command window closes, add a *pause* command at the end of the batch file. A batch file similar to this is included in the practice files for this chapter.

Once you've created your proxy class, you'll need to compile the class using the command-line compiler for the language you chose to generate (in this example, Visual C# .NET). The following listing, MakeServices.bat, shows the command-line compiler syntax to compile these classes and output the resulting assembly to the bin subdirectory of the directory from which the command is run. For this example, this should be the bin subdirectory of the Chapter_11 project. Note that this listing represents a single command and has been wrapped to multiple lines for readability. A batch file similar to this is included in the practice files for this chapter.

MakeServices.bat

```
csc /t:library /r:System.Web.dll /r:System.dll
/r:System.Web.Services.dll /r:System.Xml.dll /r:System.Data.dll
/out:bin\Services.dll AuthorsService.cs Service1.cs
```

▶ **Important**   By default, the .NET Framework and Visual Studio .NET setup programs do not add the paths to either wsdl.exe or csc.exe to the PATH environment variable. This means that to call these programs from the command line, you must either change directories to the location of the program before calling it (the technique used in the batch files contained in the practice files for the chapter), or you must add the program's path to the PATH environment variable. Instructions for adding these paths to the PATH environment variable are found in Appendix C.

Consume a Web service from Visual Studio .NET

1   Open the project for this chapter, Chapter_11, in Visual Studio .NET if it is not already open.

2   Right-click on the root of the project in the Solution Explorer, and select Add Web Reference from the drop-down menu. The Add Web Reference dialog box will appear, as shown in the following illustration.

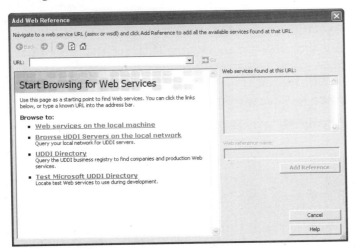

3   Type the URL to the AuthorsService.asmx file (if you followed the directions in this chapter, this should be *http://localhost/Chapter_11/ AuthorsService.asmx*) in the address text box, and click Go (you can also click *Web Services On The Local Machine* to browse for all local Web services, then select the AuthorsService service). The result should look similar to the illustration on the next page.

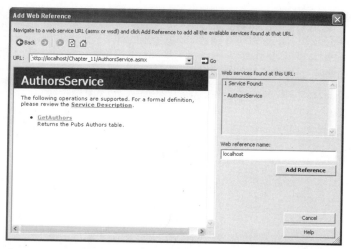

4   Click the Add Reference button at the bottom right-hand corner of
the Add Web Reference dialog box. When the Add Web Reference
dialog box closes, look in the Solution Explorer to find a new node
named Web References. Under Web References, you'll see a node
added called localhost (assuming the URL entered in Step 2 was on
the localhost domain). Expand that node (you might need to click the
Show All Files button in the Solution Explorer toolbar first). The
result should look similar to the following illustration.

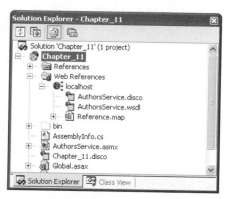

5   Right-click on localhost, and select Rename from the drop-down
menu. Rename localhost to **Authors**.

When you add a Web reference, Visual Studio .NET creates a folder
with the same name as the Web reference under the Web References
folder that is under the main project folder. There are several files
created by Visual Studio .NET in this folder. Most interesting is

Reference.cs (which is hidden by default), which contains the proxy code generated by Visual Studio for accessing the Web service.

6   Add a new Web Form. Type the name of the new Web Form as **ShowAuthors.aspx.**

7   Click and drag a DataGrid control from the toolbox to the surface of the page of ShowAuthors.aspx.

8   Press F7 to change to code view. Scroll down to the *Page_Load* method, and then modify it so that it looks like the following code:

```
private void Page_Load(object sender, System.EventArgs e)
{
    DataSet ds;
    Authors.AuthorsService svc = new Authors.AuthorsService();
    ds = svc.GetAuthors();
    DataGrid1.DataSource = ds.Tables["Authors"];
    DataBind();
}
```

9   Save and build the project.

10   Browse ShowAuthors.aspx using Internet Explorer. The output should look similar to the following illustration.

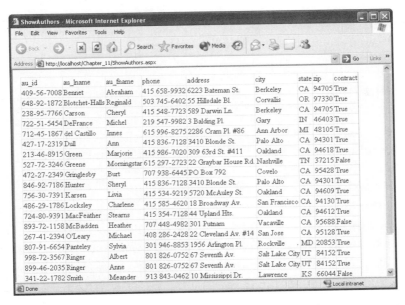

One important thing to notice about this example is that while the table we are displaying is a Microsoft SQL Server table, we do not reference *System.Data.SqlClient.* We don't have to because this application is not directly connecting to a SQL

Server database. Rather, the application connects to the Web service created earlier (which returns a generic DataSet), and from there the Web service itself connects to SQL Server. Because the project already contains a reference to the *System.Data* namespace (which is added by default to all new projects), we don't need to add any additional namespace references to use the dataset returned from the Web service.

How the Proxy Code Works

The magic behind consuming a Web service in Visual Studio .NET is not magic at all. Web services use a proxy class (just like the ones generated by the wsdl.exe utility) on the client end (in this case, the Web server) to provide access to the methods of the Web service. The proxy class is a class containing all of the methods exposed by the Web service. Rather than actual functionality (in our case, the code that connects to the SQL Server database), the proxy code descends from *SoapHttpClientProtocol* and calls out to the required Web method indirectly using its own *Invoke* method. The proxy class for the *AuthorsService* in the Chapter_11 project is called Reference.cs, and you can find it in the practice files for this chapter.

> ► **Tip**   It's important to note that Web services clients are not limited to ASP.NET Web Forms. You can just as easily consume Web services from Windows Forms applications, Console applications, Windows Services, or even other Web services.

Additional Resources

Web Services are a useful tool, particularly for providing interoperability between functionality provided by different applications, and even on different platforms. But the technology and specifications behind Web Services are still in development. For this reason, it's best to check for the latest information at sites such as the following:

- *http://msdn.microsoft.com/webservices/*   Microsoft's XML Web Services Developer Center
- *http://www.w3.org/*   The World Wide Web consortium, home of the SOAP, WSDL, XSD, and other specifications
- *http://www.uddi.org/*   Information on the UDDI specification

Chapter 11 Quick Reference

To	Do this
Create an XML-based Web service using ASP.NET	In Visual Studio .NET, create a new ASP.NET Web Service project. Visual Studio .NET will create the application in IIS and create a default Web service file with an .asmx extension.
Test a Web service	Browse the .asmx file containing the Web service from a Web browser. ASP.NET will generate documentation pages for the Web service, as well as allowing you to invoke the Web service.
Change the default namespace of a Web service	Add or modify the *WebService* attribute, adding a *Namespace?"<new URL>"* parameter.
Advertise a Web service	Either create a discovery document for your Web services and publish the document to a public location, such as your organization's Web site, or register your Web services in one of the publicly available UDDI business registries, making sure to provide the URL to the WSDL contract for each Web service you register.
Consume a Web service from ASP.NET	Use the wsdl.exe utility to create a proxy class based on the WSDL contract for the Web service, compile the proxy class, and instantiate the proxy class from your client application as you would any other .NET class. Alternatively, simply right-click on the project root in Visual Studio .NET, click Add Web Reference on the drop-down menu, and then enter a URL. If the URL is recognized and the methods available are displayed, click Add Reference.

Using Caching to Improve Performance

In this chapter, you will learn how to:

- Take advantage of output caching for Web Forms pages and user controls.

- Take advantage of caching for data retrieved with ADO.NET.

- Use the Cache APIs to get fine-grained control over the expiration, dependencies, and other properties of cached items.

The good news about ASP.NET is that its improvements—from the use of compiled languages rather than interpreted languages to the complete rewrite of the ASP.NET execution engine—make it easy for you to obtain the performance that many of your applications need. Well-designed applications written in ASP.NET will almost always be faster than the equivalent applications written in classic ASP.

However, for one class of applications these performance improvements alone will not be sufficient. These can include applications whose pages are computationally intensive (such as pages that use recursive procedures) or access large amounts of data, and applications that need to scale to large numbers of concurrent users.

ASP.NET offers new features for this class of applications, including a simple API for output caching and a rich and robust caching engine and API.

Understanding Caching

Caching is the process of temporarily storing expensive resources in memory. These resources might be expensive because of the amount of processor time necessary to render them, because they reside on disk, or because they reside in a back-end database on another machine.

Pages that are expensive to render can consume so much processor time that the Web server becomes unable to fulfill requests in a timely fashion. Retrieving pages and other content from disk is much slower than serving them from memory, and this performance difference is magnified when the server needs to fulfill many requests simultaneously. Requests for large amounts of data from a back-end database often encounter both disk-based and network-based performance delays. (Thus, calls from one server to another can be substantially more expensive than fulfilling a request on the same machine.)

For these reasons, Web applications that need high performance have long used caching to mitigate the performance costs of expensive operations. The output from recent requests, or requested data, is cached in memory. Subsequent requests are served from this in-memory cache, rather than rendering a page or querying a database again. This can substantially improve the performance and scalability of an application. In the past, unfortunately, this improvement has come at a cost. Developers using classic ASP were limited to either using the intrinsic *Session* and *Application* objects for caching or rolling their own caching engines.

ASP.NET now offers a rich, robust framework for caching both page output and arbitrary data that developers can access easily using both declarative and programmatic means. ASP.NET output caching allows developers to declaratively cache page and user control output to avoid wasting resources by repeatedly rendering content that does not need to change from request to request. The cache API provides a number of methods that allow developers to add items to the cache, remove items from the cache, and set properties that determine the lifetime of items stored in the cache.

Using Output Caching

Output caching allows you to cache the rendered output of any ASP.NET Web Forms page or user control, and to serve subsequent requests from the cache. This can substantially reduce the processor load on the Web server because the processor isn't busy rendering pages whose content hasn't changed. The two basic techniques for enabling output caching are *declarative* and *programmatic*. The declarative technique uses the @ *OutputCache* directive and its associated attributes to enable output caching; the programmatic technique uses the *Response.Cache* property to programmatically set caching parameters.

Using the @ *OutputCache* Directive

The simplest method to quickly set up output caching for a given page or user control is to add the @ *OutputCache* directive. This directive and its attributes allow you to set the length of time the content should be cached, the location where it should be cached, and any parameters to be used to cache multiple versions of a page. Table 12-1 describes the available attributes for the @ *Output-Cache* directive.

Table 12-1. @ *OutputCache* **Attributes**

Attribute	Description
Duration	Sets the number of seconds to cache the content. This attribute is required.
Location	Sets the location to be used to cache content. This can be one of the following values: ■ *Any* Content can be cached by any cache-aware application (such as a proxy server) in the request stream, by the Web server, or by the client browser. This is the default value. ■ *Client* Content is cached by the requesting client's browser. ■ *Downstream* Content can be cached by any cache-aware application downstream of the Web server fulfilling the request. ■ *Server* Content is cached on the Web server. ■ *None* No caching. You can use the *Location* attribute with Web Forms pages *only*.
Shared	New in ASP.NET 1.1, this attribute specifies whether or not a cached user control can be shared across multiple pages. If set to *true*, a single cached copy of the user control is shared among multiple pages within the application. If set to *false*, a separate copy of the user control will be cached for each page that uses the control. The default is *false*. This attribute is valid for user controls only.
VaryByControl	Sets the names of properties of a user control by which to vary the caching of the user control output. Multiple properties are separated by semicolons. You can use this attribute with user controls *only*.
VaryByCustom	Allows varying of cached content by browser user agent, browser capabilities, or custom logic. When set to any value other than *browser*, this attribute requires that the *HttpApplication.Get-VaryByCustomString* be overridden in Global.asax to implement the custom logic.

Table 12-1.   @ *OutputCache* Attributes

Attribute	Description
VaryByHeader	Allows varying of cached content based on the value of one or more HTTP request headers. Multiple properties are separated by semicolons. You can use this attribute with Web Forms pages *only*.
VaryByParam	Allows varying of cached content based on the value of one or more querystring values sent with a *GET* request, or form fields sent with a *POST* request. Multiple key or field names are separated by semicolons. You can also set the value of this attribute to * to vary by all parameters, or to *None* to use the same cached page regardless of *GET/POST* parameters. This attribute is required.

The *VaryByX* attributes are among the most important features of the *@ OutputCache* directive. These attributes make it possible to cache pages and user controls even when those pages are dynamically generated based on querystring values, form field values, HTTP header values, or even browser capabilities.

The *Duration* attribute lets you limit the length of time that output is cached. For pages that are updated periodically, but not as frequently as every request, the *Duration* attribute allows you to fine-tune the output caching so that you can maximize the benefit gained by caching while being reasonably sure that users will not get stale content. For example, if you had a page that, on average, was updated every two hours, you could set the *Duration* attribute of the *@ OutputCache* directive to *900*. This would cache the output of the page for 900 seconds (15 minutes) from the last time the page was requested (subject to the *VaryBy* attributes). This would ensure that the page would need to be rendered only once every 15 minutes, regardless of how many requests were received for the page, and that there would be only a 15-minute window in which users could get a cached page rather than updated data.

The *Shared* attribute allows you to conserve memory by making a single cached copy of a user control available to multiple pages within your application. Without setting this attribute to *true*, a separate copy of the user control is cached for each page that uses the user control.

Finally, the *Location* attribute determines where the output cache is located. Setting certain values for the *Location* attribute causes ASP.NET to set the *If-Modified-Since* HTTP header to allow caching of page or control output.

Cache Web Forms output

1 Open Visual Studio .NET and create a new Web Application project called Chapter_12.

2 Rename the initial default page WebForm1.aspx to Output-Cache.aspx by selecting it in the Solution Explorer window, then selecting File, and then selecting Save WebForm1.aspx As. In the resulting dialog box, type **OutputCache.aspx** as the new filename.

3 Add two labels to the form. Using the Properties window, change the *ID* property of the first label from Label1 to **Message**. Change the *Text* property of the second label to **The text above was rendered with an ASP.NET Label Server Control, then the output was cached for 10 seconds.** The resulting screen should look like the following illustration:

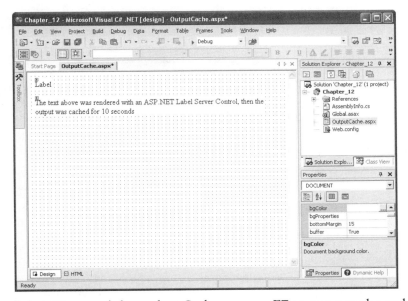

4 Select View, and then select Code, or press F7 to move to the code window.

5 Scroll down to the *Page_Load* event handler and add the following code:

```
Message.Text = DateTime.Now.ToString();
```

6 Save the open files and project, and then build the project.

7 Browse the page, and then press F5 to refresh the page in the browser. Each time you refresh the browser (as long as your refresh requests are at least one second apart), the time displayed by the first label will change.

8 Go back to OutputCache.aspx and switch to HTML view. Add an *@ OutputCache* directive at the top of the page, with the *Duration* attribute set to **10** and the *VaryByParam* attribute set to **None**. This directive should appear on the line directly below the *@ Page* directive. The complete directive should look like this:

```
<%@ OutputCache Duration="10" VaryByParam="None" %>
```

9 Save OutputCache.aspx. Because you've changed only the .aspx file, you don't need to build the project—the changed page will be dynamically compiled the next time it's requested.

10 Browse the page using Microsoft Internet Explorer, and again refresh the browser. The time displayed should change only about once every 10 seconds. The screen should look similar to the following illustration:

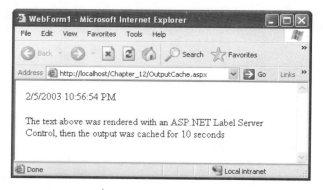

▶ **Note**   When you look at the preceding illustration, you'll notice that even though we renamed the form from WebForm1.aspx to OutputCache.aspx, the title (shown in the title bar) remains WebForm1. Microsoft Visual Studio .NET gives the filename as the default title when the form is created, but does not update that when the file is renamed. You can update the title yourself in the properties of the *DOCUMENT* object for the page, or you can edit the HTML *<title>* tag directly.

Caching User Controls

Caching the output of Web Forms pages can be very useful, but sometimes you might not be able to cache an entire page because its content is updated too frequently. Don't fret—you can still take advantage of output caching by moving less frequently updated portions of a page into one or more ASP.NET user controls, and then caching the output of the user controls.

Caching the output of user controls is nearly identical to caching page output. For user controls, you add the @ *OutputCache* directive to the user controls themselves instead of adding the directive to the page containing the user controls. As noted in the table on page 443, certain @ *OutputCache* attributes, such as *Location* and *VaryByHeader*, can be used only with Web Forms pages; they will cause an error if included in a user control.

▶ **Note**   In addition to the technique demonstrated in the following step-by-step procedure, you can also develop user controls programmatically, using the code-behind file exclusively (while the .ascx file merely has an @Control directive pointing to the code-behind file). With this technique, you can still cache the output of the user control by adding the *PartialCaching* attribute (new in ASP.NET 1.1) to the class definition for the control, as shown in the following code example:

```
[PartialCaching(30)] _
public class FragmentCache : System.Web.UI.UserControl
{
    protected void Page_Load(object sender, EventArgs e)
    {
        Message.Text = DateTime.Now.ToString();
    }
}
```

Cache user control output

1   In the same project as the previous exercise, add another item: Right-click on the root of the project in the Solution Explorer. From the context menu, select Add, then select Add Web User Control. Type the name of the user control as **FragmentCache.ascx**.

2   The default layout in User Controls in Visual Studio .NET is Flow Layout rather than Grid Layout. Add two labels (as we did in the last example, Outputcache.aspx) by dragging one label from the toolbox to the form, clicking just after the label and pressing Enter. Then add the second label. In the Properties window, change the *ID* property

of the first label from Label1 to **Message**. In the properties window, change the *Text* property of the second label to **The text above was rendered from the User Control.**

3   Switch to HTML mode and add the following @ *OutputCache* directive to the top of the HTML, just below the @ *Control* directive:

```
<%@ OutputCache Duration="10" VaryByParam="None" %>
```

4   Select View, and then select Code, or press F7 to move into the code window.

5   Scroll down to the *Page_Load* event handler and add the following code:

```
Message.Text = DateTime.Now.ToString();
```

6   Save FragmentCache.ascx and its code-behind file.

7   In the same project, add a Web Form and type its name as **Fragment-Cache.aspx.**

8   Add two labels to the form about midway down the page, leaving an equal amount of space at the top of the page as that taken up by the two labels. Using the property window, change the name of the first label from Label1 to **Message**. Change the text in the second label to **The text above was rendered from the Web Forms page.**

9   Select View, and then select Code, or press F7 to move to the code window. Scroll down to the *Page_Load* event handler and add the following code:

```
Message.Text = DateTime.Now.ToString();
```

10   Switch back to FragmentCache.aspx by clicking its tab at the top of the editor window. You should be in Design mode. If not, switch to Design mode.

11   Find FragmentCache.ascx in the Solution Explorer. Drag it onto the form. No matter where you place it, it will end up in the upper left hand corner of the design window.

12   Save FragmentCache.aspx (and any other unsaved files), and build the project.

13   Browse the page using Internet Explorer, and refresh the browser. The screen will look similar to the illustration on the next page.

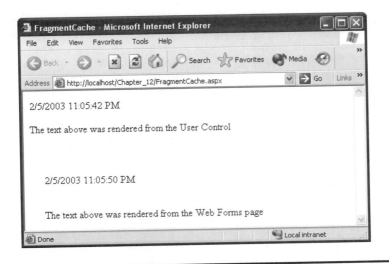

When you first browse the page, both timestamps will be the same. If you click the browser's Refresh button several times, you'll notice that the time displayed by the page is updated with each page request, while the time displayed by the user control is updated only once every 10 seconds.

▶ **Tip**   As mentioned earlier in this chapter, if you're using a user control from numerous pages within your application and want to conserve memory, you can add the *Shared* attribute to the *@OutputCache* directive, which will allow a single cached version of the control to be shared across all of the pages within your application that use the control:

```
<%@ OutputCache Duration="10" VaryByParam="None" Shared="true" %>
```

Of course, if the user control relies on input from each individual page, using the *Shared* attribute might not be appropriate. But in cases in which the output of the control will be the same for all pages, it's a handy way to avoid eating up memory unnecessarily.

Caching Multiple Versions of Output

If your page uses either querystring values (*GET* requests) or form fields (*POST* requests) to dynamically generate content, you can still use output caching by adding the *VaryByParam* attribute to the *@ OutputCache* directive with the values set to the names of the parameters by which to vary the cache. ASP.NET will cache a copy of the output from the page for each unique combination of parameters, so any user who requests the page within the period specified by the *Duration* attribute with the same set of parameters as a previous request will have that request fulfilled from the cache.

▶ **Important**   Because ASP.NET will cache a copy of the output for each unique combination of parameters, you should avoid using an excessive number of parameters to vary the cache. This can result in a significant amount of memory use. This caution applies to the *VaryByHeader* and *VaryByControl* attributes as well.

Use *VaryByParam* to cache multiple versions of a Web Form

1   In the same project as the last exercise, add another Web Form named **VaryByParam.aspx**.

2   Add two labels to the form, one above the other. Add a text box on the right of the top label. Using the property window, change the *Text* property of the first label to **Enter Your Name:**. Change the *ID* property of the textbox to **Name**. Set the *Text* property of the second label to **The text above was rendered with an ASP.NET Label Server Control, then the output was cached for 30 seconds.** Set the *Visible* property of this second label to **False.** The result should look like the following illustration.

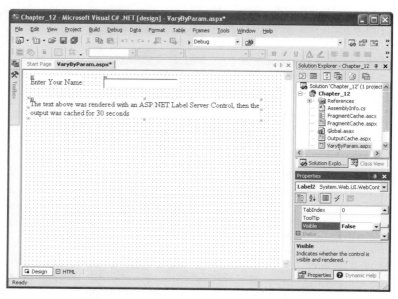

3   Switch to HTML view and add an @ *OutputCache* directive to the
    page, specifying the duration as 30 seconds and the parameter to
    vary by the name of the TextBox control:

```
<%@ OutputCache Duration="30" VaryByParam="Name" %>
```

4   Select View, and then select Code, or press F7 to move to the code
    window.

5   Scroll down to the *Page_Load* event handler and add the following
    code:

```
if (IsPostBack)
{
    Name.Visible = false;
    Label2.Visible = true;
    Label1.Text = "Hello " + Name.Text;
    Label1.Text += ". The current date and time is ";
    Label1.Text += DateTime.Now.ToString();
}
```

6   Save VaryByParam.aspx and its code-behind file, and then build the
    project.

7   Browse VaryByParam.aspx using Internet Explorer. The initial out-
    put will look similar to the following illustration.

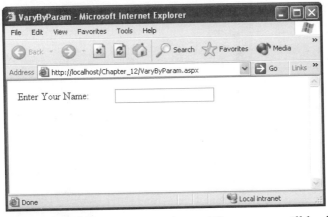

8   Enter your name and press Enter. The output will look similar to the
    illustration on the next page.

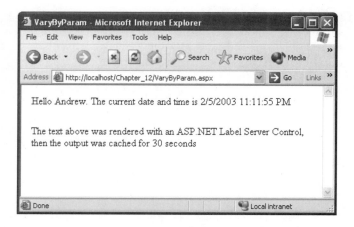

If you click the browser's Refresh button (and click Retry or OK to repost the form), the page will refresh from the cache. If you click Back and enter a different name, you will get a fresh version of the page. Try entering different names, refreshing, and then going back and entering the same names as earlier requests. You should see that all requests with the same name are cached for 30 seconds.

Using *Response.Cache*

In addition to using the @ *OutputCache* directive, you can also enable output caching for a page by using the methods of the *HttpCachePolicy* class, which is exposed by the *Response.Cache* property.

The code required to perform the same output caching as shown in the Output-Cache.aspx example is shown here. Place this code in the *Page_Load* event handler:

```
Message.Text = DateTime.Now.ToString();
Response.Cache.SetExpires(DateTime.Now.AddSeconds(10));
Response.Cache.SetCacheability(HttpCacheability.Public);
```

This code is equivalent to an @ *OutputCache* directive with a duration of 10 and a location of Any (or no location attribute). To set the cache location to client, you would use the HttpCacheability.Private enumeration member instead of HttpCacheability.Public. To turn off caching entirely, you would use Http-Cacheability.NoCache.

In addition to the *SetExpires* and *SetCacheability* methods shown in the preceding code, you can also use the *SetNoServerCaching* method in combination with the code from ResponseCache.aspx to provide the equivalent of an @ *OutputCache* directive with a duration of *10* and a location of *Downstream*.

Caching Arbitrary Data

Like the intrinsic *Application* and *Session* objects in classic ASP, the ASP.NET cache engine offers a simple, straightforward means of saving arbitrary data to the cache and accessing that data through key/value pairs. The following code shows how to add a simple text value to the cache and retrieve it:

```
Cache["myFoo"] = "foo";
Response.Write(Cache["myFoo"]);
```

An important difference is that unlike the Application and Session collection objects, which you can access by either key or numeric index, you can access cache items only by their key.

You can also use this technique to store more than just strings. For example, the code in the following example, CacheAuthors.aspx, checks the cache to see if a dataset already exists. If not, it calls a method that creates a dataset containing data from the Authors table of the Pubs sample Microsoft SQL Server database, and then it saves that dataset to the cache before setting the *DataSource* property of an ASP.NET *DataGrid* control to the default view of the first table in the dataset (0). In this example, rather than adding controls via the designer, you will add controls in HTML view and then see the results in design mode. Visual Studio .NET is a true two-way design tool.

Cache a *DataSet*

1   In the same project as the previous exercise, add a new Web Form and type its name as **CacheAuthors.aspx.**

2   Change the *pageLayout* property of the page to **FlowLayout.**

3   Switch to HTML view by clicking on the tab control at the bottom of the design window. Between the beginning and ending *<form>* tags, add the following code:

```
<asp:label id="title" text="DataSet Caching Example"
    font-name="Verdana" font-size="18" runat="server"/><br>
<asp:datagrid id="MyGrid" bordercolor="black"
    borderwidth="2" cellpadding="3" runat="server">
    <headerstyle backcolor="silver" font-bold="true"/>
    <itemstyle backcolor="black" forecolor="white"/>
    <alternatingitemstyle backcolor="white" forecolor="black"/>
</asp:datagrid><br>
<asp:label id="Message" font-style="italic" runat="server"/>
```

4   Switch to Design view by clicking on the tab control at the bottom of the design window. The resulting screen should look similar to the illustration on the next page.

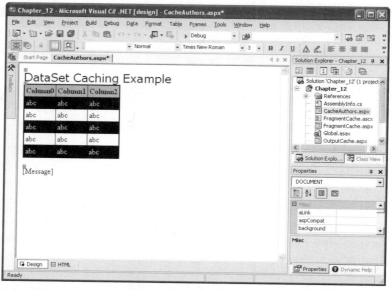

5   Select View, and then select Code, or press F7 to move to the code window.

6   Add the following *using* statement at the top of the code-behind file:
```
using System.Data.SqlClient;
```

7   Scroll down to the *Page_Load* event handler and add the following code:
```
DataSet DS = (DataSet)Cache["myDS"];
if (DS != null)
{
    Message.Text = "Dataset retrieved from cache";
}
else
{
    DS = GetData();
    Cache["myDS"] = DS;
    Message.Text = "Dataset retrieved from database";
}
MyGrid.DataSource = DS.Tables[0].DefaultView;
MyGrid.DataBind();
```

8   Add the following function definition below the *Page_Load* event handler (but above the End Class statement):
```
private DataSet GetData()
{
    DataSet myDS = new DataSet();
    string ConnStr;
```

```
// Use @ so we do not need to escape
//   backslash character.
ConnStr = @"server=(local)\VsDotNet;";
ConnStr += "database=pubs;Trusted_Connection=yes";
string SQLSelect;
SQLSelect = "SELECT au_id, au_lname, au_fname, ";
SQLSelect += "zip FROM Authors WHERE zip = '94609'";
SqlConnection mySqlConn = new SqlConnection(ConnStr);
SqlDataAdapter mySqlDA = new SqlDataAdapter(SQLSelect, ConnStr);
mySqlDA.Fill(myDS);
return myDS;
}
```

9 Save the CacheAuthors.aspx and its code-behind file, and then build the project.

10 Browse the page using Internet Explorer. The output should look similar to the following illustration. Note that the data was retrieved from the database.

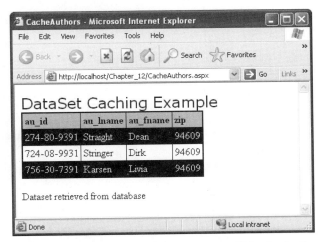

11 Refresh the browser, and the output will look similar to the illustration on the next page. Note that now the data has been retrieved from the cache. This data will remain in the cache until the app domain containing the application is recycled, or until the data is scavenged from the cache because of memory pressure. You'll learn how to programmatically remove data from the cache later in this chapter.

Caching to Improve Performance 12

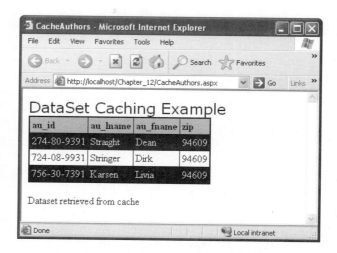

> ▶ **Note**   To use a trusted connection to connect to SQL Server (as shown in the preceding listing), you will need to either enable Windows authentication and impersonation or set up the ASPNET worker process account as a SQL Server login, as described in Chapter 9.

Using the Cache APIs

At this point you're probably wondering, "How do I remove the dataset from the cache?" There are a couple of answers to this question—one simple and one more complex. We'll leave the more complex answer for the next section. The simple answer is that you can remove an item from the cache programmatically by calling the *Remove* method of the *Cache* class and passing it the key of the item to be removed. For example, you could add an ASP.NET button to the preceding example, and then add the following line to the *Click* event handler for the button:

```
Cache.Remove("myDS");
```

This would clear the dataset from the cache and force the page to be rendered again using fresh data. (Note that because the *Page_Load* event fires before the *Click* event for the button, you might need to click the button twice before the datagrid and the label are updated.)

Understanding Expiration and Scavenging

The more complex answer to the question of how to remove items from the cache is that ASP.NET will actually do it for you. What makes this complex is that if you want to control *how* ASP.NET decides which items to remove from the cache and when it does so, you need to provide ASP.NET with that information when you add an item to the cache.

You can do this by using the *Add* or *Insert* methods of the *Cache* class. Both methods let you pass parameters that tell ASP.NET when and on what basis to expire your cached content, as well as the priority your cached content should have when ASP.NET scavenges the cache for items that can be removed to free memory.

ASP.NET determines the order in which items are scavenged from the cache based on their priority. Over time, if an item is not accessed, ASP.NET will reduce its priority periodically. When its priority reaches a predetermined point, it can be scavenged. You can set the priority of an item by passing one of the values of the *CacheItemPriority* enumeration when calling the *Add* or *Insert* method. The following code is an example of the *Insert* method:

```
Cache.Insert("myDS", myDS, null, DateTime.Now.AddMinutes(2),
   TimeSpan.Zero, CacheItemPriority.High,  null);
```

This code performs the following steps:

- Inserts a dataset stored in the *myDS* object variable into the cache with the key *"myDS"*
- Passes *null* as the *CacheDependency* parameter
- Sets the expiration for two minutes from the time when the item is added to the cache
- Sets the *SlidingExpiration* parameter to *TimeSpan.Zero* (no sliding expiration)
- Sets the cache priority for the item to *High*
- Sets the callback function for the item to *null* (no callback function)

▶ **Note** The *Add* and *Insert* methods of the *Cache* class provide essentially the same functionality, with two differences. The first difference is that all parameters of the *Add* method are required, so even if you are not using a particular parameter, you must still pass a placeholder parameter. The *Insert* method is overloaded, which makes it the easier method to use when you want to pass only some of the possible parameters.

The second difference is that the *Add* method returns an object that represents the item just added to the cache, while the *Insert* method doesn't return a value.

You can also call the *Insert* method passing just the *Key (String)* and *Item (Object)* parameters, passing the *Key*, *Item*, and *CacheDependency* parameters, or passing the *Key*, *Item*, *CacheDependency*, *AbsoluteExpiration (DateTime)*, *SlidingExpiration*, and *(TimeSpan)* parameters.

Understanding File and Key Dependencies

Another important parameter that you can pass to either the *Add* or *Insert* method is the *CacheDependency* parameter, which takes an instance of the *CacheDependency* class as its value. The *CacheDependency* class allows you to create a dependency for a cached item on one or more files or directories (known as file dependency), or on one or more other cached items (known as key dependency). The constructor for the *CacheDependency* class has the following three forms:

```
// Monitor a file or directory for changes
CacheDependency myDependency;
myDependency = new CacheDependency("myFileorDirName");

// Monitor an array of file names and/or paths for changes
CacheDependency myDependency;
string[] myFileorDirArray;
myDependency = new CacheDependency(myFileorDirArray);

// Monitor an array of file names and/or paths, and an
// array of keys for changes
CacheDependency myDependency;
myDependency = new CacheDependency(myFileorDirArray, myKeyArray);
```

Note that to set up a key dependency without any file dependencies, you must create an array of keys (even if there is only one key), pass null as the first argument to the constructor, and pass the array of keys as the second:

```
string[] Keys = new string[1];
Keys[0]="myKeyName";
CacheDependency myDependency = new CacheDependency(null,Keys);
```

Once you create the instance of *CacheDependency*, it can be passed as a parameter to the *Add* or *Insert* method of the *Cache* class:

```
Cache.Insert("myDS", myDS, myDependency);
```

Using the *Response* Object to Set Dependencies

In addition to using the *Insert* method of the *Cache* object to set up file and key dependencies, you can use helper methods available from the *Response* object—which is implemented by the *HttpResponse* class—to set up file and key dependencies for page output caching. Four helper methods are available: *AddCacheItemDependencies*, *AddCacheItemDependency*, *AddFileDependency*, and *AddFileDependencies*. Each helper method takes either a string or an *ArrayList* of strings as an argument.

The syntax for the *AddCacheItemDependency* method, which takes a *String* argument that specifies the key on which the cached output depends, is

```
Response.AddCacheItemDependency("myCacheKey");
```

The syntax for the *AddCacheItemDependencies* method, which takes an *Array-List* argument containing strings that specify the keys on which the cached output depends, is

```
ArrayList alKeys = new ArrayList();
alKeys.Add("myFirstCacheKey");
alKeys.Add("mySecondCacheKey");
Response.AddCacheItemDependencies(alKeys);
```

The syntax for the *AddFileDependency* method, which takes a *String* argument that specifies the path to the file on which the cached output depends, is

```
Response.AddFileDependency("c:\myfile.txt");
```

The syntax for the *AddFileDependencies* method, which takes an *ArrayList* argument containing strings that specify the files on which the cached output depends, is

```
ArrayList alFiles = new ArrayList();
alFiles.Add("c:\myfile.txt ");
alFiles.Add("c:\myfile2.txt ");
Response.AddFileDependencies(alFiles);
```

Invalidating the Cache Automatically on Data Change

One of the biggest challenges in using caching in your application is how to get the most out of it, even when you're dealing with data that either is frequently updated or must always be fresh. Setting absolute or sliding expiration times for a cached item can reduce—but not eliminate—the likelihood of a user getting stale data.

What you need is a way to notify the ASP.NET cache when a table has been updated, in order to remove an item from the cache. Fortunately, the *Cache-Dependency* class and the SQL Server Web Assistant make this process easy.

To force a cached copy of the *Authors* query seen in the CacheAuthors.apsx example to be expired whenever the data in the Authors table is modified, you need to first create a trigger on the Authors table that uses the SQL Server Web Assistant to write a new HTML file when the data in the table changes.

> ▶ **Note**   Because MSDE, the desktop version of SQL Server, does not support the SQL Server Web Assistant, the following example requires the use of the full version of SQL Server. If you do not own a copy, you can download or order a trial version of SQL Server at *http://www.microsoft.com/sql/evaluation/trial/default.asp*.

Create a trigger on the Authors table

1   While logged in using an account with administrative permissions to the SQL Server instance (or by using the Run As feature), open SQL Server Enterprise Manager, then drill down to and select the Tables node of the Pubs database. (This should be the Pubs database in your SQL Server instance, rather than the VSdotNET MSDE instance you've used for other examples.)

2   Right-click the Authors table in the table list, select All Tasks, and then select Manage Triggers.

3   Make sure that the *<new>* item is showing in the Name drop-down list. Add the following text to the trigger, replacing *filepath* with the path to the directory where you have saved the examples for this chapter and the filename authors.htm (for example, C:\aspnetsbs\ Chapter_12\authors.htm), and click OK.

```
CREATE TRIGGER WriteFile ON [dbo].[authors]
FOR INSERT, UPDATE, DELETE
AS
EXEC sp_makewebtask 'filepath', 'SELECT * FROM authors'
```

The second part of the process is to create the page that will use the cache by consuming the cached data.

Consume cached data

1   In the same project as the last exercise, add a new Web Form **AuthorsTrigger.aspx**. Follow the steps in the previous exercise so that AuthorsTrigger.aspx and its code-behind match the code from CacheAuthors.aspx.

2   Change the *Text* property of the title label to **Cache invalidate with trigger Example**.

3   Select View, and then select Code, or press F7 to move to the code window. Add the following line to the Imports clauses at the top of the code file:

```
using System.Web.Caching;
```

4   In the *Page_Load* event handler, replace the line that reads *Cache["myDS"]=DS;* with the following code, which adds a file dependency on the file created by the SQL Web Assistant:

```
Cache.Insert("myDS", DS,
    new CacheDependency(Server.MapPath("authors.htm")));
```

5   In the *GetData* function, modify the connection string in the file to point to the SQL Server instance where you created the trigger.

6   Save AuthorsTrigger.aspx (and its code-behind module) and build the project.

7   Browse the page using Internet Explorer. The output should look similar to the following illustration. Note that the data was retrieved from the database.

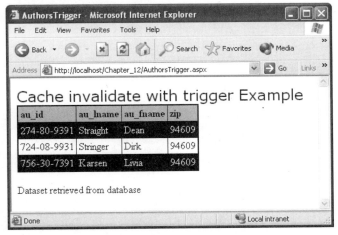

8   If you click the Refresh button in the browser, the data will be served from the cache and the output will look similar to the illustration on the next page.

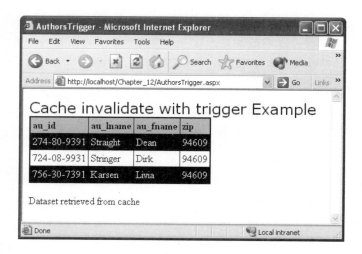

To make sure this procedure was successful, open the Authors table in SQL Enterprise Manager (by right-clicking the Authors table and selecting Open Table, Return All Rows) and change one of the values in a row in the table that matches the query criteria for AuthorsTrigger.aspx (zip=94609). (Move the cursor off the row being updated to make sure the update occurs.) Now refresh the browser. Except for any data that you've changed, the output should look like the illustration that follows Step 8.

> ▶ **Important**   While the preceding example is effective in purging the cached data when the underlying database table changes, there is a caveat to its use. Because this technique relies on the update of a file in the file system, it is possible that a problem with that file (such as incorrect permissions) could prevent the trigger from updating the file, which could lead to a blocking situation. Since what you're after with caching is improved performance and scalability, clearly blocking would be a bad thing. So if you're considering using a technique like this in your application, take care to minimize as much as possible the things that could go wrong and make sure to test the application thoroughly, particularly under loads similar to what you expect the application to bear.

Chapter 12 Quick Reference

To	Do this
Cache page or user control output	Add the @ *OutputCache* directive to the page or user control, or use the methods exposed by *Response.Cache*.
Vary the cache based on user input	Add the *VaryByParam*, *VaryByHeader*, or *VaryByControl* attributes to the @ *OutputCache* directive.
Cache arbitrary data	Insert items into the cache using either the simple syntax Cache["myKey"] = myItem; or call the *Add* or *Insert* methods of the *Cache* class.
Expire a cache item when another item changes	Insert the item to be expired with a key dependency on the other cache item.

Chapter

13

Deploying an ASP.NET Application

In this chapter, you will learn how to:

- Store application-specific configuration settings for easy deployment.
- Set up a target IIS application.
- Copy content, Web Forms pages, Web services, and assemblies.
- Deploy an application using Visual Studio .NET.

Deploying applications has been a long-standing bane of many a classic ASP developer's existence, and for good reason. While it was easy enough to deploy or replace static content and the ASP files themselves, other portions of the applications, such as components and application-specific configuration settings, required greater effort to deploy and often necessitated a shutdown of the application to replace.

Deployment is another area in which the improvements in ASP.NET truly shine. ASP.NET eliminates many of the deployment shortcomings in classic ASP, making it possible for the first time to deploy an ASP.NET application simply by copying all of the necessary files to the IIS application directory where the application will be deployed. This chapter will discuss the steps for deploying ASP.NET Web applications, both manually and through Microsoft Visual Studio .NET.

Understanding the Structure of ASP.NET Applications

Although you learned about the structure of ASP.NET Web applications earlier in the book, it is worthwhile to review this information. Understanding the structure of an ASP.NET application will make the deployment process smoother, and can help prevent unexpected errors and problems in your deployed applications.

Each ASP.NET application needs to have a corresponding IIS application root to function properly. During development using Visual Studio .NET, this process is handled for you automatically. Each time you create a new ASP.NET project in Visual Studio .NET, part of the project-creation process undertaken by the IDE is creating the folder and making it an IIS application root. The application root provides the boundary for the application. The physical file system directory that maps to the application root is the location where the root Web.config file for the application, as well as the application's bin directory (which contains all managed assemblies related to the application) and the Global.asax file (if you choose to use one), are deployed. If the IIS directory that is the root of the application is not configured as an application root, certain configuration settings can fail, and the assemblies located in the bin directory (if present) will not be loaded.

▶ **Important** Microsoft Windows XP offers multiple views of the Control Panel. The default view is called *category* view and the optional view is called the *classic* view. For this chapter, all instructions will be for the classic view. To switch from category view to classic view, click on Switch To Classic View on the left side of the Control Panel.

To determine if a directory in IIS has been configured as an application, complete the following steps.

Determine if a directory in IIS has been configured as an application

1   Open the Internet Information Services MMC snap-in (called Internet Services Manager in Microsoft Windows 2000) by clicking Start, Control Panel, Administrative tools, and then selecting Internet

Information Services. (In Windows 2000, click Start, Programs, Administrative Tools, and then Internet Services Manager.) Note that you must be logged in as an administrator (or use the Run As feature to run the snap-in) to access the full functionality of this tool.

2   Navigate to the directory whose configuration you want to check by expanding the Web site containing it and expanding other nodes as necessary. If the directory is configured as an application root, it will show an icon of a black globe in a gray box. If the directory is not configured as an application, it will either show a folder icon (for content that resides directly within the path of the parent application root) or a folder icon with a small globe (for content that resides elsewhere in the file system). The following illustration shows examples of these icons:

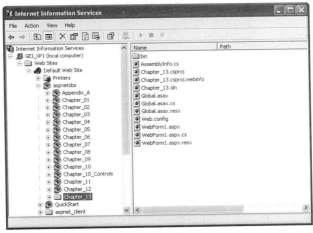

3   If the directory is not configured as an application, you can create an application root at this level. Right-click the directory, select Properties, and then click the Create button in the Directory tab (or Virtual Directory tab) of the Properties dialog box. The Properties dialog box for the Chapter_13 directory is shown in the illustration on the next page. (Note that the dialog for IIS 6.0 is slightly different in the options it presents.)

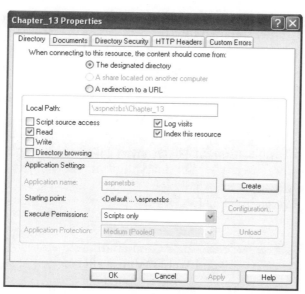

4   Click OK to update the directory with the new setting.

The directory should now show the icon for an application root, as shown in the following illustration. This step should not be necessary for directories that are the root of a Visual Studio .NET Web Application project, since Visual Studio .NET configures the root directory of this project type as an Application in IIS automatically.

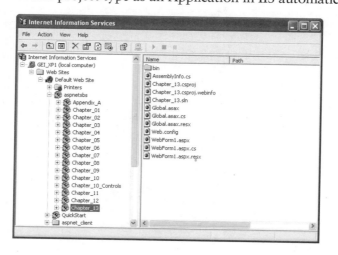

As you can see in these figures, IIS application roots can be nested one beneath the other. However, each application root defines its own application boundary. One advantage of this is that it allows you to partition your application as necessary. For example, you can provide customized configuration settings or use different versions of a private assembly with different parts of your application. The most important thing to remember, however, is that the application root is where the bin directory and Global.asax and Web.config files should be located.

Distinguishing Between Physical Path and URL

An important distinction to make when discussing deployment is between the physical path of an application (that is, the application's location within the file system of its server) and the URL of the application. This distinction becomes important when discussing the array of different tools available for deployment, some of which (such as the DOS XCOPY command) use file or network paths, and some of which (such as FTP and WebDAV) use URLs.

There is only a single file path for a given application root in IIS. However, more than one directory in IIS can map to a single physical directory in the file system. This allows you to set up URLs for both public and private access to a given application, with different IIS settings for each. If more than one IIS application root points to the same physical directory in the file system, each IIS application root will have its own IIS-specific settings. It is important to note, however, that if the physical directory contains ASP.NET-specific configuration and start-up files (Web.config and Global.asax), both IIS applications will share the settings in these files.

One important caveat regarding this sharing is that when a subfolder containing a Web.config file or a Global.asax file is defined as an application root in one of the IIS applications, it's not configured as an application root in the second IIS application. In the first case, shown in the illustration on the next page, requests to the Chapter_13 subfolder of the aspnetsbs folder will use the Global.asax file contained in the Chapter_13 folder for start-up code.

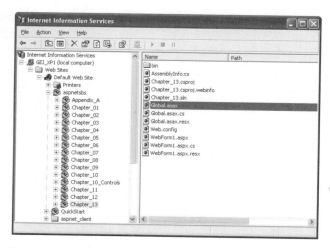

In the second case, shown in the following illustration, the Global.asax file contained within this subfolder will be ignored, since the folder is not configured as an application in IIS.

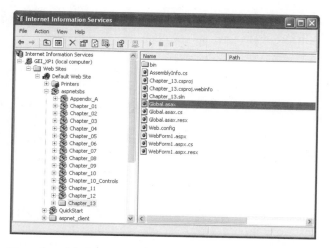

You should also note that certain settings in the Web.config file are applicable only at the application root level. For example, if the Web.config file contained in the Chapter_13 folder shown in the preceding illustration contains an *<authentication>* section, a configuration error will result because this section can be defined only at the machine (machine.config) or application root level.

The URL for a specific application root in IIS is a product of the domain name (if any) associated with the IP address that is assigned to the IIS Web site, plus the folder hierarchy between the IIS Web site and the application root. Thus, in the previous illustration, where the aspnetsbs application root resides under the default

Web site, the URL to reach the Chapter_13 directory would be either *http://localhost/aspnetsbs/Chapter_13/* or *http://servername/aspnetsbs/Chapter_13/*.

This works if you request the URL from the server containing the application, because requests for *localhost* or *servername* (where *servername* represents the name of the Web server containing the application) are automatically directed to the default Web site. If you wanted to make the content of the Chapter_13 application root available on the Internet, you'd need to create a new IIS Web site, assign a publicly available IP address on the machine to the Web site, and then create (or have a DNS provider create) a DNS entry that maps your chosen domain name (for example, *www.aspnetsbs.com*) to that IP address. Then you would create a new application root under the new Web site that maps to the Chapter_13 directory in the file system. You could access this application from the Internet using the URL *http://www.aspnetsbs.com/Chapter_13/*.

Note that if you have directory browsing disabled (the default), you will need to set a default document in the Documents tab of the Properties dialog box for the directory, in case the user does not enter a document name. The name of the default document should match the name of a page that exists in the directory. This will allow access to content using a URL that does not contain a document name, such as the preceding URLs. Otherwise, the name of the desired file must be appended, or an error will occur.

Storing Application-Specific Configuration Settings

One of the challenges of deploying most non-trivial Web applications in classic ASP is figuring out where to store application-specific configuration information. Classic ASP allowed for a number of approaches, including using custom keys in the system registry, storing configuration information in a back-end database, reading configuration settings from a custom configuration file, and building settings into components. Each approach has its own set of drawbacks that makes it less than ideal.

For example, storing configuration information in the system registry makes that information relatively secure (particularly if proper registry security procedures are followed).

However, adding that information to the registry or modifying it from a remote machine can be difficult, if not impossible, because of permission settings designed to protect the registry from remote tampering. Additionally, accessing settings within the registry can be expensive from a performance standpoint.

Neither storing configuration information in a back-end database nor storing that information in custom configuration files provides easily repeatable procedures for multiple applications. The database solution requires that changes to the Web application and the configuration database be synchronized so that users always get the correct information. The custom configuration file solution requires building logic into pages or components to parse and cache the application settings, while periodically checking to see if settings have been modified, and loading the new settings if they have been.

To simplify this situation, ASP.NET provides a special section of the Web.config and machine.config files called *appSettings*, which allows you to store application-specific configuration settings as a set of key/value pairs.

```
<appSettings>
   <add key="myConfigKey" value="myConfigValue" />
</appSettings>
```

When your application starts up, ASP.NET caches the values of the *appSettings* section in a string collection called *ConfigurationSettings.AppSettings*. You can access these settings by passing the desired key to this collection, as shown here:

```
Label1.Text = ConfigurationSettings.AppSettings["myConfigKey"];
```

In addition to automatically loading and caching these values for you at application start-up, ASP.NET monitors the Web.config file(s) for changes and dynamically reloads the contents of the *appSettings* configuration section if changes are detected.

The practice files for this chapter include an example of using the *appSettings* configuration section to store and display a simple text value. See the Web.config file for an example of storing the value; see the AppSettings.aspx file for an example of retrieving and displaying the value.

▶ **Important** While *appSettings* provides a storage location for application-specific configuration settings that is almost ideal in its ease of use and performance, note that since the values are stored as plain text in a file in the Web space, some security risk is associated with this approach.

If a vulnerability in the Web server allowed access to the Web.config file, any sensitive information stored in *appSettings* could be compromised. For this reason, never store sensitive information, such as usernames, passwords, or credit card or account numbers, in the *appSettings* section of Web.config. For items of medium sensitivity, one solution is to add the items to the *appSettings* of the machine.config file, which is not located within the Web space and thus harder to compromise. Keep in mind, however, that the *appSettings* stored in Machine.config are available to every application on the server, unless they are locked down using the *<location>* tag. (See Chapter 5 for more information on locking down configuration settings.)

For more information on storing sensitive information in Web applications, see the "Storing Secrets" section of the following security article on the MSDN Web site:

http://msdn.microsoft.com/library/en-us/dnnetsec/html/SecNetch08.asp.

Deploying a Web Application Manually

If you're developing ASP.NET applications against the Microsoft .NET Framework without the benefit of Visual Studio .NET, most (if not all) of your deployment work will be manual. The great news is that ASP.NET applications are simple to deploy. Even if you are using Visual Studio .NET, you might need to or want to deploy your Visual Studio .NET ASP.NET application manually.

Setting Up the Target Deployment Directory

To successfully deploy an ASP.NET application, the first thing you need is a target directory on the server that will host the application. You must set up this directory in IIS as an application root if you want to use the automatic loading of assemblies in the bin subdirectory or use a Global.asax file if you want to have a root Web.config file for the application. (You can't set certain configuration sections below the application level, and they will cause errors if used in a Web.config file that resides in a subdirectory.)

Copying Files to the Target Directory

Once you've set up the target directory in IIS (mapped to a physical folder on the host machine), you're ready to copy all the necessary files to the target directory. You can do this by using any number of commonly available tools, from the XCOPY command to WebDAV. You can even drag-and-drop files to and from a network share using Micorosoft Windows Explorer.

If you're using code-behind in your Web Forms pages or user controls, you'll need to decide whether to deploy the code-behind class files containing your source code to the target server. If you're using the *Src* attribute of the *@ Page* or *@ Control* directive to have ASP.NET dynamically compile your code-behind classes, you have to deploy the class files, or the application will not function. If you want to avoid deploying the code-behind class files, you can use the *Inherits* attribute of the *@ Page* or *@ Control* directive instead of the *Src* attribute. Using the *Inherits* attribute requires you to manually compile your code-behind classes and put the resulting assemblies in the application's bin subdirectory. Projects created with Visual Studio .NET will be created using the *Inherits* attribute of the *@ Page* or *@ Control* directive. As a result, you must build the project before deploying it, whether you deploy the project manually or by using Visual Studio's deployment tools.

Deploying Content

Deploying static content (such as HTML pages and images), Web Forms pages, user controls, and code-behind classes is as simple as copying them from the development application directory to the deployment target directory. For example, you would use the following command to deploy content from a local directory C:\inetpub\wwwroot\myDevApp to a remote directory for which a mapped drive, X:, has been created:

```
xcopy c:\inetpub\wwwroot\ASPNetApp1 x:\ /E /K /O
```

The parameters passed to XCOPY are as follows:

- /E specifies that all subdirectories are to be copied, whether empty or not.
- /K specifies that file and directory attributes on the destination should be set to match the source.
- /O specifies that ownership and ACL information should be copied to the destination. This is useful when using domain accounts to set ACLs.

You can find out about all of the command-line parameters available with XCOPY by executing XCOPY /?.

Deploying Assemblies

One of the areas of great improvement in deployment is .NET managed assemblies over COM components. With classic ASP applications that used custom COM components, not only did you need to copy the component file to the machine on which the application was being deployed, but you also needed to register that component in the system registry, which was difficult to do remotely. Additionally, registering a component made that component available to any application on the server, which is not allowed in a shared server environment.

Because .NET assemblies are self-describing and assemblies are private to an application by default, you can simply copy an assembly to the bin subdirectory of an application and it will be available for use by the application automatically. Private assemblies do not need to be registered to be used, and they are available only to the application in whose bin directory they reside.

Global Assemblies

The exception to the rule of XCOPY deployment applies to assemblies that you want to make available to more than one application on the server without having multiple copies of the assembly (one for each application). These assemblies need to be installed in the GAC. Remember that assemblies installed in the GAC must be strongly named. You can do this by using the al.exe command-line tool. Once you have a strongly named assembly, you can install it into the GAC in several ways:

- **Microsoft Windows Installer 2.0**   This is the preferred method for installing assemblies into the GAC because it performs reference counting and provides transactional installation, neither of which are available with the other options. See the Windows Installer documentation for more information on packaging and installing applications with Windows Installer 2.0.

- **gacutil.exe**   This command-line utility lets you add assemblies to the GAC, remove assemblies from the GAC, and list the contents of the GAC.
- **Windows Explorer**   The .NET Framework installs a shell extension that lets you simply drag-and-drop strongly named assemblies into the GAC from any Windows folder. The GAC is located at %WinDir%\ assembly.

Deployment and Assembly Versioning

One nifty thing about global assemblies that compensates for the additional overhead of installing and removing them from the GAC is that they can contain versioning information. This allows two or more versions of the same assembly to be executed side by side, and it allows client applications to request the version of an assembly they want to use, or to accept the latest revision of an assembly.

Updating Assemblies

In addition to the problems of registering COM components, IIS locked any COM component as soon as it was called. Because of this, replacing or updating a COM component often required stopping the IIS Web service, unregistering the old component, copying over the new component, registering the new component, and restarting the Web service. For many applications, this meant an unacceptable amount of downtime.

With private assemblies, this is no longer a problem because of the way ASP.NET loads assemblies. Unlike IIS under classic ASP, which loaded a component into memory and locked it on disk until the Web application (or IIS) was shut down, ASP.NET first makes a shadow copy of each assembly file and then loads and locks the shadow file instead of the original. ASP.NET then monitors the original files for changes. If changes are detected, ASP.NET fulfills any existing requests with the current copy of the assembly, and then it loads the new assembly and fulfills new requests using the updated assembly, discarding the old assembly. This allows you to easily update any private assembly used by your application without needing to shut down the Web server, even temporarily.

Setting IIS Permissions for Subdirectories

Once you've copied your content and assemblies to the target directory, it's a good idea to double-check the IIS permissions on any subdirectories in the application. Fortunately, ASP.NET actually takes care of one of the most important checks for you. It automatically removes all permissions on the bin subdirectory of the application, effectively preventing the contents of the directory from being listed, read, downloaded, or executed.

Now, preventing IIS from executing the assemblies on behalf of clients might sound like a *bad* thing, but it's not. In fact, when a request comes in for a resource that ASP.NET handles, such as an .aspx, .ascx, or .asmx file, IIS simply hands the request over to ASP.NET, which processes the request from there. Since ASP.NET alone is responsible for loading assemblies, preventing IIS from attempting to execute assemblies is a *good* thing.

If you have subdirectories that contain static content, such as images, you should ensure that the only permission allowed on these subdirectories is Read.

Most important, if you need to allow users to upload content to your Web application, it is absolutely essential that you set up a separate subdirectory for this purpose, and set only the Write permission. Read must not be allowed on this subdirectory, nor should you set the Execute permissions to anything other than None. Failure to follow these guidelines could allow an attacker to upload and execute hostile code in your application.

You can view and modify the IIS permissions for any directory by right-clicking the directory name in Internet Services Manager and selecting Properties. The permissions are set in the Directory (or Virtual Directory) tab, which is shown in the following illustration.

Deployment Options in Visual Studio .NET

If you are developing Web applications with Visual Studio .NET, you can still manually deploy your applications using XCOPY, WebDAV, and so on. However, you will probably find that it is more efficient to take advantage of one of the built-in deployment features available in the Visual Studio .NET IDE. These include the *copy project* command, which provides a fast and simple method for copying a project from one machine to another or from one directory to another on the same machine, and the Setup And Deployment Projects type, which provides much more fine-grained control over how your application is deployed.

Using Copy Project to Deploy a Web Application

The *copy project* command, which you access by clicking Project, and then Copy Project (or from the toolbar of the Solution Explorer window), allows you to copy just the files you need to run an application (only the .aspx files and related assemblies, plus any static content; code-behind class files are not copied), all of the files in the project, or all of the files in the source project folder, whether they are a part of the project or not.

You can copy files either to a URL using the Microsoft FrontPage server extensions, or to a file share. The Copy Project dialog box is shown in the following illustration.

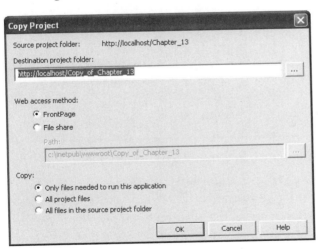

Using Copy Project is simple and straightforward, but it offers only limited control over which project files are copied and how they're copied.

▶ **Note**   The following section describes a feature available only in Visual Studio .NET Professional, Enterprise Developer, or Enterprise Architect editions. This functionality is not available with the Standard edition of Visual C# .NET.

Using a Web Setup Project to Deploy a Web Application

Another method that Visual Studio .NET offers for deploying Web applications is the Web Setup Project, which is one of the templates available in the Setup And Deployment Projects project type. The following illustration shows the Web Setup project selected in the Add New Project dialog box.

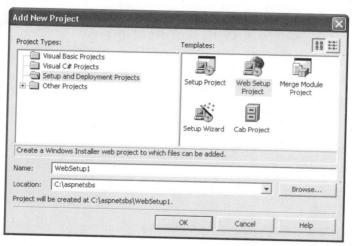

A Web Setup project allows you to specify a variety of options about how the application will be deployed, ranging from which files to include to the name of the deployed application and the location of the deployed files. When built, the Web Setup project creates a Windows Installer .msi file that can be copied to the target machine and executed to deploy the application.

Create a Web Setup project in Visual Studio .NET

1   Open an existing Web application solution in Visual Studio .NET Professional, Enterprise Developer, or Enterprise Architect editions.

2   Right-click the solution name in the Solution Explorer window, and select Add, New Project. The Add New Project dialog box will appear.

3   Select the Setup and Deployment Projects type, select the Web Setup Project template, and then click OK to accept the default project name. Make sure that Add To Solution is selected. The File System editor for the Web Setup project will appear.

4 Make sure WebSetup1 is selected in the Solution Explorer. In the Properties window, modify the *ProductName* property to match the name of the Web application project you opened in Step 1.

5 Right-click the Web Application Folder node in the left pane of the File System editor, select Add, and then select Project Output. The Add Project Output Group dialog box will appear, as shown in the following illustration.

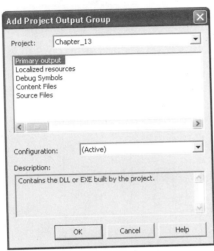

6 Select both the Primary Output and Content Files items from the list. Use the Ctrl key to select multiple items. Click OK.

7 Select the Web Application Folder node in the File System editor. Then locate the VirtualDirectory entry in the Properties window and change it to the name of a target directory on the deployment target. This directory does not need to exist—it will be created. Specify only a relative path to the virtual directory—do not use drive letters or absolute URLs.

8 Also in the Properties window, set the *DefaultDocument* property to the name of the default document for the Web application opened in Step 1.

9 Right-click the solution containing the WebSetup1 project, and select Configuration Manager.

10 In the Configuration Manager dialog box, ensure that the Build check box for WebSetup1 is checked. If it is not, check it, and then click Close.

11 Build the solution by clicking Build, and then selecting Build Solution.

12 Locate the set-up package created by the Web Setup project. It should be located in the Debug or Release subdirectory of the directory containing the Web Setup project, and will be called WebSetup1.msi if you used the default project name of WebSetup1. Copy the file to the target server and execute it. The following illustration shows the initial screen of the installation program.

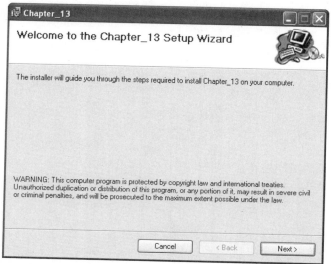

13 When you've completed the Setup Wizard, browse the newly deployed application using the URL *http://machinename/vdirname/*, where *machinename* is the name of the machine where you installed the set-up package and *vdirname* is the name that you specified for the *VirtualDirectory* property in Step 7. If the deployment worked correctly, you should see the default page for the Web application.

▶ **Important**   The installation created by Visual Studio .NET does not install the .NET Framework. You can run the program dotnetfx.exe in the dotNetFramework folder of the Visual Studio .NET Prerequisites CD before executing the installation package to allow the project to install, if the target machine does not already have the .NET Framework installed.

In addition to providing fine-grained control over the files and outputs included in the installation package, this method allows you to automatically install shared assemblies in the GAC. It also allows you to uninstall a Web application with a single command, either by right-clicking the installation package and selecting Uninstall or by locating the application's entry in the Windows Add/Remove Programs applet, which you can access from the Control Panel.

Chapter 13 Quick Reference

To	Do this
Verify that a directory in IIS is an application root	Navigate to the directory in Internet Services Manager and look at the icon for the directory. If the directory is not an application root, you can make it one by right-clicking the directory, selecting Properties, and then clicking Create in the Directory tab.
Store application-specific configuration settings	Add an *appSettings* section to your Web.config or Machine.config file, with an *<add>* tag for each item to be added to the *appSettings*.
Deploy content and private assemblies	Set up the target directory in IIS on the machine to be deployed to. Then use XCOPY, WebDAV, Windows Explorer, or another means to copy the files and folders of the application to the target directory.
Create an installation package with fine-grained control of installation items and uninstall ability	Add a Web Setup project to the solution for the Web application to be packaged, and set its properties and outputs as desired.

Tracing and Debugging ASP.NET Applications

In this chapter, you will learn how to:

■ Use tracing to learn how your application is running.

■ Debug ASP.NET applications.

■ Use the Visual Studio .NET debugger.

This book has covered a wide variety of topics related to ASP.NET development. I hope you'll be able to avoid most problems while developing your ASP.NET Web applications. Inevitably, however, there will be times when your code doesn't do what you expect it to, or you'll run into errors or problems that prevent your application from working. This final chapter will look at what to do when that happens. It's not intended to make you an expert debugger, but rather to give you an overview of the tools available for debugging in ASP.NET.

To say that classic ASP did not offer developers much support for debugging their applications would be a colossal understatement. Despite being a very simple and productive development environment, classic ASP left a lot to be desired in terms of debugging and error messages.

For example, in classic ASP you had no convenient way to access the state of the current HTTP request or of the other collections, such as the *QueryString* or *Forms* collections. ASP.NET addresses this issue through a new feature called *tracing*, which I'll discuss in the first part of this chapter.

Additionally, classic ASP error messages were often cryptic at best. If you were lucky, they told you the line of the ASP page on which the error occurred. Unfortunately, this information could be misleading. The error might have occurred in a function called by that page, but you wouldn't know that from the error message. ASP.NET provides much richer error reporting, including a stack trace of the functions that led up to an error condition, making it much easier to locate the root cause of the error.

The Microsoft .NET Framework SDK ships with its own debugger, so developers who are not using Microsoft Visual Studio .NET can attach it to the process of their ASP.NET application and step through their code to find and fix problems. Most often, however, using the debugger in Visual Studio .NET can be the most efficient way to debug your application. I'll discuss the improved error reporting and the SDK debugger in the second half of this chapter.

Tracing

As mentioned, one weakness of classic ASP was the lack of an easy way to get information about the current request. You should create reusable include files to write out the contents of the various collections of the request object, but there was no simple method of making this information available. ASP.NET provides a solution in the form of tracing, which provides a substantial amount of information about requests that have been executed, either at the page level or the application level, as well as a way to get your own custom debug information without exposing it to the users of your application.

Enabling Page-Level Trace Output

The simplest way to access trace information is through the *Trace* attribute of the @ *Page* directive. By adding the *Trace* attribute to any .aspx page, you can instruct ASP.NET to append the trace output for that page to the rendered content of the page. The following example shows how to enable tracing on a simple ASP.NET page.

Display tracing information

1   Open Visual Studio and create a new ASP.NET Web Application project called Chapter_14. Rename the default Web Page created by Visual Studio from WebPage1.aspx to **SimpleTrace.aspx** by selecting File, then Save WebForm1.aspx As.

2   Right-click anywhere on the page, and select Properties from the context menu. In the resulting dialog box (shown in the illustration on the following page), change the Page title to **Simple Trace Example**. Change Page Layout from GridLayout to FlowLayout. (If you use GridLayout, trace output and rendered page output can end up overlapping. Using FlowLayout prevents this.) Click OK.

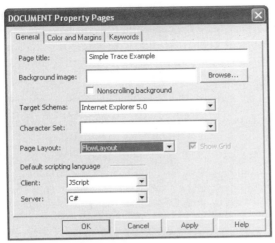

3   Add a label to the page by dragging a label from the toolbox onto the form. In FlowLayout, the label will move to the upper left of the form no matter where you place it. Change the *Text* property to **Trace is enabled for this page**.

4   Click in an empty area of the page to select the *DOCUMENT* object, locate the *trace* property in the Properties window, and set its value to *True*.

5   Save SimpleTrace.aspx and the project, and then build the project.

6   Browse SimpleTrace.aspx using Microsoft Internet Explorer. The resulting screen should look similar to the following illustration:

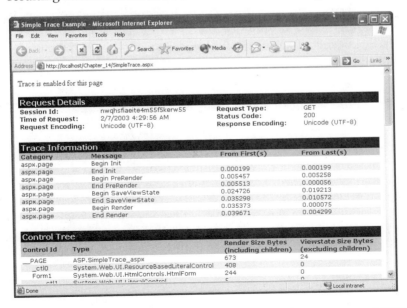

The trace output includes such information as the contents of the *cookies*, *forms*, and *querystring* collections. Therefore, page-level tracing using the *Trace* attribute of the @ *Page* directive should be restricted to non-production systems because the output is visible to any client requesting that page. Although you can use one of the configuration options detailed in the next section to configure ASP.NET to provide page-level trace output only for requests from the local system, you're best off sticking to application-level tracing on publicly available applications.

▶ **Important**   Tracing has an impact on application performance, and the information that it provides could potentially be used by malicious users to attack your application, so for both performance and security reasons you should use tracing only in development environments; disable tracing before deploying an application to a production (public-facing) environment.

Enabling Application-Level Trace Output

In addition to providing trace output at the page level, ASP.NET can be configured to log trace output for a specified number of requests for later review. The primary advantages of this approach are that it allows you to enable tracing for an entire site at once, and that when configured properly it hides trace output from users of the page, making its use on production or customer-facing systems less likely to allow malicious users access to too much information.

You enable application-level tracing by adding the *<trace>* configuration element to the Web.config file for the application and then setting its attributes to the desired values. The following example demonstrates modifying the *<trace>* element to enable application-level tracing and tells ASP.NET to log up to 40 requests. (Logged requests must be cleared manually when the request limit has been reached.) Appendix B details the attributes for the *<trace>* section.

Enable application-level tracing in Web.config

1   In Visual Studio, open the Chapter_14 project created in the previous example.

2   Edit the Web.Config file by double-clicking on it in the Solution Explorer. Then, from the Edit menu, select Find And Replace, and then select Find. In the Find What text box, type **<trace** and then click Find Next. This will move your cursor to the beginning of the *<trace>* section. Change the *<trace>* element so that it looks like this:

```
<trace
    enabled="true"
    requestLimit="40"
```

```
        pageOutput="false"
        traceMode="SortByCategory"
        localOnly="true"
  />
```

3   Save the changes to Web.config.

To allow access to the logged trace output, ASP.NET provides an *HttpHandler* that is mapped to a special URL called *trace.axd*. Appending *trace.axd* to the base URL for the application will display the list of currently available traces, as shown in the following illustration. Clicking View Details for a particular trace displays its output. Clicking Clear Current Trace clears all current entries from the trace log and allows more requests to be logged.

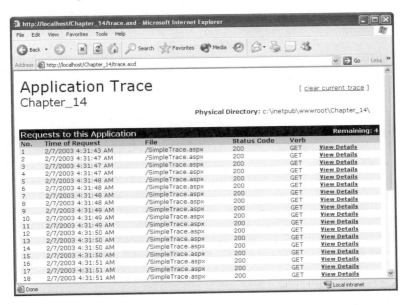

Writing to the Trace Output

At one time or another, most developers who have ever tried debugging a classic ASP application have resorted to using *Response.Write* for outputting the value of variables to the page, or for placing flags within code to determine where the code is breaking by seeing how much of the page gets executed before execution is halted. While this was (and still is) a useful technique for debugging, it is useful only for development machines that are not accessible by users—many of the aforementioned developers have gotten calls from their supervisors when they forgot to take the *Response.Write* statements out before migrating a page to a production server.

▶ **Important**   The page-level setting for trace functionality will override the setting in Web.config. So even if you have tracing enabled in Web.config, setting the *trace* attribute of the @ *Page* directive to *False* will still disable tracing for that page. Likewise, even if tracing is disabled at the application level in Web.config (or at the machine level in machine.config), setting the page-level *trace* attribute to *True* will still enable tracing for that page. For this reason, if you use page-level tracing you should always double-check your pages before publishing them to a public server to ensure that the *trace* attribute for each page has been removed or set to *False*.

ASP.NET's trace functionality minimizes this problem by allowing developers to write to the trace output instead of writing to the page output. Assuming that page-level trace output has not been enabled, this prevents end-users from seeing the trace statements written by the developer.

▶ **Important**   As noted earlier, enabling tracing for a page or for an application does carry some performance overhead. Even though the ASP.NET trace functionality allows you to leave tracing enabled without trace output being viewed by end-users, when performance is important, it is a good idea to disable tracing for an application at both the page and application level.

The trace output is exposed to developers via the *TraceContext* class, which is available from the *Page.Trace* property (which can be referred to within a page simply as *Trace*, since the *Page* object is assumed). There are two methods for writing to the trace output, *Trace.Write* and *Trace.Warn*.

Determining If Tracing Is Enabled

To keep developers from wasting time attempting to write to the trace output when tracing is not enabled, the *TraceContext* class exposes a Boolean property called *IsEnabled*, which contains the current status of tracing for the page. This is especially helpful if you are performing expensive processing or database lookups as a part of your trace logging.

Using *Trace.Write*

The *Trace.Write* method of the *TraceContext* class is overloaded, and you can call it in one of the following three ways:

```
Trace.Write(string message);
Trace.Write(string category, string message);
Trace.Write(string category, string message, Exception errorInfo);
```

■ *message* is a string containing the message to be written to the trace output.

- *category* is a string containing a description of the message (variable, statement, or whatever the developer wants as a category).
- *errorInfo* is an exception object, which allows exceptions to be logged to the trace output.

The category and errorInfo parameters allow developers to set up sophisticated application-wide tracing by defining specific categories of logged information and using them consistently across an application.

The following example shows how to create a page that tests if tracing is enabled for the page, and then writes a simple message to the trace output.

Write trace messages

1 In Visual Studio, open the Chapter_14 project used in the previous examples. Add a new page by right-clicking on the root of the project in the Solution Explorer, selecting Add, and then Add Web Form. Type the name of the form as **TraceWrite.aspx**.

2 Right-click anywhere on the page, and select Properties from the context menu. In the resulting dialog box, change Page Layout from GridLayout to FlowLayout, and then click OK.

3 Add a label to the page.

4 Change to HTML mode by clicking the HTML button on the bottom of the design window. Add **Trace="true"** to the @ *Page* directive:

```
<%@ Page Language="c#" AutoEventWireup="false"
    Codebehind="TraceWrite.aspx.cs"
    Inherits="Chapter_14.TraceWrite" Trace="true" %>
```

5 Change to the code view by pressing F7. Scroll down to the *Page_Load* event handler and add the following code:

```
if (Trace.IsEnabled)
{
    Label1.Text = "Writing 'Hello from Page!' to Trace Log...";
    Trace.Write("Hello from Page!");
}
```

6 Save TraceWrite.aspx, its code-behind file, and the project, and then build the project.

7 Browse TraceWrite.aspx using Internet Explorer. The resulting screen should look similar to the illustration on the nexy page. (Notice the hello message on the first line under the Trace Information heading.)

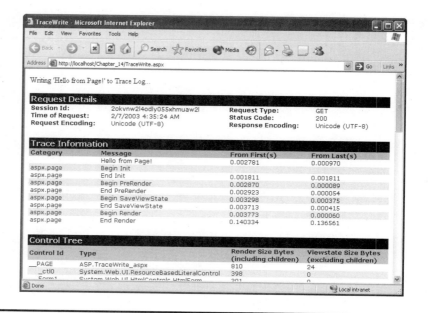

Using *Trace.Warn*

Another method offered by the *TraceContext* class for writing to the trace output is *Trace.Warn*. The primary difference between the two methods is that output written with *Trace.Warn* appears in the trace output as red text, making it ideal for highlighting important entries such as exceptions.

Understanding the Trace Output

The trace output for a page contains a great deal of information. Table 14-1 lists the sections of the trace output and describes the information contained in each.

Table 14-1.   Trace Output Sections

Section	Description
Request Details	Displays request-specific information such as session ID, request type, request status code, and encoding.
Trace Information	Displays messages relating to stages of page processing, as well as execution times for these stages.
Control Tree	Displays a tree representation of all controls on the page, including *LiteralControls* for static HTML text within the source file. Also displays the render size and *ViewState* size of each control.
Cookies Collection	Displays the name, content, and size of all cookies sent as part of the request.

Table 14-1. Trace Output Sections

Section	Description
Headers Collection	Displays a list of all HTTP headers sent as a part of the request.
Form Collection	Displays a list of the names and values of all form fields sent as part of a *POST* request.
Querystring Collection	Displays a list of the names and values of all querystring values sent as part of a *GET* request.
Server Variables	Displays a list of the server variables for the request.

Debugging

In an ideal world, all programmers would be so skilled and attentive to detail that they would write bug-free code. Unfortunately, we do not live in an ideal world. As such, debugging, or tracking down the source of errors and erroneous results, is an important task that all developers need to perform before they allow end-users to use their applications. This section will discuss some techniques for reducing the number of bugs in your code up front. We'll also look at the tools and techniques in ASP.NET and the .NET platform used for debugging applications.

Understanding Bug Categories

There are three broad categories of bugs:

- **Syntax errors**   These errors occur when code breaks the rules of the language you're using, such as a Visual Basic *Sub* statement without a closing *End Sub*, or a forgotten closing curly brace (}) in C#. These errors are the easiest to locate. The language compiler or integrated development environment (IDE) will alert you to them and will not allow you to compile your program until you correct them.

- **Semantic errors**   These errors occur in code that is correct according to the rules of the compiler, but that causes unexpected problems such as crashes or hanging on execution. A good example is code that executes in a loop but never exits the loop, either because the loop depends on a variable whose value was expected to be something different than it actually was or because the programmer forgot to increment the loop counter. Another category of errors in this area includes requesting a field from a dataset. Unless you are using a typed dataset, you have no way to tell if the field actually exists at compile time. These bugs are harder to detect and are one type of runtime error.

- **Logic errors**   Like semantic errors, logic errors are runtime errors. That is, they occur while the program is running. But unlike semantic errors, logic errors do not cause the application to crash or hang. Instead, logic errors result in unexpected values or output. This can be a result of something as simple as a mistyped variable name that happens to match another declared variable in the program (an argument for descriptive variable names rather than simple ones). This type of error can be extremely difficult to track down and eliminate, particularly since in complex programs it can be difficult (if not impossible) to reproduce a logic error reported by a user.

Preventing Bugs

Before we get into the discussion of how to debug the various errors you're apt to run into in your applications, let's take some time to look at strategies for preventing bugs in the first place. Preventing bugs is a much more efficient and much less expensive way to produce bug-free software.

The following list contains a few strategies that will help. This is not a comprehensive list by any means, but applying these strategies consistently will help you spend less time debugging your code and more time enjoying its rewards.

- **Write readable code**   Choose (or develop) and make consistent use of naming and coding standards. It's not that important which standard you use, such as Hungarian notation (*txtFirstName*) or Pascal Casing (*FirstName*) or another naming convention, as long as you use one. You should also strive for consistency in your comments and encourage liberal commenting of code. Anything that makes code more readable and easier to understand will help eliminate bugs from the get-go.

- **Create effective test plans**   The only effective way to eliminate logic errors is to test every path of your application with every possible data value (or representative range of data) that a user could enter. This is difficult to manage without effective planning. You should create your test plans at the same time you're designing the application, and you should update these plans as you modify the application design. To be effective, the test plans need to describe how to test each piece of functionality in the application. Test plans and other design documents can also help highlight design problems before they are implemented, preventing a wide array of bugs.

- **Use a rich IDE**   You don't necessarily need to use Visual Studio .NET to develop your Web applications—ASP.NET does not require it—but you should consider developing in an IDE that provides syntax checking as you type. If you develop with Notepad, it is too easy to amass a number of syntax errors that go unnoticed until you try to run the page. Then you get to spend the next half hour or more eliminating the errors, one at a time, until you finally get the code to run. This is not an efficient way to write code.

■ **Get another pair of eyes** Whether you're working on a team or building an application on your own, it is important to have someone else review your code (and test it, if possible). Developers are simply too close to their own code to catch every bug before (and sometimes even after) testing. A review by a different pair of eyes can help you catch what you've missed.

Compiling Web Forms Pages in Debug Mode

As mentioned in the introduction to this chapter, ASP.NET provides a great deal of information to developers when a bug or error halts execution of an application by throwing an exception. Some of this information, such as the stack trace, is available regardless of the mode that the code was compiled in. The following example shows what happens by default when a project created in Visual Studio .NET divides by zero in code to force an exception to be thrown.

Show the result of a divide-by-zero exception

1 In Visual Studio, open the Chapter_14 project created previously for this chapter. Add a new page by right-clicking on the root of the project in the Solution Explorer, selecting Add, then Add Web Form. Type the name of the form as **DivByZero.aspx**.

2 Add a label to the page.

3 Change to the code page by pressing F7. Add the line

```
using System.Diagnostics;
```

to the top of the code-behind file, before the class definition.

4 Scroll down to the *Page_Load* event handler and add the following code:

```
int One = 1;
int Zero = 0;
int Result;
Debug.Assert(Zero != 0, "Value of Zero will result in exception.");
Result = One / Zero;
Label1.Text = "Got past the error.";
```

5   Save DivByZero.aspx, its code-behind file, and the project, and then build the project.

6   Browse DivByZero.aspx using Internet Explorer. The resulting screen should look similar to the following illustration.

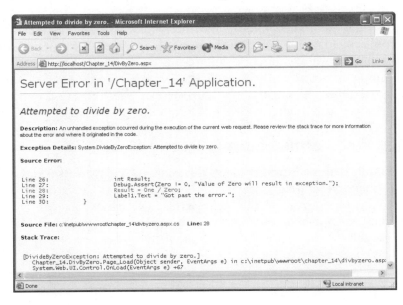

The previous illustration shows the information available when the application is compiled in Debug mode, the default when you create an application using Visual Studio .NET. Information such as the code with the error shown in context, as well as a stack trace, is available only in Debug mode. The following example shows the output when an error occurs and debugging is not enabled.

View divide-by-zero exception information without debugging enabled

1   Open the Chapter_14 project in Visual Studio and open Web.Config by double-clicking on it in the Solution Explorer.

2   Locate the *<compilation>* element in Web.Config and then change the *debug* attribute from *true* to *false*.

3   Select Configuration Manager from the Build menu. In the resulting dialog box, change the configuration for Chapter_14 from Debug to Release. Alternatively, you can change the Active Solution Configuration drop-down list to Release. You should rebuild the application whenever you change configuration settings.

4   Save Web.config and the project, and then build the project.

5   Browse DivByZero.aspx again using Internet Explorer. The resulting screen should look similar to the following illustration.

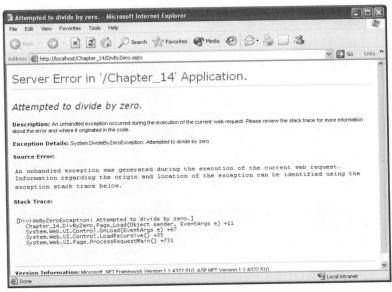

6   Reverse these steps to re-enable debugging for the Chapter_14 project.

The error message displayed this time is less informative, but this is potentially a good thing. For instance, none of the actual code is reproduced, and the stack trace is minimal. Thus, turning off debugging can reduce the risk of exposing sensitive information in your code by the occurrence of an exception. Of course, it's best to avoid having sensitive information in your code in the first place, but making sure that debugging is disabled for public-facing systems can protect both your code and any sensitive information therein.

▶ **Important**   Because even the error page returned when debugging is disabled could provide useful information to a malicious user (such as the version information for the version of the .NET Framework you are running), you should, in addition to disabling debugging, provide custom error-handling pages wherever possible, as explained in Chapter 5. At a minimum, you should set the *mode* attribute of the <customErrors> element to **On**, so that no information other than the fact that an error has occurred is returned to the user's browser.

Understanding ASP.NET Error Messages

Anyone who's seen the infamous ASP 015 error probably realizes just what a dramatic improvement the information in the previous examples represents. ASP.NET will provide descriptive information for both semantic and syntax errors, including the type of exception thrown (which allows you to provide effective and specific exception handling when you cannot completely prevent the exception) and the stack trace for the current request. As mentioned previously, you can also write to the trace output, and any trace statements that occur before execution is halted by an exception will be shown in the trace output.

Using the Visual Studio .NET Debugger

While the error information provided by ASP.NET at runtime can be useful in locating and eliminating syntax errors, most semantic and logic errors require a debugger. This tool uses the source code for a program and an executable compiled with debug symbols to let you step through your code line by line, set breakpoints, and examine the state or values of variables during program execution. You can also use the *Assert* method of the *Debug* class (part of the *System.Diagnostics* namespace) to test for certain conditions in your code and write messages to the output window of the debugger when the assertions fail.

The .NET Framework SDK comes with its own debugger, which provides rich debugging functionality for ASP.NET applications. The debugger is installed in the *drivename*\Program Files\Microsoft.NET\FrameworkSDK\GuiDebug folder (or in *drivename*\Program Files\Microsoft Visual Studio .NET 2003\SDK\v1.1\GuiDebug for Visual Studio installations) and is named DbgCLR.exe. You can execute the runtime debugger by double-clicking this file in Windows Explorer or by clicking Start then Run, and then entering the path and filename and clicking OK.

Generally, however, you will find that the integrated debugger included with Visual Studio .NET is superior to the SDK debugger. To view some of this debugger's features, let's take the DivByZero.aspx page as an example. To debug ASP.NET applications, you must be logged into the machine with an account that has administrator rights or use the Run As functionality to start Visual Studio .NET using an account with administrator rights.

Debug a divide-by-zero exception

1   Open the Chapter_14 project in Visual Studio and switch to the code-behind module for DivByZero.aspx.

2   If you have more than one project in your solution, right-click the Chapter_14 project in Solution Explorer and select Set As Startup Project. This sets Chapter_14 to be the project that is loaded when the project is run or debugged.

3   Right-click DivByZero.aspx in Solution Explorer and select Set As Start Page. This sets DivByZero.aspx to be the page that is loaded when the project is run or debugged.

4   While it's obvious what the problem is in this example, suppose you needed to determine exactly why the divide by zero exception was happening. One way to find out is to step through the code and check the values of your variables as each line executes. Start by scrolling down to the *Page_Load* event handler. Along the left side of the code window is a gray bar. Click on the gray bar to the left of the line with the Debug.Assert. A red dot indicating a breakpoint will appear on the gray bar, and the line will be highlighted. The following illustration shows the breakpoint set in Visual Studio .NET.

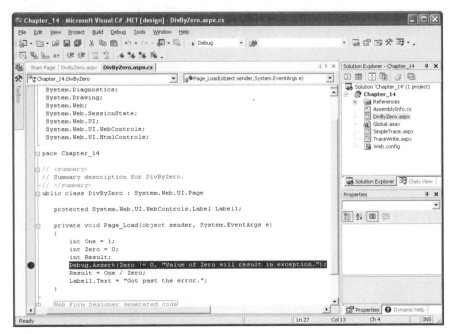

The presence of a breakpoint (or breakpoints) will cause the application to stop executing and display the debugging interface in the IDE when you run the application using the debug feature of Visual Studio. You can then examine the value of variables, step through the code line by line, and take other actions to determine why your code isn't working as you expect.

5   Run the application by selecting Start from the Debug menu (or by pressing F5). Since the breakpoint set in the previous step is in the *Page_Load* event handler, it will be reached immediately. The screen will look something like the following illustration:

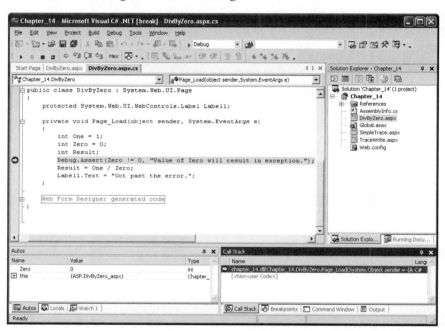

There are several ways to determine the values of variables while in the debugger. The first is to simply move your mouse over a variable and leave it there. A mouse hint appears telling you the name and value of the variable. Also, note that there is a Watch tab in the window at the bottom left of the screen just shown.

6   Click the Watch tab, and then click on the first line in the Watch
    window. You will be able to enter a variable name in the Name col-
    umn. Type **Zero**, and then press Enter. The Watch window will
    look like the following illustration. (If you don't see a Watch tab,
    you can summon the Watch window via the Debug menu. Select
    Debug, then Windows, and then Watch. Select the first Watch win-
    dow in the menu.)

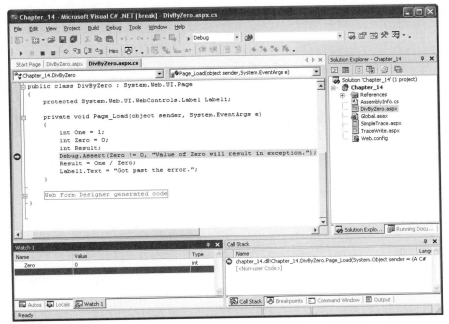

7   An easier way to see the value of a local variable is to look at the
    Locals window, by clicking in the Locals tab. This window shows all
    local variables, as shown in the illustration on the next page. (If you
    don't see a Locals tab, you can summon the Locals window through
    the Debug menu as described in the previous step.)

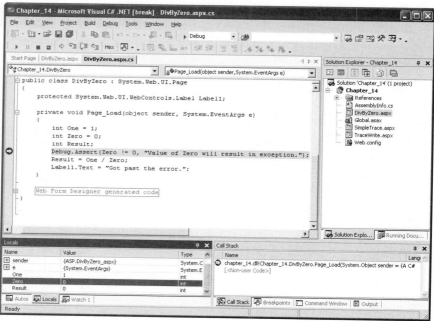

8 Press F10 to single-step through the code. In this case, you should move to the line with the actual division. The screen should look like the following illustration.

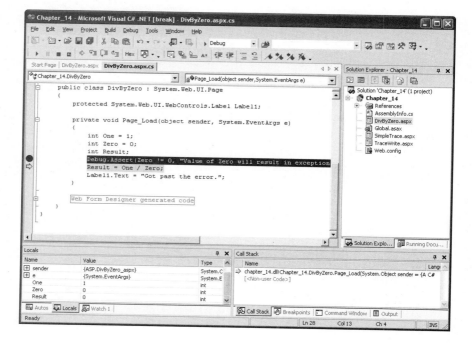

9   If the Output window is not visible, make it visible by selecting View, then Other Windows, and then Output. The output window will have the assert failure shown, as the following illustration shows. (You might need to scroll up in the Output window to see the message.)

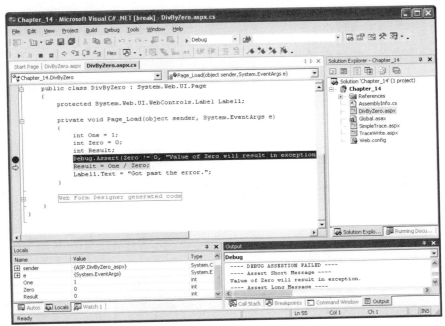

10 Seeing that the variable Zero is indeed equal to 0, we could just stop debugging. We could also change the value of the variable Zero. Highlight the line with Zero on it in the Locals window, and then click in the Value column. We can now edit the value. Change the value by typing **1** and press Enter. The value changes to 1 and appears in red. (Red is the default, but in any event, the value appears in a color defined as indicating the value has changed.)

11 Press F10 again to single-step to the next statement. If a line calls a method that is compiled for debugging and you have access to the source, you can press F11 to step into that code. Press F5 to continue. The browser screen should appear, with the message "Got past the error." displayed.

12 Close the browser.

13 Right-click on the line with the breakpoint, and select Breakpoint Properties. The form shown in the illustration on the next page will appear.

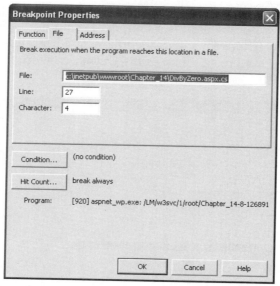

14 Click the Condition button. In the dialog box that appears, leave Condition checked, and enter **Zero <> 0** in the text box. The dialog box should look something like the following illustration. When it does, click OK.

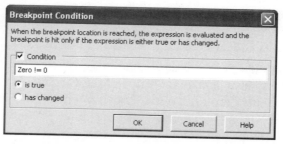

15 Click the Hit Count button. Change the value of the drop-down list labeled *When the breakpoint is hit* to break when the hit count is equal to. A text box should appear. Leave it set to 1. When the dialog box is set as shown in the illustration on the following page, click OK. Click OK again to close the Breakpoint Properties dialog box.

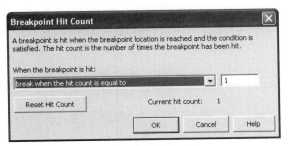

16 Run the application. It will run without breaking for the exception, and display a screen similar to the error screen you saw in the earlier DivByZero.aspx example.

17 Change the properties of the breakpoint as shown earlier, setting the condition to **Zero = 0**. Run the application. This time, the breakpoint will be reached with a condition that is true, and you will be brought to the debugger. Use F10 to single-step through the code, and you will see exactly how the exception is thrown. Seeing how the code runs by single-stepping through it can often be a huge help.

► **Note** The technique used to start debugging in this example (selecting Debug, then Start or F5) causes all projects in the solution to be built prior to debugging. You can debug a single project and skip the build of other projects in the solution by right-clicking the project in Solution Explorer, highlighting Debug, and then selecting Start New Instance or Step Into New Instance.

Using *Debug.Assert*

As shown in the previous examples, you can add *Debug.Assert* messages to your code to test certain conditions. The *Assert* method is overloaded and supports the following forms:

```
Debug.Assert(bool condition);
Debug.Assert(bool condition, string message);
Debug.Assert(bool condition, string message,
    string detailMessage);
```

- *condition* is an expression that evaluates to true or false.
- *message* is a string containing a brief message to display when *condition* returns false.
- *detailMessage* is a string containing a detailed message to display when *condition* returns false.

To call the Debug class without explicitly including the namespace, you need to import the System.Diagnostics namespace using the Imports directive, as described in the preceding examples.

Chapter 14 Quick Reference

To	Do this
Enable page-level tracing	Add the *Trace* attribute to the @ *Page* directive and set its value to *true*.
Enable application-level tracing	Add the *<trace>* configuration section to Web.config with the desired attributes. At a minimum, the *enabled* attribute is required and should be set to *true*.
Write to the trace output	Call either the *Trace.Write* or *Trace.Warn* method, passing the appropriate arguments.
View detailed error information or prepare for using the runtime debugger	Compile your page or pages in Debug mode by either adding the *Debug* attribute to the @ *Page* directive with a value of *true* or adding the *<compilation>* section to the Web.config file and setting its *debug* attribute to *true*.
Invoke the runtime debugger	Locate the file DbgCLR.exe and execute it.
Debug a page using the Visual Studio .NET debugger	Ensure that the page is set to compile in debug mode, which is the default in Visual Studio .NET. Set breakpoints by clicking on the gray bar on the left side of the code window.
Make a breakpoint conditional	Set a breakpoint as earlier in the chapter, and then right-click on the line and select Breakpoint Properties from the context menu. Set a condition (to break only when a condition is met) or a hit count (to break only after some number of passes through the line where the breakpoint is).
To disable debugging when moving an application to production	In Web.Config, in the *<compilation>* tag, set *debug* to *false*. In the Build menu, select Configuration, change the configuration for the project involved to *Release*, and then rebuild the application.

Part

5

Appendixes

Migrating from ASP to ASP.NET

In this chapter, you will learn how to:

■ Recognize issues common to the migration process.

■ Migrate a page that accesses data using ADO.

■ Use programming practices with classic ASP that will make migration easier.

The one disadvantage of moving from ASP to ASP.NET using C# is that there is not a convenient way to migrate applications bit by bit or to modify the VBScript used by ASP so that it will compile as Visual Basic C# .NET in ASP.NET. Of course, migrating VBScript ASP pages to C# is a lot harder than converting VBScript to Visual Basic .NET, but if your experience is with C++, the C# transition will be worth the effort.

Migration Overview

Almost all the issues you encounter when migrating your classic ASP applications to ASP.NET fall into two categories: page structure changes and language changes. The next two sections discuss the types of changes in each category and the ways you need to update your code to work with them.

Page Structure Changes

The page structure changes from classic ASP to ASP.NET can be broken down into two areas: changes in the structure of code blocks and changes to the syntax of page directives.

Code Blocks

As discussed in Chapter 7, there are significant changes between how code was structured in classic ASP and how it is structured in ASP.NET. These changes, which are designed to make your code more readable and maintainable, are likely to be the most common issue in migration.

In classic ASP, server-side code is written in either code render blocks, indicated by the syntax <% %>, or code declaration blocks, indicated by the *<script runat="server"></script>* syntax. Either syntax can be used anywhere in the page and can contain either statements or procedures.

One problem with classic ASP was that it can be difficult to tell the order in which its code will execute, which can cause bugs. It's also all too easy to write spaghetti code, wind up with a page covered in render blocks, and mix procedures and raw statements. This can make the code difficult to read and maintain, and mixing HTML and render blocks often negatively affects page performance.

In ASP.NET, the purpose of render blocks and code declaration blocks has been narrowed considerably. Render blocks in ASP.NET can contain only executable statements, not procedures, whereas code declaration blocks can contain only global variable declarations and procedures.

▶ **Important**   In addition to the performance and reliability implications of mixing code within render blocks and HTML, using render blocks also makes for an unclear separation of presentation and program logic. ASP.NET enables one team to work on the presentation logic (in the .aspx files) while another group works on the guts of the application logic (in the .cs files).

Another significant difference between classic ASP and ASP.NET is that in classic ASP, multiple *<script runat="server">* code declaration blocks can be used on a page. Each code declaration block could use a different language through the *language* attribute, which could be set to VBScript or JScript. ASP.NET only supports a single language per page, which is Visual Basic .NET by default.

Top-to-Bottom vs. Event-Driven Programming

Classic ASP pages using render blocks always executed from top to bottom. Code in <% %> render blocks was executed and output to the response stream as the ASP interpreter encountered it.

ASP.NET code is compiled into an instance of the *Page* class, and execution is event-based. Rather than placing start-up code in the first render block in a page, start-up code in ASP.NET is placed in the *Page_Load* event handler, which is fired when the instance of the *Page* class that represents the page is loaded into memory. Likewise, a *Page_UnLoad* event is fired just before the page is removed from memory and can be used to run any clean-up code that is necessary.

Page Directives

In classic ASP, the primary directive used in pages was the @ *Language* directive, which specified the language to be used for render blocks. Other less commonly used directives included @ *Codepage*, @ *EnableSessionState*, @ *LCID*, and @ *Transaction*.

In ASP.NET, these directives are attributes of the @ *Page* directive, which should appear at the top of each ASP.NET Web Form page. See Chapter 7 for a full discussion of the @ *Page* directive and its attributes.

One new attribute of the @ *Page* directive that is important to discuss in relation to classic ASP is the *AspCompat* attribute. By default, ASP.NET runs as a multi-threaded apartment (MTA) process. This means that single-threaded apartment (STA) components, such as those written in Visual Basic 6.0, are not compatible with ASP.NET. This includes the ADO components, which are installed to run as STA components by default. (You can modify this by running a batch file that changes the registry settings for ADO, but that is beyond the scope of this discussion.) Setting the *AspCompat* attribute to *true* forces ASP.NET to run in STA mode, making it possible to use STA components in ASP.NET pages.

▶ **Important**   Setting *AspCompat* to *true* should be considered a short-term solution when migrating from ASP to ASP.NET, because this setting can have a significant negative impact on the performance of your application. For best performance, you should rewrite components written in earlier versions of Visual Basic using Visual Basic .NET, and migrate existing ADO code to use ADO.NET.

Language Changes

In addition to changes to the structure of pages in ASP.NET, there are some significant changes when moving code from VBScript to C# that will require modifications to your code. These include the following:

- *Set* and *Let* are not needed or supported. Object references can be set by simple assignment:

```
Object1 = Object2;
```

- Parentheses are required for calling all methods in C#, including methods that do not have parameters:

```
Response.Write("Hello, World! ");
```

- All statements are terminated with semicolons.

- Blocks that are associated with control structures like *if* and *while* statements are delimited by curly braces ({ *and* }) rather than words, such as *Endif* or *End While*.

- The *Variant* data type does not exist in C# .NET. The replacement is *Object*.

- Default properties are not supported. All properties must be called explicitly:

```
MyString = TextBox1.Text;
```

- Property declaration syntax is different in C#. Instead of *Property Set*, *Property Get*, and *Property Let*, C# .NET uses the following syntax (keep in mind that *value* is a special keyword that contains the value submitted to the *set* portion of the *public variable* statement):

```
public string MyProperty
{
    get
    {
        return MyInternalVariable;
    }
    set
    {
        if ( value!=MyInternalVariable )
        {
            MyInternalVariable=value;
        }
    }
}
```

▶ **Important**   The property just shown acts as a simple shell for *MyInternalVariable*. You can use any code while setting or getting the property. In this example, I only set *MyInternalVariable* in the setter if it is different from the current value. Properties can be used to expose values that don't really exist as explicit fields in the class. For instance, you might create an Invoice class that exposes an *Invoice-Total* property that cannot be set, and when read actually totals the amounts in each invoice line. You can also use properties to expose objects that might take some time to create. By doing so, you can postpone the expensive creation until the object is first requested, allowing Just-In-Time initialization.

- By default, parameters are passed to procedures in C# by value. Parameters can be passed by reference using the *ref* keyword. You can change the value of Reference parameters in the procedure to which they're passed and then retrieve their value outside the procedure:

```
public void MySub(ref string MyValue)
{
    MyValue="Hello! ";
}
```

Migrating a Data Access Page to ASP.NET

To demonstrate some of these changes and show you how to deal with them, let's walk through the process of migrating a classic ASP page that accesses data in a SQL Server database through ADO and writes it to the page as an HTML table. You will migrate the ADO to ADO.NET and change the language from VBScript to C#. Rather than rendering a table directly, the ASP.NET version uses a DataGrid component. The following listing shows the classic ASP page you'll use to start. You will need to set the *pwd* attribute in the connection string to the appropriate password for your VSdotNET MSDE instance. You might also want to change the *uid* attribute to the name of an account with fewer privileges than the *sa* account. You can get the values of both of these attributes from your SQL Server administrator.

GetAuthors.asp

```
<%@ Language=VBScript %>
<html>
<head>
<%
Dim objConn
Dim objCmd
Dim objRS
Dim strConn

' Do NOT use the sa account in data access code, as shown in
' the connection string below! Doing so is a MAJOR security risk!
' Change the connection string to either use a trusted connection,
' or to use a less-privileged account to access the database.
strConn = "PROVIDER=SQLOLEDB;INITIAL CATALOG=PUBS; " _
    & "SERVER=(local)\VSdotNET;uid=sa;pwd=;"
Set objConn = Server.CreateObject("ADODB.Connection")
Set objCmd = Server.CreateObject("ADODB.Command")
Set objRS = Server.CreateObject("ADODB.Recordset")

objCmd.CommandText = "SELECT * FROM Authors"
objConn.Open strConn
Set objCmd.ActiveConnection = objConn
Set objRS = objCmd.Execute

Sub FormatTable

    Dim objField

    If Not objRS.EOF Then
        Response.Write "<table border=2 cellspacing=0>"
        Do While Not objRS.EOF
            Response.Write "<tr>"
            For Each objField In objRS.Fields
                Response.Write "<td>" & objField & "</td>"
            Next
            Response.Write "</tr>"
            objRS.MoveNext
```

```
        Loop
        Response.Write "</table>"
    Else
        Response.Write "No Records! "
    End If

End Sub
Sub CleanUp()
    objConn.Close
    Set objConn = Nothing
    Set objCmd = Nothing
    Set objRS = Nothing
End Sub
%>
</head>
<body>


<%
FormatTable()
CleanUp()
%>


</body>
</html>
```

The following illustration shows the output of this page.

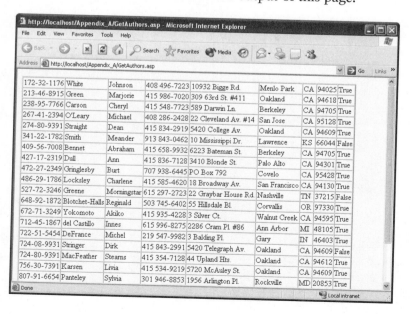

The page in the previous listing accesses the Authors table of the Pubs SQL Server sample database (in this case in the VSdotNET MSDE instance that can be installed with Visual Studio .NET), calls a render function to write the data to the page as an HTML table, and then calls a clean-up function to close the connection to the database and set the object references to *Nothing* to ensure that the COM subsystem knows these objects can be destroyed.

> ▶ **Important**   One thing this sample code has in common with much of the sample code you will encounter (and unfortunately, some production code as well) is its use of the *sa* SQL Server login account with a blank password. (This is the default for SQL Server 6.5 and 7.0 installs. You must explicitly choose a blank password to use a blank *sa* password in SQL Server 2000.) In practice, the *sa* account should always be given a strong password because this account has full administrative rights on the SQL Server machine. This includes the ability to run operating system commands through an extended stored procedure.
>
> You should *never*, under any circumstances, use the *sa* account for accessing data from a page. All it takes is a single bad page to compromise an entire server, especially when your page provides system administrator access to SQL Server.
>
> If you cannot use a trusted connection to SQL Server, you should set up one or more special user accounts for each Web application with the absolute minimum rights necessary to allow access to that application's data. This will reduce the risk of overbroad rights, which can cause data to be compromised.
>
> Another security issue in the sample is the placing of user ID and password information directly in the page. In practice, if you are connecting to a database with an explicit username and password, connection string information should be stored somewhere more secure. In order of increasing security, options include storing it as an *appSetting* in Web.config, storing it as an *appSetting* in Machine.config (not appropriate in a shared server environment), and hard-coding it as a private member of a compiled component. See the section entitled "Storing Database Connection Strings Securely" at *http://msdn.microsoft.com/library/en-us/dnnetsec/html/SecNetch12.asp* for more information on this topic.

Short-Term Migration

In the short term, your goal might be to simply move your pages over to ASP.NET while still using most of the existing logic in the page. Although this choice has performance implications, it might make your migration easier by letting you do it in stages. Making the code in the previous listing work as an ASP.NET page is largely a matter of modifying it to comply with the rules for ASP.NET code using Visual Basic .NET. The conversion from VBScript to Visual Basic .NET is beyond the scope of this book.

Long-Term Migration

Doing a quick-and-dirty conversion to allow your VBScript ASP pages to run as ASP.NET pages using Visual Basic .NET is a stopgap measure that will enable you to get the page up and running quickly. Among other compromises, you will need to modify the ASP.NET default to allow STA components to work correctly with ASP.NET. In the long run, it's best to fully migrate your code to take advantage of the features offered by ASP.NET and ADO.NET. The following steps show how to migrate the ASP page to run under ASP.NET in C#.

Migrate a page to ASP.NET

1   Open Visual C# .NET. Create a new project called Appendix_A.

2   To rename the initial default page, on the File menu, click Save WebForm1.aspx As. In the resulting dialog box, type **GetAuthors.aspx** as the new file name, and click the Save button.

3   Move the mouse pointer to the Toolbox, and drag a DataGrid onto the Web form. Change the ID of the DataGrid to **MyGrid**.

4   On the View menu, click Code, or press F7 to move to the code window.

5   Add the following line to the using clauses:

```
using System.Data.SqlClient;
```

6   Scroll down to the *Page_Load* event handler and add the following code:

```
private void Page_Load(object sender, System.EventArgs e)
{
    // Put user code to initialize the page here
    DataSet MyDS = new DataSet();
    SqlConnection MySqlConn;
    SqlDataAdapter MySqlDa;
    string ConnStr;
    string SQLSelect;
    ConnStr=@"server=(local)\VsDotNet;database=pubs; " +
        "Trusted_Connection=yes";
    SQLSelect="SELECT * FROM Authors";
    MySqlConn=new SqlConnection(ConnStr);

    try
    {
        MySqlDa=new SqlDataAdapter(SQLSelect,MySqlConn);
        MySqlDa.Fill(MyDS);
        MyGrid.DataSource=MyDS.Tables[0].DefaultView;
        DataBind();
    }
```

```
// finally block ensures that the connection will be closed,
//   even if an exception occurs.
finally
{
    MySqlConn.Close();
}
}
```

7 Save the file and its code-behind module, and then build the project.

▶ **Note** To use a trusted connection to connect to SQL Server as shown in the preceding listing, you will need to either enable Windows authentication and impersonation or set up the ASPNET worker process account as a SQL Server login, as described in Chapter 9.

8 Browse GetAuthors.aspx using Microsoft Internet Explorer. The output should look similar to the following illustration.

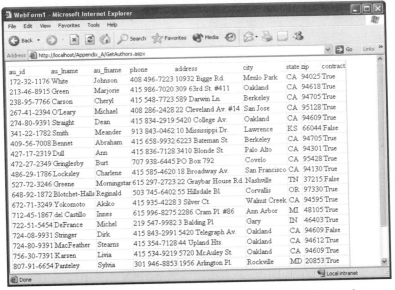

9 Switch to GetAuthors.aspx by clicking the appropriate tab near the top of the Visual Studio .NET editing window. Ensure that you are in Design mode by clicking Design on the tab control at the bottom of the Design window.

10 Right-click the DataGrid and click Auto Format on the shortcut menu. The screen that appears will look like the illustration on the next page.

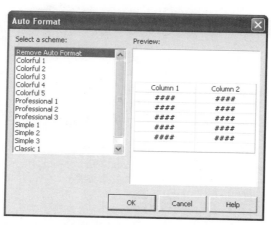

11 In the AutoFormat dialog box, click Professional 1 in the Select A Scheme box, click OK, and then save the page.

12 Browse GetAuthors.aspx again, using Internet Explorer. The screen that appears will look similar to the following illustration.

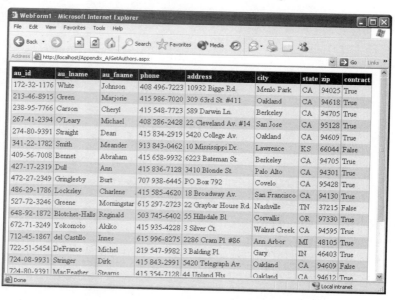

▶ **Note**   The code in the preceding listing offers better performance than a quick-and-dirty conversion of the VBScript code to Visual C# .NET because it does not rely on *AspCompat* to run. It takes advantage of ADO.NET instead of using ADO through COM Interop (which carries some performance overhead). The code could be made even more efficient by using an ADO.NET DataReader to access the data. The code in the preceding listing also provides greater flexibility for modifying the look of the rendered table. You can modify this by adding attributes to the *DataGrid* tag. Using an ASP.NET *DataGrid* also provides built-in support for paging, editing, and filtering. Fancy formatting (including alternating item formatting) is also easy to add, as shown in Step 17 of the previous procedure, using Visual Studio .NET's Auto Format. See Chapter 9 for more information on these features.

Best Practices for Preparing for ASP.NET

As you can see from this appendix, migrating from classic ASP to ASP.NET does not need to be terribly painful. However, a lot depends on how your classic ASP code is written in the first place. Code that is written with a great deal of intermingled HTML and render blocks will be more difficult to migrate, as will code that does not follow good coding practices. The following are several coding practices you can put in place in your ongoing classic ASP development to make migrating it to ASP.NET easier:

- Use *ByVal* or *ByRef* to explicitly state which type of parameter is desired in procedures that take parameters. This will remind you what types of parameters are expected when moving to ASP.NET and C#.

- Write all procedures in *<script>* code declaration blocks, rather than in render blocks.

- Use render blocks sparingly, particularly when intermingled with HTML tags.

- Do not rely on default properties. Instead, explicitly name properties such as *objRS.Value*.

- Do not use multiple languages in server-side *<script>* blocks. Choose the language you're most comfortable with and use it exclusively on a per-page basis.

ASP.NET Configuration Elements

This appendix lists the syntax for each configuration element and describes the attributes and child elements available for that element (where applicable). The names of configuration elements and their attributes are case sensitive and are in what is referred to as *camel case*. In camel case, the entire first word of a name is lowercase, and the initial letter of each additional word in the name is capitalized. For example, the *sessionstate* configuration element becomes *sessionState*. Remember that if you don't use camel case with both configuration element names and attribute names, you'll get an error when you try to access a page in the application.

<trace>

The *<trace>* element allows you to enable or disable application-wide tracing (see Chapter 14 for more information on this useful feature), as well as set the parameters for the tracing functionality. When tracing is enabled, you can review information about requests received by the Web server with the special URL *http://<servername>/<appname>/trace.axd*. The *<trace>* element has the following syntax:

```
<trace
    enabled="true|false"
    localOnly="true|false"
    pageOutput="true|false"
    requestLimit="integer"
    traceMode="SortByTime|SortByCategory" />
```

Table B-1 describes the *<trace>* element attributes in more detail.

Table B-1. *<trace>* **Element Attributes**

Attribute	Description	Options
enabled	Determines whether application-level tracing is enabled for the application.	*true*: Turns on application-level tracing. *false*: Turns off application-level tracing. The default is *false*.
localOnly	Determines whether trace information is viewable by computers other than the local Web server.	*true*: Trace output can be viewed only from the local Web server. *false*: Trace output is viewable from any machine. The default is *true*.
pageOutput	Determines whether trace output is appended to each ASP.NET page in the application or is available only through trace.axd.	*true*: Trace output is appended to each page within the scope of the configuration file. *false*: Trace output is available only by browsing the special trace.axd URL. The default is *false*.
requestLimit	Determines the number of requests that are stored for review through the trace.axd URL. Once this limit has been reached, the current trace must be cleared by browsing trace.axd to collect information on additional requests.	The default is 10, but the higher this number, the more overhead is involved in tracing. Set this number as small as is feasible.
traceMode	Determines the sort order of the requests stored.	*SortByTime*: Sorts trace information by the order in which events are processed. *SortByCategory*: Sorts trace information alphabetically by category. When used with the *Trace.Write* method, *SortByCategory* can be useful for grouping *Trace.Write* statements using the same category argument. The default is *SortByTime*.

<globalization>

The *<globalization>* element controls globalization settings for ASP.NET applications. This includes the encoding used for requests, responses, and files, as well as settings for specifying the culture to be associated with Web requests and local searches. The *<globalization>* element has the following syntax:

```
<globalization
    culture="any valid culture string"
    fileEncoding="any valid encoding string"
    requestEncoding="any valid encoding string"
    responseEncoding="any valid encoding string"
    uiCulture="any valid culture string" />
```

Table B-2 describes the *<globalization>* element attributes in more detail.

Table B-2. *<globalization>* Element Attributes

Attribute	Description	Options
culture	Determines the culture (such as language defaults) used to process incoming Web requests.	This attribute must be set to a valid culture string. For a list of valid culture strings, see the Microsoft .NET Framework documentation entry for the *System.Globalization.Culture-Info* class.
fileEncoding	Determines the type of character encoding used for parsing ASP.NET application files (.aspx, .asmx, and .asax).	This attribute must be set to a valid encoding string. If this attribute is not included in either Machine.config or Web.config, encoding is based on the machine's Regional Options setting in Control Panel.
requestEncoding	Determines the type of character encoding used to process incoming Web requests.	This attribute must be set to a valid encoding string. If this attribute is not included in either Machine.config or Web.config, encoding is based on the machine's Regional Options setting in Control Panel. The default is *utf-8*.
responseEncoding	Determines the type of character encoding used to encode outgoing responses.	This attribute must be set to a valid encoding string. If this attribute is not included in either Machine.config or Web.config, encoding is based on the machine's Regional Options setting in Control Panel. The default is *utf-8*.
uiCulture	Determines the culture (such as language defaults) used to process searches that are culture- or locale-specific.	This attribute must be set to a valid culture string. For a list of valid culture strings, see the .NET Framework documentation entry for the *System.Globalization.CultureInfo* class.

<httpRuntime>

The *<httpRuntime>* element controls several aspects of the ASP.NET HTTP runtime engine. The *<httpRuntime>* element has the following syntax:

```
<httpRuntime
    appRequestQueueLimit="number of requests"
    enableKernelOutputCache="true|false"
    enableVersionHeader="string"
    executionTimeout="seconds"
    maxRequestLength="kbytes"
    minLocalRequestFreeThreads="number of threads"
    minFreeThreads="number of threads"
    useFullyQualifiedRedirectUrl="true|false" />
```

Fully Qualified vs. Relative URLs

There are two basic types of URLs used for creating hyperlinks in Web pages: fully qualified URLs and relative URLs. Fully qualified URLs, also known as absolute URLs, contain all of the information necessary for the browser (or other client program) to locate the resource named in the URL. This includes the protocol moniker being used (*ftp://*, *http://*, *https://*, and so on), the server's domain name or IP address (on local Windows networks, the machine name can also be used), and the path to the resource. A typical fully qualified URL would look like this:

http://localhost/quickstart/aspplus/default.aspx

Relative URLs provide only the information necessary to locate a resource relative to the current document (known as document relative) or current server or domain (known as root relative). A document-relative URL used to link to the previously referenced page from another page in the same virtual directory would look like this:

default.aspx

A root-relative URL would look like this:

/quickstart/aspplus/default.aspx

Because some controls or applications might not know how to use relative URLs, at times you'll need to use a fully qualified URL.

Table B-3 describes the *<httpRuntime>* element attributes in more detail.

Table B-3.   *<httpRuntime>* **Element Attributes**

Attribute	Description	Options
appRequestQueueLimit	Specifies the number of requests that ASP.NET will queue when no threads are available to process them, before returning a "503–Server Too Busy" error message.	Increasing this value can result in unacceptably long wait times for users, so use caution and test carefully when making adjustments to this value. The default is 100.
enableKernelOutputCache	Specifies whether the http.sys cache is enabled for IIS 6.0 and higher. *New for version 1.1.*	Kernel output caching can significantly improve performance. The default is *true*.
enableVersionHeader	Specifies whether the X-AspNet-Version header is output with each request. *New for version 1.1.*	The default is *true*.
executionTimeout	Determines amount of time, in seconds, that an ASP.NET request can continue executing before being shut down.	This attribute, which is similar to classic ASP's *Server.ScriptTimeout* property, can be used to prevent hung or long-running requests from consuming more resources than necessary. This attribute should be set somewhere higher than the average time it takes to process requests, but not so high as to allow processor overutilization by errant or inefficient pages. The default is 90 seconds.

Table B-3. *<httpRuntime>* **Element Attributes**

Attribute	Description	Options
maxRequestLength	Determines maximum size of incoming file uploads, in kilobytes.	This attribute is designed to help prevent denial of service attacks mounted by uploading large files to a server. Set it to the smallest size feasible for files you expect your users to upload. The default is 4,096 kbytes.
minFreeThreads	Configures the minimum number of threads ASP.NET will keep free for processing new requests.	The default is 8.
minLocalRequestFreeThreads	Configures the minimum *FreeThreads* number of threads ASP.NET will keep free for processing requests coming from the local machine. Maintaining these free threads can help prevent deadlocks in multithreaded processing. Note that this is incorrectly identified in the current .NET Framework documentation as *minFree-LocalRequestFreeThreads*.	The default is 4.
useFullyQualifiedRedirectURL	Determines whether relative or fully qualified URLs are used for client-side redirects. This attribute allows developers to support certain mobile controls that require fully qualified URLs for client-side redirects.	*true*: Client-side redirects are fully qualified. *false*: Client-side redirects are relative. The default is *true*.

<compilation>

With 10 attributes and two child elements, the *<compilation>* element is one of the more extensive ASP.NET configuration elements and contains settings that determine how ASP.NET compiles code in your Web applications and Web Services. The settings you'll see most frequently are the *debug* and *default-Language* attributes, which are placed in your application's Web.config file by default when you're using Microsoft Visual Studio .NET. Other settings, such as the *<assemblies>* and *<namespaces>* child elements, are equally important but usually are inherited from the settings in Machine.config, unless overridden by a developer.

The *<compilation>* element has the following syntax:

```
<compilation
    batch="true|false"
    batchTimeout="seconds"
    debug="true|false"
    defaultLanguage="language"
    explicit="true|false"
    maxBatchSize="number of pages"
    maxBatchGeneratedFileSize="kbytes"
    numRecompilesBeforeAppRestart="number"
    strict="true|false"
    tempdirectory="directory" >
    <compilers>
        <compiler
            extension="file extension"
            language="language"
            compilerOptions="compiler options"
            type=".NET type"
            warningLevel="number" />
    </compilers>

    <assemblies>
        <add assembly="assembly name" />
        <remove assembly="assembly name" />
        <clear />
    </assemblies>
</compilation>
```

Table B-4 describes the *<compilation>* element attributes in more detail.

Table B-4. *<compilation>* **Element Attributes**

Element	Attribute	Description	Options
<compilation>		Determines compiler options for the application. Supports the *<compilers>* and *<assemblies>* child elements.	
	Batch	Determines whether the application supports batch compilation of ASP.NET pages. When batch compilation is enabled, ASP.NET will attempt to compile all ASP.NET pages within the application directory on the first request. This prevents later page requests from having to be compiled on request.	*true*: Batch compilation is supported. *false*: Pages will be compiled one by one as they are requested. The default is *true*.
	BatchTimeout	Determines the amount of time, in seconds, before timeout of batch compilation. If the timeout is exceeded, the compiler will switch to per-request compilation mode.	This setting will vary depending on the size of an application and the amount of time you are willing to allow for batch compilation. The default is 15 seconds.
	Debug	Determines whether debug information is included in compiled assemblies for ASP.NET pages and Web Services. This attribute should always be set to false in a production application because debug assemblies are larger and don't perform as well as release-type assemblies.	*true*: Assemblies are compiled with debug info. *false*: Assemblies are compiled without debug info. The default is *false*.

Table B-4. *<compilation>* **Element Attributes**

Element	Attribute	Description	Options
	DefaultLanguage	Determines the language(s) to be used during dynamic compilation.	This attribute is the name of a language, as specified by one of the *<compiler>* child elements. The default is *vb*.
	Explicit	Determines whether ASP.NET compiles pages written in Microsoft Visual Basic .NET using the Visual Basic Option Explicit compiler option (which forces explicit declaration of variables). Enabling this setting makes it easier to locate and fix common problems, such as misspelled variable names, that otherwise wouldn't be discovered until runtime.	*true*: Enabled. *false*: Disabled. The default is *true*.
	maxBatchSize	Determines the maximum number of pages for batch compilation.	The default is 1,000.
	maxBatch-GeneratedFileSize	Determines the maximum combined size, in KB, of the generated source files in batch compilation.	The default is 3,000.
	numRecompiles-BeforeAppRestart	Determines how many times application resources can be dynamically recompiled before the application is automatically restarted. This setting can be configured at both the application level and the global level through Machine.config.	The default is 15.

Table B-4.   *<compilation>* Element Attributes

Element	Attribute	Description	Options
	strict	Determines whether ASP.NET compiles pages written in Visual Basic .NET using the Visual Basic Option Strict compiler option (which prevents type conversions that would result in data loss, late binding, and other error-prone coding habits) to your .aspx files before compilation.	*true*: Enabled. *false*: Disabled. It's a good practice to turn this on, through either Machine.config or Web.config, through the Visual Studio .NET properties dialog box for the project (choose Build under Common Properties), or by adding Option Strict to the page or module you're working on. This makes it easier to fix common problems, such as overflows or rounding errors, that otherwise wouldn't be discovered until runtime. The default is *false*.
	tempDirectory	Determines the directory in which the temporary ASP.NET files resulting from dynamic compilation will reside.	Any valid directory.
<compilers>		Child element containing individual *<compiler>* child elements.	
<compiler>		Determines options for specific language compilers. One or more of these child elements can be contained within the *<compilers>* element.	

Table B-4.   **<compilation> Element Attributes**

Element	Attribute	Description	Options
	extension	Determines the file extension used by dynamically compiled code-behind modules for a specific compiler. The extensions for the three most commonly used ASP.NET languages (Visual Basic .NET, Microsoft C#, and Microsoft JScript .NET) are included in Machine.config, so you don't need to set them yourself unless you want to add additional extensions for one of these languages.	String representing the file extension (.vb, .cs, and so on). Use semicolons to delimit multiple extensions. This setting should match the language specified in the language attribute. This attribute is required.
	language	Determines the list of language names to be handled by a specific compiler. The names for the three most commonly used ASP.NET languages (Visual Basic .NET, C#, and JScript .NET) are included in Machine.config, so you don't need to set them yourself unless you want to add additional names for one of these languages.	String representing the language name (vb;visualbasic; vbscript). Use semicolons to delimit multiple names. This setting should match the language specified in the extension attribute. This attribute is required.
	compilerOptions	Determines any compiler-specific options to be passed along during compilation.	Consult the .NET Framework SDK documentation to determine available options.

Table B-4.   *<compilation>* **Element Attributes**

Element	Attribute	Description	Options
	Type	Determines which .NET class or assembly is used to compile resources using the language specified in the language attribute, or with the extension in the extension attribute. The types for the three most commonly used ASP.NET languages (Visual Basic .NET, C#, and JScript .NET) are included in Machine.config, so you don't need to set them yourself unless you want to modify the type for one of these languages (not recommended).	This attribute is a comma-delimited list that can include the class name, assembly name, and version information. The Machine.config file contains good examples of the syntax for this attribute. This attribute is required.
	warningLevel	Determines the compiler warning levels, which determine the types of warning messages (and the severity) that are emitted by the compiler.	The value for this attribute depends on the language compiler being configured. The default for C# is 1.
<assemblies>		Child element containing one or more of the *<add/>*, *<remove/>*, or *<clear/>* child elements.	The child elements of the *<assemblies>* element are used to add references to assemblies to be used during compilation. ASP.NET automatically links in the assemblies specified here during dynamic compilation.
	<clear>		Specifies that all current or inherited assembly references should be removed.

Table B-4. *<compilation>* Element Attributes

Element	Attribute	Description	Options
<add>	*assembly*	Specifies an assembly, by its assembly name, to be referenced during dynamic compilation.	This setting should be the assembly name, not the DLL name, of the desired assembly. You can also use the wildcard * to add all assemblies from the application's private assembly cache (by default, in the bin sub-directory).
<remove>	*assembly*	Specifies an assembly, by its assembly name, to be removed from use during dynamic compilation.	The assembly name used must match exactly the name of an assembly added by a previous add directive (for example, from a parent Web.config). You cannot use wildcards for this attribute.

<pages>

The *<pages>* element allows you to set the defaults for the page-level attributes that are more commonly associated with the attributes of the *@ Page* ASP.NET directive. The settings in this element apply to all pages for which specific attributes of the *@ Page* directive do not appear. If these attributes do appear in an ASP.NET page, their settings will override those in either the Machine.config or Web.config configuration files. As such, the *<pages>* element provides a handy way of configuring the *SessionState*, *ViewState*, and other settings at an application or subfolder level, giving you a great deal of control over your application.

The *<pages>* element has the following syntax:

```
<pages
    autoEventWireup="true|false"
    buffer="true|false"
    enableSessionState="true|false|ReadOnly"
    enableViewState="true|false"
    enableViewStateMac="true|false"
    pageBaseType="typename, assembly"
```

```
smartNavigation="true|false"
userControlBaseType="typename"
validateRequest="true|false" />
```

Table B-5 describes the *<pages>* element attributes in more detail.

Table B-5. *<pages>* **Element Attributes**

Attribute	Description	Options
autoEventWireup	Determines whether support for page events (*Page_Load* and so on) is automatically provided in an application's ASP.NET pages.	*true*: Event support is provided automatically. *false*: Event support is not provided. Event handlers must be manually wired by developers. The default is *true*. Pages created in Visual Studio .NET will have *autoEventWireup* set to *false* by default.
Buffer	Determines whether responses are buffered before being sent to the client. This setting is analogous to the classic ASP *Response.Buffer* property.	*true*: Buffering is enabled. Page output will be buffered until the page is completely processed, or until either the *End* or *Flush* method of the *HTTPResponse* class is called. *false*: Buffering is not enabled. Buffering is to the client as it is rendered. The default is *true*.
PageBaseType	Provides the type or assembly name of a class from which ASP.NET pages should inherit. In the absence of this attribute, the default is to inherit from the *Page* class of the *System.Web.UI* namespace.	You can use this attribute to provide a class derived from the *Page* class if you want to provide additional functionality not included in the base *Page* class. This is a simple yet powerful way to extend ASP.NET applications.
smartNavigation	Determines whether the SmartNavigation feature, which uses *IFrame* elements to minimize page "flash" on postbacks, is enabled by default.	The default is *false*.

Table B-5.   *<pages>* Element Attributes

Attribute	Description	Options
userControlBaseType	Provides the type or assembly name of a class from which ASP.NET User Controls (.ascx files) should inherit. In the absence of this attribute, the default is to inherit from the *UserControl* class of the *System. Web.UI* namespace.	
enableSessionState	Determines whether a new session is created by default for the current user by an ASP.NET page. Note that if the user already has a session from a prior page in which this attribute is set to *false*, this attribute will not affect that session. However, setting the attribute to *ReadOnly* will prevent the page from modifying values set in previous pages.	*true*: If the user does not have a current session when he or she requests a page, a new session will be created. *false*: If the user does not have a current session, one will not be created. If the user does have a session, it will not be affected, but its values cannot be accessed from pages where this attribute is *false*. *ReadOnly*: If the user does not have a current session, one will not be created. If the user does have a session, its values can be read from within a page where this attribute has been set to *ReadOnly*, but they cannot be modified. The default is *true*.
enableViewState	Determines whether *ViewState* (the method by which ASP.NET Server Controls store their state between page requests) is enabled.	*true*: *ViewState* is enabled. Server Controls will maintain their values from one request to the next. *false*: *ViewState* is not enabled. Server control state will be reset with each request.
enableViewStateMac	Determines whether a Machine Authentication Check (MAC) is performed on *ViewState* data when a Web Form is posted back to the server. The MAC can help identify client-side tampering with the *ViewState* hidden field.	*true*: MAC is enabled for *ViewState*. *false*: MAC is not enabled for *ViewState*. The default is *true*.

Table B-5.   *<pages>* Element Attributes

Attribute	Description	Options
validateRequest	Specifies whether request validation is enabled for pages affected by the configuration file. *New for version 1.1.*	Since the Request Validation feature can help prevent a variety of script injection attacks, it is recommended that you leave this set to *true* (the default), unless you are certain that your application properly filters and validates all user input.

<customErrors>

The *<customErrors>* element allows you to customize how your ASP.NET application responds to error conditions. In this element, you can specify whether the raw error messages generated by ASP.NET should be visible to local or remote clients, or whether to redirect the client to either a custom error page or a page specific to the error that occurred (based on the status code of the error). The *<customErrors>* element supports one child element, *<error>*, and has the following syntax:

```
<customErrors
   defaultRedirect="url"
   mode="on|off|RemoteOnly">
   <error
      redirect="url"
      statusCode="status code"/>
</customErrors>
```

Table B-6 describes the *<customErrors>* element attributes in more detail.

Table B-6.   *<customErrors>* Element Attributes

Element	Attribute	Description	Options
<customErrors>		Determines how ASP.NET errors are handled.	
	defaultRedirect	Determines the page to which a user is redirected if an error occurs.	The page to which this URL points can be either an .aspx page, in which you attempt to clean up or recover from the error, or a static HTML page, to inform the user of the error and offer guidance.

Table B-6. *<customErrors>* **Element Attributes**

Element	Attribute	Description	Options
	mode	Determines whether raw ASP.NET error messages are sent to the client.	*On*: Custom errors are enabled. When an error occurs, the client, whether on the local Web server or remote, will be redirected to the custom error page specified by the *defaultRedirect* attribute (or to a page specified in an *<error>* child element). *Off*: Custom errors are not enabled. When an error occurs, the client will see the error page generated by ASP.NET. Note that depending on how your application is designed, this can expose proprietary information to clients, so you should rarely use this setting. *RemoteOnly*: Custom errors are enabled for remote clients. When an error occurs, remote clients will be redirected to a custom error page, while clients on the local Web server will see the error page generated by ASP.NET. This allows developers to track down errors without allowing clients to see raw error pages. *RemoteOnly* is the default.
<error>		Determines redirect page for a specific error type, based on the HTTP status code for the error.	Adding *<error>* tags provides finer-grained control over error handling.

Table B-6. *<customErrors>* **Element Attributes**

Element	Attribute	Description	Options
	redirect	Determines the page to which a user is redirected if an error of the type specified in the *statusCode* attribute occurs.	
	statusCode	Determines the HTTP status code (404–Not Found, and so on) that is handled by this *<error>* child element.	

<authentication>

The *<authentication>* element controls configuration of authentication in ASP.NET. You can choose from one of three authentication methods, and you can set appropriate parameters for the method you choose or you can choose no authentication at all. The *<authentication>* element supports two child elements: *<forms>* and *<passport>*. Additionally, the *<forms>* element supports one child element, *<credentials>*, which in turn supports one child element, *<user>*, as shown in the following example:

```
<authentication
    mode="Windows|Forms|Passport|None">
    <forms
        loginUrl="url"
        name="name"
        path="/"
        protection="All|None|Encryption|Validation"
        requireSSL="true|false"
        slidingExpiration="true|false"
        timeout="number">
        <credentials
            passwordFormat="Clear|MD5|SHA1">
            <user
                name="username"
                password="password" />
        </credentials>
    </forms>
    <passport
        redirectUrl="url" />
</authentication>
```

Table B-7 describes the *<authentication>* element attributes in more detail.

Table B-7.   *<authentication>* Element Attributes

Element	Attribute	Description	Options
<authentication>		Determines how ASP.NET authentication is handled.	
	mode	Determines the authentication mode to be used. Authentication is discussed in greater detail in Chapter 6.	*Windows*: ASP.NET will use Windows authentication by default. Works with IIS's Basic, Digest, NTLM, or Certificate- based authentication methods. *Forms*: ASP.NET will use Forms-based authentication, which provides basic support for "roll-your-own" security scenarios, by default. *Passport*: ASP.NET will use Microsoft Passport as the default authentication method. *None*: No authentication will be performed by ASP.NET.
<forms>		Determines the parameters associated with Forms-based authentication.	
	loginUrl	Determines the URL to which a user is redirected if he doesn't have a valid authentication cookie.	This can be any page in your ASP.NET application that allows a user to log in. The default is *login.aspx*.
	name	Determines the name of the cookie used for authenticating a user.	Default is *.ASPXAUTH*.

Table B-7.   *<authentication>* Element Attributes

Element	Attribute	Description	Options
	path	Determines the path to set for the authentication cookie.	Default is /. This is to prevent the possibility of missing cookies because of browser case sensitivity with respect to URL paths and cookies.
	protection	Determines the methods used to protect the authentication cookie from being compromised. Your choice of which method to use, or whether to use any at all, will depend on your security needs vs. the amount of resources you're willing to devote to security. Generally, the higher the level of security, the greater the performance overhead.	*All* (default): Both encryption and data validation will be used to protect the cookie. This is the recommended setting. *Encryption*: The authentication cookie will be encrypted, but will not be validated. This leaves the cookie vulnerable to certain types of attacks. *Validation*: The authentication cookie's contents will be validated to ensure that they haven't been changed between the browser and the server. *None*: Neither encryption nor validation is used. Not recommended.
	requireSSL	Determines whether the authentication cookie will be sent with requests that do not use SSL. *New for version 1.1.*	If set to *true*, the forms authentication cookie will not be sent over a non-SSL connection. The default is *false*.
	slidingExpiration	Determines whether each request in a given session resets the expiration of the authentication cookie. *New for version 1.1.*	The default is *false*.

Table B-7. *<authentication>* **Element Attributes**

Element	Attribute	Description	Options
	Timeout	Determines the amount of time, in minutes, until the authentication cookie expires.	Default is 30. You should set this value to the minimum amount that will allow users to use your site effectively. If you use persistent cookies with forms authentication, they will not time out.
<credentials>		In conjunction with the *<user>* child element, allows you to define credentials to authenticate against within a configuration file.	If you use this method to store credentials in a Web.config file within your application scope, and your application is compromised, it might be possible for intruders to gain the passwords stored there, even if they're encrypted. Remember that no encryption method is perfect.
	PasswordFormat	Determines the encryption used for stored passwords.	*Clear*: No encryption is used. Not recommended. *MD5*: Passwords are encrypted using the MD5 hash algorithm. *SHA1*: Passwords are encrypted using the SHA1 hash algorithm.
<user>		Determines the username and password of a single user. Use one *<user>* child element for each set of credentials you want to store in the configuration file.	
	name	Specifies the username of the user to authenticate against.	

Table B-7. *<authentication>* **Element Attributes**

Element	Attribute	Description	Options
	password	Specifies the password of the user to authenticate against.	This value should be an encrypted version of the password created with the hash algorithm specified by the *passwordFormat* attribute of the *<credentials>* tag.
<passport>		Child element used to set the parameters for Microsoft Passport-based authentication.	
	redirectUrl	Determines the URL where the user will be redirected if he or she has not been authenticated.	

<identity>

By default, requests made by ASP.NET applications for resources requiring authentication, such as files secured by NT Access Controls Lists (ACLs), are made in the context of either the IUSR_MACHINENAME or IWAM_MACHINENAME accounts, depending on whether the application is configured to run in-process or out-of-process relative to IIS. The *<identity>* element allows ASP.NET applications to use impersonation, in which an application takes on the security context of the user making a request, or of a specified account. The *<identity>* element has the following syntax:

```
<identity
   impersonate="true|false"
   userName="username"
   password="password" />
```

Table B-8 describes the *<identity>* element attributes in more detail.

Table B-8. *<identity>* **Element Attributes**

Attribute	Description	Options
impersonate	Determines whether ASP.NET applications will use impersonation.	*true*: Enables impersonation of security accounts by ASP.NET applications. *false*: Disables impersonation of security accounts by ASP.NET applications.
userName	Specifies a user account that the affected ASP.NET application will impersonate.	Any valid user account. You should ensure that the account that you choose has access to only the desired resources. For example, as a rule, it is not a good idea to have an ASP.NET application impersonate an account in the Administrators group. If omitted, ASP.NET will impersonate the account of the logged on user (as provided by IIS).
password	Specifies the password for the account named in the *userName* attribute.	

<authorization>

The *<authorization>* element lets you specify which accounts or roles (groups) are authorized to access resources within the scope of the configuration file. The *<authorization>* element supports two child elements, *<allow>* and *<deny>*, both of which have three attributes. The *<authorization>* element has the following syntax:

```
<authorization>
    <allow
        users="userlist"
        roles="rolelist"
        verbs="verblist" />
    <deny
        users="userlist"
        roles="rolelist"
        verbs="verblist" />
</authorization>
```

Table B-9 describes the *<authorization>* element attributes in more detail.

Table B-9.   *<authorization>* **Element Attributes**

Element	Attribute	Description	Options
<authorization>		Determines authorization settings for an application or directory. Contains one or more *<allow>* or *<deny>* child elements.	
<allow>		Allows access to resources based on user account, group membership, or HTTP request method.	
	users	List of users (NT user accounts) granted access to the resource(s).	This attribute takes a comma-delimited list. Access to anonymous users is allowed using the ? wildcard, and access to everyone is allowed using the * wildcard.
	roles	List of roles (NT groups) granted access to the resource(s).	This attribute takes a comma-delimited list.
	verbs	List of HTTP verbs (GET, POST, etc.) granted access to the resource(s).	This attribute takes a comma-delimited list. Verbs available are GET, HEAD, POST, and DEBUG.
<deny>		Denies access to resources based on user account, group membership, or HTTP request method.	
	users	List of users (NT user accounts) denied access to the resource(s).	This attribute takes a comma-delimited list. Access to anonymous users is denied using the ? wildcard, and access to everyone is denied using the * wildcard.
	roles	List of roles (NT groups) denied access to the resource(s).	This attribute takes a comma-delimited list.

Table B-9. *<authorization>* Element Attributes

Element	Attribute	Description	Options
	verbs	List of HTTP verbs (GET, POST, etc.) denied access to the resource(s).	This attribute takes a comma-delimited list. Verbs available are GET, HEAD, POST, and DEBUG.

<machineKey>

The *<machineKey>* element allows you to specify the keys used for encryption and decryption of cookie data in Forms-based authentication. This element can be used at the machine level through Machine.config, as well as at the site and application levels through Web.config files, but it cannot be used at the subdirectory level. The *<machineKey>* element has the following syntax:

```
<machineKey
    decryptionKey="AutoGenerate|value[,IsolateApps] "
    validation="AutoGenerate|value[,IsolateApps] "
    validationKey="3DES|MD5|SHA1" />
```

Table B-10 escribes the *<machineKey>* element attributes in more detail.

Table B-10. *<machineKey>* Element Attributes

Attribute	Description	Options
decryptionKey	Determines whether the decryption key to be used is autogenerated or specifies a key value to be used.	*AutoGenerate* (default): ASP.NET will generate a random key for decryption. *New for version 1.1.* In version 1.1, the *IsolateApps* modifier is added, which ensures that each application will have a unique key generated, based on the application ID. *value*: This represents a string of characters (minimum 40, maximum 128) to be used as a decryption key. Note that 128 characters is the recommended length. For shorter-length keys, you should ensure that the key is randomly generated. This setting is necessary in Web farms to ensure that all servers are using the same keys, providing transparent user access while still taking advantage of encryption.

Table B-10. *<machineKey>* **Element Attributes**

Attribute	Description	Options
validation	Determines the type of encryption to be used by ASP.NET.	*3DES*: Data is encrypted using Triple-DES (3DES) encryption. *MD5*: Data is encrypted using the MD5 hash algorithm. *SHA1* (default): Data is encrypted using the SHA1 hash algorithm.
validationKey	Determines whether the validation key to be used is autogenerated or specifies a key value to be used.	*AutoGenerate* (default): ASP.NET will generate a random key for validation. *New for version 1.1.* In version 1.1, the *IsolateApps* modifier is added, which ensures that each application will have a unique key generated, based on the application ID. *value*: This represents a string of characters (minimum 40, maximum 128) to be used as a validation key. Note that 128 characters is the recommended length. For shorter-length keys, it is recommended to ensure that the key is randomly generated. This setting is necessary in Web farms to ensure that all servers are using the same keys, providing transparent user access while still taking advantage of encryption.

<securityPolicy>

The *<securityPolicy>* element allows you to specify one of several named security policies, or a custom policy, for code-access security based on the name and *policyFile* attributes of its *<trustLevel>* child element. The *<trust>* element, described in the next section, specifies which of the named policies is implemented for a given site or application. The *<securityPolicy>* element supports one child element, *<trustLevel>*, with two attributes, and has the following syntax:

```
<securityPolicy>
  <trustLevel
    name="value"
    policyFile="value" />
</securityPolicy>
```

Table B-11 describes the *<securityPolicy>* element attributes in more detail.

Table B-11.   *<securityPolicy>* **Element Attributes**

Element	Attribute	Description	Options
<securityPolicy>		Determines the available named security policies for sites and/or applications.	
<trustLevel>		Each *<trustLevel>* child element sets up an available named policy based on its name and *policyFile* attributes.	
	name	Specifies the name to use for the policy.	The name specified by this attribute is also used by the *<trust>* element to implement the named policy.
	policyFile	Specifies the file name of the file that contains the code-access security settings to be used under the named policy.	The file name specified by this attribute is relative to the location of the Machine.config file.

<trust>

The *<trust>* element is used to implement one of the named security policies created by the *<securityPolicy>* element. This element can be used at the machine level through Machine.config, as well as at the site and application levels through Web.config files. However, it can't be used at the subdirectory level. The *<trust>* element has the following syntax:

```
<trust
    level="Full|High|Low|None|custom name"
    originUrl="url" />
```

Table B-12 describes the *<trust>* element attributes in more detail.

Table B-12.   *<trust>* **Element Attributes**

Attribute	Description	Options
level	Determines the applicable trust level, based on a named security policy.	*Full*: Code-access security is based on the Full named policy set up by default in Machine.config. *High*: Code-access security is based on the *High* named policy set up by default in Machine.config. *Low*: Code-access security is based on the Low named policy set up by default in Machine.config. *None*: Code-access security is based on the *None* named policy set up by default in Machine.config. *custom name*: Code-access security is based on a custom named policy set up in either Machine.config or a Web.config file at the site or application level.
originUrl	Specifies the origin URL for an application.	*Optional*: This attribute can be used to support permissions for *Socket* and *WebRequest* requests that allow connectivity to the origin host.

<sessionState>

The *<sessionState>* element is used to configure the Session State *HttpModule*, including the type of state management to be used (in-process, out-of-process, or Microsoft SQL Server), the default session timeout, and whether to use cookies for associating requests with user sessions. The *<sessionState>* element has the following syntax:

```
<sessionState
   stateConnectionString="IP address:port number"
   cookieless="true|false"
   mode="Off|Inproc|StateServer|SQLServer"
   sqlConnectionString="sql connection string"
   timeout="number of minutes" />
```

Table B-13 describes the *<sessionState>* element attributes in more detail.

Table B-13. **<*sessionState*> Element Attributes**

Attribute	Description	Options
stateConnectionString	Specifies the server and port number to connect to when the mode attribute is set to *StateServer*.	This attribute is required when the mode is set to *StateServer*. The default is tcpip=127.0.0.1:42424.
cookieless	Determines whether user sessions are mapped to requests by using cookies or by adding a user's *SessionID* to the URL string for requests by that user.	*true*: SessionIDs are added to request URLs, and cookies are not used. *false*: Cookies are used to map user requests to sessions. The default is *false*.
mode	Determines the type of session state management that applications will use.	*Off*: Session state is disabled. *Inproc*: Session state is stored in-process with the application, as in classic ASP. *StateServer*: Session state is managed by an out-of-process NT Service, allowing multiple servers in a Web farm to share a single state store. *SQLServer*: Session state is managed by SQL Server database, allowing multiple servers in a Web farm to share a single state store. This mode has the added advantage of providing persistent state storage in the event of a Web server crash. The default is *InProc*.
sqlConnectionString	Specifies the connection string used to connect to a SQL Server database where state information is stored.	This attribute is required when the mode is set to *SQLServer*.
timeout	Specifies the amount of time, in minutes, before the user's session expires.	Like the classic ASP *Session.Timeout* property, this attribute uses sliding expiration. Each request by the user resets the amount of time before his session expires. The default is 20 minutes.

<httpHandlers>

The *<httpHandlers>* element allows you to assign requests of certain types or for certain resources to specific handler classes. For example, in Machine.config, the handling of ASP.NET pages (requests with the .aspx extension) is assigned to the *System.Web.UI.PageHandlerFactory* class. The *<httpHandlers>* element can also be used to prevent HTTP access to certain types of files by assigning them to the *System.Web.HttpForbiddenHandler* class, as is done by default for configuration files (*.config) and source files (*.vb and *.cs, for example).

The *<httpHandlers>* element supports three child elements, *<add>*, *<remove>*, and *<clear>*, and has the following syntax:

```
<httpHandlers>
  <add
     path="path"
     type="type, assembly name"
     validate="true|false"
     verb="verblist" />
  <remove
     path="path"
     verb="verblist" />
  <clear />
</httpHandlers>
```

Table B-14 describes the *<httpHandlers>* element attributes in more detail.

Table B-14.   <httpHandlers> Element Attribute

Element	Attribute	Description	Options
<httpHandlers>		Determines the assignment of requests to *httpHandlers* for ASP.NET applications.	
<add>		Each *<add>* child element maps a specific type of request to a given *httpHandler*.	

Table B-14.   *<httpHandlers>* Element Attribute

Element	Attribute	Description	Options
	path	Specifies the URL path this *httpHandler* will handle.	This can be a single URL, as in the case of the default mapping of the trace.axd URL to *System.Web.Handlers. TraceHandler*, or can use a wildcard to specify that the *httpHandler* should handle all requests of a given type (such as **.aspx* or **.asmx*).
	validate	Determines whether the ASP.NET runtime should attempt to load the class before the actual request is received, in order to ensure that it exists.	*true*: The ASP.NET runtime will attempt to load the class when the associated application is started up. *false*: The ASP.NET runtime will load the class only when the actual request is received. This can improve start-up time, but will delay the appearance of the error if the class does not exist. This attribute is optional.
	type	Specifies the .NET class that should handle the requests specified by the path and verb attributes.	This is a string containing a comma-separated list with the class name and other information, such as version and public key, that enables ASP.NET to locate the class in either the application's bin directory or the global assembly cache.

Table B-14.   *<httpHandlers>* Element Attribute

Element	Attribute	Description	Options
	verb	Specifies the HTTP verbs for which the *httpHandler* will handle requests.	Comma-separated list of verbs (GET, POST) or a wildcard (such as *, which specifies that all verbs should be handled).
<remove>		Removes an *httpHandler* mapping, based on the path and verb attributes specified.	
	path	Specifies path of the *httpHandler* to be removed.	This attribute must exactly match the path attribute of an *httpHandler* added by a previous *<add>* child element.
	verb	Specifies verb(s) of the *httpHandler* to be removed.	This attribute must exactly match the verb attribute of an *httpHandler* added by a previous *<add>* child element.
<clear>		Removes all *httpHandler* mappings, either those configured by the current file or those inherited from parent configuration files.	

<httpModules>

HttpModules are classes that implement the *IHttpModule* interface and are used to provide functionality to ASP.NET applications. For example, by default, the Machine.config file adds *HttpModules* for output caching, session-state management, authentication, and authorization. The *<httpModules>* element allows you to add *HttpModules* to ASP.NET applications.

The *<httpModules>* element supports three child elements, *<add>*, *<remove>*, and *<clear>*, and has the following syntax:

```
<httpModules>
   <add
      name="name"
      type="classname.assemblyname" />
   <remove
```

```
      name="name"
   <clear />
</httpModules>
```

Table B-15 describes the *<httpModules>* element attributes in more detail.

Table B-15.   *<httpModules>* Element Attributes

Element	Attribute	Description	Options
<httpModules>		Determines the *httpModules* available for ASP.NET applications within the scope of the configuration file.	
<add>		Each *<add>* child element adds a specified *httpModule*.	
	name	Specifies a name that can be used by ASP.NET applications to refer to the module identified by the type attribute.	
	type	Specifies the .NET class that implements the desired *httpModule*.	This is a string containing a comma-separated list with the class name and other information, such as version and public key, that enables ASP.NET to locate the class in either the application's bin directory or the global assembly cache.
<remove>		Removes an *httpModule*, based on the name and type attributes specified.	
	name	Specifies the name of the *httpModule* to remove.	This attribute must exactly match the name attribute of an *httpModule* added by a previous *<add>* child element.
<clear>		Removes all *httpModules*, either those configured by the current file or those inherited from parent configuration files.	

<processModel>

The *<processModel>* element configures settings related to how ASP.NET applications run, and it provides access to a number of features geared towards improving the availability of applications. These include automatic restart (which can be configured based on elapsed time or number of requests), allowed memory size, and Web garden, in which applications can be associated with specific processors in a multiprocessor machine. Note that when ASP.NET is running under IIS 6.0 in native mode, the settings in the *<processModel>* element are ignored in favor of the settings configured by the IIS administrative UI.

The *<processModel>* element has the following syntax:

```
<processModel
    clientConnectedCheck="time in hh:mm:ss format"
    comAuthenticationLevel="Default|None|Connect|Call|Pkt|
        PktIntegrity|PktPrivacy"
    comImpersonationLevel="Default|Anonymous|Identify|Impersonate|
        Delegate"
    cpuMask="number"
    enable="true|false"
    idleTimeout="time"
    logLevel="All|None|Errors"
    maxIoThreads="number"
    maxWorkerThreads="number"
    memoryLimit="percent"
    pingFrequency="hh:mm:ss"
    pingTimeout="hh:mm:ss"
    requestLimit="number"
    requestQueueLimit="Infinite|number"
    responseDeadlockInterval="Infinite|hh:mm:ss"
    responseRestartDeadlockInterval="Infinite|hh:mm:ss"
    restartQueueLimit="Infinite|number"
    serverErrorMessageFile="filename"
    shutdownTimeout="time"
    timeout="time"
    webGarden="true|false"
    username="user name"
    password="password" />
```

Table B-16 describes the *<processModel>* element attributes in more detail.

Table B-16. *<processModel>* **Element Attributes**

Attribute	Description	Options
clientConnectedCheck	Determines the frequency with which ASP.NET checks if the client is still connected while a request is queued.	This attribute takes a time value in the format hh:mm:ss. The default is 0:00:05. This attribute can be useful for preventing processor resources from being wasted on queued requests for which the client has disconnected.
comAuthenticationLevel	Specifies the DCOM authentication level.	*Default*: DCOM will determine authentication level based on its normal security negotiation algorithm. *None*: No authentication. *ConnectCall*: DCOM authenticates the credentials of the client with each remote procedure call. *Pkt*: DCOM authenticates that all received data is coming from the expected client. *PktIntegrity*: Same as *Pkt*, but also verifies that data has not been modified in transport. *PktPrivacy*: Same as *PktIntegrity*, but adds encryption. The default value is *Connect*.
comImpersonationLevel	Specifies the COM authentication level.	*Anonymous*: Client is anonymous. Not supported in the current release. *Identify*: Server can obtain the client's identity and impersonate the client for ACL checking, but cannot access system objects using the client's identity. *Impersonate*: Allows the server to impersonate the client and access system resources using the client's security context, but this context can only be passed across a single machine boundary. *Delegate*: Same as *Impersonate*, but the impersonation token can be passed across multiple machine boundaries.

ASP.NET Configuration Elements   B

Table B-16.   *<processModel>* Element Attributes

Attribute	Description	Options
cpuMask	Specifies the processors (on a multiprocessor server) that are allowed to run the ASP.NET application. This attribute works with the *webGarden* attribute. When *webGarden* is set to true, *cpuMask* determines the eligible processors for the application.	The default is 0xffffffff.
Enable	Enables or disables the *processModel* settings for ASP.NET applications.	*true*: *processModel* settings are enabled. *false*: *processModel* settings are disabled.
idleTimeout	Determines the amount of time, in minutes, before ASP.NET shuts down an inactive worker process.	Default is *Infinite*, in which case the process will not be shut down when idle.
logLevel	Specifies the types of process events that will be written to the event log.	*All*: All process events are logged. *Errors*: Only unexpected shutdowns, memory limit shutdowns, and deadlock shutdowns are logged. *None*: No events are logged. The default is *Errors*.
maxIoThreads	Specifies the maximum number of IO threads per CPU.	Any value from 5 to 100 is valid. The default is 25.
maxWorkerThreads	Specifies the maximum number of worker threads per CPU.	Any value from 5 to 100 is valid. The default is 25.
memoryLimit	Determines the maximum allowable memory size for an ASP.NET application.	This attribute takes a number representing the percentage of the total system memory that the application's worker processes can consume. If this value is exceeded, ASP.NET will launch a new process, reassign existing requests to it, and then shut down the old process.

Table B-16. *<processModel>* **Element Attributes**

Attribute	Description	Options
pingFrequency	Determines how often the ASP.NET ISAPI extension pings the worker process to see if it is running. If the process does not respond in the interval specified by *pingTimeout*, the worker process will be restarted.	The format of this value is hh:mm:ss. The default is 30 seconds.
pingTimeout	Determines the time interval after which an unresponsive worker process is restarted.	The format of this value is hh:mm:ss. The default is 5 seconds.
responseDeadlock-	Determines the time interval *Interval* after which the process will be restarted when there are queued requests, and no responses have been generated for this interval.	The format of this value is hh:mm:ss. The default is 3 minutes.
responseRestart-DeadlockInterval	Determines the time interval that must elapse before a second restart to cure a deadlock (as specified by *responseDeadlockInterval*) can occur.	The format of this value is hh:mm:ss. The default is 9 minutes.
requestLimit	Determines the number of requests an application can fulfill before ASP.NET launches a new worker process and shuts down the old one.	Default is *Infinite*, in which case the process will not be shut down, regardless of the number of requests. This setting can be used to restart the application after a given number of requests, and it can help deal with problems such as memory leaks in legacy COM components used by an application or blocked processes.
requestQueueLimit	Determines the number of requests that can be queued before ASP.NET returns the "503–Server Too Busy" status error.	Default is 5,000.

Table B-16.   *<processModel>* Element Attributes

Attribute	Description	Options
restartQueueLimit	Specifies the number of requests that are kept in the queue while the process is restarting.	Default is 10.
serverErrorMessageFile	Provides custom message for Server Unavailable error condition.	Path and file name to the desired file. If omitted, the default Server Unavailable message is used.
shutdownTimeout	Determines the amount of time that an ASP.NET worker process is given to shut itself down.	This attribute takes a time value in the format hh:mm:ss. If the time specified by this attribute is exceeded, ASP.NET will force the shutdown of the worker process. The default is 0:00:05.
timeout	Determines the amount of time, in minutes, before ASP.NET launches a new worker process and shuts down the old one.	This setting can be used to restart the application after a given period of time, and it can help deal with problems such as memory leaks in legacy COM components used by an application or blocked processes.
webGarden	Determines whether Web gardening is enabled.	*true*: Web gardening is enabled. *false*: Web gardening is disabled.
password	Specifies a password for the user account specified in the username attribute.	Default is *autogenerate*, which can be used with either the SYSTEM or MACHINE special accounts.
username	Determines the identity under which ASP.NET worker processes are run.	Default is MACHINE, which runs worker processes as an unprivileged ASP.NET service account called ASPNET. This provides a higher level of security than the beta releases of ASP.NET (which used the more privileged SYSTEM account), but can make certain techniques, such as using trusted connections with SQL Server, more difficult because the ASP.NET account is not trusted. You can also use another special account, SYSTEM, to run the ASP.NET worker processes, but for security reasons, this is not recommended.

<webControls>

The *<webControls>* element allows you to specify the location of script files used by client-side implementations of ASP.NET Server Controls, such as the validation controls. The *<webControls>* element has the following syntax:

```
<webControls
   clientScriptsLocation="path" />
```

Table B-17 describes the *<webControls>* element attribute in more detail.

Table B-17. *<webControls>* Element Attribute

Attribute	Description	Options
clientScriptsLocation	Determines where ASP.NET will look for client-side scripts for use with ASP.NET Server Controls.	This attribute is relative to the root Web of the Web server.

<clientTarget>

The *<clientTarget>* element allows you to set up aliases to be used by the *Client-Target* property of the *Page* class. The *<clientTarget>* element supports one child element, *<add>*, and has the following syntax:

```
<clientTarget>
   <add
      alias="aliasname"
      userAgent="true|false" />
   <clear />
   <remove
      alias="aliasname" />
</clientTarget>
```

Table B-18 describes the *<clientTarget>* element attributes in more detail.

Table B-18. *<clientTarget>* Element Attributes

Element	Attribute	Description
<clientTarget>		Creates aliases for specific browser user agents that can then be specified from the *Page.ClientTarget* property.
<add>		Maps a specific user agent string to an alias name.
	alias	Specifies the name of the alias.
	userAgent	Specifies the browser user agent that the alias looks for.
<clear>		Removes all aliases added (or inherited) by the current Web.config file.
<remove>	*alias*	Removes the specified alias added (or inherited) by the current Web.config file.

B

ASP.NET Configuration Elements

<browserCaps>

The *<browserCaps>* element contains settings used by ASP.NET to provide the functionality of the browser capabilities component (accessible via the *Request.Browser* property). It provides filtering processes that allow the browser capabilities component to populate its properties with information on the capabilities of a user's browser, based on the information contained in the user agent string passed by the browser. The *<browserCaps>* element supports three child elements, *<result>*, *<use>*, and *<filter>*. The *<filter>* element supports one child element, *<case>*. The *<browserCaps>* element has the following syntax:

```
<browserCaps>
    <result type="System.Web.HttpBrowserCapabilities" />
    <use var="HTTP_USER_AGENT" />
        list of default property values
    <filter>
        <case
            match="string1|string2|stringN">
            property=value
        </case>
    </filter>
</browserCaps>
```

Table B-19 describes the *<browserCaps>* element attributes in more detail.

Table B-19.   *<browserCaps>* Element Attributes

Element	Attribute	Description	Options
<browserCaps>		Allows filtering and mapping of strings within the browser user agent string to properties of the browser capabilities component.	
<result>		Specifies the result type of the configuration element.	
	type	.NET class used as the result type.	The default is *System.Web.Http-BrowserCapabilities*.
<use>		Determines the server variables used while evaluating *<filter>* and *<case>* elements.	
	var	Server variable used in evaluating *<filter>* and *<case>* elements.	The default is *HTTP_USER_AGENT*.

Table B-19. *<browserCaps>* **Element Attributes**

Element	Attribute	Description	Options
<filter>		The *<filter>* contains one or more *<case>* child elements to search for specific strings within the user agent string.	
<case>		Each *<case>* child element searches for a specific string or strings within the user agent string.	
	match	Specifies the string or strings (separated by | characters) to look for in the code.	If a specified string is found, the property assignment enclosed by the *<case></case>* tags is executed.

Setting and Retrieving Custom Application Settings

The final configuration element is a special one because it allows you to configure your own custom application settings, which can then be easily retrieved from within your ASP.NET applications.

<appSettings>

The *<appSettings>* element allows you to create your own configuration settings as key/value pairs. You can use this configuration element to store configuration information such as DSNs for data access, and then retrieve them in your application using the following syntax:

```
string DSN;
DSN = ConfigurationSettings.AppSettings["dsn "];
```

This is assuming that you've stored the DSN using "dsn" as the key.

The *<appSettings>* element has the following syntax:

```
<appSettings>
  <add
     key="string"
     value="string" />
  <clear />
  <remove
     key="string" />
</appSettings>
```

ASP.NET Configuration Elements

B

Table B-20 describes the *<appSettings>* element attributes in more detail.

Table B-20.   *<appSettings>* Element Attributes

Element	Attribute	Description
<appSettings>		Creates key/value pairs that can be retrieved using *ConfigurationSettings.AppSettings(key)*.
<add>		Adds a key/value pair.
	key	Specifies the name of the key to use to retrieve the value.
	value	Specifies the value to be returned.
<clear>		Removes all key/value pairs added (or inherited) by the current Web.config file.
<remove>	*key*	Removes the specified name/value pair added (or inherited) by the current Web.config file.

Installing Visual Studio .NET 2003

> **In this chapter, you will learn how to:**
>
> - Determine if your operating system supports building and running ASP.NET applications.
> - Ensure that Internet Information Services is installed and running.
> - Install Microsoft .NET Framework and Microsoft Visual Studio .NET.
> - Install the Pubs sample database for access through MSDE.
> - Edit the system path for easier access to tools used in this book.

To create ASP.NET applications using the Visual Studio .NET development environment, you need to install both the .NET Framework and the Visual Studio .NET software on a supported platform.

Before You Install

Although you can install the Visual Studio .NET development environment on Microsoft Windows NT 4.0, Windows 2000, Windows XP, or Windows Server 2003 (though for reasons discussed in Chapter 6, it's better to develop on Windows 2000 or XP Professional and deploy to Windows 2000 or Windows Server 2003), support for running ASP.NET is limited to platforms that support

IIS 5.0 or above. This means that to run ASP.NET applications locally, you must be running Windows 2000 (any version), Windows XP Professional, or any later version of Windows that provides support for IIS 5.0 or above.

Once you have determined that your operating system supports IIS, you should make sure that IIS is installed before you install the Visual Studio .NET development environment. If IIS is not installed before you install Visual Studio .NET, ASP.NET will not install correctly. You can do this by using the Add Or Remove Programs item from Control Panel. Note that you must be logged in as an administrator to verify and install IIS.

▶ **Note**   In addition to having IIS installed, you must install and configure the Microsoft FrontPage Server Extensions (FPSE) if you want to access projects via the server extensions. (The default access mode is File Share, but you can change this in the Microsoft Visual Studio .NET Options dialog box.) For detailed instructions on installing and configuring IIS and FPSE on Windows 2000, Windows XP, and Windows Server 2003, refer to the document \setup\Web-Server.htm on disk 1 of the Visual Studio .NET software. If your CD-ROM drive uses D as the drive letter, you would read the file using D:\setup\WebServer.htm.

▶ **Important**   The default installation of some versions of IIS includes sample files that can present a security risk if installed on production systems. When installing IIS, you can choose not to install these samples by clicking the Details button in the Windows Component Wizard, and then unchecking the Documentation check box, which will remove the samples. You might also want to uncheck the boxes for services you don't plan to use, such as the FTP, SMTP, and NNTP services, since unused services can also present a security risk. By removing these samples and services, you can eliminate a whole range of potential vulnerabilities. For more information on samples and services, and how they impact server security, see Chapter 6.

Installing Visual Studio .NET 2003

Installation of the Visual Studio .NET development environment is divided into two parts. First you must install the components from the Visual Studio .NET Prerequisites CD, which includes the .NET Framework and other software required to support the Visual Studio .NET development environment. Once you've installed the updates, you can install the Visual Studio .NET development environment.

To install the Visual Studio .NET Prerequisites or Visual Studio .NET, you must be logged in as an administrator or have access to an administrative account valid for the machine on which you want to install the software. If you are not an administrator, you will see a dialog box similar to the Windows XP dialog box shown here.

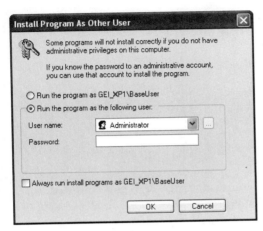

If you see this dialog box, you can either log out and log back in using an administrator account, or you can specify the user name and password of an administrative account from which to run the installation program.

Install the Visual Studio .NET prerequisites

1 Insert disk 1 of Visual Studio .NET 2003 into your CD-ROM drive. If autorun is enabled, setup will begin automatically, and you will see the dialog box shown on the next page. If autorun is not enabled, you will need to run setup.exe from the root of the CD-ROM drive (if you are not logged in as an administrator, right-click setup.exe and select Run As to open the dialog box shown in the preceding illustration, and then enter the user name and password of an administrator account to start the installation).

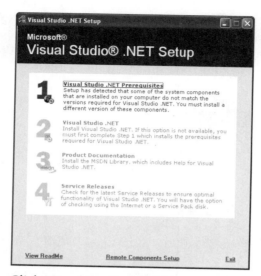

2   Click Visual Studio .NET Prerequisites. You will be prompted to insert the Visual Studio .NET Prerequisites CD, as the following illustration shows.

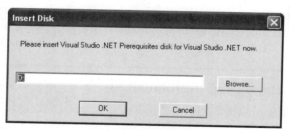

3   Insert the Visual Studio .NET Prerequisites CD into your CD-ROM drive (changing the drive letter displayed in the dialog box to the letter of your CD-ROM drive if necessary) and click OK. The End User License Agreement (EULA) for the Windows Component Update will be displayed, as in the illustration on the following page.

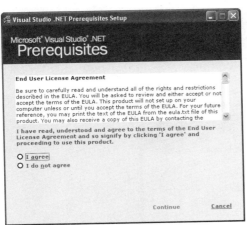

4 Click I Agree and then click Continue. (You should always read the EULA before agreeing.)

A list of the components to be installed will be displayed, as shown in the following illustration. (Depending on the system you are installing on, a slightly different list of components might be shown.)

▶ **Note** One of the components installed by the Visual Studio .NET Prerequisites is the .NET Framework 1.1. If you already have the .NET Framework 1.0 installed, the 1.1 version will be installed side-by-side with it, allowing applications to execute against either version of the framework (depending on how they're configured).

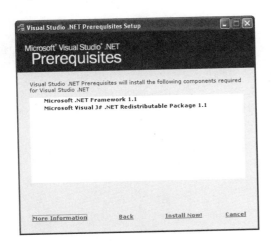

5   Click Install Now! You might be prompted to reboot to complete installation of certain components. The installation will continue after the machine is rebooted.

When the installation is complete, the following dialog box will be displayed.

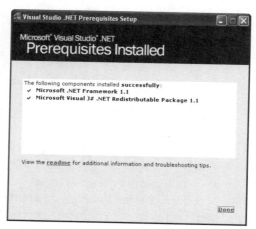

6   Click Done to complete the installation.

▶   **Note**   The steps and screen shots in the next section are based on the Enterprise Architect edition of Visual Studio .NET. The steps and screens for other editions will be similar, though there will be fewer options available in Step 4 when installing other editions of Visual Studio .NET.

Once you've completed the Visual Studio .NET Prerequisites installation, the setup dialog box for Visual Studio .NET will be displayed again, as shown in the illustration on the following page.

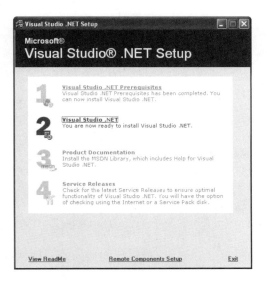

Install Visual Studio .NET

1   Begin the Visual Studio .NET installation by clicking Visual Studio .NET. You will be prompted to insert disk 1 of Visual Studio .NET, as the following illustration shows.

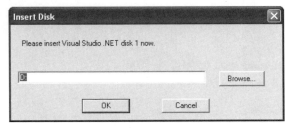

2   Insert disk 1 of Visual Studio .NET into your CD-ROM drive. (Change the drive letter displayed in the dialog box to the letter of your CD-ROM drive if necessary.) Click OK.

   The setup program will load necessary components and then display the dialog box shown on the next page.

3   Review the EULA, click I Agree, enter the product key and your name, and then click Continue to continue installing. (If you are not familiar with installing software such as Visual Studio .NET, you should click Review The ReadMe File prior to continuing the installation.)

After you click Continue, the Options page shown in the following illustration will be displayed.

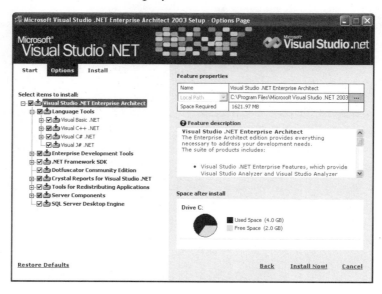

4   Review the available options. For example, you can click the ellipsis button (shown below) to change the drive on which the software will be installed. You can also select an option from the tree on the left and read about that feature in the Feature Description box on the right. Once you're satisfied with the options you've selected, click Install Now! to continue the installation.

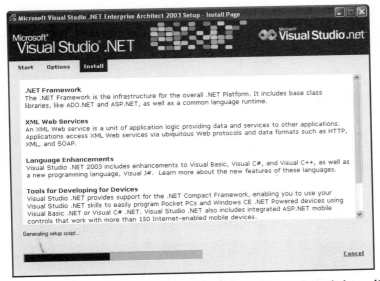

The following Install dialog box will be displayed.

5   Insert the appropriate install disk when prompted, and then click OK. Once installation is complete, the message shown on the next page will be displayed, assuming there were no problems. (If any errors occurred, you can review the setup log via the link provided to determine what the error was.)

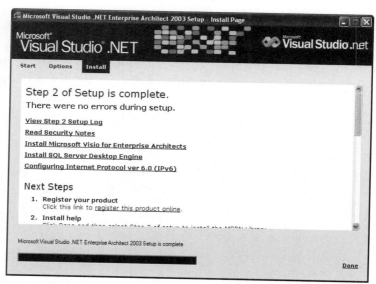

6 Review the installation notes displayed (including registering Visual Studio .NET, if desired), and then click Done to complete the installation of Visual Studio .NET Standard.

Once Step 2 of the Visual Studio .NET installation is complete and you've clicked Done, the following dialog box will be displayed.

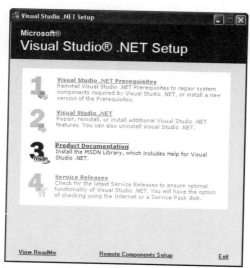

You can now install the MSDN Library, which provides product documentation and help for Visual Studio .NET.

Install MSDN Library documentation

1 Click Product Documentation.

You will be prompted to insert disk 1 of the MSDN Library for Visual Studio .NET, as the following illustration shows.

2 Insert disk 1 of the MSDN Library into your CD-ROM drive. (Change the drive letter displayed in the dialog box to the letter of your CD-ROM drive if necessary.) Click OK.

The following dialog box will be displayed.

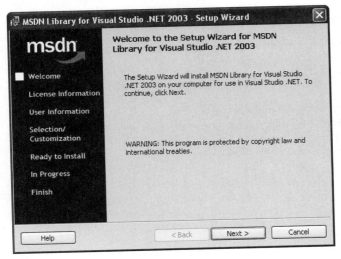

3 Click Next.

The license agreement for the MSDN Library will be displayed, as shown in the illustration on the next page.

Installing VS .NET 2003

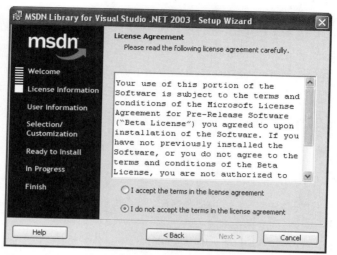

4   Read the license agreement, click I Accept The Terms In The License Agreement, and then click Next.

The User Information page shown in the following illustration will be displayed.

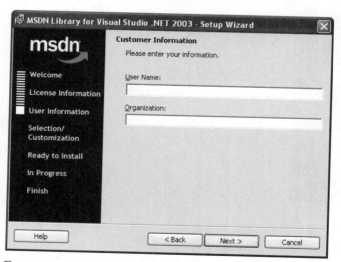

5   Enter your user name and organization name (if applicable), and click Next.

The following Setup Type page will be displayed.

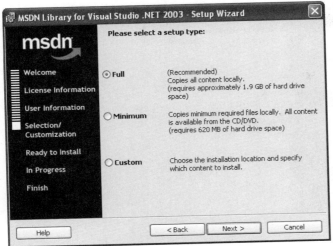

6   Select Full (or a different setup type, if desired), and click Next.
    The Destination Folder page shown in the following illustration will
    be displayed.

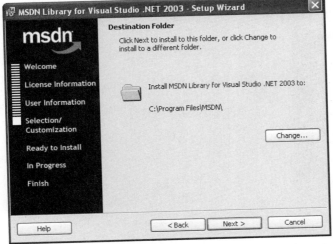

7   If desired, click Change to change the folder to which the MSDN
    Library will be installed, and click Next.
    The Ready To Install page will be displayed, as shown in the illustra-
    tion on the next page.

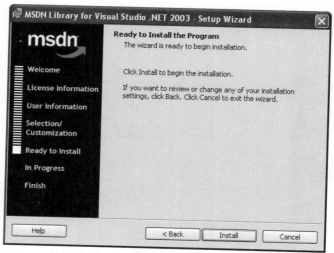

8 Click Install to begin the installation process.
The following In Progress page will be displayed.

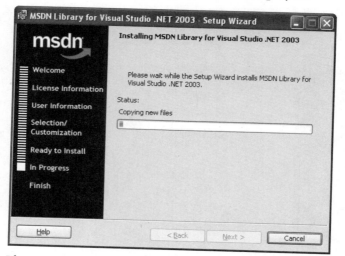

If prompted for disk 2 and/or 3, insert them when prompted. When the installation is complete, the Finish page shown in the illustration on the following page will be displayed.

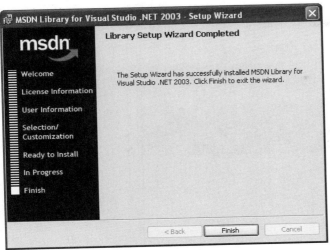

9   Click Finish to exit the MSDN Library Setup Wizard.

Once the MSDN Library installation is complete, the following dialog box will be displayed.

Visual Studio .NET Setup allows you to check for service releases (collections of patches) via the Internet to ensure that your software is up to date.

Install service releases

1   Click Service Releases.

The Service Releases dialog box shown in the following illustration will be displayed.

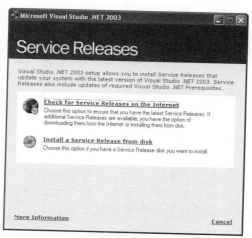

2   Click Check For Service Releases On The Internet.

If a service release is available, you will be prompted to install it. Otherwise, you will see the following dialog box.

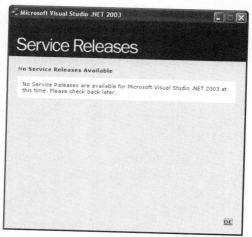

3   Click OK to dismiss the Service Releases dialog box.

4   Click View ReadMe in the Visual Studio .NET Setup dialog box if you want to read about installation and uninstallation, known issues, and other release notes. When you are finished, click Exit to exit Visual Studio .NET 2003 setup.

A Microsoft SQL Server–compatible database is required to run the database examples in this book. MSDE, the desktop edition of SQL Server, is provided with Visual Studio .NET Standard edition. The setup program for MSDE is copied to the install directory for Visual Studio .NET by default.

Install MSDE

1   Locate the setup program (setup.exe) for MSDE. The default location is C:\Program Files\Microsoft Visual Studio .NET 2003\Setup\MSDE.

2   Run setup.exe to install MSDE. As with other programs, you will need to be logged in as an administrator (or use the Run As command with an administrative account) to install MSDE.

To configure MSDE to work with the provided samples, see Chapter 6 and Chapter 9 for information on configuring users and database access in MSDE.

Before you are able to completely configure the security settings for MSDE, however, you will need to at a minimum install the Pubs sample database. Though several sample databases are included with the VSdotNET instance of MSDE, these are not installed by default. The following procedure describes how to install the Pubs sample database using the oSql command-line tool. If you have the SQL Server client tools installed, you can also use the SQL Server Query Analyzer to run the necessary SQL script.

Install the Pubs sample database

1   Log in using an account with administrator rights on the machine, or use the Run As feature in Step 2 to open the command prompt using an administrator account.

2   Open a command prompt, and navigate to the location of the inst-pubs.sql SQL script. By default, this will be C:\Program Files\Microsoft Visual Studio .NET 2003\SDK\w1.1\Samples\Setup. You might need to alter that path if you installed Visual Studio to a different location.

3   Run the oSql utility using the following command syntax (if you get the message *'oSql' is not recognized as an internal or external command, operable program or batch file.*, you may need to add the path to the oSql utility to the Path environment variable, using the techniques described in the next section):

```
oSql -S (local)\VSdotNET -E -i instpubs.sql
```

If the command is successful, the command line window should look similar to the following illustration when processing is complete.

In addition to following the setup steps described in previous procedures, you might want to complete the following procedure to make it easier to use some of the command-line tools included with the .NET Framework, such as the WSDL.exe utility described in Chapter 11, and the command-line compilers. By default, the path to these tools is not added to the Path environment variable (used by the operating system to locate commonly used commands), which means that to use the tools you must either navigate to the folder containing them, or use the full path to the tools when you call them, rather than just using the name of the tool. To add the path to these tools to the Path environment variable, follow these steps. You will need to be logged in as an administrator for this procedure to work.

Add the path to common .NET tools to the Path environment variable

1   Open Windows Explorer, locate the My Computer icon, right-click the icon, and then select Properties.

2   In the System Properties dialog box, click the Advanced tab. The dialog box will look similar to the illustration on the following page.

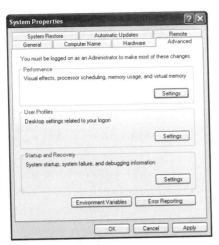

3 Click Environment Variables.

4 With the *Path* variable selected in the System Variables list box as shown in the following illustration, click Edit.

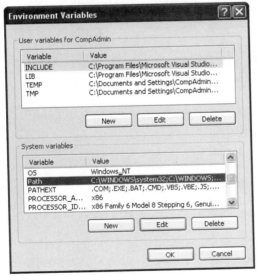

5 In the Edit System Variable dialog box, add the following paths to the end of string in the Variable value text box. You should prefix each path with a semicolon:

C:\Program Files\Microsoft Visual Studio .NET 2003\SDK\v1.1\Bin

C:\WINDOWS\Microsoft.NET\Framework*version*** (where ***version* represents the version number of the .NET Framework installed, in the format *vN.N.NNNN*)

Note that these paths assume that you have installed using the default paths, and that your Windows directory is named WINDOWS. If this is not the case, you might need to modify the paths for your system. You can locate the exact path for the .NET Framework Bin directory by doing a search for wsdl.exe, and you can locate the exact path for the command-line compilers by doing a search for vbc.exe. Use these paths for this step if they are different from the ones shown.

6   Click OK three times to accept your modifications and close all dialog boxes.

7   Test the Bin path modification by opening a command prompt from the Start menu and running wsdl /?.

If the modification was done correctly, the resulting screen should look similar to the following illustration.

8   Test the second path modification by opening a command prompt from the Start menu and running vbc /?.

If the modification was done correctly, the resulting screen should look similar to the following illustration.

Index

Symbols and Numbers

A

N

W

G. Andrew Duthie

G. Andrew Duthie is the founder and principal of Graymad Enterprises, Inc. (*http://www.graymad.com*), providing training and consulting in Microsoft Web development technologies. Andrew has been developing multi-tier Web applications since the introduction of Active Server Pages. He wrote about developing scalable *n*-tier applications in *Microsoft Visual InterDev 6.0 Enterprise Developer's Workshop*, also from Microsoft Press.

Andrew is a frequent speaker at events, including Software Development, the Dev-Connections family of conferences, Microsoft Developer Days, and VSLive! He also speaks at .NET user groups as a member of the International .NET Association (INETA) Speaker's Bureau (*http://www.ineta.org*).

In addition to his work for Graymad Enterprises, Andrew enjoys spending time with his wife, Jennifer, playing music, and smoking his meerschaum pipe. You can reach Andrew by email at andrew@graymad.com.

The manuscript for this book was prepared and submitted to Microsoft Press in electronic form. Pages were composed by nSight, Inc. using Adobe FrameMaker+SGML for Windows, with text in Sabon and display type in ITC Franklin Gothic. Composed pages were delivered to the printer as electronic pre-press files.

Cover designer:	Greg Hickman
Interior Graphic Designer:	James D. Kramer
Principal Compositor:	Donald Cowan
Copy Editor:	Lisa Wehrle
Technical Editor:	Chris Russo
Principal Proofreader:	Jennifer Carr
Indexer:	Jack Lewis, J&J Indexing

Get a **Free**
e-mail newsletter, updates,
special offers, links to related books,
and more when you

register on line!

Register your Microsoft Press® title on our Web site and you'll get a FREE subscription to our e-mail newsletter, *Microsoft Press Book Connections.* You'll find out about newly released and upcoming books and learning tools, online events, software downloads, special offers and coupons for Microsoft Press customers, and information about major Microsoft® product releases. You can also read useful additional information about all the titles we publish, such as detailed book descriptions, tables of contents and indexes, sample chapters, links to related books and book series, author biographies, and reviews by other customers.

Registration is easy. Just visit this Web page and fill in your information:

http://www.microsoft.com/mspress/register

Microsoft®
